NEGOTIATING
MASCULINITIES
IN
LATE IMPERIAL
CHINA

NEGOTIATING
MASCULINITIES
~IN~
LATE IMPERIAL
CHINA

MARTIN W. HUANG

UNIVERSITY OF HAWAI'I PRESS
HONOLULU

© 2006 University of Hawai'i Press

Printed in

11 10 09 08 07 06   6 5 4 3 2 1

LIBRARY OF CONGRESS CATALOGING-IN-PUBLICATION DATA

Huang, Martin W., 1960–
    Negotiating masculinities in late imperial China / Martin W. Huang.
      p. cm.
    Includes bibliographical references and index.
    ISBN-13: 978-0-8248-2896-7 (hardcover : al,.paper)
    ISBN-10: 0-8248-2896-8 (hardcover : al,.paper)
    1. Masculinity—China. 2. Gender identity—China. 3. Sex (Psychology)
4. China—History—Qing dynasty, 1644–1912. I. Title.
    BF175.5.M37H83 2006
    305.31'0951—dc22
                                        2005019242

University of Hawai'i Press books are printed on acid-free paper
and meet the guidelines for permanence and durability of the
Council on Library Resources

Designed by Liz Demeter

Printed by Integrated Books Technology, Inc.

CONTENTS

ACKNOWLEDGEMENTS

As in the case of all my previous works, Robert Hegel was the first reader of the manuscript for this book, and he read and commented on some of the chapters more than once. My gratitude for his advice and guidance is beyond words. I am grateful to the University of Hawai'i Press' anonymous readers for their extensive and detailed comments and critiques, which proved to be very helpful in my revision, although I was not able to implement all their suggestions.

I would like to thank all those who generously offered their help and advice in various ways when I was working on this project: Guan Daoxiong, Xiao Chi, Paul Ropp, Wilt Idema, Michael Fuller, Li Qiancheng, Beata Grant, and Hu Ying. The assistance of the interlibrary staff of the Main Library at the University of California, Irvine, and Bill Wang, the East Asian librarian there, was indispensable to my research.

Some of the research for this book was conducted during a leave in the academic year 2001–2002, made possible in part by a fellowship from the Chiang Ching-kuo Foundation. Grants from the Council on Research, Computing and Library Resources, and the School of Humanities at the University of California, Irvine, also greatly facilitated my research.

I am particularly grateful to Karen Lawrence, the Dean of the School of Humanities, and the Center for Asian Studies at the University of California, Irvine, for a subvention that made the publication of this book possible.

An earlier version of chapter 8 was published in *Chinese Literature: Essays, Articles, Reviews* 25 (2003). I thank the journal editor for the permission to reprint it here.

Finally, my gratitude goes to Pamela Kelley of the University of Hawai'i Press for her interest in my work and her professionalism and to Bojana Ristich, whose meticulous editing has saved me many errors and inconsistencies.

M. W. H.

INTRODUCTION

On March 19, in the seventeenth year of the Chongzhen period (1628–1644), Zhu Youjian, the last emperor of the Ming dynasty (1368–1644), hanged himself when the rebel troops of Li Zicheng (1605–1645; *ECCP,* pp. 491–493) were about to overwhelm the capital city. Learning of the emperor's death, the vice censor-in-chief, Shi Bangyao (1586–1644), also committed suicide. Before taking his life, Shi lamented the following in a suicide poem: "Ashamed of being unable to come up with even half a plan to defuse the present crisis / I can only choose death to return the favor I have received from my lord" (see chapter 4 for further discussion). Several decades later, when reading this suicide poem, the early Qing thinker Yan Yuan (1635–1704; *ECCP,* pp. 912–915) was moved to tears. What struck him most must have been the "feminine" helplessness evoked in Shi Bangyao's characterization of his act of loyalty/chastity.[1] The first line of the couplet is a minister's confession of incompetence, whereas the second line captures the feminine gesture of a woman committing suicide to vindicate her chastity. Elsewhere Yan Yuan insisted that the loyal Ming ministers who committed suicide after the collapse of the Ming dynasty could be remembered at best as "the chaste women of the inner chambers [*guizhong yifu*]."[2]

For Yan Yuan, the celebrated image of a chaste woman committing suicide to vindicate her chastity was becoming increasingly problematic, especially after the fall of the Ming dynasty, a tragedy Yan Yuan attributed in part to the feminization of many Confucian literati and their resultant inability to carry out their manly duties. A common rhetoric of the discourse on the fall of the Ming was that whereas a large number of chaste women had demonstrated tremendous moral courage and unflinching loyalty during the national disaster, many men, in sharp contrast, had behaved in unmanly fashion. Yan Yuan, however, seemed to question whether it was appropriate to compare these men with chaste female martyrs when "effeminacy" was precisely the issue. The fact that many officials and generals had to resort to suicide like chaste women was itself a telling indictment since suicide would not have been necessary had they been competent enough to achieve victories on the battlefield. According to people like Yan Yuan, there was something inherently feminine about the act of suicide.³

The ambivalence and anxiety associated with the image of chaste women found in Yan Yuan's writings point to one of the central issues explored in this study—namely, the complicated and often opposite roles assigned to the female "other" in a man's negotiation of his identity in late imperial China. Students of Chinese gender history have long been struck by the prominent presence of women in traditional male literati discourses of self-representation. How this apparent prominence of the feminine shaped the construction of masculinities in the late imperial discourses is a topic I seek to explore.

In most of the works examined in this study there generally are two common strategies for constructing and negotiating masculinity. The first, which I would call the strategy of analogy, is to construct masculinity in close association with the feminine; the second, or the strategy of differentiation, is to define masculinity in sharp differentiation from feminine. In both cases women bear the burden as the ultimate defining "other," although various "lesser" men could also serve as "others" in this negotiating process. In most cases, both strategies are simultaneously employed, although the emphases can vary considerably. In this study, "femininity" is a rather broad concept, denoting a wide range of gender phenomena associated with women, from the castrated (emasculated) to the marginalized and from the politically and socially destabilizing (prostitutes, plotting palace women, eunuchs, etc.) to the exemplary women celebrated in Confucian chastity discourse.

The analogy strategy is more likely to be found in texts where the image of a woman is, paradoxically, appropriated as a positive metaphor to promote the male literati author's own desirability or visibility in front of a male audience. Despite their pretense of femininity, these discourses are almost always homosocial in that they are by and for men.⁴ In a patriarchal society such as that of late imperial China, masculinity was most likely a homosocial enactment since what mattered to a man most were the judgments and scrutiny of other men, while women's opinions, if ever expressed or heard, were seldom taken into serious consideration. A man's anxiety over being perceived as not masculine enough could be alleviated only when he was persuaded that such a perception was not shared by other men.

One example of the analogy strategy is that male literati poets often performed poetic "transvestism" by presenting themselves as "neglected but still faithful wives or concubines" to vindicate their Confucian virtues or to express their frustrations so that their values as virtuous men would be better appreciated by other men in superior positions. This transvestistic rhetoric can also be found in other kinds of discourse, such as political treatises and other more personal writings of scholar-officials. Here, comparing oneself to a woman is only a masking strategy of self-re/masculinization. To profess that one is in the dominated group (like a woman) is a subtle tactic to seek approval from the dominant groups and, consequently, gain eventual domination in relation to male peers by moving oneself into a more advantageous position.[5] This is a strategy of re/positioning. In practice, however, such tactics may have many different consequences that tend to complicate the gender status of the transvestite, pointing to his dual-gender position: he is a woman in relation to the ruler or superior, and yet precisely because they recognize his feminine position, he is able to move into a more masculine place in relation to other men (see chapter 2).

Related to poetic transvestism is what I would call narrative transvestism, which characterizes many works of fiction and drama that focus on romantic love. Here it is often a woman who masquerades as a man in order to escape from an unwanted marriage or to pursue a career. Such narrative transvestism seems to assume an interchangeability between men and women. Indeed, in many novels and plays, a romantic and handsome man is almost always praised for his feminine looks and delicate manners. Here ideal male beauty is largely defined as a feminine quality. A man's fair skin, refined looks, and elegant manners—qualities supposedly admired by both men and women—testify to a man's cultural sophistication and therefore his superior moral virtue, and a feminine-looking man is often presented as the embodiment of such sophistication and virtue (see chapter 7).

This analogous gender rhetoric seems to have a basis in the *yin-yang* correlative thinking that underpinned almost all the cultural discourses in pre-twentieth-century China. *Yin* and *yang* originally referred to the shady and sunny sides of a hill. In the correlative thinking system, they are concepts describing relationships among things in the universe. Consequently, in theory, they do not have fixed meanings, despite the fact that *yin* is often associated with the female and *yang* with the male.[6] A wife is in the *yin* position in relation to her husband, while the latter is supposed to be in the *yang* position. However, this same husband occupies the *yin* position in relation to his superior. Here the *yin-yang* concept is mainly a notion of positionality. In other words, *yin* qualities do not belong to women only; by the same token, a man does not monopolize *yang* qualities. This assumed sharing of *yin* and *yang* qualities between men and women appears to have made possible the kinds of rhetorical analogies often evoked in poetry, such as that between a frustrated literatus and an abandoned woman (see chapters 1 and 2).

This interchangeability between the masculine and the feminine can also be found in traditional medical theories about the body. In a study of the concept of gender in Chinese medical history, Charlotte Furth points out the following:

> The notion that the bodies of males and females are homologous along a shifting continuum of mixed and interpenetrating substances and energies means that there are more multiple possible configurations of yin and yang within the

body that might vary in individuals according to time and circumstance. Nonetheless, even as each individual body is ideally configured as balanced between yin and yang forces, this balance is not stable, and the normal probability is that most males will tilt toward a preponderance of yang qualities, while in females an affinity for yin ones will prevail. Thus yin and yang come to name masculine or feminine aspects of the bodily nature over a range of proportions that vary according to the individual.[7]

Furth argues that traditional Chinese medical discourse conceptualized an androgynous body that "has no morphological sex, but only gender."[8] What determines an individual's gender identity, according to this theory, is the individual's specific mix of *yin* and *yang* substances. If an individual tilts toward a preponderance of *yang* qualities, then this individual is considered a male, while a female tilts toward a preponderance of *yin* qualities. The gender model envisioned here is a continuum from *yang* to *yin* rather than "either masculine or feminine." In other words, the distinctions between genders are assumed to be relative rather than absolute. Of course, in specific social and cultural practices, there are other important factors; for example, social status and social roles perform important functions in determining an individual's gender identity, which is ultimately positioned in a rigid social hierarchy. In fact, this relativistic gender model envisioned in traditional Chinese medical discourse by no means precludes hierarchization: "From one aspect male and female bodies are identical or homologous and gender difference is a relativistic and flexible aspect of the body. From another aspect the bodily powers associated with sexuality and generation participate in the gendered hierarchical ordering of the human microcosm and the macrocosm of Heaven and Earth."[9] Furth's observation should help to explain the fluid gender boundaries we have encountered in descriptions of feminine male beauty and cross-dressing, on the one hand, and the rigid gender hierarchy in the subordination of women and sexual segregation, on the other; ironically, the latter necessitates many instances of cross-dressing. While masculinity and femininity were defined less categorically, the status and power associated with an individual once his or her gender identity was determined tended to be hierarchized more rigidly.

In fact, the very discursive power of male literati writings on interchangeability was, paradoxically, closely associated with a hierarchical gender system that was based on women's subordination. When a scholar-official presented himself as an abandoned-but-still-faithful wife and protested about being neglected, he was promoting himself before his lord as a virtuous subject precisely because a woman's virtue, in this idealized hierarchical gender system, was defined almost exclusively in terms of her submission and chastity. That is, women could not have been effective metaphors in these writings had they not been the natural models of submission and chastity, yet women were significant only as metaphors. At the same time, such metaphors also complicated the male author's gender identity, and, the possibility of feminization had always to be entertained.

While the effectiveness of cross-dressing seems to point to the ill-defined boundaries between the feminine and the masculine, a woman's very need to resort to transvestism in order to free herself from her assigned gender role testifies to the rigid sexual segregation in the society. Simply put, the need to avail oneself of this interchangeability is the direct result of segregation and subordination. This is why in the end a cross-dresser has always to "undress" herself to reaffirm the hierarchical gender system her transvestism appears to have initially subverted (see chapter 3). Here we seem to have another paradox: men and women are supposed to be interchangeable in many aspects, but this interchangeability becomes meaningful or can be actualized only when it enhances or reproduces the analogous hierarchical positioning of prince versus minister and men versus women. (A minister should be as loyal to his prince as a woman is faithful to her husband.) Analogy becomes effective only when it underscores differences in social or gender status. This confirms the simple but important fact that gender relationships are in many ways power relationships.

The differentiation strategy appears to be more straightforward. Here masculinity is always defined in sharp contrast to femininity, and the distinctions are assumed to be completely stable and unproblematic. Here women are usually considered a threat to men's manhood, while romantic sentiment is always viewed with deep suspicion. Masculinity is gauged by a man's ability to distance himself from women, and implications of misogyny are almost always there; here elements from the popular discourse (in contrast to the elite discourse) are more likely to be evident. However, even in texts where the analogy strategy is obviously favored, many of the basic assumptions behind the differentiation strategy, such as the subordination of women, are always there to frame the negotiation of gender identity. The two strategies are not inherently exclusive of each other because hierarchy and social inequality are the basic principles underpinning both. Furthermore, I argue that both of these strategies are necessitated by the ambivalent status assigned to women in late imperial cultural discourses. Women had two very different functions: they could be viewed as sources of corruption and as fatal threats to men's gender integrity, and, at the same time, they could be viewed as the exemplars of many Confucian virtues (especially obedience and unconditional loyalty).

In the classic Ming novel *San'guo yanyi* (The Romance of the Three Kingdoms) these two strategies are simultaneously employed to construct the novel's intricate gender structure. *San'guo yanyi* is composed of the stories of a group of masculine heroes in the context of a protracted civil war. However, women's roles are much more important than many readers have so far realized, despite their relatively limited presence in the novel.[10] Here manliness is often defined by a hero's ability to disassociate himself from women, and especially from their perceived bad influence, which is regarded as one of the most serious threats to manhood. Yet despite the deep anxiety over bad feminine influence, a number of women are presented as the *natural* exemplars of certain Confucian virtues such as loyalty and chastity. Moreover, it appears that these exemplary women are often made to serve as excuses for some masculine heroes' apparent moral deficiencies. This draws our attention to the uneasy tension between the masculinity envisioned in the novel and the virtue of loyalty widely celebrated in Confucian discourses. The tactic of deferring the moral high ground to women is related to the perception that demands of unconditional loyalty and obedience sometimes undermine the masculinity of a male subject *(chen)* or hero in his relation to the lord *(jun)* he is serving, as Mencius (ca. 371–289 BCE) argued a long time ago (see chapter 1). In *San'guo yanyi*, a novel supposedly about male heroes, women are indispensable to the negotiation of masculinity. On the one hand, they are presented as threats to manhood; on the other hand, they are celebrated as paragons of loyalty and chastity, often more virtuous than men. The implication is that Confucian virtues such as unconditional loyalty or obedience are female virtues par excellence and therefore are probably not the most desirable masculine qualities during times of political disorder. In other words, if a lord turns out to be unworthy, a hero, unlike a woman married to an unworthy husband, is entitled to switch loyalties. Whereas a woman is defined by her unconditional obedience and loyalty, a masculine hero is characterized by his ability to choose a worthy lord to serve, as well as his right to switch to another if the chosen lord turns out to be unworthy. The ambivalent ethical meanings assigned to women and their roles in the construction of the novel's models of masculinity have considerably complicated the gender structure of *San'guo yanyi* (more in chapter 5).

Based on the generic nature of the texts under examination, my study is divided into three parts. The first explores works that fall into the category of elite discourse, where the analogy strategy is often favored. It focuses on the Confucian classics, historiography, political treatises, and collections of literati writings. I trace the changing significance of a series of feminine tropes frequently deployed in literati self-representation: from the emasculated (castrato) to abandoned women to chaste widows and finally to prostitutes. I explore what the choice of a particular trope can tell us about the gender psyche of a male literati author. One important symbolic figure examined in this part is that of a loyal minister, or *zhongchen:* how is his gender status complicated as well as problematized by the contingencies of loyalty, and how is his manhood problematized by his different and sometimes conflicting obligations to the emperor, his superiors, and his peers?

The second part concentrates on a dozen works of vernacular fiction, which often contains elements from both elite and nonelite cultures. The focus shifts to a group of related but competing models of masculinity, such as *yingxiong* (heroes), *haohan* (stalwarts), *caizi* (romantic scholars), and *shengxian* (sages), exploring how these competing models evolve and complicate one another. Here the concept of loyalty is further interrogated in terms of its gender implications, and the centrality of "loyal minister" is challenged by alternative models of masculinity.

Although women are still presented as the defining "other" in these works, much more attention is now devoted to the implications of the actual (rather than metaphorical) presence of women in a man's life. Compared with the texts discussed in the first part, the presence of women in these fictional works appears to be much less prominent. However, the central question here remains more or less the same—namely, how a man negotiates his gender identity in relation to the feminine. How to maintain an appropriate distance from women remains a crucial issue in the construction process of masculinity. Here the ambivalence of the feminine explored in part 1 begins to take on a slightly different form: a masculine hero needs to prove his manliness by distancing himself from women, and yet, at the same time, his heroic image often needs to be authenticated or enhanced by the appreciation of a beautiful woman, as espoused in the so-called hero-beauty *(yingxiong meiren)* convention. Another interesting question, arising from the several novels dominated by *caizi*, is how to interpret the gender implications of the romantic scholars' apparent resemblance to women in terms of both appearance and personality. Instead of being condemned in these novels, certain feminine qualities are often celebrated as indications of a man's cultural sophistication and sensitivity. A feminine-looking man is not necessarily considered effeminate, and a subtle distinction now appears between the feminine and the effeminate. While femininity can be a positive attribute in a man, effeminacy remains the sign of a less manly man. Whether this interchangeability with the feminine points to certain different models of masculinity is another issue explored in detail in chapters 7 and 8. Owing to its unique generic nature, fiction is more likely to deviate from the values made normative in various canonical writings such as the Confucian classics and official historiography. Even when trying hard to propagate Zhu Xi's (1130–1200) Neo-Confucian notion of masculine hero, the author of the eighteenth-century novel *Yesou puyan* (The Humble Words of a Rustic) could not help but problematize it by (perhaps inadvertently) exposing its limitations. In a work of fiction a neat Confucian doctrine is often thrown into a messy context of different contingencies where adjustments and accommodations are unavoidable. *Yesou puyan* exposes the enormous tensions generated by the conflicting demands of its author's ideal of a perfect Confucian: a romantic *caizi*, a chivalrous *haohan*, and a Confucian sage.

The third part of this study deals with prescriptive advice literature, which usually targets the social elite as its main audience. In many works of household instruction, or *jiaxun,* masculinity is often negotiated within the context of a patriarchal lineage family. Here women are almost always presented as potential threats to the stability and continuity of the male lineage since they are considered "outsiders" from another family. An acid test for a son's familial loyalty after he marries is whether he will side with his parents and brothers or his wife/wives in a family dispute. Here manliness is defined largely in terms of a man's sacred blood relationship with his male relatives. The anxiety over women that filled many works of household instruction is indeed remarkable given that women are integral to the functioning of any patriarchal family. In conduct books not focused on the family, however, the implications of the feminine tend to be much more complicated. Some of these books seem to subscribe to the hero-beauty convention in emphasizing the positive implications of the feminine in a man's attempts to come to terms with his manhood. Some of these books also draw our attention to the increasingly diverse models of masculinity available in late imperial China, as well as the resultant confusion over the blurring boundaries of many seemingly stable definitions of masculinity. It is also here that we revisit the tension between hero and sage (the two competing models of masculinity in many Confucian discourses), a topic of heated debate among the literati ever since Zhu Xi proposed his definition of a true hero.

One of the common themes in most of the works examined in this study is that masculinity is a fluid concept, and, paradoxically, a man becomes concerned with its articulation only when he feels discriminated against by other men. That is, it often becomes an urgent issue when a man feels compelled to distinguish himself from the weaker sex, while women, as the defining "other," are always needed in this re/masculinizing process, no matter what the specific strategies. Consequently, masculinity is almost always fraught with anxiety over the perceived lack of what is considered masculine. To the extent that masculinity is a construct contingent upon its lack or absence, it is an ideal that can never be completely fulfilled. In a sense, almost all strategies for constructing masculinity are also attempts to come to terms with a man's anxiety over not having what he is supposed to have.

The issue of masculinity began to attract the attention of China scholars only very recently, and almost all the important studies on this subject have been published in the new millennium. To my knowledge, there have been only three monographs in English published on this topic: Xueping Zhong's *Masculinity Besieged?* (2000); Kam Louie's *Theorising Chinese Masculinity* (2002); and Geng Song's *The Fragile Scholar* (2003).[11] Neither Zhong nor Louie focuses on pre-twentieth-century China, although the latter devotes considerable attention to the continuities in the long history of Chinese masculinities. Louie's study, which concentrates on the *wen-wu* (civil versus military) polarity, is invaluable in illuminating some of the large patterns of masculinities envisioned in both traditional and modern Chinese cultural discourses.[12] Much less ambitious and more focused on the late imperial period, my study strives to be more historical as well as more empirical. Appreciating the value and importance of theorizing and paradigms, I am, however, more reluctant to offer an overarching definition of "Chinese masculinity." Instead, I emphasize the contingencies of masculinity, although I also try to address issues such as continuities and trends. This is one of the reasons why I have avoided the term "Chinese masculinity" and instead prefer the plural form, "Chinese masculinities." The *caizi,* the focus of Song's study, are also explored in detail in the second part of this book, although *caizi* are only one of the several masculine models I examine, and my examples tend to be taken from fictional works of a later historical period. I am more interested in how the model of *caizi* interacts with other competing models. Much attention is devoted to the mutations of *caizi* as they are represented in several novels from the eighteenth and nineteenth centuries.

Compared with the studies noted above, this book focuses more on the question of *how* different models of masculinity were proposed and negotiated in relation to the feminine rather than trying to define *what* late imperial Chinese masculinities were. I hope to shed light on the intriguing question of why, in trying to come to terms with their own gender identities, many late imperial Chinese literati wrote so much about the feminine, sometimes even appealing to the interchangeability between the masculine and the feminine, while never doubting the naturalness of gender inequality.

This study is not meant to be a chronological survey of late imperial Chinese masculinities, although it is conceived as a historical study concentrating on what I consider to be several historically significant "moments" in the long late imperial period. Trained as a literary historian, I have tried nonetheless to move beyond what has usually been considered "literary" by including in my discussion works from a great variety of genres, some of which fall outside the narrowly defined domain of literature. I hope that there are enough differences and contradictions in the limited number of cases I have examined to give us a feel for the pluralistic nature of the notions of masculinity and their intricate nuances as they were constantly contested and re/invented in late imperial China.

PART 1

ENGENDERING THE LOYAL MINISTER

CHAPTER 1

From True Man to Castrato

Early Models and
Later Ramifications

Although this study focuses on the late imperial period, this beginning chapter will examine two important figures in early China, the philosopher Mencius and the historian Sima Qian (ca. 145–ca. 86 BCE), both of whom exerted considerable influence on various later discourses on masculinity. Placing their views in the larger context of the formation of the so-called *shi* class (men of professional skills) in early China, I try to account for certain shifts in the early history of Chinese masculinities that would have far-reaching implications for the late imperial period.

The Earlier Context and Later Interpretations

The Chinese character *nan* (man or male) is glossed in Xu Shen's (58–147) *Shuowen jiezi* dictionary as *zhangfu* (an adult male or, more literally, a male who has reached the height of an adult), and it is further defined as "a man laboring in the field," as suggested by the two graphs *li* (physical strength) and *tian* (field), which make up this character. Obviously *nan* emphasizes a man's physical strength. However, in his annotations to this entry in the dictionary, the Qing philologist Duan Yucai (1735–1815) calls our attention to the definition given in *Baihu tong* (attributed to Ban Gu [32–92]), where *nan* is associated with a successful career in the government *(gongye).*[1] The *Baihu tong* reference to career success seems to suggest a notion of masculinity that is defined less by physical strength. However, some scholars have argued that *nan* was originally used to refer to someone good at working in the fields rather than a noun denoting male per se and that its reference as "man" was a relatively late phenomenon. Instead, the character originally used to refer to "male" was *shi,* which etymologically refers to the male sexual organ.[2]

Indeed, the construction of masculinities in early China was closely associated with the transformation of a social group loosely known as *shi* (this same character later came to refer to members of the lower stratum of the nobility, who often relied on their professional skills for social advancement).³ Most modern scholars believe that prior to the time of Confucius (b. ca. 551 BCE), *shi* members were mostly warriors *(wushi)*.⁴ Mark Edward Lewis argues that the earlier use of the term *shi* epitomizes the idea of authority based on noble descent and martial valor. He believes that sanctioned violence in ritual sacrifices and warfare contributed to a concept of manliness that emphasized martial prowess.⁵

However, during the late Spring and Autumn Period (722–481 BCE) and early Warring States Period (480–221 BCE), a different ideology of masculinity began to take shape when *wenshi* (men of learning) started to differentiate themselves within the larger *shi* community.⁶ *Wenshi* were known for their wisdom and for specialized cultural knowledge (about matters such as rituals, music, politics, etc.) rather than for their martial prowess.⁷ Initial manifestations of this ideology could be found in Confucius' endeavor to make the question of what constituted *yong* (valor, bravery, or courage) into an issue of morality. The Master said: "To offer sacrifice to the spirit of an ancestor not one's own is obsequious. Faced with what is right, to leave it undone shows a lack of valor."⁸ Apparently Confucius was trying to combat what he perceived to be his contemporaries' tendency to overemphasize the values of *yong*. He was particularly concerned with the kind of *yong* devoid of *yi* (righteousness or morality):

> Zilu said, "Does the gentleman admire courage [*haoyong*]?"
>
> The Master said, "For the gentleman it is righteousness that is supreme. Possessed of courage but devoid of morality, a gentleman will make trouble while a small man will be a brigand."⁹

Elsewhere the Master argued that a virtuous man must also be brave, but a brave man was not necessarily always virtuous.¹⁰ He juxtaposed *yong* with *gang* (unbending) to demonstrate the possible danger of transgression if *xue* (learning) was not diligently practiced: "To love courage without loving learning is liable to lead to insubordination. To love unbending strength without loving learning is liable to lead to indiscipline."¹¹ Confucius appeared rather suspicious of *yong* and *gang*, qualities normally associated with the masculine, and he was especially wary of their transgressive potential when they were not disciplined or not under the control of *yi*.¹²

Zengzi, Confucius' disciple, is quoted in the *Lunyu* (The Analects) as saying, "A gentleman must be strong and resolute [*hongyi*], for his burden is heavy and the road is long. He takes benevolence as his burden. Is that not heavy? Only with death does the road come to an end. Is that not long?"¹³ Zengzi perceived an important connection between a gentleman's ability to carry out his task of benevolence and his masculinity (being strong and resolute, or *hongyi*).

Here it is worthwhile to look at the Song Neo-Confucian thinker Zhu Xi's reading of Zengzi since Zhu's view of masculinity would become very influential, as well as controversial, during the late imperial period, after he was canonized by the imperial government. In his reading, Zhu Xi ingeniously related Zengzi's observation on *hongyi* to his emphasis on the constant need to maintain moral vigilance:

> A supremely wise sage with his kind of moral makeup does not need much effort, and, instead of degenerating into human desire, the Heavenly principle would naturally dominate. In the case of a virtuous man, whose moral makeup is slightly inferior, he will not make too many mistakes so long as he is taught properly before he practices. When it comes to a man of average moral endowments, he will be all right only if he makes a tremendous effort and is constantly on guard to control himself. Zengzi said, "[A gentleman] takes benevolence as his burden. Is that not heavy? Only with death does the road come to an end. Is that not long?" And he also said, "In fear and trembling, as if approaching a deep abyss, as if walking on thin ice [*zhanzhan jingjing, rulin shenyuan, rulü bobing*]."[14]

Zhu Xi further associated this ability to maintain moral vigilance directly with his vision of Confucian masculinity: "Only when a man is courageous but cautious at the same time and only when a man is constantly 'in fear and trembling, as if approaching a deep abyss, as if walking on thin ice,' can he become a 'courageous man of great military skills and effectively defend the state.'"[15]

Inspired by Zengzi, Zhu Xi offered a more elaborate formulation of his concept of Confucian masculinity, centering on the constant need for moral vigilance, in his debate with the utilitarian Confucian thinker Chen Liang (1143–1194):

> I have discussed Mencius' observation that "when speaking to men of consequence it is necessary to look on them with contempt and not be impressed by their lofty position."[16] Although Mencius was not unafraid of men of consequence, he nevertheless showed contempt to those who were arrogant. Capable of this kind of courage, one should have no problem sleeping in the open, even when the roof of one's bedroom is gone. Only those who are capable of behaving like this can be considered truly heroic figures [*zhenzheng da yingxiong ren*]. However, such a hero can only be the result of one's being "in fear and trembling, as if approaching a deep abyss, as if walking on thin ice" and not being arrogant or reckless [*xueqi cuhao*] at all.[17]

As we shall see below (especially in chapters 8 and 9), Zhu Xi's seemingly unusual association of a hero, who was supposed to be fearless, with the Confucian's anxiety over moral fallibility would become an important theme repeatedly emphasized in Confucian discourses on masculinity. At the same time, it would generate heated debates on the relationship between the sage and the hero in late imperial China.

Mencius' True Man

It was Mencius who, based upon Zengzi's theories, offered a more articulate notion of Confucian masculinity that would greatly influence Zhu Xi, a fact already reflected in the latter's remark quoted above. Compared with the Master, Mencius demonstrated a much more explicit concern with the gendered meanings of *yong,* although he never failed to scrutinize its ethical ramifications.

Admiring Mencius' ability to keep his mind tranquil, Gongsun Chou, one of Mencius' students, told his teacher that he far surpassed the famous warrior *(yongshi)* Meng Ben in courage. In his reply, after carefully comparing different examples of valor or courage, Mencius concentrated on what he called the supreme courage *(dayong).* Its essential quality was "being in the right" rather than mere fearlessness. Valor or courage had always been considered a manifestation of *qi,* or vital force, and in the *Shuowen jiezi* dictionary the word *qi* is in fact used to gloss *yong.*[18] Mencius, however, chose to underscore the need for will *(zhi)* to command and control *qi* so that the latter would not be misused *(wu bao qi qi).* He proposed the transcendental notion of flood-like vital forces *(haoran zhi qi),* which were considered "vast and unyielding" *(zhida zhigang)* and which could be developed only by a man in perfect harmony with the vital forces of the cosmos.[19]

In his commentaries on *Mencius,* Zhu Xi used the term *xueqi* (blood and *qi*) from Confucius to characterize Meng Ben's *yong* as the "valor of blood and *qi* [*xueqi zhi yong*]."[20] Of course, the term *xueqi* has already appeared in Zhu Xi's observation on the association between heroism and moral caution quoted above. The original passage from *Lunyu* reads as follows:

> Confucius said, "There are three things the gentleman should guard against. In youth, when the blood and *qi* are still unsettled *(xueqi weiding),* he should guard against the attraction of feminine beauty. In the prime of life, when the blood and *qi* have become unyielding *(xueqi fanggang),* he should guard against bellicosity. In old age, when the blood and *qi* have declined, he should guard against acquisitiveness."[21]

Obviously, Confucius was deeply concerned with blood and *qi,* against which, according to him, a gentleman needed to remain constantly vigilant. It is suggested in *Mencius* that only through rigorous moral self-discipline could blood and *qi* be transformed into "flood-like *qi.*" By proposing the concept of flood-like *qi,* Mencius made *yong* into a more positive quality than Confucius had allowed. (Mencius was apparently less suspicious of *yong.*) For Mencius, *dayong* was a subtle mental power that was defined by its ethical implications. In contrast to *dayong,* Mencius proposed the notion of *xiaoyong* (small valor or small courage).[22] Once again *yong* was evaluated in terms of *yi;* in the case of a king, the question was whether his valor could benefit his country. Small valor brought no benefits to the country, and it was therefore considered to be the attribute of commoners *(pifu zhi yong).* Here a commoner's valor was understood to be typical of someone who could not control his *qi* or what Zhu Xi would later characterize as "the valor of blood and *qi.*"[23]

Da zhangfu (a great man or a true man) and *xiao zhangfu* (petty man) were another pair of important terms that Mencius used to further define his version of Confucian masculinity:

> Jing Chun said, "Were not Gongsun Yan and Zhang Yi great men [*da zhangfu*]? As soon as they showed their wrath the feudal lords trembled with fear, and when they were still the Empire was spared the conflagration of war."
>
> "How can they be thought great men?" said Mencius. "Have you never studied the rites? When a man comes of age his father gives him advice. When a girl marries, her mother gives her advice and accompanies her to the door with the cautionary words, 'When you go to your new home, you must be respectful and circumspect. Do not disobey your husband.' It is the way of a wife or concubine [*qiefu zhi dao*] to consider obedience and docility the norm.
>
> "A man lives in a spacious dwelling, occupying the proper position, and goes along the highway of the Empire. When he achieves his ambition he shares these with the people; when he fails to do so he practices the Way alone [*duxing qi dao*]. He cannot be led into excesses when wealthy and honored or deflected from his purpose when poor and obscure, nor can he be made to bow before superior force. This is what I would call a true man [*da zhangfu*]."[24]

Here Mencius tried to define masculinity in opposition to what he considered femininity. While a woman, according to Mencius, was defined by her obedience, a true man was characterized by his independence and his courage to practice the Way alone, especially under unfavorable circumstances. Once again, masculinity was measured in terms of a man's ability or determination to stand up for the sake of righteousness, or *yi,* because, unlike a woman, a true man did not bow to the powerful (politically or physically). Martial prowess and other physical attributes were not significant factors in Mencius' definitions of masculinity and femininity.[25]

The Changing Status of *Shi* and the Feminine

The apparent de-emphasis of martial valor in the Confucian ideology of masculinity has led some to argue that there was a feminine quality associated with Confucianism, despite the fact that Mencius tried to present his notion of masculinity in contrast to femininity. In his well-known essay "Shuoru" (On *Ru*), published in 1934, the twentieth-century scholar Hu Shi cited the *Shuowen jiezi* definition of *ru* (the character employed in later ages to refer to the followers of Confucius) to support his argument that people identified as *ru* were usually considered soft and feminine. In that dictionary, *ru* is glossed as "being soft" *(rou)*. Hu Shi argued that the graph *xu* had the connotation of being mild and soft. When it was used as a word, it was often interchangeable with words such as *nuo* (weak and subservient) and *ruan* (soft). He believed that *ru* originally referred to priests during the Yin dynasty (ca. sixteenth century–eleventh century BCE), and it was also associated with the "way of the mild" *(roudao,* a life philosophy many people of the Yin adopted in order to come to terms with their tragic fate as the conquered people after the Yin monarchy was toppled by the Zhou army). However, Hu Shi also noted that during the Spring and Autumn Period, Confucius and some of his followers tried to invigorate the *ru* tradition by emphasizing moral courage.[26] Hu Shi's essay has provoked some controversy among scholars, although many of them appear to have accepted his basic arguments.[27] It is probably safe to say that with the rise of Confucianism, or *rujia* (as it came to be known later), there indeed emerged a new notion of manhood, which was based less on martial prowess than on ethical courage.

Another important discursive practice emerged during the Warring States Period that contributed to the complexities of the early history of Chinese masculinity. As Mark Lewis has noted, accompanying the increasing emphasis on social hierarchy during this period, there was a "sexual re-imagining of the political realm" in which "the rule of husband over wife was regarded as the paradigm of all authority."[28] For example, in *Zhan'guo ce* (Intrigues of the Warring States; a work believed to have been compiled by Liu Xiang [79–8 BCE] based on pre-Qin sources), we can find many cases where a *shi*'s service as an official is compared to a woman married to a man.[29] In a story about the assassin Yu Rang from *Zhan'guo ce,* we come cross the statement, "A man dies for someone who really understands him, and a woman adorns herself for someone who appreciates her beauty,"[30] a saying that would be made famous by Sima Qian when he repeated it in his writings.[31]

As shown in Sima Qian's *Shiji* (The Records of the Grand Historian), such argument by analogy was quite common during the Warring States Period. For example, we are told that Wang Chu, an adviser to the King of Qi, refused the offer of a high position from the invading Yan troops because he believed, "A loyal minister does not serve two lords and a chaste woman does not take a second husband."[32] The comparison of a loyal minister to a faithful wife was to become a convention in political discourses on loyalty in the two-thousand-year history of imperial China. This "sexual re-imagin-

ing of the political realm" seems to have reached a more theoretically
refined level around the time of Sima Qian, when the centralized imperial
rule *(dayitong)* became consolidated and ruler-subject relationships began
to be conceived more rigidly in gendered terms.

The "Wenyan" commentary (believed to have been produced during the
Former Han dynasty [206 BCE–8 CE]) on the hexagram *kun* in the *Yijing*
(Book of Changes) provides a philosophical validation of such gender-
political practices: "Although [the subject of] this divided line has excellent
qualities, he [does not display them, but] keeps them under restraint. 'If he
engages with them in the service of the King, and be successful, he will not
claim that success for himself':—this is the way of the earth, of a wife, of a
minister."[33] Here the cosmic correlation among the three *kun*[a] phenomena—earth, minister, and wife—is evoked to make an ethical as well as a
political point that has profound gender implications. The Han Confucian
Dong Zhongshu (179–104 BCE) further elaborated on this correlation by
appealing to the theory of *yin* and *yang:* "In all things there must be corre-
lates. . . . The *yin* is the correlate of the *yang,* the wife of the husband, the
son of the father, the subject of the ruler. . . . Thus the relationship between
ruler and subject, father and son, husband and wife, are all derived from the
principles of the *yin* and *yang.* The ruler is *yang,* the subject *yin,* the father
is *yang,* the son *yin;* the husband is *yang,* and the wife *yin.*"[34]

The analogy between minister-ruler and wife-husband based on *yin-yang*
polarities was further strengthened by being linked with the father-son relationship in the essential "three bonds" *(san'gang).* Scholars have noted that
various *yin-yang* theories began to be associated with gender during the
late Spring and Autumn Period, as reflected in the Confucian classic *Zuozhuan* (The Zuo Commentary), although these associations were not yet
coherent or systematic.[35] By third century BCE, however, in texts such as
Lüshi chunqiu (The Spring and Autumn Annals of Lü), the gendering of
yin-yang polarities became quite common. Lisa Raphals argues that "it is
toward the end of the second and beginning of the first centuries [BCE]
that explicitly hierarchical *yin-yang nan-nü* analogies emerge, notably in the
Chunqiu fanlu and the *Li ji.*"[36]

These discursive conventions, where male political relationships in
the public realm were conceived in terms of private gender relationships
between husband and wife/concubines, considerably complicated the conceptualization of masculinity in imperial China. To better understand this
complication, we have to look more closely at the changes in the *shi* community from the Warring States era, when China was divided into many
competing states, to the subsequent two centuries, when China was united
under a centralized government.

If it is true that the social structure of the Warring States Period became
more hierarchical compared with the earlier Spring and Autumn Period—

as Mark Lewis has argued—then it is probably equally true that the demand for the services of *shi* was also much greater during the later period, when all the states were constantly engaged in large-scale warfare for domination or survival. Mencius' famous political theory on the relative independence of ministers at the expense of a ruler's absolute authority was related to the higher status the *shi* were enjoying during his time. For Mencius, the hierarchical husband-wife relationship was not the appropriate model for the ruler-minister relationship. The right model, he suggested, was that of student-teacher, and he insisted that a ruler should treat his minister with utmost respect, just as he would treat his teacher. Such respect, according to Mencius, was essential to a *shi*'s gender identity as a true man *(zhishi* or *yongshi)*.[37] Here we may recall Mencius' insistence on the distinction between masculinity *(da zhangfu),* which was defined as a man's courage to stand up for his ideals, and femininity *(qiefu zhi dao),* which was characterized by obedience. Now if a minister was relegated to a position from which he could only obey or placate rather than teach or advise his prince, then he was being reduced to the status of a woman. Although Mencius never explicitly used gender metaphors to discuss the ruler-subject relationship, he came quite close when he characterized those who only wanted to please the princes they were serving as *rongyue zhe* (a man who always tries to please).[38] Obviously, loyalty and obedience, which, according to Mencius, were the main attributes of a woman, were not the first things he looked for in a minister. On the contrary, Mencius asserted that when a prince repeatedly rejected his minister's advice, the latter should simply leave him.[39] What was important to Mencius was whether a ruler was worthy of the service of a *shi* and the right of the latter to choose whom he wanted to serve.

For many, Mencius' image of an independent-minded and almost arrogant *shi* gradually became only a remote memory after China was united under a centralized imperial monarchy. Advising the First Emperor of Qin (r. 221–202 BCE) about strengthening the central government and tightening control, the famous (or notorious) legalist minister Li Si (ca. 280–208 BCE) argued, "In the past, the feudal rulers vied with one another in inviting wandering scholars to their courts and treating them generously. But now all under heaven has been pacified and laws and ordinances proceed from a single source. The common people in their homes devote their efforts to agriculture and crafts, while gentlemen [*shi*] study the laws and ordinances and practice how to avoid prohibitions."[40]

Although the Qin monarchy did not last long, its centralized imperial system was continued and perfected during the succeeding Former Han dynasty, especially after the power of various princes and feudal lords was steadily reduced during the reigns of Emperor Wen (r. 180–157 BCE), Emperor Jing (r. 157–141 BCE), and Emperor Wu (r. 141–87 BCE).[41] The courtier and jester Dongfang Shuo (153–94 BCE) was keenly aware of the changes in the status of a *shi:*

In Su Qing and Zhang Yi's time, the House of Zhou was in complete ruin; the feudal lords failed to appear in audience at court; they instead waged war for dominance and tried to conquer others by force. Twelve states emerged through annexation and none of them could triumph in total victory. He who received the service of gentlemen became powerful, and he who lost the service of gentlemen was condemned to defeat [*deshi zhe qiang shishi zhe wang*]. . . . But this is not the case today. Our sage emperor is able to spread his virtue. And everyone under heaven is in fear [of his power] and all feudal lords submit and obey. . . . Had Su Qin and Zhang Yi been born together with me in the present age, they would not even have been clerks, let alone Gentlemen-in-Attendance (like me). This is because in different times, things are different.[42]

Most scholars agree that the convention of comparing a frustrated *shi* (often an official) to an abandoned woman in Chinese literary tradition was initiated by the poet Qu Yuan (fl. third century BCE) in his *Lisao* (Encountering Sorrow).[43] While in the first half of this long poem the poet adopts the female persona longing for her lover (his patron or king), in the second half, the king becomes a maiden pursued by the poet. In later literary works apparently influenced by Qu Yuan, rarely do we find examples in which the metaphor of the feminine is used to refer to one's patron or superior. Whereas in this poem from the Warring States Period we can still find evidence suggesting that the male-female polarities did not *always* correspond to that of ruler-minister (that is, sometimes the politically powerful person was compared to a woman), in later literary works the hierarchy of power was always rendered as an unequal gender relationship in which the less powerful had always to be metaphorically represented by the weaker gender. Increasingly, gender differences (often inequalities) were appropriated for the sake of emphasizing and justifying political hierarchy or vice versa. This new gender rigidity, one is tempted to speculate, might have been in part a result of the new centralized political structure, where social and political hierarchy became increasingly prominent features.[44] One thing seems certain: in early imperial China, subservience or obedience, which Mencius had defined as an essential feminine quality, came increasingly to define the position of a *shi* in relation to the monarchy he was supposed to serve. Now let us turn to Sima Qian, whose tragic life and problematic gender identity might have symbolically captured the fate of many *shi* in early imperial China.[45]

Castration and the Reinvention of Masculinity

In 98 BCE, Sima Qian was sentenced to death for offending Emperor Wu when he tried to defend Li Ling, a general who had surrendered to enemy troops after suffering serious defeats on the battlefield.[46] During the Han dynasty, under certain circumstances, a death sentence could be commuted to castration. Sima Qian appears to have asked for commutation and it was granted.[47] How to apologize for the decision of choosing castration over death, a great shame in the eyes of many of his contemporaries, became Sima Qian's obsession in his postcastration life. His most eloquent apology was his famous "Bao Ren Shaoqing shu" (A Letter in Reply to Ren Shaoqing). This letter, full of gender anxieties, can be read as its author's painstaking attempt to reclaim his male identity, an endeavor of self-re/masculinization.

At first glance, Sima Qian seems to have submerged himself in anguish and self-loathing. In addition to *chi* (shame), *ru* (humiliation) appears sixteen times in the letter. He told his friend Ren Shaoqing that as a castrato (*xingyu zhi ren;* literally, one who has suffered physical mutilation), he was now looked down upon by everyone, and therefore he was not in a position to say anything in front of the emperor on Ren's behalf. He even went so far as to carefully catalogue many important historical figures who had refused to be associated with castrati or eunuchs, among whom was Confucius.[48]

Sima Qian insisted that a brave man did not necessarily have to commit suicide for the sake of honor, while even a coward would do anything to gain the recognition of being righteous; moreover, whether an act could be judged courageous or cowardly to a large extent depended on the specific circumstances. He offered the following explanation for his decision to seek commutation: "The reason I have not refused to bear these ills and have continued to live, dwelling in vileness and disgrace without taking my leave, is that I grieve that I have things in my heart which I have not been able to express fully, and I am ashamed to think that after I am gone my writings will not be known to posterity."[49] Then he provided another lengthy list of great historical figures who had achieved eternal fame by writing great books only after serious setbacks and sufferings.[50] Among them again was Confucius. Sima Qian claimed that he had chosen castration over death precisely because he wanted to emulate the Master and become a great author so that he would not be forgotten by posterity like an insignificant ant *(louyi).*[51] Sima Qian was setting up a paradox: as a castrato, he was attempting to regain his deprived "manhood" by emulating someone who had generally shown great contempt for castrati.[52] Sima Qian tried to resolve this apparent paradox by redefining the implications of physical dysfunction: "Those like Zuo Qiu, who was blind, or Sunzi, whose feet were amputated, could never hold office [*bukeyong;* more literally, not usable] so they retired to compose books in order to set forth their thoughts and indignation, handing down their theoretical writings in order to show to posterity who they were. I too have ventured not to be modest but have entrusted myself to my useless writings [*kongwen*]."[53]

In "Taishigong zixu" (The Grand Historian's Postscript), Sima Qian also used the word *kongwen* to refer to *Chunqiu* (The Spring and Autumn Annals) as a work Confucius wrote only after he had failed to prevail on any ruler to accept his service.[54] By comparing his traumatic experience as a castrato to the Confucius' setbacks, Sima Qian implied that Confucius also suffered from dysfunction. Great writings, known as *kongwen*, which might not be appreciated in their authors' lifetimes, were somehow related to the authors' physical dysfunction, as in the cases of Zuo Qiu, Sunzi and Sima Qian himself. The "emptiness" of the writing paralleled the author's physical deficiency.[55] In this regard, the reference to Sunzi, or Sun Bin (ca. 378–301 BCE), is particularly revealing. In Sima Qian's "Sunzi Wu Qi lie-zhuan" (The Biographies of Sunzi and Wu Qi), we are told Sun Bin's feet were amputated owing to a trick by someone who was jealous of his talent. Later, when appointed by King Wei of Qi as a general to command an army to go to the rescue of the state of Zhao, Sun Bin declined on the grounds that as a *xingyu zhi ren*, it would not be appropriate for him. Instead he accepted the position of adviser (*shi*[a]; also meaning teacher) and sat in a wagon directing the battle.[56] (*Xingyu zhi ren* was the same phrase Sima Qian used to describe himself as a castrato, as we mentioned above.) Sun Bin was also known for a treatise on military strategy. Obviously, in the eyes of posterity, his physical limitation (which was emphasized by the fact that he had to be carried in a wagon when he was directing battles) was more than compensated for by his texts and the military victories he had helped to win.[57]

In fact, Sima Qian was claiming more: instead of emasculating a man, physical mutilation such as castration could render a man more masculine (becoming a cultural hero like Confucius) than a man with merely normal sexual function. In other words, the removal of his genitals, the bodily signifier of his masculinity, paradoxically served only to enhance his manhood. Separating his sexed body from his gender, Sima Qian tried to erase the physical un-manning by celebrating it as a force that motivated him to accomplish the most masculine of tasks—bringing honor to his ancestors and attaining fame. This becomes especially ironic since by allowing himself to be castrated he appeared to have committed two great unfilial sins in the eyes of a Confucian: harming his body, which was a sacred gift from his parents, and depriving himself of the ability to produce male offspring (most likely Sima Qian did not have any male heirs).[58] Yet Sima Qian claimed that by virtue of this seemingly unfilial act, he was in fact accomplishing the greatest filial act—bringing honor to his ancestors by completing the unfinished work of his father. This was the ultimate act of masculinity.[59]

Sima Qian's traumatic experience of castration could also be understood in a larger context as an important historical event in that it might have forced many of his *shi* contemporaries to confront the emasculating nature of imperial politics: they were repeatedly reminded that the time was long gone when they could command even more respect than the princes.[60] Now they were reduced to the low status of the emperor's jesters or entertainers (*changyou*), a term Sima Qian used to characterize the low status of his father as an imperial astrologer—his father was only a plaything for the emperor, to keep the latter entertained.[61] Here we may recall Mencius' contempt for ministers who knew only how to please and entertain their lords.

Interpreted in this light, Sima Qian's reference in his letter to the maxim "A gentleman dies for the person who understands him, and a woman adorns herself for the person who appreciates her beauty" should help us to better understand the plight of his *shi* peers: they had to do everything possible to keep the emperor pleased or entertained, just as a woman had to adorn herself in order to please her husband/lover. The marginalizing experience shared by many of Sima Qian's *shi* contemporaries was probably one of the major factors that contributed to the unusually pervasive presence of the feminine in works of *fu* (rhapsody), an important literary genre during the Former Han dynasty.[62] A main theme of these writings was the frustrations of a political career *(shi buyu)*.[63]

Sima Qian's castration became a historical event capable of even more potent cultural implications if we look at how his subtle strategies of self-re/masculinization gave rise to an alternative redeeming notion of masculinity for *shi* members who were feeling emasculated by their increasingly marginalized status. Now they could reclaim their lost manhood by producing "empty writings," even though these writings might be regarded by their contemporaries as completely trivial or feminine, because these writings were meant for posterity. Posthumous fame—or rather the prospect of such fame—could effectively help an emasculated man to regain his lost manhood. Sima Qian's notion of masculinity seems to have been a particularly powerful force for re/masculinization since it defied temporal limitations. Of course, the notion already had support from another source: the theory of the three kinds of cultural immortality, or *san buxiu*, which advocated the attainment of virtue; achievements in public service; and the creation of words *(lide, ligong, liyan)*, first proposed in *Zuozhuan*.[64] There was nothing more masculine for an educated man than immortality in the eyes of posterity through the texts he had authored.

For the *shi* convinced of their talents and moral virtue, it was now acceptable not to be appreciated or employed by the government. They still deserved the honor of true men if they could write about how they had been forced to become "women." As Sima Qian had argued all along, an emasculating experience could lead to the enhancement of masculinity if it could be turned into a motivation for producing "empty writings." In Sima Qian's case, the writing brush was a substitute for the penis.

Clearly Sima Qian had intended "Bao Ren Shaoqin shu" and "Taishigong zixu" to be the authoritative reading guides for his monumental history. Many later readers considered his castration one of the most important interpretive factors when reading his *Shiji*.[65] In fact, many of them followed Sima Qian's own guidelines rather faithfully in their interpretations of this work. This is particularly significant since what interests us most in this study is how the castration became a symbolic event in the history of Chinese masculinities. To better appreciate its symbolic significance to men of later ages, in the following readings from *Shiji*, while following Sima Qian's own guidelines, I sometimes corroborate my interpretations with those of many other readers, especially those from the late imperial period.

Let us begin with Sima Qian's much anthologized "Lian Po Lin Xiangru liezhuan" (The Biography of Lian Po and Lin Xiangru), about two figures from the Warring States Period. It begins with an interesting juxtaposition in which *wen* and *wu* were carefully contrasted: "Lian Po was an able general of Zhao. In the sixteenth year of King Huiwen [283 BCE], he led the Zhao army against Qi and routed its troops, taking the city of Yangqin. Then he was promoted to be the rank of chief minister. He was known for his valor [*yong*] among all the feudal lords. Lin Xiangru, a man of Zhao, was the servant of the chief eunuch, Mu Xian."[66] The contrast between the two could not be more obvious: Lian Po was a famous general, known for his military prowess, while Lin Xiangru was the retainer of a eunuch. Here Lin Xiangru's association with a eunuch is particularly significant since Sima Qian himself as a castrato was given the position of *zhongshu ling* (secretariat director) by Emperor Wu; the position was usually occupied by a eunuch at that time. No wonder Lian Po was furious when he learned that Lin Xiangru had also been promoted to chief minister and was even ranked higher than he (Lin had risked his life several times and successfully defended the honor of the king in a number of diplomatic missions): "I am a general who has done much in the battlefield for the country. All Lin Xiangru did was wag his tongue, and yet he was promoted to be above me, despite his lowly background [*jianren*]. This is humiliating, and I would never serve below such a fellow."[67]

Here *jianren*, or a man of lowly origins, was apparently used to emphasize Lin Xiangru's status as the employee of a eunuch. (Sima Qian in his letter to Ren Shanqin had painfully pointed out how men of honor all disdained castrati.) Lian Po's insistence that Lin Xiangru's promotion was based on his speaking ability rather than his military prowess also emphasized Lin Xiangru's supposed lack of manliness compared to Lian. However, the purport of Sima Qian's biography was to demonstrate precisely how Lin Xiangru as a "lesser man" was eventually able to win total respect from Lian Po, the more "masculine" hero, by virtue of his impeccable manly actions.[68] While Lin Xiangru's courageous actions had already struck fear deep in the hearts of the powerful enemies of the state of Zhao, he also managed to keep his composure and avoid confrontations with the unreasonable Lian Po in the interest of the country. For this reason he should be admired as a paragon of valor as well as wisdom. Finally, Sima Qian called our attention to the fact that many people were capable of bravery, or *yong*, since a man who knew he had no choice but to die would naturally become brave. While dying was not a difficult act in itself, how to die and for what reason to die were indeed difficult issues.⁶⁹ A proper decision on whether and how to die was an indication of an even more profound bravery. Indeed, death, and especially suicide, were issues with which Sima Qian had had to wrangle ever since he had decided to accept castration over death. Consequently, for Sima Qian, to die or not to die became a central issue in defining manhood.

In "Wu Zixu liezhuan" (The Biography of Wu Zixu), Wu Zixu's father was imprisoned by King Ping of Chu, who demanded that Wu Zixu and his brother go to Chu as a precondition for their father's release. Knowing that they both would be killed along with their father if they went, Wu Zixu chose to flee in order to wait for an opportunity for revenge, while his brother went to Chu with the understanding that he would die with their father. Many years after the death of his father and brother, Wu Zixu was able to lead an army to attack Chu. By the time his army conquered Chu, however, King Ping had also died. All Wu Zixu could do was to dig up the former king's grave and whip his corpse with three hundred blows. In his comments, Sima Qian argued, "Had Wu Zixu died with his father, there would have been no difference between himself and an ant," implying that by choosing to live, Wu Zixu got an opportunity to avenge his father (albeit in only a symbolic manner), thus securing his own name in history. The rhetoric here is reminiscent of that in Sima Qian's letter to Ren Shaoqing, where he defended his own choice of castration over death. He characterized Wu Zixu's choice as "setting aside a small principle of righteousness [*xiaoyi*] and taking revenge to wipe clean a great shame [*dachi*]." Wu Zixu "endured disgrace to achieve great deeds and fame, and none but a true man [*lie zhangfu*] could have done this."⁷⁰ Interestingly, for Sima Qian, *yi*, or righteousness, could be considered small or insignificant and could therefore be ignored if personal honor and revenge were at stake—a far cry from the emphases on *yi* seen in Confucius and Mencius.

At the end of "Lu Zhonglian Zou Yang liezhuan" (The Biography of Lu Zhonglian and Zou Yang), Sima Qian tried to justify the inclusion of Lu Zhonglian in *Shiji* even though many would question Lu's morality: "Although Lu Lian's [another name used by the author] views were not necessarily in accordance with the great principles of righteousness, I gave him credit for eloquently arguing his ideas while not being intimidated by the feudal lords and commenting on contemporary affairs in defiance of ministers in high positions."⁷¹ "The great principles of righteousness" (*dayi*) did not weigh too much on Sima Qian when he was judging this historical figure. Apparently, he shared Lu Zhonglian's view that "those who cling to small virtue [*xiaojie*] will not attain fame and glory, and those who cannot bear small shame [*xiaochi*] will not achieve great things."⁷² Lu Zhonglian's word *xiaojie* certainly reminds us of Sima Qian's *xiaoyi*, or small principles of righteousness. We have reason to believe that Sima

Qian's notion of *yong* was a significant departure from those of Confucius and Mencius, where *yi* was a defining quality. Instead, to be able to endure temporary disgrace for the sake of accomplishing great deeds and achieving fame, according to Sima Qian, was a hallmark of true manliness.

In his biography of the famous Han general Han Xin, Sima Qian tells us a revealing anecdote about the early years of his subject. Once Han Xin was willing to crawl between the legs of another man just to avoid fighting a duel. Consequently, people considered Han Xin a coward.[73] However, when Han Xin eventually became a renowned general, cowardice was the last quality people would associate with him.[74] Another hero who had suffered humiliation in his early years was Zhang Liang, a famous Han minister. Zhang was rewarded with a copy of a treatise on military strategy by an old man because he had respectfully picked up the old man's shoes under a bridge when the old man rudely ordered him to do so.[75] As we shall see in our discussions in chapters 8 and 9, both Han Xin and Zhang Liang would become masculine models celebrated in late imperial cultural discourse for their ability to endure humiliation for the sake of achieving something much greater.

Similar demonstrations of true manliness can be found in Sima Qian's presentation of another Han general, Ji Bu, in "Ji Bu Luan Bu liezhuan" (The Biography of Ji Bu and Luan Bu), where Sima Qian again reiterated the importance of a man's being able to endure humiliation: "In order to find opportunities for his unfulfilled potential, he was able to endure disgrace without feeling ashamed. This was why he eventually became a famous general of the Han. Wise men regard the issue of death with great seriousness. Even lowly people such as slave women and concubines are capable of committing suicide out of passion, not because they were brave, but because they were at the end of their wits."[76] What must have struck a chord with Sima Qian was the fact that Ji Bu, in order to avoid being arrested, was willing to endure the humiliation of being sold as a slave, with his head shaved and his neck chained *(kunqian)*.[77] Particularly interesting is the word *xinglu*, which Sima Qian chose to describe Ji Bu's physical humiliation.[78] This word was usually used to refer to severe punishment such as a death sentence; *kun*[b], or head shaving, was an extremely humiliating punishment since one's hair was often considered an important part of one's sacred body (sacred because it was a gift from one's parents), and head shaving was regarded as tantamount to tonsorial castration.[79] By later becoming a famous general, Ji Bu redeemed far more than the manhood he was supposed to have lost (the humiliation of being sold as a slave)—just like our historian.

Sima Qian's biography of Ji Bu has inspired many autobiographical interpretations from later readers. The Ming writer Mao Kun (1512–1601; *DMB*, pp. 1042–1047) was convinced that Sima Qian was giving vent to his own pent-up emotions, while the pseudonymous commentator Huainanzi pointed out that all the tortuous logic about "one should not die casually" and "one should not be afraid of dying" was meant to defend Sima Qian's own decision.[80]

Writing about how other men were able to regain or enhance their manhood by enduring temporary disgrace became an important vehicle of self-re/masculinization for Sima Qian. In this regard the story of Nie Zheng in "Cike liezhuan" (The Biographies of the Assassins) is especially revealing. After assassinating his patron's nemesis, Nie Zheng mutilated himself to ensure that no one would identify him and that the cycle of revenge would stop. Nie Zheng's sister, Rong, after learning of his death, came forward to claim his corpse because she did not want her brother to remain an unknown hero, even though her public acknowledgement would surely endanger her own life. Before her suicide, she declared, "He mutilated himself to hide his identity because I was still alive. However, how can I, out of fear of death, allow my noble brother to perish in anonymity?"[81] By virtue of this act of transmission, the sister, according to many, also achieved fame for herself. Likewise, by committing the heroism of someone else to writing, Sima Qian was able to bring fame to himself. In Rong, we can feel the reverberations of Sima Qian's claim to masculinity as a transmitter (historian) of others' masculine behavior.[82] The female gender of Rong, with whom Sima Qian appeared to identify, was particularly significant, given his experience as a castrato and his role as a historian who had to rely on "empty writing" to claim fame and honor. For Sima Qian, masculinity was apparently a quality that did not necessarily always belong to a man. Though usually demonstrated by great men, it could sometimes transcend gender boundaries to be found in a feminine-looking man, a castrato, or even a woman. This reminds us of Sima Qian's curious mention at the end of the biography of Zhang Liang that he was rather surprised by a portrait of Zhang. He was a very feminine-looking man, he noted; yet he had always thought that Zhang, a famous minister and military strategist, must be a very imposing masculine figure. This led Sima Qian to caution that one could never be judged merely on the basis of physical appearance or bodily attributes.[83] By implication, the reader should not judge our historian's manliness based on his emasculated body.

Xiang Yu and the Feminine

The images of heroic masculinity presented in *Shiji* do not always have to be interpreted with reference to Sima Qian's agenda of re/masculinization. One of the most imposing figure of masculinity in *Shiji* is Xiang Yu (d. 202 BCE), known as the Hegemon King of the Chu (Chu bawang); he eventually lost to the founder of the Han dynasty, Liu Bang (Han Kaodi; r. 202–195 BCE) in an epic struggle for control after China's first empire, the Qin, collapsed. As represented in *Shiji*, Xiang Yu was virtually a paragon of masculine strength. We are specifically told that he was over eight feet tall (Sima Qian seldom mentioned the height of his historical figures). He was so powerful that he could lift a bronze cauldron with little trouble. His glare and his bellowing were often intimidating enough to send his enemies on the run (a physical feat to be repeated by many masculine heroes in later historical and fictional works).[84] Many times, he was able to single-handedly kill hundreds of enemy soldiers. However, often his killing frenzies went too far. He was said to have slaughtered thousands and thousands of prisoners of war, as well as innocent residents of the areas he conquered, thus probably preventing many people from surrendering peacefully. His famous song before he finally committed suicide was revealing:

> My strength could uproot the hills,
> My *qi* could dominate the entire world;
> But the times were against me,
> And my horse runs no more.
> When my horse runs no more,
> What then can I do?
> Ah, Yu, my Yu,
> What will your fate be?[85]

Chased by the advancing troops of the Han, the once mighty hero Xiang Yu was reduced to asking a woman what he should do. His brutal physical strength proved to be of little use at this junction, although, before committing suicide, he still insisted on killing a few more enemy generals and several hundred more enemy soldiers—probably just for show, since such killings would not enable to him to break through the multilayered encirclement. The word *qi* in his song was significant. In his comments at the end of "Ji Bu Luan Bu liezhuan," Sima Qian also made note of Xiang Yu's enormous *qi* when he observed that Ji Bu demonstrated tremendous valor *(yong)* because he seemed to possess the kind of *qi* that Xiang Yu had demonstrated.[86] As mentioned above, Mencius believed that the cultivation of *qi* was crucial to the attainment of great valor, or *dayong*. Obviously, Xiang Yu's tragic failures had a lot to do with his having allowed his *qi* to get the better of him or his having abused his *qi*, something against which Mencius had already warned. Han Xin, the famous general, called Xiang Yu's valor only that of a commoner *(pifu zhi yong)*, again a term already used by Mencius.[87]

At the beginning of Sima Qian's biography of Xiang Yu, there was a revealing passage about his early years:

> When Xiang Yu was young, he tried to study to be a scribe [*xueshu*]. Failing in this, he took up swordsmanship [*xuejian*]. When he failed in this too, Xiang Liang was upset with him, but Xiang Yu said, "Writing is good only for keeping records of people's names. Swordsmanship can only enable one to defeat a single adver-

sary [*di yiren*]. It is not worth learning. What I want to learn is the skills that would enable me to defeat ten thousand enemies [*di wanren*]."

Then Xiang Liang began to teach him military strategies, which pleased Xiang Yu tremendously. However, Xiang Yu refused to complete his studies after mastering only the general outline.[88]

Xiang Yu was ambitious, but he did not persevere in what he did. Although he expressed a desire to learn the skills that would defeat ten thousand enemies and although occasionally he could even be a brilliant military strategist, he made many fatal strategic errors. What posterity remembers about Xiang Yu is precisely that he possessed only the skills to defeat a single enemy *(di yiren)*, the same words Mencius had used to describe physical valor.[89]

"Xiang Yu benji" (The Basic Annals of Xiang Yu) and "Gaozu benji" (The Basic Annals of Emperor Gaozu) are probably two of the most controversial biographies in *Shiji*, largely because they are full of ambiguities and inconsistencies. The reader's interpretations are further complicated by conflicting references to these two historical figures elsewhere in *Shiji*.[90] Our historian sometimes appeared to have been fascinated with Xiang Yu's physical prowess and heroic feats.[91] But at other times, he was quite straightforward in condemning Xiang Yu for his failure to heed the sound suggestions of his advisers, for his senseless killings, and for his reliance on physical force alone.[92] One of Sima Qian's implicit criticisms was that Xiang Yu was unable to endure disgrace or humiliation. Encircled by the Han troops, Xiang Yu decided, against the advice of others, to commit suicide rather than return to face the people of his native land in shame. As a result, he forfeited the opportunity to regroup and probably even the chance for an eventual come-from-behind victory. This was another example of being unable to endure a temporary disgrace for the sake of final glory.[93]

Even so, Xiang Yu must have appealed to Sima Qian tremendously, in part because the latter was such a giant figure among tragic failures. As he mentioned in his letter to Ren Shaoqing, almost all of Sima Qian's heroes were failures in one way or another. Confucius could also be considered a failure since his offer of service had been rejected by many feudal lords. Here we may recall the image of the Master as captured in *Lunyu:* "Is that the person who keeps working toward a goal the realization of which he knows to be hopeless?"[94] For Confucius and probably for Sima Qian as well, the ultimate test of manhood was whether a man could continue to do what was considered right even though there was absolutely no hope of success.

Finally, let us look at the significance of a woman in Xiang Yu's life, Lady Yu, or Yu Ji, in complicating his image. Throughout history, largely thanks to Sima Qian's biography, Xiang Yu was mostly known for his physical prowess, anger, ferocity, and above all his *qi*.[95] In several Ming historical novels, the accounts of Xiang Yu lifting the cauldron became much more elaborate, apparently to further emphasize his astonishing physical strength.[96] The term Chu bawang (Hegemon King of the Chu) became almost synonymous with masculine physical strength.

Sima Qian's brief reference to Lady Yu helped to stir the imagination of many later writers. In his account of Xiang Yu, Sima Qian mentioned only briefly that after realizing that he was defeated by the Han troops, Xiang Yu sang a song to Lady Yu in despair. Although she was said to have sung a song in reply, her song was not quoted. Sima Qian's Lady Yu was almost completely silent. Furthermore, there was no mention of her suicide. However, in many later writings, she was given a distinct voice, and her song, expressing her determination to commit suicide to prove her faithfulness to Xiang Yu, was fully quoted.[97] In these popular fictional writings, Lady Yu spoke a lot about her love for Xiang Yu and her determination to remain faithful. She even pretended to prepare to masquerade as a man to follow her lover, apparently in order to coax him into giving her his sword, with which she would eventually slit her throat. The love between the two now began to receive much more attention.[98] Lady Yu, a beautiful and frail woman, became an indispensable stage prop that helped to bring the tragedy of a great hero to a more moving climax. Probably nothing was more effective in underscoring the tragic futility of a masculine hero than the image of a helpless but chaste woman committing suicide alongside him. Now the tragic legend of a great hero and a stunning beauty was completed. Consequently, the pairing of such a hero with a beautiful woman was to become an important element in the construction of masculinities in late imperial cultural discourse (more in chapter 8).

Whereas for some people the devotion of a beautiful woman served effectively to validate Xiang Yu's masculine heroism, for others, this same romantic association pointed to his fallibility. This sentiment is captured in the common saying, "The courage of a hero dwindles with romantic attachment" *(yingxiong qiduan, ernü qingchang)*.[99] One could infer from Xiang Yu's romantic involvement with Lady Yu that a truly masculine hero should not associate with any women at all—an ideology of masculinity that would find its fullest expression in the Ming classic novel *Shuihu zhuan* (Water Margin; examined in chapter 5). The narrator of another famous Ming novel, *Jin Ping Mei* (Golden Lotus, or The Plum in the Golden Vase), even blamed Xiang Yu's attachment to Lady Yu as part of the reason behind Xiang's eventual fall, implying that her constant companionship might have distracted him during important military campaigns. Of course, in *Jin Ping Mei*, Xiang Yu's relationship with Lady Yu is presented mainly as an example (though a far-fetched one) to show how even great heroes suffer defeat and humiliation for the sake of a woman *(qu qi zhi qi)*.[100]

Paradoxically, Sima Qian's most famous masculine hero was also an emotionally vulnerable man. No one can forget the tearful last-minute exchange between Xiang Yu and Lady Yu, which bespeaks the tender side of an otherwise ruthless man of brutal physical strength. The two seemingly contradictory readings of Xiang Yu's association with Lady Yu should prepare us for a better appreciation of two major competing notions of masculinity in late imperial cultural discourse—one that defined itself *against* the feminine and the other seeking to validate itself *through* the feminine. These two different but related notions of masculinity, shown in the case of Xiang Yu, were not necessarily always mutually exclusive, and they were sometimes simultaneously present in the construction of a particular model of masculinity. In fact, it was these two competing notions that gave rise to the analogy and differentiation strategies outlined in the introduction.

CHAPTER 2

From Faithful Wife to Whore

~~

The Minister-Concubine
Complex in Ming Politics

In chapter 1 I discussed the analogy between the gender status of women and the political status of *shi* in early Chinese political discourse, where *chen* (minister or subject) and *qie* (woman or concubine) were often juxtaposed to underscore their shared servile relationship to their respective "superiors." In this chapter I shall examine how this analogy worked itself into Ming political discourse and how differently scholar-officials made use of it to negotiate their own male gender identities.

The Politically Castrated

Originally, the character *chen* meant male slaves, and *qie* meant female slaves and criminals. When the two characters are combined as a noun, *chenqie* can also refer to slaves or subordinates; as a verb, it refers to the act of enslaving or ruling over someone.[1] The graph of *chen* describes the posture of subservience.[2] A minister's loyalty and obedience to his ruler began to be characterized as absolutely unconditional in some political theories during the Warring States Period and especially in those proposed by the legalists. Later during the Former Han dynasty, Dong Zhongshu and others incorporated such legalist elements into their new version of Confucianism, based on a correlative cosmological system, to accommodate the new monarchy's need for an effective central government. This revised Confucianism was eventually embraced by the Han monarchy as an important part of its imperial ideology.[3] However, the emphasis on a minister's unconditional subservience to his ruler was not completely compatible with some specific teachings of Confucius and especially those of Mencius, as we discussed in chapter 1. These incompatibilities should help us to appreciate better the complicated implications of the masculine and the feminine, as well as the subtle status of *shi,* in Chinese imperial politics.[4]

There was a tension inherent in the image of women in Chinese impe-

rial political discourse. On the one hand, the metaphor of a faithful wife/
concubine was always the one to be appropriated when the emphasis was
on a minister/subject's loyalty or obedience to his ruler. Furthermore, when
an official fell out of favor with the ruler or with the superior he was serving, he often compared himself to an abandoned wife or concubine to
underscore his being unappreciated. Here *chen* and *qie* became almost synonymous, and their statuses were equated by virtue of their similar subservient positions. On the other hand, in imperial politics, women (especially a ruler's wives and people associated with them) were regarded as
problematic because they were perceived as competitors with the ministers
for the attention of the ruler. "Women and ministers were mutually exclusive because they stood in an identical relation to the ruler; if one occupied
the slot, then the other had to be removed."5 It was often believed that
when a ruler began to listen to his wives or palace ladies instead of his ministers, the country would suffer disaster. Here *chen* and *qie* were irreconcil-
able political entities, and the rhetorical relationship between them was
often characterized by its antonymous nature in formal political discourses.

In Confucian political theories, women, whose proper place was in the
emperor's inner court, were supposed to be completely excluded from the
politics of the outer court. Emperor Wu of the Han dynasty was so wary of
the potential meddling of his women that as soon as he decided on which
one of his sons would be the crown prince, he ordered the boy's birth
mother put to death.6 Having supposedly learned from the usurping of
power by Emperess Lü soon after the death of Han Gaozu (Liu Bang),
Emperor Wu insisted on strict gender distinctions between the inner and
outer courts *(neiwai youbie)*. Emperor Wu's ruthlessness in keeping women
out of imperial politics was admired by many historians as far-sighted,
despite its extremity.7

More than a thousand years later, in one of his memoranda to the throne,
the Song Neo-Confucian thinker Cheng Yi (1033–1107) urged the emperor
to avoid the company of the inner court as much as possible, although he
never came close to suggesting that he would have condoned Emperor
Wu's extreme measures: "Generally speaking, if in the course of a day the
emperor is in the close company of worthy scholar-officials *(shidafu)* much
of the time and is in the close company of eunuchs and concubines *(siren
gongnü)* only a small part of the time, his character will automatically be
transformed and his virtue will become perfect."8 Of course, the worthy
scholar-officials were *chen* of the outer court, just like Cheng Yi himself (significantly eunuchs were grouped together with the emperor's concubines in
the inner court).

The tension between the outer and the inner courts deepened considerably during the Ming dynasty, although it was now the eunuchs rather than
the *waiqi* (imperial wives and their relatives) who became the major threats
to imperial political order. Later historians often considered the perceived

decline of the power of the outer court during the Ming dynasty as a phenomenon closely parallel to the rising power of the inner court—especially
that of the castrati, also known as *neichen* (literally, ministers of the inner
court), in opposition to the virile *waichen* (ministers of the outer court; also
known as *chaochen*). The distinctions between these two kinds of ministers
were related to the more general gender implications of the *neiwai* opposition: a woman was properly defined by her domain in the inner *(nei)* space
(the private space inside a house or palace), and a man in the outer *(wai)*
space, or the public realm.[9]

In the political treatise *Mingyi daifang lu* (Waiting for the Dawn: A Plan
for the Prince), written soon after the fall of the Ming dynasty, the thinker
and historian Huang Zongxi (1610–1695; *ECCP,* pp. 351–354) cited the pervasive interference of eunuchs in imperial politics as one of the main reasons behind the collapse. He argued that the problem of eunuchs during the
Ming was much worse than in previous dynasties because by the Ming
dynasty, eunuch participation in imperial politics had become almost institutionalized. Huang referred to scholar-officials as *tingchen* (literally, ministers at the imperial court). When he was criticizing the emperor's confusion of scholar-officials with eunuchs, Huang chose *waichen* and *neichen* to
refer to the two respectively, apparently to underscore the reality as well as
the serious nature of such confusion, pointing to the implicit gender ramifications of the tension between these two competing forces. Obviously when
the emperor was interested only in ensuring his own power, both scholar-
officials and eunuchs were his subjects, or *chen,* while the crucial *neiwai* distinctions were often meaningless to him. However, when a ruler could not
distinguish *nei* from *wai,* many were convinced political disorder was bound
to follow. To make it much worse, a significant group of scholar-officials,
according to Huang Zongxi, accepted the *neiwai* confusion as unavoidable
and even started to behave like eunuch-castrati themselves. Eventually,
they began to assume the position of the castrated in their relation to the
emperor. In other words, they became politically passive and accepting.[10]
This is probably why Huang Zongxi often directly compared these politically castrated ministers to the feminine elements of the inner court—concubines and eunuchs:

> To act solely for the prince and his dynasty, attempt to anticipate the prince's
> unexpressed whims or cravings—this is to have the mind of a eunuch or impe-
> rial concubine [*huan'guan kongqie*]. . . .
>
> It may be asked, is not the term "minister" always equated with that of
> "son"? I say no. Father and son share the same vital spirit. . . . The term "prince"
> and "minister" derive from their relation to all-under-Heaven. If I take no
> responsibility for all-under-Heaven, then I am just another man on the street. If
> I come to serve him without regard for serving all-under-Heaven, then I am
> merely the prince's menial servant and concubine [*puqie*]. If, on the other hand,

I have regard for serving the people, then I am the prince's friend and teacher. Thus with regard to ministership the designation may change. With father and son, however, there can be no such change.[11]

The Mencian influence on Huang Zongxi was quite obvious here.[12] For our present discussion the similar gender rhetoric adopted by both Mencius and Huang Zongxi is particularly interesting. As we mentioned in chapter 1, Mencius defined a woman in terms of her total obedience to her husband *(qiefu zhi dao),* while a true man *(da zhangfu)* was characterized by his courage to stand up for his moral ideals. Here gender distinctions between the feminine and the masculine were conceived in terms of the political differences between servile obedience and unyielding for the sake of one's moral ideals. Now, according to Huang Zongxi, when a minister decided to abandon his Confucian duty of serving all under Heaven and chose instead to serve the ruler like a slave or concubine, he began to take on the political gender identity of the feminine. In other words, in this complicated gender/political relationship, if a minister allowed himself to act like a eunuch or concubine, his Confucian manhood was seriously compromised. If elsewhere Huang Zongxi was only implicitly challenging the ruler-minister and husband-wife/concubine analogy, he explicitly asserted here that the father-son relationship was fundamentally different from that between ruler and minister. This was quite significant because Huang Zongxi was openly questioning the basic rationale behind the influential theory of *san'gang* (three bonds, or the relationships between husband and wife, father and son, and subject and ruler), which had been part of the imperial orthodoxy since the Former Han dynasty (see chapter 1). In addition to the political castration of many scholar-officials, Huang Zongxi attributed the poor governing record of the Ming to the drastic curtailing of the power of ministers, which had been engineered and institutionalized by the founder of the Ming dynasty, Zhu Yuanzhang (1328–1398; *DMB,* pp. 381–392).[13]

In 1380, to further consolidate his absolute power, Zhu Yuanzhang abolished the prime ministership, something quite unprecedented in the long history of imperial China. The emperor himself became the de facto prime minister, in direct charge of the daily business of governing the entire empire. However, the administrative burden soon proved to be too much for future emperors, and they began to rely more heavily on the so-called Grand Secretaries (Da Xueshi) from the Hanlin Academy. It was during the Yongle period (1402–1424) that the institution known as *neige* (literally, the inner cabinet), or the Grand Secretariat, began to take shape. It was usually composed of a number of Grand Secretaries, who worked for the emperor in the capacity of private advisers and secretaries. The power of its members increased dramatically during the later Ming dynasty. However, its members never attained the power enjoyed by a prime minister because they lacked institutional support. Consequently, they depended much more on the whims of a particular emperor at a particular time since they were merely his private secretaries or personal servants and nothing more. In the eyes of some, they occupied a position not that much different from that of a eunuch. In fact, for many officials serving in the so-called six ministries, the *neige,* as its name suggested, was an institution of the inner court, where imperial concubines and eunuchs dwelled.[14]

Starting with the Xuande period (1426–1435), eunuchs began to be formally trained in government practices and precedents, and they were allowed to get more involved in imperial politics. In their capacity as personal servants, eunuchs had more immediate and easier access to the emperor and therefore found it easier to win his favor, especially when he was reluctant to get directly involved in the daily administration of the government. By the mid-Ming the Grand Secretariat had become fully established as an institution of executive power, and one of the main duties of its members was to render opinions of approval and disapproval *(piao'ni)* on various memorials submitted by officials. Their opinions, in turn, were supposed to be signed off in vermilion ink by the emperor himself. However, the eunuchs served as go-betweens. The director from the most powerful eunuch agency, known as the Directorate of Ceremonial (Sili jian), was often the de facto spokesman of the emperor. Consequently, a large chunk of Ming imperial politics involved the constant conflicts and tension between the Grand Secretariat and the Directorate of Ceremonial.[15] In this regard, Huang Zongxi's somber reflections on the power structure of the Ming imperial government tell us something about the awkward position of the members of the Grand Secretariat, supposedly the most powerful civil officials at the court:

> It may be argued that in recent times matters of the state have been discussed in cabinet [*neige*], which actually amounted to having prime ministers—even though nominally there were no prime ministers. But this is not so. The job of those who handle matters in the cabinet has been to draft comments of approval and disapproval [on memorials], just like court clerks. Their function was inconsequential enough to begin with, yet, worse still, the substance of the endorsement came from those closest to the emperor and was then merely written up in proper form. Could you say that they had real power?[16]

Huang Zongxi concluded that the members of the Grand Secretariat were often at the mercy of the so-called palace menials *(gongnu),* or castrati. He argued elsewhere that one of the fundamental problems in Ming politics was that a ruler always took his personal interest to be the common interest of all under Heaven and considered his ministers his servants or slaves rather than public officials.[17]

Abandoned but Still Faithful

Huang Zongxi's observations should help us better appreciate the significance of a famous conversation between the official Fang Xiaoru (1357–1402; *DMB*, pp. 426–433) and the Prince of Yan, Zhu Di (1360–1424; later known as the Yongle Emperor [r. 1402–1424]; *DMB*, pp. 355–365). As recorded in many histories of the Ming dynasty, Zhu Di led a three-year rebellion (1399–1402) to "clear up" disorders *(jingnan)* in the reign of his nephew, Zhu Yunwen, the Jianwen Emperor (1377–ca. 1402; *DMB*, pp. 397–404). After defeating the emperor's troops, he planned to install himself as emperor, and he ordered Fang Xiaoru, who had once served as one of the emperor's confidants, to draft a decree announcing his succession to the throne. The prince defended his apparent act of usurpation in front of Fang Xiaoru:

> "I only tried to emulate the Duke of Zhou, who served King Cheng."
>
> Fang Xiaoru asked: "Where is King Cheng?"
>
> The prince said: "He burned himself to death."
>
> Fang asked: "Why don't you establish King Cheng's son as emperor?"
>
> The prince answered: "The country needs a mature ruler."
>
> Fang asked: "Then why don't you establish King Cheng's younger brother as ruler?"
>
> The prince replied: "These are the private matters of our family." [18]

Fang Xiaoru refused the prince's request, and as a result, he and his "ten families" were put to death. Fang's death was one of the most celebrated events in Ming history, largely because it was considered proof of his unwavering loyalty to the deposed sovereign. However, a deep irony lies in the prince's insistence that the issue of who should succeed to the throne was a private matter of the royal family, while Fang Xiaoru asserted that it was a public matter concerning the entire empire. After ascending the throne, the Yongle Emperor was going to make sure that all his ministers were fully aware that they were indeed his *personal* servants and he could destroy or promote any one of them at his whim.

Most court officials who had served under the Jianwen Emperor were not as stubborn or as loyal as Fang Xiaoru. Facing the harsh political reality, they conveniently accepted the triumphant prince's claim that this was a private matter of the royal family and duly acknowledged him as the legitimate new emperor. Among these "more realistic" officials was Huang Huai (1367–1449; *DMB*, pp. 665–667), who was representative of the many *puqie* ministers (to use Huang Zongxi's word) during the early Ming. Before we examine these ministers' self-representation in terms of their "concubine complex" *(qiefu xintai)*, we should take a brief look at early Ming imperial politics.[19]

The founding of the new dynasty ruled by a Han Chinese sovereign did not bring many new career opportunities for *shi*, who had supposedly suffered much neglect in the previous alien Yuan dynasty (1271–1368).[20] In fact, the early years of the Ming monarchy were very difficult for the *shi*, in large part because of the extremely autocratic style of two strong-willed emperors, Hongwu and Yongle. Rising from the humble origins and with little education, the Hongwu Emperor, Zhu Yuanzhang, was rather ambivalent in his dealings with the scholar-officials. He seems to have been deeply suspicious that someone was always conspiring to challenge his autocratic rule. This suspicion led him to take the unprecedented measure of abolishing the prime ministership so that he could more effectively have every aspect of the government within his direct control. Always on the lookout for every possible sign of challenge, he would not tolerate the slightest dissent. He even declared that reluctance to serve in his government was a serious crime punishable by death. Two Confucian scholars from the Suzhou area were put to death simply because they had declined to serve.[21] For the first time in Chinese history the most scared gesture of independence available to a *shi*—withdrawal from politics—was formally pronounced a criminal act punishable by death. No wonder Zhu Yuanzhang was particularly annoyed by Mencius for advocating a *shi*'s independence and for his emphasis on the relative equality between ruler and minister. Zhu Yuanzhang once insisted that Mencius' tablet be removed from the Confucian pantheon. Moreover, displeased with Mencius' teachings about the "rights" of ministers, he ordered a scholar to prepare an expurgated edition of *Mencius* in which all the seditious passages were censored.[22] Zhu Yuanzhang's message was clear: a minister could not be allowed to behave as the sovereign's friend or mentor, as Mencius had advocated. A minister could only be a servant/concubine *(puqie)*, exactly as Huang Zongxi would later complain. Notorious for putting many of his high officials to death for no apparent reason, Zhu Yuanzhang never hesitated in reminding his ministers of their subservient status.[23] The Yongle Emperor, Zhu Di, Zhu Yuanzhang's son, was equally ruthless, though less heavy-handed. It was during his reign that the Eastern Depot was established, an infamous eunuch spy agency that was to terrorize many scholar-officials for many years to come during the Ming. Like Zhu Yuanzhang, the Yongle Emperor was equally unpredictable in his wrath.

Given such a harsh political environment in the early Ming, Huang Huai was indeed quite remarkable in being able to continue his career as long as he did. Huang Huai and another member of the Grand Secretariat, Xie Jin (1369–1415; *DMB*, pp. 554–558), once enjoyed such favor from the Yongle

Emperor that he often consulted with them deep into the night in his own bedroom.[24] However, later remonstrations by Xie Jin were considered intolerable by the emperor, and he was left to die in prison.[25] Huang Huai was also incarcerated, presumably because of his involvement in the struggle for the throne among the princes. He was eventually imprisoned for ten years, based on some quite trivial charges, and the Yongle Emperor never showed any willingness to intervene on his behalf. Huang Huai was released from prison only after the crown prince, whom he had once tutored, assumed the throne.[26]

During his ten years in prison, Huang Huai composed quite a few poems, which were later assembled in a collection entitled *Xingqian ji* (A Book of Reflections on Mistakes). In fact, the prevailing sentiment in this collection was as much regret over his so-called mistakes as his anguish over being misunderstood and neglected. In "Qie boming" (The Ill-Fated Woman), Huang Huai, in the voice of an abandoned woman, reminisced about how deeply in love she and her husband had been when they first married and how sad the long separation had been after he abandoned her, although she remained faithful to him. The sharp contrast between the happy early days of the marriage and the sad separation only underscored the unpredictability of the husband's temperament (therefore, the unpredictability of the emperor's whims).[27] In this slim volume (containing only two *juan*), there are at least ten poems focusing on the image of an abandoned woman; in almost every one of them we can find the male poet's allegorical self-reference as a minister now out of favor.[28]

Huang Huai's poetic predilection to present himself as an abandoned woman was understandable, since his long and resilient political career, despite some significant interruptions, was the best testimony to his skills in avoiding saying or doing anything that might upset the emperor—the skills a dutiful and obedient concubine was supposed to master. The same was true of several of Huang's peers, three members of the Grand Secretariat who shared the last name Yang and were collectively known as the "Three Yangs" (San Yang): Yang Shiqi (1365–1444; *DMB*, pp. 1535–1538), Yang Rong (1371–1440; *DMB*, pp. 1519–1522), and Yang Pu (1375–1446; *DMB*, pp. 1537–1538). All three had remarkable political durability, and all three served in important positions under several emperors. Their long careers must have been at least in part the result of their being able to read the emperor's mind and their success in presenting themselves as obedient ministers.[29] After a reading of Huang Huai's poems in *Xingqian ji*, Yang Shiqi, probably the least slavish among the three Yangs, became even more aware of the unavoidable dangers a minister faced and therefore the need to be careful.[30] Yang Rong's career maxim was "An official in a high position needs to be extra cautious."[31] Having witnessed many tragedies of ministers losing their lives for speaking their minds, Yang Rong sighed; "Whenever I saw an official suffering tragedy because he was too stubborn, I was deeply troubled. Serving a ruler/master, one has to follow certain rules, and when remonstrating, one has to choose the right method." Then he used a specific example to illustrate his point: if the emperor misread a phrase from a book, one should not correct him directly but should wait until an opportunity presented itself, correct him, and even then do it only indirectly.[32] In a word, all three Yangs tried to be good *puqie* ministers, although none of them was as self-conscious of their feminized position as Huang Huai was in his poetic self-representations. However, the interchangeability between minister and concubine had become such an important part of the rhetorical conventions in scholar-officials' self-representations, that even ministers who were not so subservient would in times of despair resort to them to air their frustrations.

Compared with the Hongwu and Yongle Emperors of the early Ming, the emperors of the mid-Ming, such as Wuzong (r. 1488–1505), were much less domineering. These relatively weak emperors seem to have emboldened many scholar-officials to speak out on what they believed. However, the ministers now also had to contend with the even more emboldened "ministers of the inner court"—the eunuchs. Several generations younger than the Three Yangs, Li Mengyang (1473–1529; *DMB*, pp. 841–845), the most famous among the so-called Former Seven Masters in Ming literary history, was known for his fearless spirit and his heroic struggle with the powerful eunuch Liu Jin (d. 1510; *DMB*, pp. 941–945). Li Mengyang was imprisoned several times for courageously condemning eunuchs and corrupt officials. He prided himself on being doubly masculine *(chonggang)* and unyielding *(xingzhi)*,[33] and his writings have always been praised for their masculine style.[34] And yet in his writings we can still encounter quite a few poems where he resorted to the image of an abandoned woman to give vent to his political frustrations.

Learning that several important upright officials had been demoted or banished for their opposition to Liu Jin, Li Mengyang composed the poem "Qufu ci" (The Song of an Abandoned Woman). To make sure that this love poem was read as a political allegory, the poet provided readers with all the necessary background information in a preface to the poem. The poem proper starts with the sadness of sudden abandonment: "Peacocks flew south while wild geese glided north/I left you with eyebrows furrowed and tears running down." Then the female "I" begins to refer to her husband's cold heart: "While I don't mind being thrown away like a bucket of water/You indeed had a cold heart to take such a sudden departure." Thereafter the poem's focus moves back and forth between the sadness of separation and memories of happier days. It concludes with the following couplets:

Who could understand my sorrows and anguish?
Dancing and singing, you should pity yourself in vain.

Since Governor of Guiji you are certainly not,
How could I act like his wife, wavering in my loyalty to you?[35]

Please take good care of your own precious health,
While I only pray that your newly found love is not as good as the
one before.[36]

While insisting on her faithfulness, even after being abandoned, the female "I" cannot help wondering whether the new love will serve and love her husband as she herself had. Of course, Li Mengyang's message was that the emperor would soon regret his decision to demote so many loyal ministers. Compared with Huang Huai's poems, Li Mengyan's poem is more concerned with protest than with demonstrating loyalty.

The tone of protest against the emperor's injustice was even stronger in another of Li Mengyang's poems, "Handan cairen jiawei siyang zu fu" (A Handan Beauty Was Married to a Lowly Soldier." The first half of the poem reads as follows:

From a poor family I originally came,
And by mistake I entered the palace.
Three thousand beautiful palace ladies
 All have dazzling smiles.
What the lord loved was singing and dancing,
And yet I was too young to sing and dance well.
Once the lord was upset,
I was discarded like a fallen leaf.[37]

Although this time the poet did not provide a contextual note or preface, the first couplet immediately reminds the reader of a proverbial observation that frequently appeared in early Chinese texts: "Whether beautiful or ugly, a woman will be subjected to jealousy once she enters the palace; whether talented or mediocre, a *shi* will incur resentment once he begins to serve at the court."[38] The poet hints that he should not have served as an official in the first place (Li entered officialdom by mistake, just like the woman who mistakenly entered the palace), while the title of the poem strongly suggests that the poet's talents are completely unappreciated, as is the case of his female persona, who was apparently forced to marry an unworthy husband.

If these poems focusing on the images of a neglected woman were not what people normally would have associated with "masculine" writers such as Li Mengyang, then even more surprising were several poems of a very similar nature by Li's more famous contemporary Wang Yangming (1472–1529; also known as Wang Shouren; *DMB*, pp. 1409–1416). Wang Yangming was the founder of a school of Ming Neo-Confucianism known as

Xinxue (the School of the Mind), an important intellectual movement during the mid- and late Ming. (In addition to being an influential Confucian thinker, Wang was also known for his military expertise. It was Wang who led the imperial army to successfully quell the rebellion of Prince Ning in 1520.) In Wang's collected writings, rather unexpectedly, there were five poems grouped together under the title "Qufu tan" (The Songs of an Abandoned Woman). The first four poems were quite conventional, presenting the male poet as a wife who, originally from a poor family, was abandoned by her fickle husband because he had found a new love. However, the last poem is especially interesting since it focuses on the theme of sad music. It concludes with the couplet: "You are known for your wisdom and insights/ Then why should you still hear such sad music?"[39] The poet, instead of blaming everything on "her" ill fate, was openly questioning the wisdom of the ruler, wondering if he himself should accept the status of a concubine.[40]

These poems demonstrate what setbacks in political life could do to the poetic style and even gender psyche of a scholar-official. Wang was not known for being a sentimental poet. In 1506 he was stripped of his official title after he became involved in the struggle against the powerful eunuch Liu Jin. He composed these poems in exile after he was banished to a dispatch station in northwestern Guizhou, just before he experienced his famous "epiphany" (an important event in the intellectual history of late imperial China, known as *Longchang wudao,* or "The Epiphany in the Longchang Dispatch Station"). In fact, we could almost say that the birth of Wang Yangming's Xinxue philosophy, which would take the late Ming intellectual world by storm in the next century or so, could be considered at least in part a result of his political frustrations or, as described in his poems, his bitter experience as an abandoned woman. In other words, Wang Yangming turned to the sage alternative of self-cultivation *(neisheng zhi dao)* only after he had experienced deep disappointment with "the kingly way" *(waiwang zhi dao).*[41]

Here we may want to take a look at the broader context of the political emasculation of many *shi* during the sixteenth and early seventeenth centuries and the role of Wang's teachings in their attempts to come to terms with their experience. Wang Yangming's new theory of self-cultivation seems to have provided many late Ming *shi* with important spiritual as well as psychological support in the face of the ever more depressing, and oppressive, reality of contemporary politics (incompetent emperors and the corrupting influence of the eunuchs). It enabled them to believe that ultimate moral authority resided within each individual rather than in the teachings of the sages of past ages or the imperial government—thus the possibility of self-empowerment (i.e., re/masculinization) at a time when they felt that they were being increasingly marginalized as well as emasculated. The examples of Li Mengyang and Wang Yangming seem to demonstrate that the metaphor of an abandoned but faithful wife had become such a part of the poetic convention that different officials/poets turned to it for many different reasons. Some emphasized their faithfulness/loyalty, and others underscored the mistreatment to which they had been subjected. Furthermore, in protesting mistreatment, some of them, such as Li Mengyang, also began to show some doubt about the wisdom of engaging in imperial politics, a feeling that would become much more dominant in some late Ming writings, where the metaphor of women underwent more significant changes.

From Unhappy Wife to Reluctant Prostitute

Wang Yangming's contemporary, Xu Zhenqing (1479–1511; *DMB*, pp. 569–570), chose to employ the woman metaphor to represent himself in a rather different context. Deeply humiliated when, owing to his homely appearance, he was assigned to a lowly official position just after he had passed the national examinations, Xu sought to express his frustrations and anger in a poem entitled "Chounü fu" (Rhapsody on a Homely Woman).

It is very likely that "Chounü fu" was meant to be a parody of classic Han rhapsodies on beautiful women, such as "Meiren fu," attributed to Sima Xiangru (179–117 BCE), which exerted a great influence on the presentation of women in later literati poetry.[42] A brief look at Sima Xiangru's "Meiren fu" should help us better to appreciate Xu Zhenqing's unique agenda. At the beginning of "Meiren fu," we are specifically told that the Prince of Liang delighted in Sima Xiangru because he was handsome and elegant. However, later someone accused Sima Xiangru of trying to use his good looks to seduce women and warned the prince against allowing Sima Xiangru to wander into his inner palace. To vindicate himself of accusations of lechery, Sima Xiangru related to the prince how he was able to resist the seduction of a beautiful female neighbor. The bulk of the rhapsody is about how Sima Xiangru remained unperturbed in the presence of an attractive woman.[43]

Now let us turn to Xu Zhenqing's "Chounü fu," which starts with the poet's bitter self-deprecation in the voice of an ugly woman. The creator has made a gross mistake by giving her the face and figure she now has; as a result, the female "I" in the poem is ugly to the degree of being almost grotesque. Despite her appearance, however, she tells the reader that she is virtuous, diligent, and talented in all kinds of work a woman is supposed to do. Unfortunately, no one has wanted to marry her, and now she is thirty years old. In contrast, her female neighbor is just the opposite. She is very pretty but morally reprehensible. Moreover, she is lazy. Yet numerous suitors are after her. The female "I" then begins her bitter complaint: the morals of this world have declined so much that people seek only beautiful appearance while ignoring virtue *(haose jiande)*. She goes on to catalogue several rulers in history who suffered disasters because their heads were turned by seductive women.

Of course, it has usually been assumed that women appealed to men because of their *se* (beauty of a woman), while a male *shi* won recognition from his superiors through virtue and talent. When Confucius said that he had not noticed that people appreciated virtue as much as they did pretty women *(haose ru haode)*,[44] he was implicitly acknowledging that most men tended to be attracted more by *se* than *de* (virtue). Apparently, Xu Zhenqing was protesting being treated like a woman since as a male *shi*, he should be judged in terms of virtue and talent rather than appearance. Xu's insistence on his masculinity here should lead the reader to question Sima Xiangru's gender identity in "Meiren fu" since Xu's "Chounü fu" could be read almost as a deliberate critique of Sima Xiangru's femininity. (Remember that Sima Xiangru found favor with the prince mainly because of his own *se*—a way of seeking favor implicitly denounced by Xu Zhenqing as feminine.) Furthermore, by declaring his innocence in not being seduced, Sima Xiangru's poetic persona appears to have symbolically castrated himself, denying the ability to seduce the prince's palace ladies. This emasculating process, as we will see, is reversed by Xu Zhenqing in "Chounü fu" in that he vindicates his masculinity by presenting himself as an ugly but virtuous woman who in the end turns out to be a man in disguise.

Xu Zhenqing deliberately mimics Sima Xiangru by employing the similar trope of a beautiful but morally questionable female neighbor to underscore his own virtue, which is supposed to have quite different gender implications from Sima Xiangru's. Particularly intriguing is the way the poet describes "her" ugliness:

> The fierce *yin* took advantage of the *yang,*
> While the feminine weakened the masculine.
> Dark eyebrows with large neck,
> Protruding nose bridge above an upward tilted nose.
> Eager to talk but unable to speak clearly,
> Snoring very loudly when asleep.
> Her figure was like that of a dead pig,
> Clumsy but full of strength.[45]

This woman is just as astoundingly ugly as Sima Xiangru's female neighbor is astonishingly beautiful. However, the woman's ugliness tends to problematize her female gender identity. In many ways, this is a picture that projects a masculine, though rather unrefined, figure, as if the appearance of a woman was imposed on a man. What has made this ugly woman's appearance so grotesque is that it is a result of the feminine, or the *yin*, overpowering the masculine, or the *yang (liyin chengyang)*. Most likely, this woman was originally a man, but the strong feminine elements have somehow distorted him into a woman *(nü duo nan zhi)*. Her ugliness is the result of a tortuous mixture of the feminine and the masculine (a disorder of *yin* and *yang*). Xu Zhenqing seemed to be implying that he had been misjudged by a world where the *yin-yang* cosmic order had already been disrupted. This was why he had been judged by the standards for a woman rather than those for a man. However, the reader is still supposed to be able to discern an undeniable masculine quality even in "her" ugliness. This quality, while making the woman ugly, also renders her both virtuous and talented. After all, this poem about an ugly woman was meant to prove the poet's under-appreciated masculinity. In other words, the "I" is undesirable only because others have used the wrong gender standards. The poet has been forced to become an ugly woman.

As a poet, Xu Zhenqing was known for his short lyrics on refined senti-ments. As one of the "Four Masters of the Middle Wu" from the South, he was often contrasted by later literary historians with Li Mengyang, who was supposed to represent the style of the North, which was characterized by its masculine qualities.[46] Interestingly enough, the eccentric "Chounü fu" anticipated a new trend in the use of metaphor of the feminine in late Ming writings, where the focus would be on the anguish of emasculation rather than on docile femininity to win back the heart of one's lord or superior.

While many late Ming scholar-officials continued to use the minister-concubine analogy when they wrote about their political frustrations, some began to do so for a different reason. A scholar-official might still compare himself to a concubine, but not to protest that his talent was being neg-lected; the issues of loyalty and faithfulness were no longer the focus of dis-cussion. Instead, the concubine metaphor was now evoked to underscore the humiliation and pain of being an official. Entering officialdom was now considered a humiliating experience of emasculation, nothing more. The weaker sex was not evoked to solicit sympathy or pity from one's superiors but as a caution to one's peers against becoming an official.

As we have discussed, many early and mid-Ming scholar-officials com-pared themselves to an abandoned woman or neglected concubine because they wanted to be "reclaimed" by the ruler. In other words, in their poems, an abandoned woman still wished to reunite with her husband. Her wife/concubine status would remain the same even when reunion was indeed granted. In the writings of some late Ming scholar-officials, the concubine status itself was presented as undesirable and to be avoided at all costs. The role of concubine was often described as something imposed on a *shi*. This change reflected a profound disillusionment with late Ming politics and a search for alternatives to validate *shi* status as members of the elite.

The conflicts between the Wanli Emperor (r. 1573–1620) and his minis-ters had been simmering for so long and the animosity was so deep that the sovereign decided in 1587 to simply ignore his ministers by not holding reg-ular morning audiences. It was said that for the next twenty or more years, he simply refused to see his ministers.[47] He resorted to this approach of *wuwei zhi zhi* (rule through nonaction) mainly because he realized that brutal suppression such as physical torture (known as *tingzhang*, or whipping at the court), imprisonment, or even death would never stop determined Confucian scholar-officials from remonstrating about his failures as a ruler.[48] This was a time when the emperor was trying to deprive his ministers of any opportunity for martyrdom, so to die as a result of remonstrations against the emperor was probably the most heroic (and therefore masculine) act a minister could perform.[49] It was testimony to his status as a mentor/friend to his sovereign, the relationship envisioned by Mencius and many other Confucian thinkers. The Wanli Emperor meted out punishment to his ministers in his own strange way; for example, he refused to fill many vacant positions, sometimes bringing the government to a state of semiparalysis. Moreover, with the emperor refusing to serve as the ultimate arbiter, factional fighting among scholar-officials soon reached epidemic proportions. Withdrawal from politics became a widespread phenomenon, although very few scholar-officials succeeded in complete withdrawal since officialdom was such an integral part of their careers.[50]

In the writings of the late Ming writer Yuan Hongdao (1568–1610; *DMB*, pp. 1635–1638), the leader of the literary movement known as the Gong'an school *(Gong'an pai)*, a constant theme was the undesirability of officialdom, despite the fact that Yuan repeatedly had to go back to governmental service because of various pressures, especially from his relatives.[51] Precisely because of the enormous pressures on him to serve, his frustrations at not being able to free himself from the shackles of officialdom were all the more exasperating.

In his complaints about the hardships of officialdom, Yuan Hongdao repeatedly used the conventional analogy between concubine and minister, although in a rather different manner. For him the image of a concubine almost always contained negative connotations. Commenting on the mess created by factional fighting, Yuan Hongdao noted, "This was just like the situation where wives and concubines started quarreling over bedchamber matters (*chuangdi jian shi* [i.e., who is entitled to sleep with the husband on a particular night]) moments after their home had been robbed."[52] Here the author was not identifying with the wives and concubines. Instead he was comparing narrow-minded officials involved in factional fighting to lustful and jealous wives and concubines, from whom the author himself apparently wanted to keep a distance. This distance signaled a different self-perception on the part of some late Ming literati in their relation to the long-standing "other"—the conventional metaphor of the feminine.

In another of Yuan Hongdao's poems, "Suimu jishi" (The End of the Year), we can see how this distance became a crucial aspect of the author's self-identity. The entire poem focuses on the poet's lonely life as a district magistrate. The second half of the poem reads as follows:

My interest in officialdom withers just like the frosted grass,
And a homesick heart is trying to catch the flying evening bird.
Who cares to be that young woman
Who once asked if her eyebrows were painted properly? [53]

The last couplet is obviously an allusion to the Tang poet Zhu Qingyu's
(b. 791) famous poem, "Jinshi Zhang Shuibu" (On the Eve of the Examinations, to Director Zhang of the Bureau of Waterways and Irrigation):

Last night in the wedding chamber stood the red candles;
In the morning the bride will pay respects to your parents.
Finishing my morning toilet, I ask you timidly:
Are my eyebrows painted in fashion? [54]

Zhu Qingyu sent this poem to his mentor, Zhang Ji (ca. 776–ca. 829), on the
eve of the government examinations as a subtle proof of his competence
and as a way of asking him whether he thought his protégé would be able
to pass. The poet ingeniously compares his own anxiety before the examinations to that of a bride who was supposed to pay respects to her parents-in-law the morning after the wedding. It was said that Zhang indeed sent a
reply poem to Zhu in which he praised the "woman's beauty and singing
voice," implying that Zhu had enough talent and should not worry about
the examinations. [55] The anxiety and fears of a bride were precisely what
Yuan Hongdao did not want to experience, although he knew that an official had to constantly worry about whether "my eyebrows are painted in
fashion."

The different meanings assigned to the image of a bride certainly testify
to the rather different attitudes toward officialdom exhibited by Yuan Hongdao and Zhu Qingyu. Unlike Zhu Qingyu, for the late Ming literati, the
image of a timid bride was just the opposite of what they were pursuing.
According to his younger brother Yuan Zhongdao (1570–1624), Yuan
Hongdao believed that "a true man [*da zhangfu*] is someone who acts on
his own initiative and who is capable of doing whatever he plans to do. He
mustn't allow himself to be led by others or be directed by others' opinions." [56] Once again we are reminded of Mencius' definition of a true man
as someone who "practices the Way alone," as discussed in chapter 1.

Reviewing changing prose styles through the ages, Yuan Zhongdao associated masculine writing with the notion of *zhen* (genuineness and authenticity) popular among his contemporaries and contrasted it with what he
considered to be the writing style typical of a bride:

Wanting to express himself, a true man is concerned only that the limited
medium will not allow him to fully articulate what is unique within him. How
can he act as timidly as a bride who has just been married three days? [In writ-

ing] one can be either moderate or completely uninhibited. Being imitative is pure hypocrisy. . . . The people from Chu do not have to seek moderation when writing their essays, nor do they have to be hypocritical. They just have to present their true selves [*zhenren*] so that their writing can authentically reflect them.[57]

Consequently, masculinity was associated with spontaneity and femininity with artificiality.

For Yuan Hongdao, serving as an official was an artificial act since an official had to take on the role of a concubine against his "natural" inclinations as a man. In a letter to a friend, Yuan Hongdao writes about the unpleasantness of the job of a district magistrate: "[Often] I have to lower my head to serve my superiors [*dimei shiren*];[58] I work hard like a horse or an ox and always have to conduct myself as meekly as a concubine."[59]

This comes very close to the image of a slave or concubine that Huang Zongxi described in his famous political treatise, as discussed above. Imperial concubines were almost always presented in a negative light in formal writings on imperial politics. However, in scholar-officials' personal self-representations, this same metaphor was usually appropriated to construct a positive image of a loyal but unappreciated minister (just like an abandoned woman). Now, significantly, there was a new twist in Yuan Hongdao's self-presentation. Here the concubine experience was presented as humiliating and definitely emasculating—and he wanted to escape from it. The theme of a minister's/concubine's loyalty, so important in early and mid-Ming works, now became entirely irrelevant. Yuan Hongdao even compared officialdom to prostitution and considered his behavior as a magistrate so unnatural that he found it totally disgusting: "I have to behave like a slave before my superiors and act like a prostitute when there are visitors passing through."[60]

Jiang Yingke (1533–1605), one of Yuan Hongdao's close friends, also used the prostitute metaphor to describe the humiliating experience of officialdom: "I have been suffering constantly under the burden of administrative duties. . . . I always have to lower my head [*dimei*] just like a whore who is entertaining her important-looking clients. I don't dare to show any sign of displeasure, nor can I smile. I have always to hold my breath and bend my knees when walking."[61] Jiang Yingke was also known for his aversion to officialdom, and yet, like Yuan Hongdao, he served in many official positions.[62] To make his job more tolerable, he tried to take it less seriously by adopting the approach of *liyin* (enjoying the pleasures of withdrawal while serving as an official).[63] However, as the tortuous oxymoron *liyin* suggests, it was not easy to enjoy withdrawal while serving as an official. The burdens of officialdom soon caught up with him. Using the same metaphor once employed by Li Mengyang—"A Handan beauty was married to a

lowly soldier,"—Jiang Yingke compared his entrance into officialdom to a
forced marriage to an unworthy husband or to the ill fate of a beautiful
courtesan who married a poor peasant and had to suffer the abuse of her
parents-in-law.[64]

Jiang Yingke's complaints about officialdom became especially vocal
when one of his friends drew his attention to the long poetic tradition of
comparing a frustrated minister to an abandoned woman:

> Thank you for showing me the essay "On Allegorical Interpretations." Was this
> written for the amusement of self-mockery? This would not be necessary if you
> were just trying to air your frustrations at being unable to find someone to appre-
> ciate your talent [*buyu*]. Allow me to make a few comparisons: a *shi* is just like
> a woman [*shi you nü ye*]. If she is pretty, then she will be considered a boudoir
> beauty. Consequently, why should this beauty worry about being unable to find
> a husband? Instead, she should rather worry about marrying the wrong husband.
> A stunning beauty deep in the inner chamber, she excels in composing poetry,
> playing music, and doing needlework. However, she is predestined to suffer. If
> she enters the palace, she will probably have to be rated low since she will not
> be considered so beautiful when compared with the three thousand palace ladies
> in the imperial harem. If she is married to a merchant or a peasant, stripped of
> her earrings and necklaces, she has to clean the chamber pot in the morning and
> fetch water from the well in the evening. Any slight mistake will turn her into a
> target for scolding by her husband or in-laws. The hardships will drive her to con-
> template suicide. Then she will start to think in regret that she should not have
> gotten married in the first place. Since I entered officialdom . . . I have been los-
> ing weight and my hair is turning gray. And yet, many times I have been the tar-
> get of rebuke by my superiors. I am beginning to feel like a poor woman who is
> regretting that she ever married in the first place.[65]

Obviously, Jiang Yingke was telling his friend that the sentimental allegorical convention was no longer valid or refreshing enough in their present
situation. The problem was not that talent was unappreciated but rather,
that appreciation always brought disaster. Having reached the painful conclusion that a *shi*'s political identity was defined by his need to seek employ-
ment in government and that he was thus condemned to occupy the unfor-
tunate position of a woman, Jiang was suggesting that the only possible
salvation was to refuse to marry in the first place so that there would be no
"husband" to please or obey.

The despair we often encounter in early and mid-Ming writings where
the minister-concubine analogy dominates was now transformed into play-
ful self-mockery in Jiang Yingke's writings. In such playfulness, however,
we still discern a deep sense of total helplessness—he still had to serve,
despite his disgust with officialdom. For people like Yuan Hongdao and

Jiang Yingke, officialdom became a business of double deception: being an official meant having to fake obedience to one's superiors, and at the same time one had to *pretend* that he liked the business of faking. This was probably why "prostitute" came to replace "concubine" as a metaphor in some late Ming writings. Despite the switch of roles, entering governmental service remained the same emasculating experience. However, one important difference was that a prostitute did not care with whom she slept so long as she was paid, while a concubine was supposed to remain faithful to her husband even after he had abandoned her. One at least had some choices, while the other had none whatsoever. For people like Jiang Yingke, officialdom was just a means for making a living, and the Confucian ideal of serving all under Heaven (in Huang Zongxi's words) remained only a lofty but remote ideal. Yuan Hongdao, for example, once declared that he did not mind being an official so long as it did not prevent him from practicing Chan Buddhism and enjoying women and wine (an apparent contradiction).[66]

In the long run, it was difficult for scholar-officials such as Yuan Hongdao and Jiang Yingke, who had long been trained in Confucian moral teachings, to maintain such a cynical view of politics and trivialize officialdom in such a manner. The issue of authenticity [*zhen*] became all the more urgent for these people precisely because of the prostituting nature of their experience in politics. Wang Yangming's "mind only" theory of self-cultivation seems to have provided them with the means for finding a viable alternative, and it certainly contributed to the rise of interest in the notion of authenticity during the late Ming. This was why Yuan Zhongdao associated masculinity with authenticity and femininity with hypocrisy. Metaphorically, being a woman meant obedience (taking orders but not speaking what was on one's mind), while being a man meant just the opposite—being one's own master and showing one's true feelings. Of course, this definition again sounds Mencian. No wonder that in Jiang Yingke's writings we often come across topics such as seeking authenticity *(qiuzhen)*, valuing the genuine *(guizhen)*, or the loss of the self *(sangwo)*.[67] Nothing was more a loss of self than having to prostitute oneself.

Finally, in analyzing the changes in the use of the wife/concubine/prostitute metaphor, we have to consider that the early and mid-Ming works we have discussed were written mostly by high officials serving in the central government, while for the late Ming, we have focused on scholar-officials in much less important positions at the local levels. In other words, the latter group was located at the periphery as far as the imperial political structure was concerned. To a certain extent, our shifting focus from the center to the periphery reflects the changes in the intellectual world during the second half of the Ming dynasty: those at the periphery began to have a more dominant role in setting the nation's cultural agenda. A significant group of nationally renowned cultural figures, such as Li Zhi (1527–1602; *DMB,* pp.

807–818) and the three Yuan brothers, either served only as low-level officials or stayed out of governmental service for a large portion of their lives.
It also appears that those at the periphery were more likely to feel the need
to reassert their masculinity and felt more the urge to renounce their feminized positions in relation to their superiors, as if the distance from the the
center of imperial power had enabled them to feel more like a man. However, what is telling about the changing feminine tropes—from eunuchs to
abandoned women and finally to prostitutes—is that the changes reflect
an intricate relationship between the writers' self-perceptions as gendered
beings and their increasingly marginalized status in imperial politics.

CHAPTER 3

The Case of Xu Wei

~~

A Frustrated Hero or a
Weeping Widow?

In this chapter we shall conduct a case study of one individual figure at the margins of the Ming elite community: Xu Wei (1521–1593), a dramatist, painter, and poet. It will allow us to explore in a much more focused manner how a disenfranchised Ming literatus tried to come to terms with his problematic manhood and the specific masculinizing strategies he employed in negotiating his gender identity. The fact that Xu Wei, unlike all the scholar-officials discussed so far, was never an official should provide us with a good opportunity to examine some of the unique challenges he faced as a commoner *(buyi)* and their impact on his gender psyche.[1]

In his biography of Xu Wei, Yuan Hongdao made the following observation on Xu's poetry:

> In him there was unbending spirit, as well as the frustrations of a hero who could find no place to turn [*yingxiong shilu, touzu wumen*]. This is why his poems are sometimes full of laughter and sometimes of anger; they sometimes read like roaring water gushing through a narrow valley, the subtle sound of plants sprouting from under the soil, the weeping of a widow in the middle of the night [*guafu zhi yeku*], and the [sighing] of a lone traveler after waking up in a cold night.[2]

Particularly intriguing is Yuan Hongdao's reference to a weeping widow. How can a frustrated hero's poems be compared to a widow's weeping? How did Yuan Hongdao see in Xu Wei's poems two completely opposite images, one the ultimate figure of masculinity—a hero—and the other that of a helpless widow? If there are indeed two opposite images, what is the relationship between them? How are they related to Xu Wei's self-image as a man, and what could repeated frustrations do to the gender psyche of a hero? These are some of the questions we seek to answer in this chapter.

The Marginal and the Feminine

Reading through the more than two thousand poems in Xu Wei's collected works, *Xu Wei ji,* one has to conclude that the predominant images are those of masculine heroes.[3] Xu Wei's heroes are often bold figures—for example, the famous assassins Jing Ke and Yu Rang from the Warring States Period —or triumphant military officers; many were his contemporaries or even acquaintances.[4] Quite a few of his works (including prose) are devoted to *xia* (knights-errant and chivalrous men) he admired.[5] In fact, Xu Wei was quite obsessed with swords. Many of his poems are explicitly devoted to the topic of swords and knives, while references to these weapons also abound in many poems that are concerned with other topics.[6] In a word, there is an unmistakable obsession with martial heroics in his writings. Of course, this can be explained by some "simple" facts in Xu Wei's life, such as his long association with the military, although the exact implications of these "facts," as well as the significance of the images of swords and knives in his writings, are anything but simple and clear.

Xu Wei was a native of Shanyin (now part of Shaoxing in Zhejiang Province). His birth mother was a slave girl from the aboriginal Miao area. His father, a petty official, died when he was only one hundred days old. He was raised by his father's second wife, Miaoshi (née Miao), whom his birth mother served as a maid. Although Miaoshi, childless herself, treated Xu Wei almost as her own son, his childhood was not a happy one.[7] There were constant frictions between Miaoshi and Xu Wei's two elder brothers, who, many years his senior, were his father's children by his first wife.[8] When Xu Wei was ten, the family's financial situation worsened, so his birth mother was sold. The ensuing separation must have been devastating for him.[9] Xu Wei was not able to reunite with his birth mother for almost twenty years.[10] Following the death of his stepmother, when he was fourteen, the family financial situation deteriorated even further; his two brothers squandered most of what was left of the family fortune. Xu Wei could not afford to marry since in his hometown the betrothal gifts a groom was supposed to give to the family of the bride were quite expensive.[11] Finally, he had to accept an uxorial marriage with a daughter from the Pan family, and he moved to his wife's home as a live-in son-in-law *(ruzhui).* The marriage, though short (his wife died of childbirth complications), was a relatively happy one. However, his having to live in his wife's home must have been a feminizing experience. In his memoirs of his wife, Panshi, Xu Wei mentioned that she had always been very considerate and tried her best to avoid any topic that might hurt his self-esteem because of his *ruzhui* status.[12] The emasculating implications did not become fully clear to him until a few years later, when he lost a legal dispute to inherit his elder brother's property after the latter's death. His loss was presumably due to the assumption that he had voluntarily renounced his right as a male heir in the Xu family when he allowed himself to be married (like a woman) into a family of another surname.[13] The fact that his birth mother was a slave girl might have been another factor.

Despite his literary precocity (by his own account, he was already able to compose eight-legged exam essays at the age of nine), Xu Wei did not get his *xiucai*, or licentiate degree, until he was twenty, and he failed to pass the provincial examinations in as many as eight attempts.[14] The loss of his right to inherit within the Xu family, which amounted to almost a patrilineal excommunication, coupled with his repeated frustrations in examinations, must have been sources of deep humiliation for Xu Wei, forcing him to search for alternative ways to vindicate himself.

All these factors must have contributed to Xu Wei's unusual interest in the military. A significant portion of his life was devoted to activities associated with the military, and many of his friends were generals and military officers. Probably the most immediate factor was that his hometown region had been plagued by invading Japanese pirates and their Chinese accomplices for a considerable period. Xu Wei was deeply involved in the military defenses of his hometown. In the winter of 1558, he formally joined the staff of Hu Zongxian (ca. 1511–1565; *DMB*, pp. 631–638) as a private secretary *(muyou)*, when Hu was the supreme commander of the Zhejiang region, leading the imperial government's military campaigns against the increasingly threatening pirates.

Apparently, Xu Wei prided himself on his knowledge of military affairs.[15] His longing for distinction as a true man in a military career found expression in many of his poems celebrating the military heroics of *others:*

> From the arm hang the golden official seals;
> Around the waist is the jade belt carved with the pattern of peach blossoms.
> This is what a true man should achieve;
> I laugh at myself—what did I get from reading books?[16]

In this poem celebrating the military triumphs of the famous general Qi Jiguang (1528–1588; *DMB*, pp. 220–224), Xu Wei explicitly asserted that one's masculinity was defined by victories on the battlefield rather than book learning. Similar sentiments can be found in many other poems. Xu Wei was especially envious of one of his friends who, as a *shusheng* (scholar) serving as private secretary for an official, was able to distinguish himself on the battlefield:

Four Victory Songs in Honor of Mr. Cao

No. 1

> You once joined the staff of an official on an expedition southward;
> Like flying stars fast came the call to arms.
> Deep among the soldiers, the report says,
> Leading the charge was a young scholar.

No. 3

In a contest of martial arts the literary men compete;
On the backs of peach blossom horses, they fought with golden spears.
From ancient times among those really successful
Whose successes depended on their writing brushes?[17]

On other occasions, however, Xu Wei seems not to have completely accepted the assertion that book learning was irrelevant in assessing one's masculinity: "Who but men could take care of things in this world? Nothing should be beyond the reach of a scholar."[18] After all, despite his aspirations to be a military hero, Xu Wei was viewed by most of his contemporaries as a *wenshi* or *wenren* (both meaning "a literary man"), and he was known to posterity mainly as a versatile *wenren* artist who excelled in drama, poetry, painting, and calligraphy. Xu Wei was able to win the respect of his patron, Hu Zongxian, not because of his brilliance in military strategizing but because of his literary skills. That is, Hu hired him as a literary man rather than a military adviser. It was said that some of the Taoist-style elegiac essays *(qingci)*, written by Xu Wei and other private secretaries of Hu Zongxian and accompanying various auspicious gifts Hu presented to the throne, pleased the Jiajing Emperor (r. 1522–1566). The emperor enjoyed them so much that he often commented on and underlined sentences he liked and had them collected in a little book.[19]

A revealing conversation between Hu Zongxian and Xu Wei is recorded in a late Ming collection of anecdotes: "When Xu Wei served as one of his private secretaries, Hu Zongxian treated him quite well. Once Hu jokingly told Xu, 'You are merely a literary man [*wenshi*]. Without me, fame would always be beyond your reach.' 'Although you are a great hero,' replied Xu, 'your name will never be remembered by others without my writing about you.'"[20] People might doubt the authenticity of this conversation, but it is certain that Hu Zongxian respected Xu Wei for his literary skills rather than anything else. Xu Wei, however, was probably not too thrilled with this situation, since he perceived himself as competent in both military and civil affairs *(wenwu shuangquan)*. Some of Xu Wei's friends, such as the poet Shen Mingchen (fl. mid-sixteenth century), who once also served as a private secretary on Hu Zongxian's staff, indeed praised him as someone who was good at both book learning and swordsmanship and who had the ability to outmatch ten thousand people *(xueshu xuejian di wanren)*.[21] In fact, Xu Wei once used this same phrase *(xueshu xuejian)* to compliment one of his friends.[22] Terms such as *xueshu* (book learning), *xuejian* (swordsmanship), and *di wanren* (a match for ten thousand) can be traced back to Mencius and Sima Qian's famous biography of Xiang Yu, the ultimate martial hero in Chinese history (see chapter 1), and Xiang Yu was one of the historical figures Xu Wei appears to have found most fascinating.[23]

Despite his interest, and probably competence, in military affairs, Xu

Wei was successful in claiming attention only to his talent as a *wenshi*. The opposing attraction of books and swords must have been one of the important sources of tension in Xu Wei's life, and it explains in part why the sword is such a dominant image in his writings. He could at least write about the sword, even if he did not have an opportunity to use it. The fact remains that he could write only about the glorious swordsmanship of others, while he himself was never able to practice it in real battles. The weapon available to Xu Wei as a *muyou* was his tongue or his brush. He once complained that as a *muyou*, he could use only his tongue as a sword to fight battles *(yishe weidao)*.[24] His main job was to offer advice to his patron and prepare documents for him. As a *wenshi*, he was allowed to play only the passive role of a witness or a recorder rather than someone directly at the center of action. Later, looking back on his life, Xu Wei had to acknowledge that he had failed to achieve anything in either book learning or swordsmanship.[25]

Serving as a private secretary for an important official such as Hu Zongxian appears to have produced in Xu Wei a feeling of deep ambivalence. For one thing, Hu Zongxian's apparent appreciation of his literary talents must have given him a tremendous sense of fulfillment. It had to be a boost to his much-bruised masculine ego. In a letter to Hu Zongxian, "Xie Dufu Hu gong qi," Xu Wei profusely thanked Hu for showing him respect as a man of great ability *(guoshi zhi dai),* for enabling him financially to take good care of his birth mother, and for making arrangements for him to marry again. (This time, instead of Xu's being married into his wife's family, his wife was married into his, and she came to live in his house.)[26]

Despite Hu Zongxian's appreciation and respect, we can find traces of Xu Wei's ambivalence toward his *muyou* experience in many of his writings. In a farewell letter to one of his friends, who was about to begin his own *muyou* career, Xu Wei started out by emphasizing how lofty the profession of *mu* (serving on the staff of an official) had been during ancient times because *mu* candidates at that time were selected according to individual talents. He deplored that the selection in his own times, in contrast, was no longer exclusively based on one's talents. Even if a talented man happened to be selected, there would not necessarily be any opportunities for him to show his abilities.[27] Elsewhere, Xu Wei complained that while it was possible in ancient times for many people (even those of the most humble origins) to rise to fame and distinction after joining the staff of an official, this had now become virtually impossible because the staff members of an official were no longer regarded as part of the bureaucratic institution.[28] Here Xu Wei alluded to an important change during the mid-Ming from the practice of *muliao zhi* (the government recognizing and paying the staff of an official) to *muyou zhi* or *muke zhi* (an official paying his staff members directly as private helpers and therefore *you* [friends] or *ke* [guests]). No longer enjoying recognition and salary from the government, staff members felt their positions to be much more precarious since their relationships with their employer were now a purely private matter. At the same time, chances for advancement were now virtually nonexistent.[29] Consequently, according to Xu Wei, the status of *mu* had been drastically reduced in the transition from *muliao zhi* to *muke zhi*.[30] Taking advantage of the occasion when Hu Zongxian presented him with the gift of a silver pheasant, Xu Wei composed a short poem where he implicitly compared his *muyou* experience to that of a bird imprisoned in a small cage.[31]

As noted, Xu Wei's main duty as a private secretary was to draft documents and write perfunctory poems and essays in his patron's name for various occasions. Later Xu Wei often felt that he needed to apologize for these writings:

> In ancient times, people rarely asked others to ghostwrite for them because those capable of writing were either very important people themselves or recluses. In the case of important people, one could not even seek audience with them, not to mention commission writings from them; as for recluses, one would have a hard time seeking them out, let alone asking them to write on his behalf. Unfortunately, I labored over writing like a horse tilling the field because I am neither an important person nor a recluse. This is why people could ask me to write for them, a fate I could hardly avoid. On the other hand, what is in vogue nowadays are examination essays. Those who have become officials by passing the civil service examinations usually are not very good at old-style poems and essays. Even if some of them are, now the demand for perfunctory writings for various occasions has become so great that they have to commission others to write for them. Being no recluses, these ghostwriters must have been unsuccessful in their own careers. That is why these commissioned writings could at least help their readers understand the people and the world.[32]

This is by no means a very effective apology; the concluding remark is especially unconvincing and even somewhat out of place. The only justification Xu Wei managed to offer for his willingness to ghostwrite was that his humble status left him with no other choice but to offer his brush for hire. However, ghostwriting could be exasperating and even feminizing. It could be much worse than the usual frustration a literatus commonly complained about—that is, that one's talent was not being recognized. In the case of a *muyou*, often one's talent was given some recognition, and sometimes one was even granted opportunities to demonstrate and use one's talent. However, the talent could be exercised only in someone else's name—the patron's. Serving as a *muyou* for an influential official such as Hu Zongxian, Xu Wei was close to power, yet he was barred from exercising it in his own name. A *muyou* was entitled only to a ghostly existence defined by the needs of the one who had hired him.

A favorite metaphor among *muyou* used to characterize their frustrations was that of a girl who was too poor to marry but who had to make beautiful wedding dresses for rich girls, an image made famous by the late

Tang poet Qin Taoyu (fl. late ninth century) in his poem "Pinnü" (A Poor Girl). The concluding couplet of this famous poem reads as follows: "How sad every year I have to do needlework /And yet all the gowns I make are for the weddings of other girls [*wei taren zuo jiayishang*]." This poem has become a classic because of its subtly evoked image of a *pinshi* (a poor and frustrated literatus), and the interchangeability between *pinshi* and *pinnü* has been an important theme in Chinese poetic tradition.[33] Xu Wei composed a similar poem comparing himself to a girl who was too poor to marry and yet always labored for the weddings of rich girls.[34] It is here that we begin to feel the feminine presence of the "weeping widow" that Yuan Hongdao detected in Xu Wei's writings.

Self-Castration and Re/Masculinization

Xu Wei received an even more serious blow when his patron, Hu Zongxian, was arrested in 1563 as a result of the downfall of the notorious grand secretary Yan Song (1480–1565; *DMB,* pp. 1586–1591) and his clique, with whom Hu was closely associated. Two years later Hu died in prison (he probably committed suicide). This was an important turning point in Xu Wei's life. For him, the implications of the downfall of Yan Song and his clique, however, were much more complicated than the fact that he now needed to find another job. Having worked for Hu Zongxian, Xu Wei was inevitably sucked into the controversies surrounding his former patron, and he suddenly found himself in a quandary that was soon to drive him over the edge. He was torn between his antagonism toward the Yan Song clique and his gratitude and loyalty to his former patron.

Making the dilemma even more painful was the fact that one of Xu Wei's friends and fellow townsmen, Shen Lian (1507–1557; *DMB,* pp. 1182–1185), was persecuted and eventually put to death by Yan Song and his people. The persecution was apparently triggered by Shen Lian's outspokenness. He often spoke out publicly against the "criminal" deeds of the Yan Song clique and even once sent a memorandum to the throne demanding that Yan Song and others be impeached. In "Jipu" (The Chronology of an Eccentric's Life), Xu Wei listed Shen Lian in the section on "best friends" *(jizhi).*[35] In fact, Xu Wei believed that Shen Lian was one of the few who "had respected [him] as a man of ability [*guoshi zhi dai*]." As I mentioned above, this was the same phrase Xu Wei had used to describe how he had been treated by Hu Zongxian. Xu Wei's admiration for Shen Lian was attested to by the frequency with which he mentioned him in his writings. The painful fact was that Shen Lian and Hu Zongxian, the two people who had shown the most understanding of Xu Wei's ability and talents, were respectively affiliated with two opposing political factions locked in a brutal power struggle that had dominated the political scene of the last two decades of the Jiajing reign (1522–1566). After Shen Lian's much celebrated and tragic death, Xu's admiration for him deepened to the point that he began to worship him as a great hero.[36] Understandably, in several of his poems composed in memory of Shen Lian, Xu Wei associated his hero with the sword, his favorite symbol of masculinity.[37]

In his biography of Shen Lian, Xu Wei listed in detail all of Shen's heroic deeds. What he most admired was what he termed Shen's three extraordinary or marvelous qualities: his great writings, his daring remonstrations with the emperor, and his stubborn straightforwardness. He compared Shen's loyalty and tragic death to those of Qu Yuan; at the same time, he compared himself to Song Yu, Qu's disciple who mourned his master, thus showing his deep respect for Shen.[38] It should be pointed out here that in the eyes of others Xu Wei was also an extraordinary man *(qiren)*.[39] Moreover, *qiren* was a self-image Xu Wei cherished, as indicated by the title of his "autobiographical chronology," "Jipu."

In several poems Xu Wei compared Shen Lian to Mi Heng from the Three Kingdoms Period (220–265). Mi was known for his open defiance of the powerful warlord Cao Cao (155–220) and for castigating Cao in front of his guests after Cao tried to humiliate Mi by assigning him to the job of a drummer.[40] It is beyond doubt that Xu Wei wrote the play *Kuang gushi Yuyang sannong* (Three Performances of "Yuyang Roll" by the Mad Drummer), one of four plays in his *Sisheng yuan* (Four Cries of a Gibbon) play cycle, to celebrate Shen Lian's heroic defiance of the evil Yan Song.[41]

The eventual downfall of Yan Song and his people, which began in 1563, made it possible for Shen Lian's family to have the imperial government officially rehabilitate his name, something Xu Wei must have welcomed wholeheartedly. However, the disgrace of Yan Song also meant the downfall of Hu Zongxian. As a ghostwriter who had drafted many documents sent to Yan Song in Hu Zongxian's name, Xu Wei had reason to fear repercussions. After Hu Zongxian was arrested, Xu Wei was invited to join the staff of Li Chunfang (1511–1585; *DMB,* pp. 818–819), the minister of rites, who was apparently impressed by Xu's ability to compose Taoist-style elegiac essays, to which the Jiajing Emperor had taken such a liking. In fact, Li Chunfang's quick rise to power can be attributed in large part to his winning the emperor's favor with his own *qingci* essays. Xu Wei went to the capital and accepted the job. However, he soon learned that Li Chunfang was closely associated with the new chief grand secretary, Xu Jie (1503–1583; *DMB,* pp. 570–576), who had played a direct role in the initial downfall of Hu Zongxian and who was apparently engaged in an ongoing effort to further persecute Hu and his associates. Reluctant to serve someone who might have had a hand in the tragedy of his former patron, Xu Wei decided to quit. However, Li Chunfang was not happy with Xu Wei's request to terminate their *muyou* contract. Only after repeated interventions by some of Xu Wei's important friends in the capital and only after he had gathered enough money to return the *pinjin* (initial bonus; it was sixty taels of silver) was he released from the contract.

This ordeal must have given Xu Wei even more reason to fear that he would be targeted for persecution because of his close relationship with Hu Zongxian. In his autobiographical chronology, Xu Wei used the term *shengbu* (blackmailing or threatening) to describe Li's attempts to force him to rescind his decision to quit.[42] He also noted that in the following year he began to suffer from a mysterious illness, or *bing* (insanity?), and he repeatedly tried to harm himself physically.[43] Modern scholars have hotly debated whether Xu Wei was really insane or was just faking insanity in order to avoid persecution.[44] What we do know with certainty, however, is that Xu Wei tried to commit suicide. He made clear his intent in the epitaph he wrote before his attempt:

> People said that Xu Wei did not have to die because morally he, as a *wenshi*, was blameless. However, they did not know that there were many *wenshi* who died even though they were morally impeccable in their duties as private secretaries for their patrons. I want to end my own life rather than allow others to have me killed. When righteousness was not an issue, I always behaved freely without being constrained by the Confucian moral code. However, when it came to right-eousness, I always adhered to my sense of personal honor and would rather die than be forced to do what I did not want to do. Therefore, none of my relatives will mourn my death, and none of my friends will understand my death. Since I have not been very good at making a living, after my death there will not be much money left for my funeral, except for a few thousand volumes of books, two chime stones, some ink stones, several swords, and a few paintings, plus some manuscripts of my own writings. I have asked one of my fellow townsmen to sell the swords and paintings; the money should be enough for a [simple] funeral. I have also entrusted one of my friends with my manuscripts.[45]

This certainly reads like a suicide note. What is puzzling, however, is the specific way Xu Wei carried out his mission. According to Tao Wangling (b. 1562; *jinshi*, 1589), Xu's young fellow townsman, Xu Wei did not try to kill himself by slitting his throat with a sword or via some other more "manly" means. This was curious given his lifelong obsession with swords, which he did not forget to mention even in his "suicide note." Instead, he attempted to pierce his ear with an awl and smash his testicle(s) with a hammer.[46] This was indeed a very ineffective as well as strange way of trying to kill oneself. It was a slow and excruciating process of self-mutilation rather than an instant act of suicide.

One is tempted to think that in fits of delusion, Xu Wei must have been tormented by something closely associated with his ears (the hearing function) and testicles (the physical denominator of his masculinity). The attempt to destroy his ears was probably related to his fear of hearing any

more bad news about the persecution of Hu Zongxian's followers or associates, as if only by becoming deaf could he insulate himself enough from the
witch hunts. His act of self-castration might have been a strange acknowledgement of his "emasculated" status. With the demise of Hu Zongxian,
Xu's importance as a man of talent had suddenly disappeared. Moreover,
Xu Wei seems to have felt that if he had acted with the courage of a true
man (as had Shen Lian) and had confronted Hu Zongxian about his association with such evil people as Yan Song, he could probably have saved his
patron from tragedy. This is the sentiment implicitly expressed in Xu Wei's
eulogy for Hu Zongxian:

> How sad! Had you been good at self-discipline, you could have become aware
> of your own mistakes [in time], while people would have remembered all your
> good deeds after you saved them from suffering [caused by the pirates]. Unfor-
> tunately, neither of these is the case, and that is why disaster eventually hit you.
> How sad! At the beginning, when you were alive, I failed to discipline myself to
> serve you well; in the end, after you passed away, how could I expect people to
> consider me qualified to ask them to think only of your achievements? As lowly
> and humble as I am, I have failed in both instances [serving you well while you
> were alive and asking others to remember your good deeds after you were dead].
> Full of gratitude, I can only shed tears in this desolate world.[47]

Unlike in a typical eulogy, which was supposed to heap praises upon the
deceased, Xu Wei was expressing his wishes about what might have been if
he and Hu had had a second chance to do things differently. It is a eulogy
full of belated regrets and blame for himself as well as for the deceased.

Furthermore, the death of Hu was an emasculating event for Xu Wei at
a yet more subtle level. It must have exerted tremendous pressure on him
to do something more heroic, such as to end his own life out of loyalty and
gratitude, as a chaste widow was supposed to do after the death of her husband. Elsewhere Xu Wei observed, "In ancient times, a man would look forward to the chance to offer his life if he could find someone who really
appreciated him."[48] Read in this context, we could interpret Xu Wei's assertion in his "suicide note" that there were many *wenshi* who died as a result
of the downfall of their patrons as an indication of the degree to which he
himself felt pressured to resort to some radical act to prove his loyalty. In
other words, these *wenshi* died because, Xu Wei believed, they felt that they
were supposed to make some radical gesture of loyalty after their patrons'
deaths.

Xu Wei's sense of guilt that he had not done enough for his patron must
have been compounded by the fact that his close friend and colleague, Shen
Mingchen, who had also been treated well by Hu Zongxian when Shen was
serving him as a *muyou*, did something much more heroic and much more
worthy of the honor of a loyal minister. Shen risked his own life by plead-
ing with all the important officials who were willing to listen to him and pre-

senting them with a eulogy he had written for Hu Zongxian, insisting that his former patron had been the victim of great injustice.[49] Likewise, the famous writer Mao Kun, who had also once served on Hu Zongxian's staff, took great risks to make similar public protests on Hu's behalf. Mao Kun's son, Mao Guojin (*jinshi*, 1583), would later point to these actions with great pride in his biography of his father. Mao Guojin argued that after Hu's arrest, almost all his former followers disappeared, and only his father, out of anger and a strong sense of justice, wrote to the higher officials, insisting that Hu's contributions to the country far outweighed the wrongs he was supposed to have committed.[50] In comparison with the daring protests of Shen Mingchen and Mao Kun, Xu Wei's silence was indeed conspicuously embarrassing, especially given his enormous gratitude to Hu, as expressed in his earlier writings.[51] Others may have perceived Xu Wei's joining the staff of Li Chunfang, Hu's enemy, as an act of betrayal. Commenting on Shen Mingchen and Xu Wei almost a century later, the early Qing poet Zhu Yizun (1629–1709) contrasted Shen's selfless deeds of loyalty with Xu's insanity as a result of his fear of being implicated. He came to the conclusion that Shen was far superior to Xu in terms of moral character.[52]

It is in the aftermath of Hu Zongxian's downfall that we should search for possible clues to account for Yuan Hongdao's seemingly puzzling association of Xu Wei, someone extremely conscious of his masculine image, with a weeping widow. The sudden downfall of Hu Zongxian appears to have left Xu Wei all alone in the world, just like a widow who had suddenly lost her husband. The fact that Xu Wei took great trouble to withdraw from service to Li Chunfang can be interpreted as an indication of his guilt for being "unfaithful" to the deceased. His attempts at self-mutilation must have been, at least in part, an extreme expression of such guilt.

Before examining further the paradoxical implications of Xu Wei's attempts at self-castration, we may benefit by a close look at his views on real chaste widows. Unlike many of his literati contemporaries (see chapter 4), Xu Wei was surprisingly sympathetic to widows who did not commit suicide to prove their chastity. In "Gongshi zhuan" (The Biography of Gongshi), Xu Wei related the story of a woman who rejected the plea of her dying husband to die with him. After his death and later the death of their daughter, she refused to remarry when her mother tried to pressure her. She even cut off all of her hair to demonstrate her determination to remain a faithful widow (also an act of self-mutilation, though not as violent as Xu Wei's). Xu mentioned a detail in her life when she was only a child: after hearing that her uncle had become a martyr for the country, she praised him as having died a worthy death, an indication of her virtue even before she had grown up. Xu Wei commented:

> Since ancient times, chaste widows and loyal ministers have been able to demonstrate their virtue because such virtue was already seeded in them from the time

their mothers, in ominous dreams, became pregnant with them; this virtue did not start to exist at the moment they decided to deface themselves or slit their throats. Just like a piece of jade: it would rather be broken into pieces than abused. This is because it already possesses its fine characteristics when it is being formed in the wild; one does not need to throw it hard onto the ground to verify these characteristics.[53]

Here Xu Wei was arguing that the virtue of a chaste widow or a loyal minister did not necessarily have to be proven through a radical act; such dramatic acts as suicide were almost irrelevant as far as one's loyalty or chastity was concerned. (We are reminded again of Sima Qian's decision to not choose death and his apology for his decision.)

Among the chaste women he wrote about, Xu Wei appears to have been particularly obsessed with the tragic case of a certain widow Zhou. He mentioned her repeatedly. In his poems "Zhoushi nü ershou" (Two Poems on the Woman Zhou), Xu Wei detailed how Zhou, after the death of her husband, was prevented by her parents-in-law from remarrying. They insisted that she retain her chastity as a widow. Furthermore, they repeatedly mistreated her and even physically abused her. They eventually took away her son. When reunited with his mother after almost a decade of forced separation, the son did not even know who she was because his grandparents told him that she was merely his wet nurse.[54] No longer able to endure the suffering, widow Zhou committed suicide. However, her suicide brought glory and honor to her husband's family, and, ironically, she was now celebrated as a chaste widow.[55]

It is particularly interesting that Xu Wei repeatedly criticized such inhuman insistence on widow chastity by associating it with the image of a loyal minister that was often celebrated in conventional political discourse:

> Pitying the grass, the evil wind I blame;
> One faults the snow to promote the purity of the pine tree.
> A grand event promoting social morality you want to turn this into,
> And yet a "loyal minister" is not what I want to become.[56]

Elsewhere, Xu Wei compared a widow to an ancient Confucian sage: "Like the Baron of the West [later King Wen of the Zhou], whose loyalty only brought him tragedy, how many women and ministers since ancient times have suffered the same fate?"[57] In "Jiefu pian" (On A Chaste Woman), Xu again ridiculed this insistence on widow chastity by comparing it to the pressures on a minister to commit suicide when it was absolutely unnecessary because there was no national disaster: "Although we did pledge to live together forever, I won't seek a national tragedy just to have a chance to be a loyal minister."[58]

Of course, as we discussed in chapter 2, the minister-concubine rhetoric had long been part of conventional political discourse in imperial China.

Consequently, it is not surprising that Xu Wei compared what he considered excessive insistence on widow chastity to the equally excessive demands of loyalty imposed on a minister. However, the ironic and often negative context within which the metaphor of a loyal minister is invoked in these poems about female others is indeed unusual, and it should alert us to the possible presence of Xu Wei's own agenda. Although there is not enough evidence for us to date these chaste widow poems with accuracy, it is very likely that at least some of them were written after the downfall of Hu Zongxian, when Xu Wei was feeling the pressure to show his loyalty to his former patron.[59] What drove Xu Wei insane—if he indeed became insane, as he and others claimed—at least in part was the enormous pressure on him to demonstrate his "chastity" in the aftermath of Hu Zongxian's fall, and such pressure might not have been all self-imposed. His failure to stand up as a real man for his patron, as Shen Mingchen and Mao Kun had apparently done, only added to his feeling of being feminized. His eventual violent act of self-castration was only a radical reaction to such emasculating pressure, as if he, in a moment of insanity, had managed to convince himself that the destruction of his testicles could help to alleviate this pressure, which was impinging on him by underscoring what was removed but had originally been there.

Xu Wei's subsequent killing of his wife, Zhangshi, however, seems to point to an entirely different kind of response (at least on the surface) to the emasculating pressure. Many theories have been proposed to account for why Xu Wei killed his wife.[60] It is certain that Xu Wei was convinced that his wife was unfaithful to him. Whether his suspicion was justified is more difficult to determine, although his suspicion must have been fueled by his painful awareness of the limitations of his self-mutilated body. For Xu Wei (and many others), there was probably nothing more threatening to one's manhood than the shame of being cuckolded. Xu Wei bitterly characterized his wife's "affair" as "a shame that would make one hold one's nose [*yanbi zhi xiu,* or extremely revolting]."[61] In a way, killing his wife was a desperate effort to defend his honor as a man at a time when he himself (as well as others) were questioning his manhood and his male body had been disfigured. As noted, his marriage had been arranged, and probably paid for, by Hu Zongxian; consequently Zhangshi was a symbolic reminder of Xu's past successes. With the downfall of Hu Zongxian, Xu Wei must have felt that his wife's affair was a deliberate reminder of his now diminished manhood, which, ironically, was supposed to have been symbolized by what he had presumably destroyed in his suicide attempt. He believed that uxoricide was the only way for him to prove to others as well as to himself that he was still a man.

It is interesting that Xu Wei's crisis of manhood provoked two seemingly different responses: self-castration (a deliberate violent act to deny his manhood) and killing his adulterous wife (a radical attempt to defend his male honor). However, both can be understood as the responses of a man tormented by serious doubts about his manhood. Self-castration was probably an admission that he was not a worthy man—or, more probably, a reassertion of his manhood by the physical destruction of what he had always possessed as a man; he imposed a brutal "absence" on himself only to underscore what originally had always been present. Killing his wife was only a logical further effort to prove his male status. All this can be understood as Xu's attempts to assert or reassert his agency and authenticity as a male subject.

Cross-Dressing and the Need to Undress

We need to return briefly to Xu Wei's play *Kuang gushi yuyang sannong*, which, as noted, was apparently written in memory of his friend Shen Lian. Interpreted in light of Xu Wei's attempted self-castration, a small detail in the play becomes more significant, even though we cannot determine accurately whether the play was written before or after he attempted this violent act (more about the dating of his *Sisheng yuan* play cycle below). In most versions of Mi Heng's story, as recorded in history and fiction, Mi Heng is said to have insisted on being naked in Cao Cao's presence to show his defiance when the latter ordered him to change clothes to perform for his guests. In his play, Xu Wei added a subtle but rather curious detail to emphasize the masculine courage symbolized by Mi Heng's open defiance. In the play, when Mi Heng is a bit slow in changing his clothes, one of Cao Cao's subordinates yells at him:

> Beast, how could you bare yourself in front of the prime minister! As they say, a donkey's prick [*lüliaozi*] points toward the east while a horse's prick [*maliaozi*] points toward the west.
>
> [Mi Heng replies:] Your bald-headed prime minister's prick points toward the south and my prick points toward the north.[62]

Here Cao Cao's subordinate quotes a vulgar proverb about the proper directions for a donkey's and a horse's penis in order to remind Mi Heng that he should remember his status as an entertainer in front of the prime minister.[63] Mi Heng replies that he indeed understands that Cao Cao is in the position of the powerful (his penis pointing toward the south, or *chaonan*), while he himself is in the position of the less powerful (his penis pointing toward the north). However, by merely mentioning the simple fact that he has a penis, just as Cao Cao does, Mi Heng is suggesting that their different power positions are not that important or relevant. Instead, he is facing Cao Cao just as one man faces another man.

Given Xu Wei's particular attention to Mi Heng's genitalia and to their symbolic relationship to a *wenshi*'s Confucian manhood in this play, his own attempted self-castration, even though it might have been carried out in a state of insanity, should not be interpreted simply as a crazy act by a deluded person that was devoid of gender implications.[64]

In Xu Wei's other plays gender anxiety is manifested in different ways. In fact, Mi Heng's undressing at the beginning of *Kuang gushi yuyang sannong* should help us to better understand the significance of cross-dressing, which served as the basis for plot development in two of the other plays in Xu Wei's *Sisheng yuan* play cycle. It is indeed remarkable that Xu Wei, who was under constant pressure to prove his manliness in the face of many adversities, should have authored two plays about how a woman is able to achieve public honors and personal happiness by cross-dressing as man: *Ci Mulan tifu congjun* (The Female Mulan Joins the Military in Place of Her Father; hereafter *Ci Mulan*) and *Nü zhuangyuan cifeng dehuang* (A Female Prima Gets a Male Phoenix after Declining a Female One; hereafter *Nü zhuangyuan*).[65]

The two female protagonists in these plays, Mulan and Huang Chongjia, achieve success mainly because they manage to persuade others, via cross-dressing, to accept their newly acquired gender identities as men. That is, it is often people's perceptions of one's gender identity rather than one's actual talents that determine whether one is successful. This stance appears to have reflected a fairly modern view of gender equality. In fact, many modern scholars have complimented Xu Wei for his "progressive" views on women as expressed in these two plays. However, in light of Xu Wei's own gender anxiety, this apparent sympathy for women can be more fruitfully interpreted as an attempt by the male playwright to vindicate his denied masculinity. There is an unmistakable autobiographical dimension in the two female protagonists. The celebration of female success here is no more straightforward than the sympathy Xu expressed for chaste widows.

In *Ci Mulan*, Mulan offers to enlist in the military in place of her aging father by cross-dressing as a young man. After twelve years of service, Mulan returns home with honors and distinction. This two-act play focuses on the moments before and after Mulan assumes her false gender identity, while her military triumphs as a "male" soldier are mentioned only briefly at the end of act 1.[66] A significant portion of the first act is about how Mulan assumes a male identity. In other words, the play chooses to concentrate on Mulan's experience as a woman, even though it is her "male" experience that brings her honors and distinction. Such a focus tends to emphasize Mulan's gender status as a woman and therefore questions the legitimacy of her having to assume the false gender identity of a man.

The concluding lines of the last aria sung by Mulan are quite revealing: "They have looked at me thousands of times, and yet none of them could tell whether I was a male or a female. I have just come to realize that those who can tell male from female do not rely on their eyes." Even more revealing is the last couplet of the play's concluding chorus: "How many things in this world are muddled? This play is meant to criticize those who cannot tell male from female."[67] Here the term *cixiong* (female and male) takes on the additional meaning of "to see who is more capable," as expressed in the phrase "to have a contest to see who is a real man/male [*jueyi cixiong*]"; the latter term was quite common in late imperial writings. In other words, this play is an explicit protest against those who have failed to recognize talent because of their blind faith in fake gender appearance (relying too much on what they can see on the surface).

While *Ci Mulan* is about how a woman is able to distinguish herself on the battlefield, *Nü zhuangyuan* is about how a woman, also by masquerading as a man, is able to achieve top honors in the civil service examinations and become an important official. Whereas Mulan offers to enlist in the military out of her filiality, Huang Chongjia decides to sit for the examinations because she has no means of supporting herself after the death of her parents.

Unlike *Ci Mulan,* which dwells only briefly on Mulan's military career, the five-act *Nü zhuangyuan* is fairly detailed about Huang Chongjia's literary triumphs. If act 1, which is about how she successfully passes the civil service examinations, serves only as a preview of her poetic talent, act 4, where she is said to have composed various poems in different genres, is a detailed account of her literary accomplishments. Furthermore, as some modern critics have pointed out, the specific references to Huang Chongjia's talents in literary composition (especially the demanding *siliu wen,* a special kind of parallel prose), music, painting, calligraphy, and chess are meant to reflect the playwright's own accomplishments in these areas.[68] Such detailed accounts of Huang Chongjia's literary talents seem also to have been necessitated by the explicit critique of the examination system in act 2, where one of the candidates complains that the grading of an essay is purely a judgment call on the part of the examiner: "There has been no uniform standard in judging essays since ancient times, and the only thing that is important is to win the tacit approval of the examiner." He further reminds people of the saying, "It is much better for an examinee to win the heart of the examiner than the praise of all the people under Heaven."[69] Here Xu Wei's own frustrations with the examination system appear to have boiled over (all of his eight attempts to pass the provincial exams failed). However, by ridiculing the arbitrary nature of the examination system, our playwright also casts doubt on his female protagonist's literary talent—she, too, might have passed out of sheer luck or the bias of the examiner. That is why, in addition to the detailed account of her literary talents in act 4, Xu Wei goes out of his way to have her pass another "test" in act 3, where she solves three difficult legal disputes as a judge.

If *Ci Mulan* can be interpreted as an expression of Xu Wei's own aspirations toward a distinguished military career *(wu),* *Nü zhuangyuan* was meant to showcase his literary talents *(wen).* Despite Xu Wei's aspirations to distinguish himself on the battlefield, his ultimate goal was to achieve distinction as a civil official by first passing the civil service examinations. Mulan, even after all the glories on the battlefield, still feels that she might be unworthy of her future husband, who is a civil official.[70] This certainly reflects the value system of Xu Wei's times, which tended to prize the civil over the military.

One particularly interesting aspect of *Nü zhuangyuan* is its constant references to the story of Mulan. Mulan is obviously a model Huang Chongjia tries to emulate. When she feels embarrassed at being exposed as a female cross-dresser, her future father-in-law, Prime Minister Zhou, reminds her that what Mulan did is worthy of a hero and that no one would mention shame in connection to her.[71] In act 4, Prime Minister Zhou asks Huang Chongjia to compose an essay in parallel prose to celebrate the building of a temple in honor of Mulan. The audience is reminded of the possible autobiographical implications of the play when Prime Minister Zhou praises Huang Chongjia for immortalizing the life of Mulan: "She was originally a girl before joining the military, and you have captured in detail her heroic spirit in your essay of parallel prose."[72] Of course, Xu Wei had already authored a play about Mulan, performing the same "duty" that Huang Chongjia is now performing in *Nü zhuangyuan,* which also happens to have been authored by Xu Wei.

In her essay on Mulan, Huang Chongjia emphasizes the original message of *Ci Mulan*—namely, what is important is one's talent rather than one's gender appearance: "It is difficult to tell a male rabbit from a female; a horse is a great horse regardless of its colors or whether it is male or female."[73] This echoes Mulan's insistence in *Ci Mulan* that what should matter is one's ability rather than others' perceptions of gender identity. Having achieved glory on the battlefield, Mulan reminds the audience that "This is an illusion from whatever perspective it is viewed, and there is nothing to brag about. I killed the bandits and captured their leader simply because I was able to dress as a man. I have accomplished all this without too much effort."[74] This insistence on exposing the misleading nature of gender appearance is reinforced at the end of the play, when the audience is told that the ability to tell male from female has nothing to do with what can be observed by the naked eye.

Xu Wei seems to protest that for his contemporaries, all that mattered was appearance and perception because his female protagonists have to assume a fake gender identity to demonstrate their talents. For Xu Wei, being feminized or being relegated to the feminine position of the marginalized amounted to a deprivation of opportunities to show his worth as a real man (*cixiong;* whether he had real talent) since he was condemned to being a "woman" by his unappreciative times.

It is here that the elaborate description of Mulan unbinding her feet at the beginning of the play becomes significant. Bound feet are supposed to be the ultimate gender marker of Mulan as a woman. The audience is told that it took Mulan several years to have her feet bound into feminine shape, and now she is worried that once unbound, her feet will lose their shape forever. She begins to feel relieved only when she realizes that her family has a magic liquid with which she can wash her feet back into their feminine shape once the time comes when she has to think about marriage. Here we are reminded of the artificiality of gender attributes such as bound feet. This unbinding episode suggests that bound feet are not completely natural; rather they are the result of long-time cultivation. Furthermore, Xu Wei's anachronism is particularly interesting: during the Han dynasty, the historical period in which Mulan was supposed to have lived, the practice of foot binding had yet to become popular. Xu Wei was apparently attributing to Mulan the female gender qualities typical of his own times. While Xu Wei was not necessarily expressing doubts about the naturalness of foot binding as a female gender attribute, such an anachronism alerts the audience to the fact that gender differences are conditioned by particular historical times. Xu Wei seemed to be insisting that gender differentiation was often a matter of perception and could be manipulated, and cross-dressing was only one of the more explicit examples of such manipulation.

At the same time, Xu Wei appears to have also acknowledged that there was a limit to such manipulation since both of his female cross-dressers eventually "undress" themselves and return to their original roles as women. In fact, Huang Chongjia's wet nurse, Aunt Huang, has to literally undress herself, exposing her large breasts, in order to convince others that she is a real woman—she had long taken on the false identity of a man—and that her mistress's virginity has never been compromised.[75] In contrast, Huang Chongjia needs to undress herself only "poetically" by acknowledging her "true" female gender identity in a poem addressed to Prime Minister Zhou; the latter accepts her as a woman without further ado. In a polite society, one can establish one's masculine identity by passing the civil service examinations with "good poetry" or reclaim feminine identity by the same poetic means. The wet nurse, however, without any poetic talent, has to resort to much more demeaning means to reclaim her female gender status. Her female gender identity can be reaffirmed only through a physical inspection of her body.

This kind of "undressing" at the end of these two plays serves as an interesting parallel to Mi Heng's undressing at the beginning of *Kuang gushi*, where undressing *(luoshang)* and exposing himself are Mi Heng's symbolic gestures to reassert his manliness in open defiance of Cao Cao.[76] Frustrated with others' doubts about his manhood because of the feminine/marginal position to which he had been relegated, Xu Wei was ridiculing his contemporaries' inability to tell the male from the female and their blind trust in the "dressed up." Xu Wei was desperate for a chance to "undress" himself or to "bare it all" in order to reclaim his denied masculinity. Paradoxically, the impossibility of "undressing"—that is, the lack of opportunity to reassert his dignity as a man—might have contributed to his insanity, leading him to take the radical action of self-castration. His male organs as gender markers were significant only to the extent that they could be "shown" to others. In Xu Wei's mind being denied the opportunity to show his worth, must have amounted to being castrated. For Xu Wei (insane or not), self-castration was probably the only potent means to protest the blind trust in gender appearance. By mutilating his physical gender marker, Xu Wei was demanding attention to what he believed he had always possessed and what people had refused to see or pretended not to see. What was the significance of possessing this physical symbol of manhood if people refused to acknowledge its existence, not allowing him to "undress" as Mi Heng had done?

CHAPTER 4

Manhood and Nationhood

~~

Chaste Women and the
Fall of the Ming Dynasty

Xu Wei's views on female chastity were rather atypical among his male peers in that he considered widow suicide not necessarily praiseworthy. However, his deep interest in this topic was by no means unusual for a male literatus. In fact, male literati played a crucial role in the cult of chaste women, which reached an unprecedented scale during the Ming dynasty.[1] In male literati writings on chaste women—such as biographies, epitaphs, and memoirs—profuse praise of female chastity was often accompanied by laments over the moral deficiencies of male literati. In other words, the heroic deeds of the chaste women, these authors believed, highlighted the failure of educated men, supposedly the moral backbone of society, to live up to their own ethical standards.[2]

The famous late Ming essayist Gui Youguang (1507–1571; *DMB*, 759–761) was quite straightforward in his praise of chaste women, and he simultaneously castigated male moral deficiencies: "Although I grew up near the seashore, I have not traveled to many places. But I have encountered several dozen cases of village women committing suicide for the sake of their deceased husbands, and I have duly recorded these [virtuous] deeds. However, when there was a national crisis, very few high officials chose to commit suicide. Is this because the moral energy of Heaven and Earth privileges women?"[3] Gui Youguang appears to suggest that women are by nature morally superior to men. Almost a century earlier, the scholar-official Luo Lun (1431–1478; *DMB*, 986–985) was even more extreme on this subject:

> What is the purpose of learning for a gentleman? To enlarge his mind, to restore its [original] brightness, and to perfect its moral integrity. Although they are not scholars, why are only women able to perform such heroic acts? . . . During times of peace, a gentleman would be very upset if he were to be compared to a woman, but during a time of national crisis his behavior pales in comparison with that of a woman. Therefore [one should look for] moral integrity in the [female]

sex rather than the other sex. Why? If only all male literati gentlemen were women, how could any disaster possibly befall the nation? I wrote this account of chaste women to shame those disloyal ministers/subjects.[4]

As we discussed in chapters 1 and 2, the analogy between a chaste woman and a loyal minister was part of the long-standing rhetorical convention in traditional political discourse. A minister was expected to demonstrate his loyalty to the ruler just as a woman was supposed to prove her chastity to her husband. What bothered Gui Youguang and Luo Lun was a perceived collapse of this analogical relationship: they were convinced that in reality there were far fewer loyal ministers than chaste women.

Anxiety over the erosion of this moral analogy began to take on different meanings around the mid-seventeenth century, when the Ming state was violently toppled. The urgent issue of how to prove one's loyalty to a fallen monarchy seems to have dramatically enhanced the rhetorical power of the familiar trope of chaste women. Death became almost a daily issue many male literati had to confront during the violent dynastic transition. Furthermore, failure to die (not being killed and especially not killing oneself) became a constant source of anxiety for the surviving literati, who still considered themselves the loyal subjects of the fallen Ming *(yimin)*. For the surviving loyalists, writing about the heroic deeds of chaste women inevitably became a redemptive occasion for self-examination as well as apology. It was in such a process of soul-searching that the subtle contradictions inherent in the analogy began to become painfully visible to some of the literati.

A hotly debated issue among the Ming literati before the fall of the dynasty was whether it was appropriate for a betrothed woman to commit suicide if her future husband died before they could marry.[5] Gui Youguang was representative of those who argued that a woman should not commit suicide for her future husband: "If a betrothed woman, before the marriage takes place, commits suicide or pledges never to marry another man because her future husband has died, she is taking an action that does not accord with the principles of propriety."[6] It was not appropriate, according to Gui Youguang, largely because the woman's first obligations before marriage were to her parents, and she became bound by her obligations to her future husband only after the marriage.

Jiang Yingke, however, vehemently defended suicide by unwed women. He compared an unwed woman's suicide for the sake of her deceased fiancé to the case of a literatus already registered to become an official, who had yet to receive a salary as an official, but who nevertheless committed suicide out of loyalty to the fallen monarchy:

> There should be no question as to whether we should praise those ministers who have committed suicide to show their loyalty when the monarchy they have been serving has toppled and whether we should condemn those officials who fail to do so. However, there are those who have passed the examinations and have

been registered to become officials but have not received salaries and have yet to be formally appointed. One of them might ask: "I have been registered and I should be treated as an official. If I decide to commit suicide to show my loyalty to the fallen monarchy, how could a historian fail to praise me in the same manner as he praises those salaried ministers who have committed suicide out of loyalty to the fallen monarchy?"[7]

Here the act of a chaste woman is defended in terms of a loyal minister's expression of integrity.

Such a relatively innocent comparison of chaste women to loyal ministers was complicated considerably in the early Qing dynasty, when many literati chose life over death in the aftermath of the collapse of the Ming dynasty. Gui Youguang's great-grandson, the writer Gui Zhuang (1613–1673; *ECCP*, p. 427), who did not commit suicide during the violent dynastic changeover as many of his generation of loyal Ming subjects had done, also argued that a betrothed woman should not commit suicide merely because her fiancé had died.[8] He insisted that chastity was more difficult than martyrdom, believing that a woman did not have to resort to suicide just to be on the list of worthy women.[9] It is difficult not to relate Gui Zhuang's view on the chastity of unwed women to his own status as a Ming loyalist who had chosen not to die.

Similar remarks can be found in the writings of the loyalist historian Zha Jizuo (1601–1676). In a collective biography of several women who committed suicide to retain their chastity ("Fulie"), Zha related the story of a young woman named Wannu. Beautiful and talented, she was married to a poor young man, Zhang, who worked as a retainer for a rich and powerful man. The rich man tricked Wannu into going to his room and then kept her under house arrest. Zhang was too fearful to reason with his employer, although he voiced his unhappiness to others. Zhang soon disappeared when his "benefactor" began to make threats against him. Wannu repeatedly lamented that this would not have happened to her if she had been a man. Realizing that her husband was too timid or too weak to win her release, before committing suicide, she made herself a set of men's clothing, insisting that she was going to wear it in the next life. It seems that her insistence on being reborn as a man was intended in part to be a protest against her husband's "effeminacy" or his inability to protect his woman. It is particularly ironic that Wannu's martyrdom *(lie)* was in large part necessitated by her husband's low social status; her desire to become a man in the next life was a protest against the kind of effeminacy society imposed on her husband. What she failed to realize was that she would be "feminized" again if she happened to be reborn as a poor man in the next life. Even more interesting is Zha's comment at the end of this biography:

Seeking martyrdom is a momentary act, while the maintenance of chastity is a more difficult act that lasts an entire life. Many of the women who are able to maintain their chastity throughout their lives are often from families of the well educated, where moral discipline tends to be stricter. As for women from poor families, it is rather difficult for them to maintain their chastity without the benefit of education and strict discipline. This is why many of them prefer such radical acts of the moment. A man is often judged harshly by the people of later ages for cherishing his life/body [ai qi shen] during a time of violent political changes, and he is often despised by the members of the inner chambers.[10]

Zha Jizuo argues that some women preferred martyrdom because of the unfavorable environment in which they found themselves. Here *ai qi shen* (cherishing one's life/body) is a rather ambiguous phrase; it can mean either "clinging to life" or "cherishing one's integrity." It probably betrays Zha's intention of apologizing for his own choice of not dying for the fallen nation: to live under the new alien rule as a Ming loyalist while maintaining his integrity, an act of *ai qi shen,* was in fact a more difficult decision than the momentary act of dying as a martyr. As a Ming loyalist, Zha had to negotiate carefully between maintaining his political integrity and avoiding persecution by the new alien regime.[11]

How to justify not committing suicide was a major topic in the literati discourses on chastity and loyalty in the aftermath of the fall of the Ming.[12] The well-known essay "Sijie lun" (On Suicide in the Name of Moral Integrity), by the Ming loyalist thinker Chen Que (1604–1677), was probably the most sophisticated argument against the post-Ming suicide "frenzy" among the literati. The fact that his teacher, the famous Neo-Confucian philosopher Liu Zongzhou (1578–1645; *ECCP*, pp. 532–533) and many of his closest friends had all committed suicide out of loyalty to the fallen dynasty was a tremendous psychological burden on Chen Que, who, however, had chosen to live as a *yimin.* Despite his repeated expressions of regret, Chen Que explained that the reason he was "too cowardly to commit suicide" was that he needed to fulfill his filial duty and take care of his aging mother.[13] Or in the words of another famous disciple of Liu Zongzhou, Huang Zongxi, who made the same choice of not committing suicide, "one had to humble oneself so as to take care of one's mother [*qushen yangmu*]."[14]

Here we are confronted with the limits of the image of a chaste woman as a useful metaphor for male *yimin* literati. Whereas a male literati loyalist could humble himself *(qushen)* so that he could continue to take care of his parents, such a choice was simply not available to a chaste woman. Once violated and humiliated *(qushen),* she had to commit suicide, even if she had aging parents to look after. Her humiliated body had to be destroyed for the sake of female chastity, while male loyalty did not always have to be enacted physically. Consequently, despite the rhetorical analogy, the notion of *shishen* (surrendering one's body; more literally, losing one's body) had very different implications for a chaste woman and a male Ming loyalist literatus.[15]

In "Sijie lun" Chen Que criticized from a different perspective what he considered to be the abuse of the concept of chastity/loyalty and the craving for (the fame of) suicide:

> Alas! To commit suicide for the sake of integrity is not easy! If [the reason behind] the suicide is in accordance with righteousness [yi], then it is an act of moral integrity [jie]. Otherwise, it is only an act of indifferent death [wangsi] rather than moral integrity. One cannot drag out an ignoble life [wangsheng], nor can one seek death for a far-fetched reason. . . .
>
> Why? Life and death are issues everyone has to face, and no one can avoid death. There is nothing unusual about this. What is difficult is to be able to die for a good reason. . . . Not understanding this, many fame-seekers resorted to different means of suicide . . . such as a betrothed woman committing suicide for her fiancé or a man dying for someone he hardly knows. . . . This is why Confucius said, "You do not understand even life. How can you understand death?"[16] Nowadays scholars jump at this last resort so casually that they share with prostitutes and bandits the platform of virtue and chastity. There is nothing more confusing than the concept of dying for the sake of integrity [sijie]. How painful this is![17]

Elsewhere, Chen Que complained that widows chose to die rather than live to fulfill their duty of raising their sons merely because they desired the fame of a chaste woman, a tragic result of the chaste widow cult promoted by the male literati.[18]

Unlike Chen Que, the Ming loyalist poet and historian Qu Dajun (1630–1696; *ECCP*, pp. 201–203) was much more ambivalent about the moral implications of a betrothed woman committing suicide. However, Qu was more explicit about the relevance of this issue to his own choice of not committing suicide as a Ming loyalist. Like Chen Que, Qu Dajun was haunted throughout his life by the fact that his teacher had died for the cause of the fallen monarchy while he himself had failed to do so. He tried to defend himself by appealing to the theory that suicide was required of a man to show his loyalty if he had been an official serving the fallen monarchy (a view shared by many *yimin* literati including Chen Que): "All men are subjects [under the emperor]. However, there is a distinction between those who have served as officials and those who have not. Those who have served should die for their lord, whereas the priority for those who have not served should be their filial duties. This is only appropriate according to the Way."[19] Writing about chaste women, especially betrothed women who had resorted to suicide, Qu Dajun could not help being reminded of his personal choice, and his ambivalence was obvious:

> There is a distinction between a married woman and an unwed woman. A married woman could choose to avoid death and to prove her chastity by serving the interests of her husband's family; a betrothed woman could choose to end her life

to show her chastity. . . . Alas! I have compiled *The Biographies of the Martyrs of the Four Reigns Period* [*Sichao chengren lu*]. Since the death of the [Chongzhen] emperor, many commoners have been committing suicide to show loyalty to the deceased emperor even though they were not officials! When it comes to female chastity, there are these eleven women, whom I have selected as models of female virtue. Compared with those who have refused to be humiliated when captured and who have faced death with great dignity, these commoners and betrothed women have probably chosen an even more difficult course of action [therefore more praiseworthy]. People usually think that a betrothed woman does not have to die for her deceased fiancé since she is not his wife yet and that a literatus does not have to die for the deceased emperor if he has not served as an official during his reign. [Given this theory,] it is indeed difficult to talk about the best way a woman and a literatus should behave.[20]

Apparently, Qu Dajun felt that it was indeed a virtuous act for an unwed woman to commit suicide for her deceased fiancé, as worthy of praise as the act of a commoner/literatus choosing suicide to show his loyalty to the fallen dynasty. However, others were not to be blamed if they made different choices. There was no uniform standard that could be applied. Despite his ambivalence, Qu's painstaking compilation of the Ming martyrs who had chosen to die for the fallen monarchy might have been an important symbolic act of self-redemption, betraying his deep sense of guilt. To immortalize these heroic acts by recording them was almost as important as the acts themselves, though not necessarily as heroic.[21] Such self-redemption, however, was simply not available to a woman—again testimony to the limits of the analogy between ministers and chaste women.

The famous late Ming official and poet Qian Qianyi (1582–1664; *ECCP*, pp. 148–150), instead of dying for the fallen dynasty, surrendered to the new alien regime. According to various sources, when the short-lived Southern Ming monarchy was about to collapse, Qian's concubine, Liu Rushi (1617–1664), once a famous courtesan, urged him to commit suicide with her. Qian agreed; however, he changed his mind at the last moment.[22] Instead, he surrendered to the Manchus. Qian Qianyi had to carry the stigma of "a minister who served two dynasties" [*erchen*] the rest of his life. Precisely because of his *erchen* experience, Qian Qianyi was reluctant to write on the subject of chaste women.[23] In one of the few pieces he did write, "Ming jingbiao jiefu cong zumu Xushi muzhiming" (The Epitaph of the Honorable Chaste Lady Grandma Xu), he apologized profusely that he did not have enough qualifications to write about these virtuous women because of his own past: "I have done shameful things; I was a disloyal minister and unfilial son." He reluctantly agreed to write this piece only because he did not want the chaste women from his own clan to be forgotten by posterity. Yet Qian did not forget to defend his past. He first pointed out that a wife choosing to die to follow her deceased husband and a minister dying for his lord are both difficult acts of loyalty. Then he praised the female protagonist of his article for choosing to live the long and hard life of a chaste widow in order to take care of the old and raise the young. After referring to several famous male figures in ancient history who had chosen to live on after the death of their benefactors in order to better repay them, Qian observed:

> These people did not choose to die because they wanted to achieve something important and because they had great plans for the future. Compared with those who resorted to a quick death, are their choices easier or more difficult? [In answering this question], we have taken into account what one has specifically pledged to do in making such a choice. Nevertheless, [we have to conclude that] only after having acted like this chaste woman can one be justified in choosing to avoid death. At the same time, a chaste woman has to choose life over death before she even has the opportunity to offer reasons to justify the choice of not dying.[24]

By inference, the reader is supposed to realize that if Qian Qianyi himself had chosen to die, he would not have been able to help those anti-Manchu campaigns, such as the one led by Zheng Chenggong (Coxinga, 1624–1662; *ECCP*, pp. 108–110), and he would not have been able to accomplish other important tasks, such as preserving Han culture, as he believed he had done. The problem, according to Qian Qianyi, was that he first had to make the difficult choice of life before he could justify such a choice (by performing specific deeds). In other words, to judge him only on his choice to live without considering what he had done since that choice was unfair as well as unreasonable. For Qian Qianyi, writing about a chaste woman became a redeeming act of apology.

The trope of a chaste woman became even more ambiguous when some early Qing literati, in soul-searching attempts to explain the seemingly sudden collapse of an almost three-centuries-old dynasty, began to discern something even more troubling in the analogy. This was not so much because of the failure of the male literati to show the same kind of moral courage as the chaste women had shown but because of their realization that the Ming monarchy appeared to have collapsed precisely because its male subjects, especially the male literati, had acted *too much* like women. The fact that these loyal ministers had resorted to suicide, like chaste women, was the inevitable result of their failure to carry out their *manly* duties of defending the empire in the first place. Though courageous, suicide was an act of desperation and hopelessness. In their failure to defend the country, male loyalty was turned into a morally courageous but politically ineffective gesture of *female* chastity. At this point the appropriateness of the analogy itself became questionable.

For the early Qing Confucian thinker Yan Yuan, the pervasive analogy between chaste women and loyal ministers only underscored the crisis of masculinity the male literati were experiencing. It drew attention to the feminization of the literati, which, he believed, had contributed significantly to the fall of the Ming.[25] In Yan Yuan's radical critique, a major point of attack was that the Song Neo-Confucianist introvert approaches and their neglect of practical learning had feminized male literati and rendered them totally unable to function in the "real" world. The collapse of the Ming monarchy was a direct consequence of the emasculating process accelerated by the Song Neo-Confucians:

> The decline of Confucian learning started a long time ago. . . . Since the Han and Song dynasties, men have been solely concerned with philological studies, quiet sitting, reading classified dialogues [*yulei*], and writing eight-legged essays. These [bookish] men have been everywhere, from the administration of the central government to the local magistracy. The schools are filled with pale-looking bookworms who possess no talents or practical skills. They are as soft and as fragile as a woman and lack any manly qualities whatsoever.[26]

Yan Yuan repeatedly characterized the teachings of Song Neo-Confucians as *kongyan* (empty words) or *kongwen* (empty writings),[27] and he contemptuously compared literati bookish learning to a woman's needlework *(nügong)*.[28] Yan Yuan further argued that the effect of too much reading and writing was to physically emasculate or feminize a man: "Nowadays those who confine themselves to their studies [*zuo shuzhai ren*] are physically so frail that they are a laughingstock among soldiers and farmers. Is this what we call masculinity [*nanzi tai*]?"[29] Using the famous Song Neo-Confucian thinker Zhu Xi's complaints about his back pains as "evidence," Yan Yuan even proposed a theory that too much reading and writing could drain a man's vital male energy or semen, just as excessive sex could pose a serious health hazard for him (a warning often found in traditional Chinese medical discourses):

> Anyone with some knowledge of medicine knows that a man who has sex too often will suffer from back pains, a result of the loss of too much vital energy. However, people do not know that those who like to read, write, and talk too much will also suffer from back pains owing to the loss of vital energy. *The Inner Canon* [*Neijing*] clearly states: "One's kidneys are connected to one's brain." If vital energy is the essence of blood and bone, then this same energy is more concentrated in one's brain. My friend Mr. Diao has seminal emissions [*yijing*] every night, even though he doesn't like sex and has not had sex for a long time. This is only because he has been doing too much reading and writing. All these frail and sickly scholars of today must be the result of the favors bequeathed [*yize*] by Zhu Xi.[30]

Note Yan Yuan's sarcastic choice of the word *yize*, which is apparently a pun on *yijing* because in addition to "favor" or "grace," the character *ze* can also mean "a pool of water," while the character *yi* (handing down or emitting) is found in both words. This was probably why Yan Yuan insisted that the literati's obsession with book learning and trivial philological studies had brought disaster to the country.[31]

Yan Yuan's disciple Wang Yuan (1648–1710; *ECCP,* pp. 842–844) was equally harsh and even more explicit on the irrelevance of book learning to a man's job of defending the empire: "People of later ages tried to govern the world with civil arts and literary skills. Has anyone found a case in which poetry has been used to successfully thwart an enemy attack or in which *Great Learning Arranged in Chapters and Sentences* [*Daxue zhangju*] has helped the country to avoid the kind of disastrous defeat the Song troops suffered at the hands of the Mongol army at Yashan?"[32]

Yan Yuan associated this male incompetence and feminization directly with the teachings of the Song Neo-Confucians: "Since the Song and Yuan dynasties, Confucian literati have become very feminized [*xicheng funü tai*]. What a shame! They dwelled on [the impractical] topics of mind/nature when nothing was happening to the country. When the country was in deep crisis, they could only commit suicide to show their loyalty to the emperor."[33] For Yan Yuan, there was something inherently feminine about suicide. Nothing confirmed this belief more than the dying words of loyal Ming officials who committed suicide. He was particularly troubled by the often-quoted suicide poem of the Ming official Shi Bangyao, who killed himself after the fall of the capital:

> I could not help crying when I came cross the following couplet in *The Records of the Martyrs of the Year 1644* [*Jiashen xunnan lu*]:
>
> "Ashamed of being unable to come up with even half a plan to defuse the present crisis, I can only choose death to return the favor I received from my lord."[34]

It is the "feminine" helplessness (i.e., total male incompetence) captured in this poem that saddened Yan Yuan most.

Of course, not everyone considered loyalist suicide a feminine act. During the final days of the Northern Song dynasty, the Song general Liu Ge explicitly characterized his refusal to surrender and to commit suicide as an act of true men: "A chaste woman does not marry twice, and a loyal minister does not serve two different rulers. Furthermore, a minister feels disgraced if his lord becomes worried, and the minister has to die if his lord feels disgraced. 'It is the way of a wife or concubine to consider obedience and docility the norm.' This is why I have to commit suicide."[35] "It is the way of a wife or concubine to consider obedience and docility the norm" is a direct quotation from *Mencius.* Mencius believed that obedience was the behavior code to which a woman should subscribe, and it was deliberately contrasted with the way a man [*da zhangfu*] should behave (see chapter 1). Liu Ge, however, first changed the meaning of the key word, *shun,* from "being obedient," as used in *Mencius,* to "surrender" or "comply with the demands of surrender." Second, despite his initial comparison of "loyal minister" to "chaste woman" or the determination to act like a chaste woman, he was insisting that suicide out of loyalty was a manly act in contrast to the feminine act of *shun,* or surrender.

If people of the Song dynasty still viewed suicide out of loyalty as an unproblematic act of manly valor, by the mid-seventeenth century, perceptions began to change.[36] For Yan Yuan, no matter how morally courageous, suicide was a quintessentially futile act of femininity. This change in perceptions was probably one of the reasons behind the assertion by one of Yan Yuan's friends that Song Neo-Confucian scholars could be praised as "filial daughters" but not "filial sons." Yan Yuan concurred, lamenting that loyal Ming ministers who had committed suicide could be remembered only as "the chaste women of the inner chambers [*guizhong yifu*]."[37]

Yan Yuan was not the first to express concern over what was perceived to be the feminization of the literati, although his remarks pointed to its changed implications in the aftermath of the fall of the Ming. Quite a few people had already made similar observations, although they did not necessarily blame the Song Neo-Confucians. The famous Ming official Hai Rui (1513–1587; *DMB,* pp. 474–479) complained: "Those Confucian scholars were so impractical as to be totally incompetent, their learning useless. Some of them would still perform the ritual of taking off their caps in front of enemy troops while the city was being surrounded; others would be at a loss as to what to do. They could only cling to the code of loyalty and wait to be slaughtered. The sages have never talked about this kind of principle or this kind of loyalty."[38] Hai Rui's characterization of literati incompetence certainly anticipated the much harsher criticism by early Qing critics such as Yan Yuan and Wang Yuan. Concerned with the "decadent" fashion of wearing refined and colorful clothes, prevalent among the literati, the writer Li Le (*jinshi* 1568) complained that it had become very difficult to distinguish men from women by their dress: "It was scholars who all dressed up in women's clothes."[39] Another scholar-official, Shen Defu (1578–1642), also observed that many officials liked to use heavy makeup just like women, and he lamented that "nowadays men with swords prefer to view themselves as palace ladies."[40]

The famous radical thinker Li Zhi not only associated literati incompetence with femininity, but also asserted that such feminization had been going on for a long time [*qianwan shi zhi ru jie wei furen*]. He even traced the feminization of the literati to Confucius' neglect of military matters, as revealed in *Lunyu:* "Duke Ling of Wei asked Confucius about military formations. Confucius answered, 'I have, indeed, heard something about the use of sacrificial vessels, but I have never studied the matter of commanding troops.' The next day he departed."[41] According to Li Zhi, Confucius' neglect of military competency was an important factor behind the subsequent feminization of the literati.[42] Huang Shu (fl. seventeenth century), a friend of the famous writer and Ming loyalist martyr Chen Zilong (1608–1647; *ECCP,* pp. 102–103), made a similar complaint about the male literati's effeminacy and ineptitude and added that their knowledge was limited to a few commentaries on the Confucian classics.[43]

Echoing Li Zhi's complaints about the effeminacy of the literati, the famous late Ming recluse Chen Jiru (1558–1649), though declining to serve in the government himself, deplored the incompetence of governmental officials:

> All the men under Heaven have become women. Dancing and singing continued unabated in the palace while the territories were being conquered piece by piece by the enemy. High officials acted as if nothing had happened, while many were losing their lives on the battlefield. Incapable of fighting the enemy on the battleground, we, as scholars, could turn only to writing in our yearning to save the country, hoping that [by reading these writings] those effeminate men [*xumei er furen zhe*] would eventually straighten themselves out.[44]

A similar condemnation of the effeminacy of the late Ming literati can also be found in a biography by the early Qing historian Zou Yi (fl. 1645) of a chaste female impersonator, Kong Silang. Kong was the lover of a military officer, Chang Shoujing, stationed in the capital. After a peasant rebellion, troops led by Li Zicheng occupied the capital, and after Chang was put to death, one of Li Zicheng's generals ordered Kong to entertain them. Failing in an attempt to kill the general during the night, Kong committed suicide by slitting his own throat. Zou Yi observes:

> As a female impersonator, Kong Silang had to use his body to please others. Yet he refused to serve the bandits and even sacrificed his life in order to avenge the death of Shoujing. His deed was indeed magnificent. In many historical writings Kong Silang's deeds have been recorded in the section on women. However, Silang was a man! Even women's chaste deeds have been praised as acts worthy of a true gentleman. Who would consider it inappropriate to praise him as a righteous man? [At the same time,] many men nowadays like to powder their faces and pluck their beards, indulging in male-male passions. In fact, all men in this world have turned into women. Given the chastity Silang demonstrated, he could certainly be considered a virtuous woman as well.[45]

With the introduction into the picture of a female impersonator, whose gender identity was far from clear, the anxiety over the feminization of male literati was further complicated. The distinctions between the masculine and the feminine became even more problematic when gender boundaries became increasingly blurred. For some early Qing literati thinkers such confusion about gender boundaries only added to the urgency for re/masculinization. Yan Yuan was the most articulate in deploring literati effeminacy and exploring the gendered implications of the fall of the Ming. He was also the first clearly to see the possible ironies in literati writings on chaste women; the sheer incompetence of the literati lay precisely in their inability to envision themselves beyond the role of a chaste woman.

The despair of Ming loyalists and their humiliation as reluctant subjects under the new alien regime only added to literati feelings of emasculation. At the symbolic level, probably nothing was more emasculating than the Manchu policy of forcing Han Chinese men to show total submission by shaving the front parts of their heads and wearing a queue at the back.[46] Qu Dajun as a Ming loyalist seems to have been particularly obsessed with, as well as vocal about, the question of hairstyles, and he dwelled on the topic in many of his writings. Like many Ming loyalists, Qu Dajun initially tried to avoid wearing the Manchu hairstyle by becoming a monk. However, he had to resume his identity as a layman because, he insisted, he had to take care of his aging mother. In his autobiographical essay, "Jiren shuo" (A Man Who Wears His Hair in a Bun), Qu proudly recounted how heroically he had resisted the pressures to wear the Manchu hairstyle. At one point, he says, he even began to envy a woman because she could at least still wear her hair in a bun. He deplored that he was living in an age when a man could neither wear his long hair down (as a real man) nor become a woman so that he could wear his hair in a bun, implying that the Manchu hairstyle blurred the sacred gender distinctions.[47] Qu Dajun even asserted that a man whose hair was shaved would have no need for a beard or brows either. "Beard and brows," or *xumei,* was commonly used to refer to a man or masculinity. Qu Dajun was obviously suggesting that a man would no longer be regarded as a man once his hair was shaved, as if he were symbolically castrated.[48] Indeed he once directly compared the Manchu imposition of head shaving to *xingyu* (the punishment of castration).[49]

By a twist of logic, Qu Dajun was implying that the humiliation of the male subjects of a defeated country could be measured by the degree to which they were forced to feel like women. The alien Manchu regime eventually succeeded in forcing its hairstyle upon all Han Chinese men, while it failed to enforce the ban on footbinding among the Han women. The discrepancy only added to literati feelings of emasculation, as suggested in the ironic saying, "Only the men surrendered, but not the women" [*nanxiang nü buxiang*].[50] For some Han male literati, insisting on women's footbinding became a desperate compensatory gesture of trying to cling to a precarious sense of masculinity when the country (or, for that matter, their manhood) was supposed to have already been lost, but the irony implied in the gesture was difficult to miss.[51]

Here we may recall the mid-Ming scholar-official Luo Lun, who claimed that the country could avoid disaster if only "all male literati could become [chaste] women." It is not difficult to see the irony of this remark in the aftermath of the fall of the Ming. In fact, the scenario of "men becoming women," celebrated by Luo Lun almost two centuries earlier, was exactly what Yan Yuan believed to have *already* happened during the seventeenth century, and this was precisely what saddened him most. In one of his biographies of chaste women, Yan Yuan emphatically expressed his concern over the feminization of men: "Graduate Zhang from Shanzuo once composed the couplet: 'I haven't heard any morally edifying remarks in this country for a long time/Why should there be so many great Confucian scholars among the womenfolk?' Alas! If all the women have become great Confucian scholars, this is indeed something our country should celebrate. However, if all the great Confucian scholars have become women, this instead is something over which our country should grieve."[52] Here Luo Lun's analogical rhetoric is reversed. The resemblance between a chaste woman and a loyal minister, instead of meriting celebration, becomes deplorable. The trope of female chastity was now appropriated for a different purpose—to expose the feminization of men or men acting *too much* like women. Men were criticized not for failing to act like chaste women but for failing to come up with other more *manly* alternatives, such as the effective defense of the country, which would make the feminine gesture of suicide unnecessary. In other words, the male literati were now being castigated for not acting more *differently* from women.

As I pointed out at the beginning of this chapter, deploring men's moral deficiencies was a common topic in literati writings on chaste women. However, by the mid-seventeenth century, the moral superiority of a chaste woman began to provoke a different kind of uneasiness in some literati. Yan Yuan seems to have touched on the potential danger of the chaste woman trope for exposing male weaknesses in literati discourse. For people like Yan Yuan, the very obsession of the literati with this trope became a symptom of their diminished masculinity.[53] Furthermore, the analogy between chaste women and loyal ministers only highlighted the painful confusion of gender roles. Chaste women were indeed praiseworthy, but they were no longer considered the right models for men to emulate.

For other early Qing literati, gender confusion was simply a painful testament to the moral disorder, as well as an inauspicious sign of an age of disaster, as revealed in Yan Yuan's bitter complaint that a country was to suffer disaster when the gender/moral distinctions between women and great Confucian scholars became blurred. In Gui Zhuang's celebration of female chastity we can also detect a deep concern over the implications of female moral superiority:

Reading the *Gazetteer of Tianchang County,* I have found very few records of virtuous men; only Zhu Shouchang of the Song dynasty is mentioned as a filial son. . . . However, more than thirty chaste women are listed. . . . Ever since ancient times, extraordinary acts of chastity and filiality have been extremely rare. Yet in [the short span of] the last fifty years, there are already two chaste women recorded [in the gazetteer]. Alas, is this because moral virtue is found solely in women during an age of rapid decline?[54]

As I mentioned above, almost a century earlier Gui Zhuang's great-grand-father, Gui Youguang, asked a similar question as to why moral energy should favor women. In the aftermath of the fall of the Ming, Gui Zhuang was sensing something much more disturbing. For him, the superiority of the feminine (even though morally edifying) was, paradoxically, symptomatic of an age in rapid moral decline because in the end it was the men who had to defend the country.

The early Qing Neo-Confucian thinker Sun Qifeng (1585–1675; *ECCP,* pp. 617–672) offered a slightly different explanation as to why so many people were complaining about men degenerating into women:

> Filial sons, loyal ministers, and chaste women are all similar [in their moral integrity]. Whereas exemplary chastity can often be found in women from remote areas, it is rather difficult to find the acts of loyalty expected of a minister in many well-educated men of great fame. These important-looking men, steeped in Confucian teachings, often pale miserably [in terms of moral courage] when compared with women of the boudoir, owing to the workings of *yin* and *yang* forces that have been going on for a long time. Ever since ancient times, there have always been more days of disorder than days of order and more inferior men than gentlemen. Aware that *yang* cannot match *yin,* one has to admit that the *yin* forces often dominate the *yang* forces. Exasperated, one could say that in this world all men have turned into women or that all those serving in the government have turned into women. This is because people, deeply disturbed by the large number of effeminate men [*guan er ji zhe*], have to look up to manly women [*ji er guan zhe*] just to maintain a certain moral order in this world.[55]

It appears that lamentations such as "All men have turned into women" were quite common among the literati during the late Ming and early Qing. Sun was suggesting that the constant praise of chaste women could be read as an indication of concern over the ineptitude of increasingly effeminate men who were supposed to defend the empire. In other words, the more enthusiastically a literatus praised chaste women, the deeper his anxiety over "effeminate" men was likely to be. The large number of "manly women" reflected the existence of an even larger number of effeminate men.

This situation becomes even more ironic when the dominant *yin* figure of a chaste woman is juxtaposed with the equally dominant *yin* figure of a shrew (this time a completely negative female image); the juxtaposition often appeared in seventeenth-century narrative literature.[56] According to the author of the seventeenth-century novel *Xingshi yinyuan zhuan* (A Marriage Destined to Awaken the World), which is about how men are dominated by their shrewish wives, the abnormal phenomena of shrewish wives and henpecked husbands are only the symptoms of a more profound social malaise or moral disorder. In the words of Judge Wu in the novel, it is a world of *yangxiao yinzhang* (the *yang* element weakens while the *yin* element is on the rise): "In a world where *yang* is dominated by *yin,* where men of virtue are in fear of men of mean character, and where people are in fear of ghosts, how can a husband not be afraid of his wife?"[57] This is a world morally turned upside down, where Confucian gender hierarchies are completely disrupted.

The rising cult of chaste women during the late Ming and early Qing appears to have been accompanied by an increasingly deeper anxiety among male literati that men were being dominated by their shrewish wives; such women were the worst examples of *yin* forces running wild. In this period men seemed to be living in an increasingly shrinking space between the two dominating feminine figures of the chaste woman and the shrew. In any case, the superiority of *yin* spelled serious trouble for the country because, according to people like Yan Yuan, a national crisis was a crisis of masculinity (manhood equals nationhood). The predominance of chaste women and shrews was only one of the most obvious symptoms of this crisis. The impact of the fall of the Ming dynasty on the gender psyche of contemporary literati could be felt even in some early Qing commentators' readings of *San'guo yanyi,* a novel whose models of masculinity are examined in the next chapter.

PART 2

HEROES AND OTHER COMPETING MODELS

CHAPTER 5

From *Yingxiong* to *Haohan*

~~

Models of Masculinity in
San'guo yanyi and *Shuihu zhuan*

In the Ming novel *San'guo yanyi* the presence of chaste women, though limited, is still prominent enough to complicate and problematize many aspects of the novel's much more dominant masculine models. In addition, the novel contains many stories about how a masculine hero's political career is ruined or almost ruined because he fails to maintain a proper distance from women. This apparently conflicting image of the feminine is especially significant since *San'guo yanyi* had such an important role in shaping the notions of a masculine hero in the popular imagination of late imperial China.

Before we examine *San'guo yanyi* itself, it might be helpful to take a brief look at the historical period the novel reflects and its significance in terms of the "history" of the concept of "hero." During the Three Kingdoms Period the concept of *yingxiong* (hero) began to achieve prominence in various cultural discourses.[1] Indeed there seems to have been an explosion of discourses on the subject during this period.[2] It was first evidenced by a semihistorical work entitled *Yingxiong ji* (Records of Heroes), by Wang Can (ca. 177–ca. 217); it was composed of short biographical sketches of contemporaries whom Wang considered outstanding in talent and achievement. Although no longer extant, this work was one of the important sources from which the historian Pei Songzhi (372–451) frequently quoted in his copious annotations to Chen Shou's (233–297) standard history of this period, *San'guo zhi* (A Chronicle of the Three Kingdoms).[3]

Liu Shao (ca. 172–ca. 250), a contemporary of Wang Can, even titled an entire chapter "Yingxiong" in his *Renwu zhi* (A Study of Human Abilities) and devoted it to a theoretical discussion of what constituted a *yingxiong*. At the beginning of the chapter he offered the most elaborate definition of *yingxiong* to date: "The best among the trees and plants is called *ying,* and the animals that stand out from their groups are called *xiong.* Therefore men who have extraordinary civil and military abilities are called *yingxiong.* Consequently, those whose wisdom is outstanding are considered *ying,* and those whose strength and courage are superior are regarded as *xiong*."[4] Then Liu Shao went on to discuss in detail the different kinds of *yingxiong,* using as examples some well-known historical figures. An ideal hero was both *ying* and *xiong* (outstanding in both wisdom and courage/physical prowess), although Liu attached more importance to *ying.* He believed that Liu Bang, the founder of the Han dynasty, embodied the ideal hero in terms of the perfect balance between *ying* and *xiong.* Of course, Liu Bang has long been a controversial figure in Chinese history, mainly because many later Confucians considered some of his deeds to be unethical—for example, his apparent disregard of his father's life in his fight with Xiang Yu. Liu Shao also considered Xiang Yu a hero, though of much less stature, presumably because the latter was much more *xiong* than *ying.*[5] One of the complaints of later Confucians about Liu Shao's unqualified celebration of *yingxiong* is that he downplayed virtue in judging whether one was a great hero.[6]

Possibly the earliest account of a conversation on *yingxiong*—between Liu Bei (161–223), founder of the Kingdom of Shu, and Cao Cao, founder of the Kingdom of Wei and much celebrated in histories and legends, can be found in the biography of Liu Bei in *San'guo zhi.* According to Chen Shou, after having thwarted an assassination attempt on his life, Cao Cao spoke to Liu Bei, who had yet to achieve any distinction as leader: "'Right now only you and I can be considered *yingxiong.* People like Benchu don't really count.' Liu Bei had just finished his meal, and he dropped his chopsticks."[7] Although Chen Shou's narrative is rather terse, later writers filled in details about the possible reasons that Liu Bei dropped his chopsticks.[8] Liu Bei apparently did not want Cao Cao to know that he was shocked by Cao's acknowledgement, implying that Cao was fully aware that Liu Bei was his major competitor, and he dropped the chopsticks to cover his surprise. Clearly in this context, a *yingxiong* is someone who has the potential to be a contender for the throne. Indeed Liu Bei would eventually become one. Chen Shou praises Liu Bei for possessing the qualities of a hero.[9] Cao Cao was quite happy when he was characterized as "an evil man in a world of peace but a hero in a world of disorder."[10] Cao Cao believed that in a world of disorder a hero could find many opportunities for great achievement, while the issue of good and evil was almost irrelevant. Such an obsession with heroics was no doubt related to a widely shared belief in the close association between "hero" and "disorder."

Obviously, disorder was considered an important precondition for the emergence of heroes, as understood in the common saying *luanshi chu yingxiong* (disorder gives birth to heroes). Almost four centuries after China had been united under a centralized imperial government around the late third century BCE, the empire began to fall apart again: "At the end of the Han dynasty, there was widespread disorder, and many ambitious strong men began to emerge."[11] With the collapse of the Han, those good old days when the service of a *shi* was in great demand—the time about which Dongfang Shuo and Yang Xiong had been so nostalgic (see the discussion in chapter 1)—seem to have suddenly returned. Many members of the *shi* class began to believe that they could regain respect from those ambitious enough to try to establish themselves as contenders for the imperial throne. Cao Cao's famous "Qiuxian ling" (Directives to Seek the Worthies) was one of the best testimonies to this great demand for men of talent during an age of disorder.[12] At the same time, there emerged a new prince-minister relationship in which ministers began to enjoy much more equality with their princes, reminiscent of the Warring State Period, when *shi* occupied a much more central position in the political arena. In a word, in the Three Kingdoms Period men of outstanding talent, or *yingxiong,* were sought and embraced, and the *shi,* marginalized under Han imperial rule, seem to have been granted new opportunities to assert their masculine heroism.

In late imperial China, probably no other work (historical or fictional) stirred the imagination about this "heroic" period as much as *San'guo yanyi.* Most likely begun during the early Ming and relying heavily on various previous written sources, *San'guo yanyi* attained its final textual stability in the so-called Mao Zonggang commentary edition in the early Qing. It should shed much light on the complexities associated with the long historical reception of the Three Kingdoms Period as an age of *yingxiong.*[13]

Gender Disorder versus Political Disorder

As is apparent from its composition, the term *yingxiong* is inherently a concept of masculinity: the character *xiong* also denotes "male." *Yingxiong* literally means "an outstanding [*ying*] male [*xiong*]." That is, a discourse on the hero is often a discourse on how a man proves that he is an outstanding male (in relation to females and other males). However, this very need for a proof of masculinity also implies that manhood is a contested issue because it is a very fluid construct.

San'guo yanyi, a novel about many *yingxiong* trying to prove their masculinity in an age of disorder by restoring peace and order to the empire, begins fittingly with an account of the political chaos of the last years of the Han dynasty, and it is dominated by images that have deep gender implications. Here political disorder, which is considered a necessary precondition for the emergence of many heroes, is first of all a disorder of genders. Abnormal phenomena are listed as ominous signs suggesting that the empire is rapidly collapsing—for example, hens have become cocks (*ciji hua xiong;* 1.2). In addition to symbolizing political disorder, such gender disorders in the animal world point directly to the gendered nature of the political crisis in the human world. Mao Zonggang emphasizes that these are a direct reference to the disastrous political interference of the eunuchs during the last years of the Han: a castrated man is like a male turned into a female *(ci),* and a eunuch's meddling in imperial politics means that the female (the castrato) has usurped the position of a male (1.2). Here political disorder is interpreted as a disruption of political gender hierarchy. With the not-so-distant fall of the Ming still fresh in his mind—a fall that was blamed by many on the disastrous meddling of the eunuchs (see discussion in chapter 2)—Mao Zonggang seems to have been particularly sensitive to the perceived damage to the Han caused by the eunuchs more than fifteen hundred years ago.[14] To emphasize the notion of eunuch meddling, in his commentary edition Mao Zonggang goes out of his way to alter some key expressions in the original version of the novel. For example, he inserts the phrase that the emperor "blindly trusted the eunuchs" *(chongxin huanguan)* and changes the wording in Cai Yi's remonstration to the emperor from *furen ganzheng* (women meddling in imperial politics) to *fu si ganzheng* (women and eunuchs meddling in imperial politics) (1.2).[15] Of course, in traditional Chinese political discourse, nothing is more suggestive than eunuchs (castrati) as symbols of disorder in both gender and imperial politics.

In chapter 4 of the novel, when Dong Zhuo's people force Emperor Shao to commit suicide by drinking poisoned wine, the imperial concubine Tang offers to drink the wine on behalf of the emperor. Sensitive to the gendered nature of the political crisis here, Mao Zonggang points out that "this woman is more commendable than all the civil and military officials in the imperial court" (4.43), implying that all the officials have failed to fulfill their duties as male subjects of the emperor. This comment could also be Mao's implicit indictment of Ming officials whose incompetence, many believed, brought about the downfall of the Ming. Before drinking the wine, Emperor Shao asks to be allowed to say farewell to his mother, and he begins to compose a poem. This provokes another interesting comment from Mao Zonggang: "This emperor is indeed a prolific poet! He has just composed a poem before, and now he composes another one, this time a suicide poem. Unfortunately, writing cannot save one from disaster. I cry for the emperor, and I cry even more for writing" (4.43). This is reminiscent of Yan Yuan's bitter comment on the suicide poem of the Ming official Shi Bangyao (see chapter 4). Writing a suicide poem, or suicide itself, according to Yan Yuan, was ultimately a feminine act of helplessness and despair, reflecting a man's incompetence. Though viewed by many as an act of heroism, suicide, Yan Yuan insisted, paradoxically often reflected the absence of the spirit of *yingxiong* and the painful reality of men being feminized. Both Yan Yuan and Mao Zonggang appear to have associated the tragic fall of the Ming with the effeminacy of its male subjects.

Mao Zonggang's reading and editing of the novel should remind us that *yingxiong* is first of all a concept of masculinity that defines itself *against* what is perceived to be feminine and what is associated with women. In *San'guo yanyi*, the masculinity of many heroes is measured in terms of their ability to disassociate themselves from women or their ability to resist the "evil" influence of the feminine. The most prominent example of how a *yingxiong*'s manly spirit is sapped by women is Lü Bu. By comparing this character in other written sources, we can see clearly that the author of *San'guo yanyi* has taken great pains to construct a mighty hero whose tragic fall is the direct result of his inability to resist the corrupting influence of the feminine.

In *Sang'uo zhi pinghua* (The Plain Tale of the Three Kingdoms), a popular narrative dating from the early fourteenth century and a source on which the author of *San'guo yanyi* probably relied, Lü Bu, although known for his martial prowess, is said to be less powerful than Zhang Fei. During a second fight with Zhang Fei on the battlefield, Lü retreats because he is intimidated.[16] However, in *San'guo yanyi,* we are told that even Guan Yu and Zhang Fei together could not overpower Lü during a fight. Lü retreats only when Liu Bei joins Guan Yu and Zhang Fei to fight against him (5.60–61). The alteration in *San'guo yanyi* is apparently intended to underscore the tragedy of Lü's subsequent downfall at the hands of a woman, the beautiful Diao Chan. That is, Lü Bu's martial prowess, unrivaled among men, is rendered totally ineffective once he is "entrapped" by a woman. In the novel, Lü Bu is tricked into killing his adoptive father, the evil minister Dong Zhuo, by Wang Chong, who gets Lü and Dong to fight over Diao Chan through a series of elaborate plots. To drive a deep wedge between Lü and Dong, Wang Chong has deliberately promised Diao Chan to both of them, without either knowing that the other has been made the same promise. However, according to Lü's biography in *Hou Hanshu* (History of the Latter Han Dynasty), he killed Dong Zhuo because he began to feel insecure after having an affair with one of Dong's maids; there is no mention of a woman named Diao Chan.[17] In *San'guo zhi pinghua,* Lü Bu indeed kills Dong Zhuo because of Diao Chan, who used to be one of his concubines and who is now being taken away by Dong owing to Wang Chong's ruse.[18] In other words, in *San'guo zhi pinghua,* Lü Bu's claim to Diao Chan is completely legitimate, while she is only an unwilling pawn in a plot by Wang Chong.

Many details of this episode are altered in *San'guo yanyi.* Now Diao Chan is the adopted daughter of Wang Chong rather than one of Lü Bu's concubines who happens to have been separated from him because of war. Both Dong Zhuo and Lü Bu are so captivated by Diao Chan that their rivalry finally drives one to kill the other. The novelist has made all these changes to emphasize Lü Bu's vulnerability to *se* (sex or women). Ironically, in the novel Lü Bu himself views this fight over a woman as a test of his worthiness as a *yingxiong:* he tells Diao Chan that he should not be counted as a *yingxiong* at all if he cannot win her (8.92). However, Lü Bu's yardstick for measuring masculinity is also the result of Diao Chan's deliberate persuasion. She convinces him that his status as a *yingxiong* (and *yingxiong* is the exact term she uses; 8.92) is going to be compromised considerably if he cannot protect a helpless woman from a man she does not want to marry. Paradoxically, in the end Lü Bu's claim to *yingxiong* status is discredited precisely because of his insistence that being able to get the woman he loves is a hallmark of manhood.

The novelist demonstrates that Lü Bu's political career was greatly undermined as a result of his killing Dong Zhuo. After Dong Zhuo's death, Lü Bu had to constantly switch alliances among different powerful warlords just to survive. To drive home the message that Lü Bu's tragic downfall was the direct result of his vulnerability to women, the novelist provides another example (this time with some historical basis): he shows how easily Lü's wives could get him to adopt their suggestions for military actions rather than those of his insightful adviser Chen Gong.[19] Lü Bu is captured by Cao Cao mainly because he refuses to act on the advice of Chen Gong after his wife Yanshi raises objections to Chen's plan that they should take the initiative and attack Cao Cao's troops first (19.232–233). Lü Bu's subordinates repeatedly complain that he "listens only to his wives and concubines but not his generals" (19.238), implying that he has ignored the scared gender distinctions between men and women by allowing women to meddle in the affairs of men. Lü Bu himself is shown to be part of the gender disorder, echoing the novel's gendered descriptions of the political disorder. Perhaps there is nothing more telling in how far this once mighty hero has fallen than his own belated confession upon looking at his withered image in the mirror: "Too much sex and wine have ruined my health" (19.236).

At one point in this chapter, Mao Zonggang calls the reader's attention to the different attitudes of three characters in the novel—Lü Bu, Liu Bei, and Liu An—toward their wives. (Liu An is a young hunter and Liu Bei's kinsman; 19.227.) Several times in the novel, when chased by his enemies, Liu Bei chooses to abandon his wives *(qiqi)* in order to escape more efficiently with his troops. When his sworn brother Zhang Fei tries to commit suicide after suffering a defeat on the battlefield, Liu Bei stops him by making the famous (or infamous, depending one's view) claim that "Brothers are like one's own arms and legs, while wives are like clothes. When clothes are worn out, they can be patched up. When one loses an arm or a leg, it cannot be replaced" (15.173–174). Mao also directs the reader's attention to similar cases where Liu Bei shows more concern for his sworn brothers than his wives (19.228 and 25.311). Caring far less about his wife than even Liu Bei, Liu An presents a much more extreme case. Having no food left at home, he kills his wife *(shaqi)* and has her flesh cooked so as to feed Liu Bei![20] Here Lü Bu's attachment to, or "favoritism" toward, his wives *(lianqi),* is contrasted with the attitudes of Liu Bei and Liu An. Clearly, Liu Bei's placing the interests of his brothers ahead of those of his wives represents an important aspect of *yingxiong,* in contrast to Lü Bu's *lianqi,* while Liu An's brutal act might be too extreme to be exemplary. (It is condemned as "too cruel" by one commentator, Li Yu; 19.228.)

In the Ming chantefable *Hua Guan Suo zhuan* (The Story of Hua Guan

Suo; likely the Ming reprint of a Yuan text), in order to make sure that all the men are wholeheartedly devoted to one another as sworn brothers, Guan Yu and Zhang Fei agree to kill each other's family members to address Liu Bei's concerns over the possible negative effects that the burdens of family might have on their brotherhood. (Liu Bei himself is said to be unmarried at that time.) [21] The act of killing wives or family members as a way of asserting one's *yingxiong* masculinity (the inclination toward violence) tends to be celebrated more in literature associated with the oral tradition, probably reflecting aspects of a rather different notion of masculinity at a more popular level (a point to which I shall return in the discussion of *Shuihu zhuan*). In *San'guo yanyi*, a sophisticated novel by a literati author, Liu Bei's readiness to abandon his wives for a political cause is apparently presented as the most appropriate expression of one's *yingxiong* qualities.

In contrast to Lü Bu, Guan Yu as a character in *San'guo yanyi* is probably best known for maintaining his integrity by resisting sexual temptation, a quality underscored by the pains the novelist has apparently taken to ignore some unflattering facts regarding the historical Guan Yu. According to Pei Songzhi's annotations in *San'guo zhi* (and based on accounts in *Shuji* [Records of the Kingdom of Shu]), Guan Yu once got Cao Cao to promise that after the defeat of Lü Bu he would be given the wife of Qin Yilu, one of Lü Bu's subordinates. After the victory, Guan Yu repeatedly reminded Cao of his promise, but Cao changed his mind. He began to suspect that Qin's wife must be unusually beautiful (otherwise Guan Yu would not have mentioned their deal so many times). Indeed after seeing the woman, Cao Cao decided to keep her for himself, and this greatly upset Guan Yu. [22] This tells us that Guan Yu, as he was represented in history, was quite different from the *yingxiong* Guan Yu celebrated in folk legends and fiction. [23]

In *San'guo yanyi*, Guan Yu reluctantly agrees to surrender to Cao Cao; the latter, instead of being a love rival, tries hard to enlist Guan's services by giving him ten beautiful women. Much to Cao Cao's admiration, Guan Yu immediately orders them to serve his two sisters-in-law (two of Liu Bei's wives), who are with him at the time. In his commentary Mao Zonggang inserts the now famous episode of "holding the candle till dawn" *(bingzhu dadan)*. [24] We are told that to create a dilemma for Guan Yu, Cao Cao deliberately provides him and his two sisters-in-law with only one room as a residence. Guan Yu chooses to stay outside the room, candle in hand, throughout the night to avoid any appearance of impropriety (25.308). In the earlier (Jiajing) edition of the novel, Cao Cao is said to have given Guan Yu an entire building. Guan Yu divided it into two parts and chose to live in the outer part. [25] The change in the Mao Zonggang edition from an entire building to one room should give the reader some idea as to how the image of a *yingxiong* capable of resisting all sexual temptations had evolved in the different stories associated with Guan Yu. [26]

Zhao Yun, another heroic general under Liu Bei, also exemplifies the male integrity of being able to resist sexual temptation. In chapter 52, after his generals have been defeated, the governor of Guiyang, Zhao Fan, surrenders to Zhao Yun. He and Zhao Yun swear brotherhood with each other. During the banquet that follows, Zhao Fan asks a beautiful woman, his sister-in-law, to serve the wine, telling Zhao Yun that he would like to be the matchmaker for him and his sister-in-law, who is now a widow. Much to everyone's surprise, the marriage proposal angers Zhao Yun, who accuses Zhao Fan of trying to lead him into an incestuous relationship since he and Zhao Fan have become "brothers." When Liu Bei and Zhuge Liang later ask Zhao Yun why he has rejected the marriage proposal, Zhao Yun offers additional reasons: he will not cause a widow to give up her life of chastity, and he does not want a woman to distract him from his job of securing the newly conquered areas. Liu Bei responds, "Now our cause is secure. I can arrange for you to marry this woman." Zhao Yun replies, "There are many women under Heaven. I am concerned only that I won't be able to establish my reputation, and I am least worried about being single." This moves Liu Bei to say, "Zilong [Zhao Yun] is a true man" (52.652). The origin of the story about Zhao Yun's rejection of the marriage proposal can be found in Pei Songzhi's annotations to the biography of Zhao Yun in *San'guo zhi,* but it does not have Liu Bei's praise that Zhao Yun is a true man.[27]

New Heroic Possibilities: No Longer a Concubine?

One of the perennial appeals of *San'guo yanyi* to readers of later ages (especially the better educated) is its detailed dramatization of a new prince-minister relationship, which is believed to have emerged during the Three Kingdoms Period. This new relationship seems to have restored to many *shi* a strong sense of masculine empowerment—without their services no one could hope to become a serious contender for the imperial throne during a time of great opportunities. Now men of talent had the luxury of choosing a lord to serve, a choice rarely available during the previous four centuries under centralized Han rule. The common perception that the Three Kingdoms Period was an age of *yingxiong* was closely associated with this strong sense of the *shi*'s right to choose. The right to choose one's lord and how to choose him are an important part of the novel's thematic concerns.

Trying to persuade Lu Su to offer his services to Sun Quan, Zhou Yu asks him to recall "the words of Ma Yuan to Emperor Guang Wu: 'In times like these not only does the lord choose the man, but the man chooses the lord'" (29.367; Roberts, p. 227).[28] The novel seems to present a world where the assumed analogy between *chen* (minister) and *qie* (concubine) in traditional cultural discourse, as discussed in previous chapters, is being reexamined, although such a reexamination is never explicit. One prominent theme is that a *yingxiong* has the right to choose a lord to serve, and how he makes his choice becomes a test of his masculinity as a *da zhangfu*. This kind of choice is obviously unavailable to a concubine—that is, she cannot choose which husband to marry, not to mention the fact that there is no possibility of remarriage if the first husband turns out to be unworthy. In the novel, a *shi*'s changing sides or switching alliances to a worthier lord is often presented as the act of a true man.

In chapter 14, trying to persuade Xu Huang to switch his alliance to Cao Cao, Man Chong argues, "Haven't you heard the saying that a smart bird chooses its branch and a wise minister his prince? One cannot be considered a true man [*da zhangfu*] if he allows a chance to serve a worthy lord to slip away" (14.164).[29] Man Chong's argument is convincing, and Xu Huang finally agrees to switch sides, swearing loyalty to Cao Cao. Similar sentiments about the importance of the right to choose are expressed by Tian Feng after he realizes that his days are numbered because his lord, Yuan Shao, has suffered a serious defeat as a result of having refused to take Tian's advice: "Standing between Heaven and Earth, a true man [*da zhangfu*] is responsible for his own misjudgment if he has chosen the wrong lord to serve" (31.386). Tian Feng has to pay with his life for having chosen the wrong lord; dying, according to him, is the appropriate punishment for his "blindness."

In contrast, gratified that he has found a worthy lord to serve, Zhou Yu feels that his manhood has been completely corroborated: "As a man of honor living in this world, I have the good fortune to serve a lord who really appreciates me. Our relationship is based on the mutual understanding between lord and minister as well as the attachment between kinsmen. What I say, he does. What I propose, he approves. His misfortunes and his blessings are mine as much as his" (45.472; Roberts, p. 348). Zhou Yu goes out of his way to point out that Sun Quan is not only the lord he is serving, but also his brother-in-law since their wives are sisters. Zhou Yu feels like a *da zhangfu* because Sun Quan treats him like a brother and respects him as a teacher.

Zhou Yu's self-congratulatory remarks symbolically capture the nature of many of the novel's prince-minister relationships, which tend to emphasize equality and mutual respect. One of the most prominent examples is of course Liu Bei's relationship with Guan Yu and Zhang Fei. After surrendering to Cao Cao and learning that Liu Bei is safe and sound, Guan Yu begins to think about being reunited with his sworn brother. Zhang Liao asks Guan Yu, "How does your relation with me differ from that between you and Xuande [Liu Bei]?" Guan Yu replies, "You and I are just friends. Xuande and I are friends to begin with, brothers in the second place, and finally, lord and minister. The relationships are not comparable" (26.324; Roberts, p. 203; translation modified). The emphasis on brotherhood considerably complicates the prince-minister relationship here, and for many readers, it adds to the appeal of the novel. Throughout the novel, Liu Bei repeatedly puts his obligations to his sworn brothers Guan Yu and Zhang Fei ahead of his responsibilities as a "future emperor."

Liu's stance contrasts sharply with the relationship between Cao Pi and his brother Cao Zhi as it is represented in the novel. After Cao Cao's death his elder son, Cao Pi, assumes the throne of the Kingdom of Wei, and his relationship with Cao Zhi begins to worsen considerably. Cao Pi even reminds Cao Zhi that their relationship is above all one between lord and minister, despite the fact that they are brothers (79.965). For Liu Bei, his "brothers" are more important than his empire. After learning that Guan Yu has been captured and killed by Sun Quan, Liu Bei is overwhelmed with anger. He immediately decides to launch an expedition against the Kingdom of Wu to avenge Guan's death. Zhao Yun argues against such an impulsive decision and this upsets Liu Bei greatly: "Sun Quan murdered my brother. . . . Until I've gnawed [the] flesh and exterminated [the] clans [of Wu] my humiliation will not be effaced. Why would you stand in my way?" Zhao Zilong [Zhao Yun] replies: "War against the traitors to Han is a public responsibility. War for the sake of a brother is a personal matter. I urge Your Majesty to give priority to the empire" (81.984; Roberts, p. 612).

Here Zhao Yun alerts the reader to the tension between the different claims of the public *(gong)* and the personal *(si)*. This pairing parallels two other important concepts in the novel, *zhong* (loyalty) and *yi* (personal honor). Guan Yu's controversial release of Cao Cao is certainly a case where the conflict between loyalty and personal honor is fully dramatized. In chapter 50, having completely surrounded the escaping Cao Cao and his entourage, Guan Yu could easily have had Cao Cao captured or killed. However, to repay Cao Cao for his kind treatment in the past, Guan Yu decides to let him go.

It is worth pointing out that during their conversation, Cao Cao deliberately appeals to Guan Yu's sense of honor to persuade him to allow him to escape: "A true man should value reciprocity and honor. With your profound understanding of the *Spring and Autumn Annals,* you must be familiar with the story of the apprentice Yugong Zhisi, who pursued his archery instructor, Zizhou Ruzi, only to release him, unwilling to use the man's own teaching to destroy him" (50.628; Roberts, p. 384; translation modified). In his commentary, Mao Zonggang quickly comes to Guan Yu's defense, attributing his apparently controversial action to his disposition as a true man or a man of righteousness (50.622). In the context of the novel, proving one's masculinity or personal honor is evidently more important than loyalty.

Honorable acts such as this, despite or precisely because of their controversial nature, must have added much to Guan Yu's image as a *yingxiong*. The fact that Guan Yu is not punished for this deliberate dereliction of duty underscores the special nature of his relationship with Liu Bei, which is much more than that between minister and prince. That is, Guan Yu can allow the "honorable release" of Cao Cao without incurring serious personal consequences because of his position as a "brother"; it is quite different from a minister/concubine relationship, which is defined by unconditional loyalty and complete subservience. As the "elder brother," Liu Bei has to show understanding for his younger brother's sense of personal honor (he has to respect the "manliness" of another man, his equal), while the dereliction of duty by a true subordinate (a minister or a concubine) would have been a crime much more difficult to pardon. In both cases— Guan Yu's release of Cao Cao and Liu Bei's decision not to punish Guan for such an action—the private takes priority over the public.

In contrast to the concept of *yi,* which tends to emphasize reciprocity among friends or brothers, *zhong* is primarily defined by a hierarchical relationship in which the subordinate is supposed to be completely subservient and faithful to his superior. In the novel, when a man insists on being loyal to his lord, he is implicitly accepting a position analogous to that of a woman in relation to her father or husband. For example, Zhang Ren, a general under Liu Biao, is one of a limited number of *yingxiong* who would rather die than switch sides when captured or pressured by the enemy. When Liu Bei asks him to surrender, Zhang declares, "How can a loyal minister serves two different lords?" (64.792). Zhang's declaration is reminiscent of the famous saying, "A loyal minister does not serve two princes, and a chaste woman does not marry twice" (discussed in chapter 1).[30] The analogy between a minister and a married woman in terms of their subservient positions becomes most explicit when it comes to *jie* (loyalty and chastity). Mao Zonggang has an interesting observation on this issue:

> The fact that the Three Kingdoms Period was an age of many outstanding talents can be confirmed by looking at not only the men, but also the women [from that time]. A man of talent does not always need to demonstrate his *jie.* However, a woman without *jie* is considered untalented [regardless of whether she really has any talent]. Therefore, when we talk about a man, talent and *jie* are separate issues, and when it comes to a woman, talent is always judged together with *jie.* This is why it is more difficult for a woman to show her talent. (118.1422)

Mao seems to be arguing that while it is possible for a man without virtue to be considered a *yingxiong,* a woman would have no chance of being praised as outstanding if she failed to demonstrate *jie,* even if she indeed possessed great talent. Here masculinity appears to be largely defined as talent and ability, whereas femininity is defined as the virtue of selfless devotion and absolute subservience.

This disparate definition is probably one of the reasons why in *San'guo yanyi,* a novel dominated by images of heroic masculinity, the burden of *jie* often falls on women. In other words, *jie,* which emphasizes subservience and selfless sacrifice, is more often presented as an inherently feminine quality. Although there are many examples in the novel where men suffer serious setbacks owing to the negative influence of women, there are also quite a few cases where women's influence proves to be positive. In fact, it is often shown that women tend to be more conscious of the obligations of loyalty than men. Women are often presented as the more natural exemplars of loyalty and chastity. The most famous case is that of Xu Shu's mother, who commits suicide just to prevent her son from serving Cao Cao, whom she considers an evil man (chapter 37). In chapter 107, Xin Chang seeks advice from his sister, Xin Xianying, about whether he should help General Cao Shuang to fight against Sima Yi, who is plotting a coup to usurp the power of the imperial court of Wei. Despite her clear understanding that Cao Shuang is incompetent and no match for Sima Yi and that consequently anyone who helps Cao Shuang might end up paying with his life, Xin Xianying nevertheless urges her brother to side with Cao Shuang because "A man's primary obligation is to perform the duties of his office. Even a stranger in trouble deserves our sympathy. To deny the service owed to one's master is an evil thing to do" (107.1309; Roberts, p. 829). Later the victorious Sima Yi is so touched by Xin Chang's loyalty to Cao Shuang that he chooses not to punish him after all. Among those executed by Sima Yi is Cao Shuang's stepbrother, Wenshu. Now widowed and having no children, Wenshu's wife, when pressured by her father to remarry, cuts off her ears to mark her determination to remain chaste. When pressured further, she cuts off her nose, explaining, "I have been taught that 'humanity' means keeping one's chastity [*jie*] in times good or bad; honor means an unchanging heart and mind even if one's life is at stake. How can I abandon them in their hour of destruction? I will not behave as beasts do" (107.1302; Roberts, p. 832; translation modified). Once again, Sima Yi is so moved by a woman's acts of *jie* that he eventually decides to arrange for her to adopt a child so that the family line of the Caos can be continued.[31]

In chapter 117, Lady Li becomes suspicious that her husband, Ma Miao, who has been assigned by the Shu government to defend the city of Jiangyou, is not taking his job seriously. Her husband explains:

> "The son of Heaven listens to no one but Huang Hao. He is steeped in depravity and his end is near. If Wei troops arrive, we will do best to surrender. So why concern ourselves?" In great anger, Lady Li spat on Ma Miao's face and cried, "It is wrong for a man with such disloyal and dishonorable thoughts to accept rank and office from his liege. For the sake of my own dignity, I shall not see you again!" Ma Miao was too ashamed to reply. (117.1415; Roberts, p. 904)

Later when Ma Miao indeed surrenders to the Wei troops, Lady Li hangs herself in order to shame her husband.

It appears that in the novel women are more likely to choose suicide as an act to prove their moral superiority, as if it were almost a woman's priv-

ilege. For example, Madame Sun, one of Liu Bei's wives, also commits suicide after she mistakenly believes that her husband has died (84.1027).[32]
These cases seem to support the view shared by people such as Yan Yuan
that suicide was largely a feminine act, as we discussed in chapter 4.

A Model of *Wen* Masculinity

Now we move on to Zhuge Liang, whose relationship with Liu Bei fully
illustrates the validity of the belief that a wise man should be careful in
choosing the right lord to serve. The most celebrated part of their relationship, as it is represented in *San'guo yanyi*, is that Liu Bei paid three visits to
Zhuge Liang to secure his services (chapters 37 and 38). All the elaborate
details of these three visits are designed to show that Liu Bei humbles himself before Zhuge Liang in order to enlist his help. Throughout their relationship, Liu Bei treats Zhuge Liang as a teacher (*yi shili dai zhi;* 39.494)
rather than a *puqie* (servant/concubine, to use Huang Zongxi's terms, as
discussed in chapter 2). Zhuge Liang's willingness to serve is predicated
upon the assurance that he has the full trust and respect of his lord and that
this prince-minister relationship will never force him into the role of a
puqie. In fact, it is precisely Zhuge Liang's sense of masculinity to which Liu
Bei constantly appeals in order to secure his services: "How can a true man
[*da zhangfu*] with the ability to shape the world such as you waste himself
among the groves and springs? I beg you to consider the living souls of this
land, enlighten me, and free me of ignorance and folly for their sake"
(38.477; Roberts, p. 291; translation modified).

In *San'guo yanyi*, the image of *yingxiong* is complicated with the representation of men of wisdom, whose masculinity is measured in terms of *ying*,
rather than just men of martial prowess, whose masculinity is measured in
terms of *xiong* (to use Liu Shao's definition). Zhuge Liang is certainly the
most famous hero whose masculinity is defined by his brain; his image in
San'guo yanyi points to a more subtle aspect of the novel's overall *yingxiong*
ideology: its implicit de-emphasis of physical prowess in defining a hero.

The de-emphasis of physical prowess can also be seen from the fact that
Zhang Fei, a man of martial prowess, is much less important in *San'guo
yanyi* in comparison with his role in popular dramas, especially those from
the Yuan dynasty, while Guan Yu, who is supposed to like to read the Confucian classics and is believed to be much better educated than Zhang, has
become more prominent. Some scholars have argued that the difference is
in part the result of a Confucianizing process that the novel apparently
underwent in its textual evolution.[33] Guan Yu is even sometimes praised as
a *rujiang* (a Confucian general).[34] Zhuge Liang is also celebrated by many
as a *rujiang*, but he is very careful to distinguish himself from those he
regards as merely bookish Confucian scholars:

Those knowing only how to labor over the texts of the classics are merely useless pedantic Confucian scholars.[35] How can they revive our nation or further our
cause? And what of the ancient sages—Yi Yin, who tilled the soil in Shen, or
Jiang Ziya, who fished the River Wei? What of men like Zhang Liang and Chen
Ping, Zheng Yu and Geng Yan? These worthies sustained their lords in times of
peril. What canons did they master? Do you really think they simply spent their
days confined between the pen and the inkstone like some bookworms [*shusheng*], arguing over texts, flourishing words, wielding brushes? (43.546; Roberts,
p. 332; translation modified)

Zhuge Liang apparently despises those who can write long and eloquent
essays but who are short on useful ideas (43.547).

In the novel many seem to share Zhuge Liang's contempt for *shusheng*.
When Lu Xun is introduced to Sun Quan as someone who could successfully
lead the Wu army to repel the advancing Shu troops, some of Sun Quan's
aides express their doubts because Lu Xun is viewed merely as a *shusheng*
(83.1012–1013). Even Lu Xun presents himself as a *shusheng* (83.1014).
However, despite his background as a scholar, Lu Xun soon proves to be an
excellent military strategist, and he leads the Wu army to victory over the
superior Shu troops.

The second half of *San'guo yanyi* is increasingly dominated by images of
military strategists *(junshi)*, such as Lu Xun, Jiang Wei, and Sima Yi, whose
heroic status, like that of Zhuge Liang, is the result of their brains rather
than their martial prowess. I would argue that while in general the first half
of the novel tends to reflect the more "macho" type of *yingxiong*, the second
half is increasingly dominated by a Confucianized vision of masculinity that
emphasizes the importance of virtue as well as the intellect.[36] In other words,
the emphasis shifts from *wu* and the utilitarian to *wen* and the ethical. Such
a shift can also be seen in the subtle transformations that Zhuge Lian undergoes in the second half.

If the Zhuge Liang of the first half of the novel is characterized by his
brilliance and self-confidence as a military strategist, the Zhuge Liang of the
second half is cautious and more concerned with his position as a loyal prime
minister.[37] After Liu Bei formally declares himself the emperor of Shu,
Zhuge Liang's position becomes formalized, and accordingly their relationship becomes more hierarchical. Liu Bei's son, Liu Chan, succeeds his
father, and despite the fact that he respects Zhuge Liang almost as a father
figure, Zhuge becomes even more aware of his position as a minister/sub-
ject. At the same time, his image as an invincible military strategist begins to
be challenged. Sima Yi's criticism of Zhuge's misjudgement of his own generals, such as Ma Su (95.1165), is justified by the eventual loss of the important city of Jieding to the Wei kingdom. Zhuge Liang even has to rely on
Jiang Wei's strategy to overrun the enemy-controlled city of Chencang after
his own plan has failed to work (97.1189).

In his "contest" with Sima Yi, Zhuge Liang is not always the victor the reader has come to expect. Desperately trying to engage in a direct fight with the defending Wei troops, directed by Sima Yi, Zhuge Liang sends Sima Yi a big box that contains a maiden's headress and a widower's mourning garment. Enclosed also is a letter, which states basically that if Sima Yi were a real man, he would come out and fight: "If a spark of self-respect still burns inside you and if your breast still holds a manly heart, reply to me at once and face me on the field at a time of your choosing" (103.1265; Roberts, p. 801; translation modified). However, Sima Yi refuses to be entrapped, even when he is accused of behaving like a timid woman. Not bothered by the humiliation of being laughed at as unmanly, Sima Yi proves his manhood by gaining the advantage on the battlefield. Zhuge Liang and his troops eventually have to retreat without achieving victory. Zhuge Liang has to admit in the end that Sima Yi has seen through his tricks (103.1265).

In the second half of the novel, Zhuge Liang seems to have become increasingly pessimistic, even though he continues to work diligently. Despite the warnings of the historian and astrologer Qiao Zhou that Zhuge Liang's expedition against the Wei is headed for disaster, Zhuge Liang insists that he has to launch the expedition because of his pledge to the deceased Liu Bei. His famous self-characterization in his farewell remarks to the second emperor is quite revealing: "I am bound to unremitting toil during my remaining time, until I am no more" (102.1245; Roberts, p. 787). Apparently Zhuge Liang is also aware of the inauspicious nature of the omens observed by Qiao Zhou, despite his dismissal of the warnings. In other words, Zhuge launches the expedition not because he is going to achieve victory but because it is an obligation he has to fulfill out of loyalty. Here we may recall the kind of masculinity associated with the Master himself: "keeps working toward a goal despite the knowledge that it is completely hopeless" (as discussed in chapter 1). Zhuge Liang's appeal as a literati hero is mainly his unwavering loyalty in the face of adversity (the tragic dimension of his image as a *yingxiong*). Zhuge's heroics are all the more admirable because all his efforts are expended with the perfect knowledge that he is going to fail; it is an unbending masculine spirit also championed by Sima Qian in *Shiji*.

Haohan: The Economy of Masculinity in *Shuihu zhuan*

The fact that both *San'guo yanyi* and *Shuihu zhuan* are concerned with masculine *yingxiong* apparently caught the attention of some Ming publishers. During the Chongzhen period (1627–1644), there appeared a combined edition of the two novels entitled *Yingxiong pu* (literally, a manual for heroes). Clearly the publisher was attempting to promote sales of the two novels by claiming that the two classics combined could serve as a complete "guide" for those trying to recruit heroes or to be heroes themselves.[38]

Equally obsessed with the images of heroes, *Shuihu zhuan* provides some rather different models of masculinity, however. Its heroes, the so-called *haohan* (stalwarts, strong men), many of whom are from *pingmin* (plebian) backgrounds, can be very different from their predecessors in *San'guo yanyi.* Instead of courts or military camps, where political and military intrigues are often played out in *San'guo yanyi,* the settings of *Shuihu zhuan* are now *jianghu* (literally, rivers and lakes; places where commoners live and gather). *Jianghu* as a geocultural concept denotes a more private and plebian domain that is often beyond the control of the government. While most heroes in *San'guo yanyi,* many of whom are aristocrats, are vying for legitimate membership in a new or future monarchy, the *Shuihu* heroes—at least in the first two-thirds of the novel (in the 100-chapter or 120-chapter editions)—are trying only to resist the control of the imperial government. Consequently, a typical *haohan* is often characterized by his lack of ties with the government and by his plebian qualities, and he thrives in the *jianghu* setting. Although quite a few of these men were once governmental officials, they acquire the full status of *haohan* only after severing their ties with the government for one reason or another. (This begins to change in the last part of the novel after the Liangshan rebels have received amnesty from the imperial government.)

Whereas *San'guo yanyi* reads like an interesting work of fictionalized historiography, *Shuihu zhuan,* with its new focus on quotidian details and private lives, reads much more like a novel. The concept of *yi,* or personal honor, which has played an important role in defining a hero in *San'guo yanyi,* takes on special materialistic implications in *Shuihu zhuan,* as if heroic virtue can literally be quantified like money.[39] Here personal honor is closely associated with the handling of material goods, as captured in the expression *zhangyi shucai* (ready to offer financial help to others for the sake of personal honor and reciprocity), frequently used in the novel. The ultimate paragons of *yi* unanimously admired by *haohan* heroes are apparently those who have demonstrated their virtue by constantly helping others with money and other material goods. The implied message is that wealth is often considered most expressive when it is used to support personal honor. Of course, to be able to give away money, one has to have money to start with. In other words, without money, one would be severely limited in proving one's personal honor effectively. No wonder that two of the three characters most closely associated with *zhangyi shucai* in the novel are wealthy landlords, Cai Jin and Chao Gai; the third, Song Jiang, is a government clerk. Their widespread reputation as men of great honor is largely based on their generosity in dispensing their wealth. That is why Chao Gai and Song Jiang eventually become the leaders of the Liangshan rebels, while other *haohan,* despite their impressive martial prowess (such as Lin Chong and Lu Da), are ranked much lower in the Liangshan hierarchy. Before joining the

Liangshan rebels, whenever a *haohan* passes by or visits the residences of Cai Jin and Chao Gai, they will supply him with large sums of money and treat him to a banquet. This virtually becomes a ritual performed daily. Although much less wealthy than these two, Song Jiang is even more generous with his money. He is said to treat money like dirt (18.245).[40] His first meetings with Wu Song and Li Kui, are punctuated with the rituals of money giving (and the novel's narrator never fails to inform us of the specific number of taels of silver being given each time; see 23.316–317 and 38.548), but some of his acts of generosity may not be completely justifiable. One reason Li Kui feels so indebted to Song Jiang is that Song has given him money even for gambling while his other friends would not. The seventeenth-century commentator Jin Shengtan has alerted the reader to Song Jiang's close association with money/silver and Jin's criticism that Song Jiang has no other heroic qualities except for being able to buy people's gratitude is certainly to the point (a criticism echoed by other traditional commentators).[41]

When the military strategist Wu Yong tries to recruit the Ruan brothers to join Chao Gai and his people in their scheme to intercept Governor Liang's expensive birthday gifts to his father-in-law, Grand Tutor Cai, the Ruan brothers are even more straightforward in characterizing the friendships among *haohan* as "an exchange relationship": "We sell our hot-blooded selves only to someone who can really appreciate our worth!" (15.204). The value of personal honor evidently can be measured accurately only in monetary terms, and what ultimately persuades the Ruan brothers to join Chao Gai and Wu Yong is the prospect of sharing wealth.

The popularity of generous heroes such as Chao Gai and Song Jiang serves as a testament by default to the importance many *haohan* attach to money and material goods. For some of them, material well-being is one of the major attractions of being a *haohan*. For example, Wang Lun, the leader of the Liangshan bandits, tries to persuade Yang Zhi to join them by reasoning with him in this way: "You have already committed a crime. Although you have been pardoned, you will never recover your former rank. Besides, the rogue Gao Qiu is now in charge of the military. How could you expect him to let you off the hook easily? You'd better stay in our small stronghold. Be a stalwart like the rest of us. Among ourselves we could divide lots of gold and silver by using a big scale and eat meat and drink wine to our hearts' content by using big bowls" (12.163). Being a *haohan* here is equated with having lots of money and eating and drinking in large quantities. (The same rhetoric is used later by Hua Rong to persuade Qin Ming to switch sides and join the rebels; 34.491.) Note especially the specific references to quantity, such as "a big scale" and "big bowls." Such references to large quantities also appear in the descriptions of Chao Gai's reception of visiting *haohan*. They are always treated to "large servings of meat and wine" (14.168). The same vision of material well-being is repeated by one of the

Ruan brothers when he enviously talks about the Liangshan rebels: "They fear neither Heaven nor Earth, nor the authorities; they have so much gold and silver to divide among themselves that they have to use a large scale, and they wear fine clothes. They are able to drink wine in big jars and eat lots of meat. How happy they must be!" (15.203). Once again, one is struck by the emphasis on the quantities of material goods. Drinking good wine and eating good food become almost indispensable aspects of being a *haohan.*

Eating and drinking, moreover, are said to play an important role in maintaining and enhancing a *haohan*'s physical prowess. The previously starving Lu Da feels much more fit physically after eating some cakes given to him by his friend (6.90). Wine plays an even more prominent role. Being a good Samaritan, Lu Da attempts to save the daughter of a certain Mr. Liu from bandits. Before fighting the bandits, Lu Da demands wine to drink. His heavy drinking worries Mr. Liu, but Lu Da assures him, "When I'm one-tenth drunk, I can use only one-tenth of my strength, but when I'm ten-tenths drunk, I'm able to use 100 percent of my strength" (5.77). Later Wu Song successfully slays a mighty tiger single-handedly, and the feat is partly attributed to the fifteen bowls of wine he has just drunk (23.319).[42] Intoxicated, Wu Song has apparently become oblivious to fear. Later, when preparing to fight with Jiang, the Gate Guardian Spirit, Wu Song again wants wine to drink. He even repeats Lu Da's famous remark about the relationship between wine and a *haohan*'s physical strength, claiming that he simply cannot fight without drinking some wine (29.414). The close relationship between his impressive victory and his heavy drinking is captured in the second line of the chapter title couplet: "The Drunken Wu Song Beats up Jiang, the Gate Guardian Spirit." In other words, in both cases Wu Song might have suffered defeat if he had not been drunk. Another *haohan* who is also known for his brutal strength and heavy drinking is Li Kui. However, in his case, drinking is often a problem. How to remain sober often becomes an important issue in Liu Kui's career as a *haohan* (39.571). Wu Song's heavy drinking occasionally causes him problems as well. (For example, he is captured by the Kong brothers because he is too drunk to fight; 32.455.)

For better or worse, drinking is presented as an inherently masculine undertaking and a part of the lifestyle of a *haohan.* Although this is also true of many heroes in *San'guo yanyi,* drinking becomes a much more important aspect of masculinity in *Shuihu zhuan.* Here one's capacity for wine is often assumed to be in proportion to one's physical prowess. Every true *haohan* is supposed to be a good drinker, and taverns are often the places where many important events take place.[43] In chapter 29, on his way to fight Jiang, the Gate Guardian Spirit, at Happy Grove, which is about fourteen miles from the East Gate (where he is currently), Wu Song is told that there is almost one tavern per mile (29.414). The social life of a *haohan* would simply come to a complete stop without wine.

Wine, but Not Women.

In Chinese popular culture, wine has always been closely associated with sex—as indicated by the word *jiuse* (drinking and sex)—in the belief that the two are mutually stimulating. Someone who is crazy about sex is often a heavy drinker or vice versa. *Shuihu zhuan,* however, seems to insist that while many *haohan* are heavy drinkers, they have absolutely no interest in women. In this regard, there is probably no better example than Lu Da. Early in the novel, Lu Da repeatedly plays the good Samaritan who often rescues women in distress. Jin Shengtan observes the following:

> Lu Da gets into trouble three times, and each time the direct cause is a woman. The first time, he became a monk only because of the trouble he caused as a result of his trying to rescue the daughter of the old man, Mr. Jin. The second time, after becoming a monk, he again got into trouble because of his attempt to save the daughter of another old man, Mr. Liu. The third time, for saving Liu Chong's wife, he had to give up being a monk. All three incidents took place after he had just drunk a lot of wine. All this is designed to emphasize that a truly great hero, though loving wine, always keeps his distance from women.[44]

"Love for wine but not women" is also true of Wu Song. Like Lu Da, he is a heavy drinker, yet not only did he once rescue a woman from abuse by a Taoist priest (321.451–452), but he has also proven his *haohan* character by thwarting the seduction attempts of his notorious sister-in-law, Pan Jinlian (chapter 24). Wu Song's initial encounter with Pan Jinlian is perhaps one of the most famous stories of a *haohan* successfully proving his manhood by rejecting the repeated advances of a seductress.[45]

Thus an important litmus test for a *haohan* in *Shuihu zhuan* is how he conducts himself in relation to women. As we have mentioned, in *San'guo yanyi,* a hero's associations with women can sometimes become detrimental to his heroic status (as in the case of Lü Bu). However, at the same time, there are many positive images of women in that novel. In contrast, the images of women in *Shuihu zhuan* are so consistently negative that many modern scholars believe that it must have been written by a misogynist. Many important women characters are either adulteresses (such as Pan Jinlian and the wives of Yang Xiong, Lu Junyi, and Song Jiang) or they inadvertently bring trouble to their men (such as Lin Chong's wife). In the life and career of a *haohan,* women are at best distractions. Sex is considered an act that will drain the male energy from a hero, so a *haohan* should keep a safe distance from women. One of the few Liangshan bandits failing to subscribe to this theory is Wang the Dwarf, who always seems to be after women. When Wang plans to take the wife of an official he has just kidnapped, Song Jiang attempts to stop him by appealing to his sense of personal honor, reminding him that people will laugh at him if he is perceived to be suffering from the disease of "wasting one's marrow" (*liu gusui;* 32.464). Song Jiang himself, though living with a woman out of compassion (he is supporting her financially), is supposed to have little interest in women: "Song Jiang is truly a *haohan*. He is obsessed with martial arts, while sex to him is not that important at all" (21.287). Lu Junyi is also said to be quite indifferent to women since he is always cultivating his bodily strength (62.921). However, precisely because Song and Lu are not interested in sex, their women feel neglected. Both of them find lovers and even conspire against their men, causing serious problems for these two *haohan*. Consequently, having little interest in sex is not enough; one has to stay away from women altogether.

The best solution for a *haohan,* the novel seems to suggest, is to remain as distant as possible from all women. Chao Gai is a good example: "He is fond of playing with weapons, and physically he is quite strong; unmarried, he concentrates on cultivating his bodily strength all the time" (14.185). Here Chao Gai's excellent physical condition is directly attributed to his abstinence. This is probably why so many *haohan* in the novel remain single. Here we may recall Jin Shengtan's observations on Lu Da—namely, that he became a monk because he rescued a woman, and later he had to give up the priesthood because of a similar chivalrous act. Being celibate is of course one of the requirements for being a Buddhist monk. For Lu Da, who is not in the least interested in women, celibacy is not a clerical requirement but simply his "natural" way of life as a *haohan.* Becoming a monk or returning to the life of a layman will not affect his abstinence. It is all the more ironic since all this is triggered by his chivalrous acts of saving women from unwanted marriages.

If stalwarts such as Lu Da, Wu Song, and Li Kui indeed have no interest in women, what about the potentially romantic Yan Qing, who is at least equally chaste in his dealings with women in the novel? Interestingly enough, Yan Qing's nickname is *langzi* (a prodigal or womanizer), and he is said to be familiar with all the arts of entertainment, in both the theater and the pleasure quarters; he is even praised as number one among the romantics. In contrast to Lu Da and Li Kui, who are tall, robust, and often intimidating in appearance, Yan Qing is known for his fair skin and slender figure and is considered a romantic and handsome young man (74.1091). In order for Song Jiang to gain access to the emperor, Yan Qing pays a visit to the famous courtesan Li Shishi because the emperor is one of her patrons. Impressed with this handsome lad, Li Shishi makes repeated advances, even urging him to undress, giving the excuse that she wants to have a look at his beautiful tattoos. Compared with Wu Song's dealings with Pan Jinlian, Yan Qing's situation is far more challenging since he cannot afford to offend Li Shishi; otherwise there would be no hope for Song Jiang to gain access to the emperor. Fortunately, Yan Qing comes up with the ingenious proposal that he and Li Shishi swear to regard each other as sister and brother. At this juncture, the narrator observes, "Anyone else beguiled with wine and women in this situation would have ruined the grand plan. But this shows precisely what an iron will Yan Qing possessed. He was a true man!" (81.1184). As far as the "grand plan" to meet the emperor is concerned, it probably would not have been affected negatively even if Yan Qing had complied with the courtesan's wishes because then she would have been even more willing to help arrange a meeting. However, such compliance would have seriously compromised Yan Qing's standing as a *haohan*. For this reason Yan Qing is anxious to convince his peer, Dai Zong, that nothing has been going on between him and the courtesan: "If a real man forgets his principles just because of wine and women, then he is no better than a beast. May I be cut into pieces by ten thousand swords if I indeed had this intention" (81.1184). Apparently it is more an issue of personal honor than of the "grand plan." In other words, being able to resist sexual temptation is an important test of a *haohan*'s manhood. Thus Yan Qing seems to be an even better model of masculinity than those represented by Lu Da and Li Kui. Yan Qing resolves his dilemma successfully because he has the iron will to control himself, while Lu Da and Li Kui appear to have never liked women in the first place.

Revenge, Violence, and Masculinity

Revenge is often prompted by a man's sense of personal honor. In *San'guo yanyi,* as revenge for the killing of his sworn brother Guan Yu, Liu Bei is even willing to risk the future of his own country by leading an expedition against the Kingdom of Wu—against the advice of many of his councilors. Despite the fact that the Kingdom of Shu suffers a crushing defeat (as we discussed above), the Ming writer Zhu Guozhen (1558–1632) insists that by placing the need for personal honor above the interests of his nation, Liu Bei demonstrated his true heroic character since for him brotherly love was even more important than his throne.[46] For people like Zhu Guozhen, revenge is absolutely crucial for the vindication of one's manhood.

Revenge occupies an even more prominent place in *Shuihu zhuan.* Being unable to take revenge is often considered a stigma on a *haohan,* as if his manhood were in doubt. Revenge is so important to Chao Gai that after being fatally pierced in the face with an arrow, he leaves a will stating that the *haohan* who avenges his death should succeed him as the leader of the Liangshan rebels. The commentator of the *Rongyu tang* edition of the novel praises Chao Gao's dying instructions as reflecting the true character of a *yingxiong* (60.893).

Wu Song's revenge killing of his sister-in-law for murdering his brother, Wu Da, is probably one of the most disturbing stories in the novel because the revenge is extremely violent: he cuts open her chest; pulls out her heart, liver, and entrails; and places them on the memorial tablet of his deceased brother (26.382–383). The rites of revenge often have to be marked with the body parts of the enemy in honor of the deceased victim, who is appropriately avenged with the brutal death of the perpetrator. Even if the wronged individual has not died at the hands of an enemy, when that enemy is captured by a *haohan*, "cutting open the stomach and cutting out the heart" is still often deemed a necessary part of the revenge ritual, an evidenced by Hua Rong's killing of Liu Gao on behalf of Song Jiang (34.485), Yang Xiong's killing of his adulterous wife (46.686), and Lu Junyi's killing of his adulterous wife and servant (67.988). Even cannibalism is justified as a part of the revenge ritual. When Huang Wenbing (the official who has tried to arrest Song Jiang) is captured, Li Kui first slices pieces of flesh from his body, then barbecues and eats them; later Li Kui cuts out Huang's heart and liver and enjoys them as snacks with his wine. Even the commentator of the *Rongyu tang* edition complains that Li Kui has gone too far (41.601).

In *Shuihu zhuan* revenge almost always takes the form of violence. In fact, many modern readers have complained about the violent nature of many episodes in the novel. *San'guo yanyi* also contains many stories of violence, but few readers are bothered by them largely because of the abstract way in which the violence is presented. What may be too savage about *Shuihu zhuan* to a modern reader is its detailed descriptions of various killings and the sometimes apparent delight of the narrator (or at least his lack of restraint) in depicting the extremely violent acts. Liu Kui is certainly one of the characters that is most prone to violence. He seems to kill people simply because he is bloodthirsty, and he seems to take particular delight in butchering them—he kills the toddler son of an official, slices up a captured enemy for revenge, and kills Yizhang Qing's family. The list goes on and on, and many of his victims are absolutely innocent.

Whether a *haohan* is helping the weak and defenseless or avenging himself or a friend, violence is always necessary. After successfully preventing the two escorting guards from killing Lin Chong on their journey to Cangzhou (the place of exile), Lu Da insists on escorting him to the final destination because he believes that "to kill a person one has to draw blood, and to rescue a person one has to see him to safety." Paradoxically, here saving a life is equated with killing in that both require thoroughness. Both taking life and saving life are imbricated with violence in a *haohan*. In the novel "in a moment of rage" *(yishi xingqi)* is often used to characterize a *haohan*'s impulsive killing (for example, Yang Zhi's killing of Nie Er; 12.166). One commentator argues that such impulsive killing is the cause of trouble for many heroes as well as villains.[47]

In the novel a *haohan*'s proclivity to violence is supposed to be in proportion to his disinterest in women. In other words, the most violent *hao-*

han are often those who are the least interested in women.[48] Some of them, such as Wu Song and Li Kui, are known for their ruthless killing of adulterous women—and such killing is certainly one of the main story lines of the novel—while others, such as Chao Gai, Song Jiang, and Lu Junyi are simply too obsessed with weapons and the martial arts to be interested in women. There appears to be a subtle link between the novel's apparent misogynism and the violent image of masculinity on which it dwells. For these men, women represent a constant threat to their *haohan* manhood. Even faithful women, such as the wife of Lin Chong, may inadvertently cause trouble simply because their beauty attracts unwanted attention from some evil but powerful people.

Finally, a few words about the image of literati in the novel. Compared with *San'guo yanyi*, the representation of educated men or scholars *(wenren)* in *Shuihu zhuan* is much less flattering. In contrast to the elaborate first appearance of Zhuge Liang in *San'guo yanyi*, the introduction of the strategist Wu Yong (in chapter 14) is unceremonious, to say the least. Aside from his strategizing ability, Wu Yong has almost nothing else to boast of. Civil officials *(wen'guan)*, referred to as "big-hat officials" *(datoujin)*, are often the targets of ridicule by the Liangshan heroes. For example, Wang the Dwarf asserts that "the *datoujin* are the root cause of all the troubles in this world" (apparently a belief shared by many *haohan*), thus justifying his intention to force the wife of the civil commandant Liu to marry him (32.464), while the military commandant, Hua Rong, argues that military officers are mistreated by civil officials so as to persuade Qin Ming to abandon his superior (a civil official) and join the Liangshan rebels (34.491). Even Song Jiang, a well-educated man, likes to play with weapons.

Such slights against the educated in *Shuihu zhuan* are related to the novel's obsession with violence, partly because the degree to which violence is shunned in a novel is often in proportion to the degree to which it is literati-ized *(wenren hua)*. As Liangyan Ge has observed, recent scholarly emphases on *Shuihu zhuan* as a sophisticated literati novel, although well founded, tend to give the impression that its indebtedness to the oral tradition is significant only when it is examined as the basis for ironic manipulation.[49] One needs to be reminded that the folk elements in *Shuihu zhuan* retain their own independent ideological status and meaning without necessarily having to serve as the targets of "deflation." As we have learned from the late Ming and early Qing commentaries on the novel and other sources from the period, many *Shuihu* characters—such as the violent Li Kui and the lusty Wang the Dwarf—were appealing to the literati readers of that time not because of their potential for ironic readings but because of their symbolic power as the "genuine" and the "primitive," concepts that many literati, tired of the refined sophistication of their own culture, found unexpectedly refreshing.[50] The robust and often violent *haohan* figures, such as

Wu Song and Lu Da, despite their potential for ironical deflation, are at the same time models of masculinity with tremendous appeal for many readers, even some sophisticated literati, who might have come from a cultural background that did not readily celebrate violence or reckless knight-errantry per se. As we shall see in our discussion of the eighteenth-century novel *Shuo Tang quanzhuan* in the next chapter, the unsophisticated and crude can also be appropriated to satirize and deflate the values cherished by the sophisticated literati culture.

CHAPTER 6

Reconstructing *Haohan* in Three Novels from the Sui-Tang Romance Cycle

In this chapter, we look at three novels from the so-called Sui-Tang romance cycle to explore how the image of *haohan* made famous in *Shuihu zhuan* underwent significant changes in the fictional works of later ages.[1] I have chosen these three novels—*Suishi yiwen* (Forgotten Tales of the Sui Dynasty, 1633); *Sui Tang yanyi* (The Romance of the Sui and Tang Dynasties; first published 1695); and *Shuo Tang quanzhuan* (Complete Stories about the Tang, 1736)—mainly because they, with extensive intertextual borrowings among them, are all long fictional narratives about roughly the same group of heroes in the same historical settings. Furthermore, all three novels are substantially indebted, in varying degrees, to *Shuihu zhuan* in their conceptualizations of masculinity. These retellings of the same story form a trajectory of changing images of *haohan,* pointing to a fascinating re/negotiating process of masculinity.

The Wild *Haohan* Tamed in *Suishi yiwen*

The late Ming novel *Suishi yiwen* draws heavily on *Shuihu zhuan.*[2] Both novels focus on the so-called "heroes in the wilds" *(caoze yingxiong),* men who wage battles without the sanction of, or even against, the government. (Many of them are regarded by the imperial government as bandits.)[3] Both novels are preoccupied with constructing models of martial heroes. However, the models presented in *Suishi yiwen* are significantly different from those in *Shuihu zhuan.* In this regard, *Suishi yiwen*'s departures from *Shuihu zhuan* are often so deliberate that we have to read the former as a self-conscious revision of the latter in an attempt to present a considerably different notion of masculinity.

Qin Qiong (better known as Qin Shubao in legends and popular literature) was a famous military commander who helped Li Yuan (566–635) and his son Li Shimin (599–649) found the Tang dynasty in the seventh century.

Suishi yiwen is a lengthy narrative of how Qin Shubao matures into a famous general. At the very beginning of the novel, the narrator calls the reader's attention to the uniqueness of his story: this is not a story about an already established hero. Instead, much of the novel is about the protagonist's life before he achieved fame and success. It is a bildungsroman of how Qin Shubao develops, often by learning from his own mistakes, into a real hero. The role of environment (especially the influence of friends) in Qin Shubao's life is the focus of a large portion of the novel. In his fine analyses of *Suishi yiwen,* Robert Hegel has noted that Qin Shubao's friends can roughly be divided into two large groups: *haojie* (outstanding men) and *xia* (swordsmen or knights-errant). To a large extent, the maturation of Qin Shubao is also about his choosing "the values of the *haojie,* the dignified, resourceful and conscientious 'outstanding man' over those of reckless and unruly 'swordsman,' or *xia.*"[4]

A central issue in *Suishi yiwen* is indeed knight-errantry, but its representation is often complicated by the novel's main agenda to redefine *haohan.* Despite his apparent fascination with *xia* and especially heroic altruism, our novelist also appears to have been particularly concerned with the knights-errants' tendency toward unruliness and recklessness.[5] To the extent that *Suishi yiwen* can be read as a revisionist reading or rewriting of *Shuihu zhuan,* its most important story is about how the unruly and reckless *Shuihu* types of *haohan* are gradually tamed, as exemplified in its new heroic model Qin Shubao.

Like many *Shuihu* heroes, Qin Shubao possesses impressive martial skills and physical prowess. However, unlike them, he seldom allows himself to misuse them. Like many *Shuihu* heroes who are eager to be good Samaritans, Qin Shubao loves to help people in distress. He receives his greatest reward after he comes to the rescue of Li Yuan and his family when they are facing immediate danger from attackers sent by the evil minister of war Yuwen Shu. Qin Shubao eventually becomes one of the most important generals under Li Yuan and Li Shimin. Consequently, unlike his counterparts in *Shuihu zhuan,* Qin Shubao, despite his close association with *caoze yingxiong,* is able to find the ultimate *zhenzhu* (true ruler) to whom he can offer his services. (The search for *zhenzhu* is also one of the themes in *San'guo yanyi,* as discussed in chapter 5.)

If *Shuihu zhuan* is about how heroes such as Lin Chong join the Liangshan rebels because they have no other alternative given the constant persecution of corrupt officials, then *Suishi yiwen* is about how Qin Shubao is able to remain "a good citizen" despite all the adversities, persecution, and even humiliation. He does join the rebels on Wagang Ridge for a brief period, but he soon switches to the Tang troops led by Li Yuan. The fact that Li Yuan, originally an important official in the Sui imperial government, eventually becomes the founder of another dynasty (as suggested in the saying "The one who succeeds is recognized as the king, while the one who fails is condemned as a bandit"), seems to elevate his followers to a status well beyond that of "heroes in the wilds."

One of Qin Shubao's most important virtues, which sets him apart from the *Shuihu* heroes, is his capacity for *ren*. There is no exact equivalent in English for the Chinese notion of *ren*, which can mean being tolerant, patient, and accommodating; showing self-restraint; and enduring hardship, humiliation, or other adversities. An early, though by no means perfect, demonstration of *ren* is Qin Shubao's handling of adversity when he is stranded penniless in an inn, during a mission to escort some prisoners to Luzhou. Wang Xiao'er, the innkeeper, soon begins to treat Qin Shubao less courteously once he discovers that Qin is short of money: "A man of heroic spirit, how could Qin Shubao endure [*ren*] this slight at the hands of such a petty person? However, after thinking it over, he decided that he had to be accommodating since he was short of money" (6.49). Eventually, Qin Shubao is forced to sell his horse. Now, with some money in his pocket, he visits a wine shop. Because of his unimpressive dress, he is stopped at the door and has to push his way in. Once inside, he is asked to put down a deposit before he can order food and wine. Even after all this humiliation, he is treated to only cold food and wine. Again he is able to restrain himself, reasoning that he would be a laughingstock if he resorted to fighting only because he had no money (8.64). Later, when Wang Xiao'er complains that Qin has returned too late during the night, Qin Shubao is again about to explode. However, he manages to control himself once more because he is worried that if he beats the innkeeper, he will do damage to his image as a *haojie*. Qin Shubao's motto is the Master's famous caution as recorded in *The Analects*: "The lack of self-restraint in small matters will bring ruin to great plans" (8.67–68).[6] In fact, Qin Shubao later explicitly proposes a redefinition of *haohan* to include self-restraint: "One can be considered a *haohan* only if he does not seek confrontation with others and only if he understands the importance of self-restraint *(ren'nai)* and is able to endure what ordinary people cannot endure" (21.161). In this context of the importance of *ren*, the reference to the famous historical figure Han Xin of the Han is significant. Unlike the innkeeper Wang Xiao'er, his wife is quite compassionate and often helps Qin Shubao in secret while he is stranded in their inn. Qin Shubao is so grateful to her that he compares her to the washerwoman from Huaiyin (6.50), who once fed the hungry Han Xin before he went on to become a famous general under Liu Bang. According to Sima Qian's famous biography, Han Xin was known for his capacity to endure humiliation (see the discussion in chapter 1).

Of course, self-restraint and accommodation are the last things a *Shuihu* hero will exhibit. The reader will recall that Wu Song once erupted into a violent rage when he became suspicious that he was being treated with less courtesy than someone considered more important by a wine shop owner and how he beat the hell out of that "important person" (chapter 30). In other words, Qin Shubao's repeated demonstrations of *ren* in dealing with the innkeeper would be utterly unimaginable for most *haohan* in *Shuihu zhuan*, who would not tolerate disrespect or humiliation. A reader who admires the "heroic" *haohan* spirit in *Shuihu zhuan* may find Qin Shubao rather pathetic. Many times in the novel he is beaten by his superiors for one reason or another—again something a typical *Shuihu* hero would not tolerate. Moreover, Qin often cries when he is in distress.

As we discussed in chapter 5, in *Shuihu zhuan* Lu Da is admired for his deeds as a good Samaritan and especially for rescuing two women from unwanted marriages. In *Shishi yiwen,* Qin Shubao and his friends perform a similar deed, but the end result is disastrously different. In their short sojourn in the capital, Qin Shubao and his friends learn of the abduction and rape of a young girl by Yuwen Huiji, the son of Yuwen Shu. Outraged, Qin's friends decide to punish the culprit. Before he knows it, Qin Shubao is dragged into this act of knight-errantry, despite earlier warnings that he should avoid trouble in the capital. Qin Shubao eventually kills Yuwen Huiji. Incensed by the death of his son and unable to apprehend his killer, Yuwen Shu immediately orders that the girl and her mother be put to death. Consequently, Qin's chivalry has inadvertently caused the deaths of the victims. More significant, the narrator goes out of his way to associate Qin Shubao's reckless behavior with the so-called "four vices":

> In this world, the four worst vices are wine, sex, money, and anger [*jiu se cai qi*]. While people vulnerable to wine and money are often laughed at and ridiculed as drunk and greedy, many admire those who indulge in sex and anger as romantic and chivalrous. However, these admirers fail to understand that such indulgence can be the seed of disaster. Take, for example, Shubao's outrage at that moment [when he learns of the criminal deeds of Yuwen Huiji]. How can we not say that it is an expression of a hero's altruism? But think about this: although they were able to kill one person, Yuwen Huiji, the girl's entire family was put to death as a result. Furthermore, had Shubao failed to escape from the capital, he could have lost his own life and died far away from home. Who would take care of his aging mother and young wife? Why should one try to win credit as a real man this way? (24.183)

Here Qin Shubao's chivalry is denounced because Qin succumbed to anger. Qin himself apparently shares this view when he later has a chance to reflect on his actions: "Although this was an honorable act, the death of Yuwen Huiji did not bring any benefit to the girl. If I had failed to escape, my life would have been the price paid for Yuwen Huiji's death. This would have been the end of the career of a great hero. Who was going to take care of my mother and wife? This was sheer recklessness rather than chivalry"

(28.220). From this incident Qin Shubao learns a lesson on the importance of self-discipline, an aspect of the virtue of *ren* central to the growth of our protagonist.[7]

In addition to having the virtue of *ren*, Qin Shubao is also said to be compassionate and soft-hearted *(duoqing de ren)*, which may not always be pluses for him. He does not have the heart to refuse when Qi Guoyuan and other bandit chiefs of the Wagang Ridge insist on going to the capital with him. Ultimately these fellow journeymen drag him into the aforementioned disastrous knight-errantry. Quite different from the *Shuihu* heroes, Qin Shubao shows considerable compassion even on the battlefield. In a campaign against the rebels, Luo Shixin (Qin Shubao's protégé) and his troops successfully ambush the fleeing rebels and almost completely annihilate them: "Looking at the corpses of the enemy soldiers, Qin Shubao found the death scene appalling. He then went to caution Luo Shixin: 'Brother, as generals, you and I should consider it our first duty to save people rather than to kill them. In the future, so long they are fleeing and are not attacking you head-on, you should let them go'" (39.318). In *Shuihu zhuan*, such caution against unnecessary violence is rarely heard among the *haohan*, even when they are confronted with Li Kui's frequent brutal massacres of the innocent. Given the close intertextual relationship between *Shuihu zhuan* and *Suishi yiwen*, Qin Shubao's sensibility and sensitivity have to be interpreted as deliberate critiques of the *Shuihu* heroes prone to extreme violence.

In contrast to *Shuihu zhuan*, revenge is often problematized in *Suishi yiwen*. Shan Xiongxin's tragic end is largely attributable to his insistence on avenging the death of his brother, who is accidentally killed by Li Yuan. Despite Li Yuan's apology and the accidental nature of the killing, Shan stubbornly refuses to forgive Li and his people. The refusal leads him to associate with the wrong camp in the brutal civil war, and he eventually pays with his own life.

The maturation of Qin Shubao is also a process of his becoming more Confucianized—his deliberate attempts to conduct himself in a manner expected of a Confucian scholar rather than a *haohan*, although the reader is repeatedly told early in the novel that Qin Shubao does not like to read or study (3.20–21). For example, his decision to become a hermit and his subsequent short sojourn as a recluse (chapter 35) remind the reader of a scholar/hero such as Zhuge Liang rather than a *haohan*.

Qin Shubao's life as a recluse does not last long. When Li Shimin tries to persuade him to join his camp in the fight for control of the country, Qin Shubao finds himself in a quandary since he has already pledged loyalty to Li Mi and his camp. The way he pleads his case to Li Shimin sets him further apart from the macho image of a *haohan*. Qin Shubao now is first of all a *chen*, or a Confucian minister, rather than a "hero in the wilds." Here a minister's loyalty, as usual, is articulated in terms of a woman's faithfulness to her husband: "I won't be able to lightly pledge this body of mine to Your Excellency today." Qin's feminized position is further emphasized by the narrator's comments in the form of a poetic couplet: "It is not my mind that is too difficult to change/I cannot promise you my body yet just because I have been deeply indebted to you" (49.409).[8]

The conflicts between loyalty (zhong) and personal honor (yi) that dominate both *San'guo yanyi* and *Shuihu zhuan* are also problems that Qin Shubao has to face. In the last part of the novel, no longer a chivalrous *hao-han*, Qin Shubao has become a mature general, a loyal subject under a new imperial monarch. When conflicts arise between loyalty to one's lord and one's personal honor, Qin Shubao seems to side with the former with little hesitation. For example, when his sworn brother Shan Xiongxin, who has helped him many times in the past and who happens to be associated with the enemy camp, is captured by the army of the Tang and ordered to be executed, Qin Shubao asks the Prince of Qin, Li Shimin, to show leniency by sparing his life, but the latter flatly refuses. Qin Shubao accepts Li's refusal without much protest and makes no further effort to save his sworn brother. Instead, Qin merely promises Shan that he and others will provide for his family after his death.

Before Shan is put to death, Qin Shubao and his close friends gather at the execution ground and perform a strange farewell ritual. They each slice strips of flesh from their thighs, roast them, and present the pieces to Shan to eat, declaring: "We brothers have sworn before to live and die together, but today we are unable to follow you. If in the future we fail to keep our promise to take care of your family, may we be butchered and roasted just like this flesh" (59.496). This statement is full of irony. By refusing to die with Shan Xiongxin—contrary to their earlier pledge of brotherhood—Qin Shubao and the others have already broken their word. Therefore, according to the pledge they are making now, they should have been butchered and roasted. Furthermore, if Qin Shubao and the others have failed to keep their past promise, how is one expected to believe that they will not break the pledge they are making now? This pledge is only an excuse for having broken their word before. The ritual of butchering and roasting, which is supposed to symbolize the ties of brotherhood, in fact functions only to expose the hypocrisy of the participants, reminding the reader of the unpleasant fact that Qin Shubao is now too "realistic" and "mature" to pursue the empty title of *haohan*. Even in *San'guo yanyi*, where personal honor has figured less prominently, Liu Bei was willing to sacrifice his country for the sake of his sworn brother. Here Qin Shubao, as a mature general, places his own future ahead of his obligations to his sworn brother. Of course, this is done in the name of loyalty (*zhong* to one's lord rather than *yi* to one's sworn brothers). The farewell ritual among the sworn brothers becomes a mockery of the very idea of brotherhood. As we shall see, some future "rewriters" of

Qin Shubao's story will find it necessary to revise this rather unpleasant episode, which tends to compromise considerably Qin's image as a *haohan*.

The Feminine and the Heroic in *Sui Tang yanyi*

In *Sui Tang yanyi*, the notion of masculinity is further complicated. Robert Hegel has convincingly demonstrated that the first two-thirds of *Sui Tang yanyi* is heavily indebted to *Suishi yiwen*.[9] In fact, most of *Suishi yiwen* was copied almost verbatim by Chu Renhuo (1635–ca. 1719) into his own novel, *Sui Tang yanyi*, a fact Chu indirectly acknowledged in his preface to the novel. Consequently, the overall image of Qin Shubao remains unchanged in *Sui Tang yanyi*, although there are numerous minor alterations. Since Chu Renhuo added many elements from other sources, as well as from his own imagination, the context is significantly different. While *Suishi yiwen*, a much shorter novel of 60 chapters, is largely a bildungsroman concentrating on one individual, Qin Shubao, the 100-chapter *Sui Tang yanyi* has a much wider focus. Accordingly, our reading of *Sui Tang yanyi* will take these new elements into account, and we will also explore the changes Qin Shubao has undergone, no matter how subtle or minor.

Compared with *Suishi yiwen*, *Sui Tang yanyi* lays even more emphasis on loyalty, while personal honor, though still celebrated, is relegated to a more subordinate position. As I have tried to demonstrate, the author of *Suishi yiwen*, through the example of his protagonist, attempted to Confucianize as well as moderate the tough *haohan* masculinity prevalent in *Shuihu zhuan*. Nevertheless, as some scholars have noted, *Suishi yiwen* is still a predominantly "masculine" novel in the sense that, like *Shuihu zhuan*, it is almost exclusively about men and their aspirations. If misogyny characterizes many *haohan* in *Shuihu zhuan*, the same certainly cannot be said of *Suishi yiwen*, although women still occupy minor positions. *Sui Tang yanyi*, however, becomes considerably more "feminine" with the inclusion of many stories about women, and the Confucianizing process appears to have quickened its pace.[10] In *Sui Tang yanyi*, women not only become much more prominent, but also they often outshine the men in talent and especially in virtue.

One important theme emphasized in the stories associated with women is loyalty, which is often expressed in terms of *jie* (chastity, fidelity, and integrity). In his rewriting of materials from an earlier novel, *Sui Yangdi yanshi* (The Merry Adventures of Emperor Yang), Chu Renhuo adds several stories about how many palace ladies chose heroic death to prove their loyalty to Emperor Yang.[11] For example, when soldiers sent by coup leader Yuwen Shu surround the palace, Lady Zhu Gui'er openly denounces them for their act of treason. She pays with her life for her heroic defiance. Another palace lady, Yuan Bao'er, ridicules Emperor Yang for his cowardice before she commits suicide (47.486).[12] In chapter 48, several palace ladies deface themselves in order to show their determination to remain chaste for the sake of the deceased emperor. One of them declares that the heroic deaths of Zhu Gui'er and Yuan Bao'er are eloquent proof that men do not monopolize the honor of a loyal minister (48.496).

The novelist's persistent emphasis on the loyalty and chastity of women makes one wonder if it was related to his personal reaction to the fall of the Ming dynasty, the bitter memory of which must have been still fresh when he was writing the novel. (Chu Renhuo was about ten when the Ming monarchy collapsed.) As discussed in chapter 4, in national crises, some literati tended to use the metaphor of chaste women to chastise their male peers for their failure to defend the nation as men. Here we may also recall the observation of Mao Zonggang in his commentaries on *San'guo yanyi* (discussed in chapter 5) that women tended to be judged in terms of morality rather than talent, as if moral virtue were their natural quality. Of course, it is very possible that both Chu Renhuo and Mao Zonggang, who were friends, had the fall of the Ming dynasty on their minds when they were working on their respective novels. As we discussed, chastity became a more prominent issue in the Mao Zonggang commentary edition of *San'guo yanyi*.

Robert Hegel has discussed the possible loyalist sentiments in *Sui Tang yanyi*, and he in particular alerts the reader to the novel's story of the legendary woman warrior Hua Mulan, who disguised herself as a man to join the military in place of her aging father. An important detail that cannot be found in any previous legends or stories associated with Hua Mulan was apparently added by Chu Renhuo: when summoned to serve in the harem of a Turkish khan, Mulan calmly commits suicide. Her suicide is particularly baffling since at the time she is not in love or engaged to anyone and since she is only half Chinese (her father is Turkish, but her mother is Chinese). Hegel provides the possible explanation that this is intended to be a loyalist message: "Even a half-Chinese woman would prefer death by her own hand to serving a foreign ruler."[13] Also worth mentioning here is Mulan's explanation for why she has masqueraded as a man to join the military: "Feeling ashamed that there were not many loyal subjects and filial sons among men, I decided to take the risk to dress myself as a man" (57.590). Here Mulan is apparently blaming the incompetence of men as one of the reasons that she felt compelled to join the military. In other words, there would have been no need for her to do so if men had been competent enough to fulfill their duties. (Here we are reminded of similar complaints about male incompetence in the fall of the Ming, as examined in chapter 4.)

In this context, *Sui Tang yanyi*'s different rendering of Qin Shubao's response to the death of his benefactor and former superior, General Zhang Xutuo, becomes even more interesting. In *Suishi yiwen*, the narrative of Qin Shubao's mourning for Zhang Xutuo is straightforward and factual (45. 369–370). Apparently feeling that Qin Shubao is not completely blameless when he deserts Zhang Xutuo and joins the rebels of the Wagang Ridge, however, Chu Renhuo adds quite a few important details that are far less flattering of Qin. After Zhang Xutuo is killed by the rebel forces that Qin has just recently joined, Qin Shubao goes to the temple where Zhang's coffin is to pay homage to the dead general. Seeing that many of Zhang Xutuo's former subordinates are dressed in white mourning clothes, Qin thinks to himself, "Even these foot soldiers are acting honorably. What kind of person would I be if I were not following the codes of honor and loyalty?" Only then does Qin change into mourning dress. To further shame Qin Shubao for his "betrayal," the novelist inserts a brief episode in which another of Zhang Xutuo's former subordinates, Tang Wanren, commits suicide out of loyalty in front of the coffin. (In *Suishi yiwen,* Tang is said to have been killed in battle.) Before his suicide, as he walks toward the coffin Tang refuses to acknowledge Qin Shubao when the latter tries to talk to him. Moreover, Tang delivers an emotional speech before he slits his throat. His speech, about how deeply indebted he is to Zhang, is obviously meant for Qin: "Standing nearby, listening to him saying these words in tears, Shubao understood that every word he said was meant to ridicule him. Feeling as if he was being pierced by needles all over his body, he was too ashamed to go to Tang to console him" (46.464).

Tang's suicide leaves Qin Shubao no alternative but to at least make a gesture of suicide. However, others stop him just in time with the reminder that he still has an old mother to take care of, and it is a sufficient justification for him not to follow Tang's example. As discussed in chapter 4, having to take care of an aging mother was a common excuse among many Ming loyalists to justify not dying for the fallen monarchy. Here the novel's implicit reference to the painful choice of life or death, which many Ming loyalists faced, is difficult to miss. Ming loyalists such as Huang Zongxi, Chen Que, and Qu Dajun all chose to live using this same excuse, even though their teachers or mentors had given their lives for the hopeless cause of the Ming. (In the novel Zhang Xutuo can certainly be considered Qin's mentor.) The trouble Chu Renhuo has taken to alter this episode from the version in *Suishi yiwen* should alert the reader to the new importance attached to loyalty and the significance of Qin Shubao's failures in this regard.

Another interesting loyal character in the novel is Wang Yi. Wang is a dwarf presented to Emperor Yang as a "gift" by the ruler of a foreign country. He soon wins the emperor's favor thanks to his wit. Wang is so grateful to Emperor Yang for the favors he showers on him that he even plans to have himself castrated so that in the future he can always serve the emperor close by as a eunuch. The intended castration is stopped when Wang Yi is summoned to the palace by the emperor. The gesture has moved the emperor tremendously. As if to help Wang to reassert his manhood, Emperor Yang rewards him with a wife, deliberately reminding people of the castration that did not take place. Eventually, instead of demonstrating his loyalty with the physical marker of his manhood, Wang Yi demonstrates it with his life. He and his wife later commit suicide at the graveside of the emperor.[14] When someone expresses doubt that Wang could endure the pain of castration and whether he was serious when he made the promise of castration, Wang asks, "How can a real man be untrue to his own words?" (27.267). Apparently in Wang Yi's mind, castration in no way diminishes his manhood. Instead, it enhances his status as a true man because here masculinity is defined exclusively as loyalty and the determination to return favors.[15]

Compared with *Suishi yiwen, Sui Tang yanyi* contains significantly more romantic elements. Now almost every important hero is involved with a beautiful girl. (Qin Shubao is one of the few exceptions since he is married at the beginning of *Suishi yiwen.*) Adding romantic touches to the images of male heroes is one of the major aspects of Chu Renhuo's rewriting from many previous sources. For example, in chapter 16, the novelist inserts the famous love story of Hongfu and Li Jing; in chapter 41, Li Mi, who is then a rebel leader in distress, is said to be engaged to Wang Xue'er, the daughter of an old man living in a remote mountainous area; in chapter 49, Princess Dou Xianniang falls in love with the young general Luo Cheng, and their love story lasts several chapters; in chapter 51, the imprisoned Li Simin, the Tang Prince of Qin, is rescued by Li Huying, the daughter of the warden, and later Li marries her as a concubine; in chapter 58, the military strategist Xu Moagong is engaged to Yuan Zhiyan, a former palace lady. Emperor Yang's involvement with many women, though often understood as one of the reasons that he eventually loses his empire, is sometimes presented with a good deal of sympathy. As mentioned above, some of the palace ladies die heroically while others resort to self-mutilation to maintain their chastity for the sake of their deceased emperor/lover. The sometimes conflicting images of these palace ladies—most of them are talented and loyal and yet they have also caused the emperor to neglect his duties as a ruler—may be part of the novelist's effort to emphasize the conflicting obligations and demands that many people have to face in life, an important theme of *Sui Tang yanyi.*[16]

Most of the romantic episodes are fairly brief, yet there are so many of them that they become an important pattern of the plot development. The episodes could be characterized as one of the novel's central story lines— that of *yingxiong meiren* (heroes and beauties)—suggesting a new concept of masculinity that is substantially different from those in *Shuihu zhuan* and *Suishi yiwen.* Here, instead of being presented as the possible sources of disaster for men (as is often the case in *Shuihu zhuan*), women play important and positive roles in the lives and careers of many heroes. Even in the case of Emperor Yang, most of the palace ladies are presented as virtuous, loyal, and talented. Some of them have tried desperately to call his attention to the rapidly worsening political situation, but the emperor has refused to listen. He even has one palace lady executed for daring to remind him of the political troubles (47.482–483). The message is clear: Emperor Yang is responsible for his own demise, not his palace ladies. In *Sui Tang yanyi*, masculinity is not defined *against* but in close association *with* the feminine. Often the image of a hero is considered complete only when it is complemented by the admiration and love of a beautiful woman. (Here we are reminded of Yuji's role in the legend of Xiang Yu, as examined in chapter 1.)

Sui Tang yanyi was probably completed in the 1670s, and it was first published in 1695.[17] The second half of the seventeenth century was the heyday of the so-called scholar-beauty fiction, and we can certainly see evidence of it in *Sui Tang yanyi* (more about scholar-beauty fiction in chapters 7 and 8).[18] A look at this genre's influence on the novel should help us to appreciate the novel's significance in terms of the changing conceptualization of masculinity as reflected in the fiction of this period.

In chapter 5 of *Suishi yiwen*, Li Yuan and his family seek refuge in a temple, where they meet a young man named Chai Shao. Li is deeply impressed by Chai's knowledge of military affairs and the martial arts, and he immediately decides to engage his daughter to this promising young man. This entire episode was copied into *Sui Tang yanyi*. However, Chu Renhuo added quite a few new details, making it into a romantic story. In *Suishi yiwen*, Li Yuan's daughter is silent; in fact, she never makes an appearance in the novel. Everything is decided *for* her. In *Sui Tang yanyi*, however, she plays an essential role in the decision-making process. Now Li Yuan's wife, the future Empress Dou, consults their daughter before deciding on the marriage. Not shy at all, the daughter insists that her future husband be a hero with military skills. For her, good looks and talent are not enough since superficial literary skills amount to nothing during a time of political disorder.[19] Even after being assured that Chai Shao excels in the martial arts and is very knowledgeable about military affairs, she insists on testing him on her own terms. Chai Shao must recognize the different military formations presented by her maids and engage in a mock fight with these female warriors. In the end, he passes all her tests with flying colors. Chu Renhuo removes a small but significant detail from this episode as it is told in *Suishi yiwen*: the background information that Li Yuan's daughter likes to read only books on military strategy but not books like *Lienü zhuan* (Biographies of Chaste Women), which was considered a must-read for educated girls from respectable families.[20] Such a detail would not fit comfortably in the new context of *Sui Tang yanyi*, where chastity and loyalty are the main female virtues to be celebrated.

Another romance in *Sui Tang yanyi* associated with female warrior(s) is the much more elaborate love story of Dou Xianniang and Luo Cheng. These two young people fall in love when, representing opposite camps, they engage in a fight on the battlefield. A male warrior and a female warrior from opposite camps falling in love on the battlefield comprise a familiar plot in a fairly large group of traditional Chinese novels that C. T. Hsia has dubbed "military romances."[21] Possibly the earliest such plot can be found in chapter 98 of the 120-chapter edition of *Shuihu zhuan,* where Qiongying, who can throw pellets with deadly precision, marries Zhang Qing, who possesses the same pellet-throwing skills. Since this chapter (among the so-called Tianhu chapters) is usually believed to be a late addition to *Shuihu zhuan,* this brief romantic story may not be part of the original novel, which is dominated by misogyny. Earlier in *Shuihu zhuan,* the lusty Wang the Dwarf (Wang Ying) becomes infatuated with the beautiful female warrior Hu Sanniang (Yizhang Qing), although Wang proves to be no match for her on the battlefield. Later Song Jiang imposes their marriage when Hu Sanniang is taken prisoner by the Liangshan rebels—a rather antiromantic episode devoid of any elements of genuine love. Needless to say, the love story of Dou Xianniang and Luo Cheng as described in *Sui Tang yanyi* contributed substantially to the romantic tradition celebrated in many later military romances.[22]

Dou Xianniang is the daughter of Dou Jiande, the self-styled King of Xia, and Luo Cheng is the son of Luo Yi, a powerful warlord who has recently allied himself with Li Shimin, the Tang Prince of Qin. Both Dou Xianniang and Luo Cheng excel in military strategy and the martial arts. When Dou Jiande sends troops to attack Luo Yi and his people, Dou Xianniang and Luo Cheng, who are generals of their respective camps, confront each other on the battlefield. After fighting a dozen rounds without being able to get the upper hand, Luo Cheng begins to admire Dou Xianniang's martial skills. Not to hurt his enemy, Luo shoots a headless arrow at Dou as a warning, a signal Dou Xianniang does not miss. In return, she shoots a pellet at Luo in a harmless manner. Now attracted to each other, they begin to seek key information (age, marriage status, etc.) directly from each other while still on horseback. Before long, they begin to pledge love, and the headless arrow and pellet, which each has kept, become "engagement rings." Before they part, Luo Cheng promises Dou Xianniang that he will ask one of her father's best friends, Chamberlain Yang Yi, to be their matchmaker.

Some time later, after the death of Chamberlain Yang, Dou Xianniang worries that her father will not allow her to marry the son of his enemy without the persuasion of a matchmaker who commands his respect and trust. After unexpectedly intercepting Lou Cheng's letter asking Qin Shubao to find a matchmaker for him, Dou Xianniang, out of selfless love for Luo Cheng, rewrites part of the letter to give the impression that Luo Cheng wants to marry another girl. Her determination not to marry Luo Cheng is further strengthened after the Xia army is soundly defeated by the Tang troops and Dou Jiande is taken prisoner by Li Simin. She decides to ask Hua Mulan, her sworn sister, to send a "severance" letter to Luo Cheng.

Now the romance between Luo Cheng and Dou Xianniang begins to involve two other women: Hua Mulan and her younger sister Hua Youlan. Chu Renhuo reworks the legend of the famous female warrior into his novel, where she has become Dou Xianniang's sworn sister after Dou has captured her on the battlefield. More significant, the ending differs from the endings of most of the Hua Mulan legends (as noted above). In *Sui Tang yanyi,* while Mulan is moving her parents to live with her at Dou Xianniang's place, she is summoned to the harem of a Turkish khan. Despite an armed escort on her way to the khan's harem, Mulan manages to commit suicide. (Compared with her mother's remarriage after the death of her father, Mulan's chaste act becomes quite ironic.) However, before leaving for the harem, Mulan has entrusted her sister Hua Youlan with Dou Xianniang's letter, requesting that she deliver it to Luo Cheng.

Youlan, like her elder sister, masquerades as a man and sets off on her journey as a messenger. Significantly, Youlan impersonates a handsome scholar rather than a warrior (60.631). After delivering the letter, Youlan is invited to stay in the Luo residence, and she and Luo Cheng soon develop a very close relationship. Much to his delight, Luo Cheng accidentally learns from one of Youlan's maids that Youlan is actually a girl. Feigning ignorance of Youlan's gender, Luo Cheng drinks wine with her and then insists on sharing the same bed. Compelled to reveal her true identity, Youlan convinces Luo Cheng that at present they should abstain from any physical relationship and that she can marry him as a concubine only after securing consent from his would-be formal wife Dou Xianniang. Although she sleeps in the same bed with Luo Cheng for two months, Youlan maintains her chastity, which is later "authenticated" by Empress Dou with a jade-testing bead, a magical instrument that can verify a girl's virginity. Youlan's impeccable "test results" move not only Dou Xianniang, but also the Tang emperor, and consequently she is finally allowed to marry Luo Cheng. The romantic story ends happily: both girls, Dou Xianniang and Hua Youlan, are married to Luo Cheng (61.640 and 62.661). Readers acquainted with the conventions of scholar-beauty fiction no doubt find many familiar elements in this romantic episode in *Sui Tang yanyi:* cross-dressing, the perseverance of chastity, the verification of virginity by an empress, references to the concept of "norms" and "expediency" (*jingquan;* 61.637 and 639), marriages arranged by the emperor, and two beautiful girls marrying the same young man.[23]

To make this romantic episode more plausible, Chu Renhuo has made quite a few important changes from *Suishi yiwen.* For example, instead of being executed after he is taken prisoner (as is the case in *Suishi yiwen*), Dou Jiande is pardoned by the Tang emperor and allowed to become a monk (in *Sui Tang yanyi* he is presented in a much more positive light). Dou Xianniang herself is adopted by Empress Dou as a niece. These changes are necessitated by the prescribed happy ending of the romance between Dou Xianniang and Luo Cheng. The pains Chu Renhuo has taken to make these changes attest to the importance of this episode of "a romance on horseback" (*mashang di yinyuan,* a phrase in the title of chapter 49) in relation to the new thematic concerns of the novel.

With its male protagonists mostly generals and strongmen rather than scholars (as in scholar-beauty fiction), *Sui Tang yanyi* represents a major effort to tame or humanize the macho heroes with whom we have become familiar in *San'guo yanyi* and especially *Shuihu zhuan.* Now the emphasis is on these heroes' romantic sentiments. Some of them, such as Luo Cheng, even resemble the feminine-looking scholars (with fair skin and ruby lips, for example) in the scholar-beauty novels. Interestingly enough, this effort to "soften" the image of martial heroes is paralleled by a similar attempt to "harden" the image of scholars in a few scholar-beauty novels of roughly the same period—such as *Huatu yuan* (see chapter 7)—where handsome scholars are purportedly knowledgeable in military affairs and even proficient in the martial arts. *Sui Tang yanyi* and these scholar-beauty novels represent a new and important trend in the development of Chinese fiction—a conscious endeavor to construct a new masculinity that is characterized by intellectual abilities, physical prowess, sensitivity, and, most important, the capacity for romantic sentiments. This trend picked up momentum in many novels of the late eighteenth and early nineteenth centuries, as we will explore in chapter 8. Before examining how masculinities begin to be renegotiated in these novels, however, let us take a look at *Shuo Tang quanzhuan* to see how the masculine models of *Shuihu* reassert themselves but yield some different implications.

Haohan Caricatured in *Shuo Tang quanzhuan*

Like two of its predecessors, *Suishi yiwen* and *Sui Tang yanyi,* the pseudonymous eighteenth-century *Shuo Tang quanzhuan* (hereafter *Shuo Tang*) also concentrates on the figures and events of the Sui-Tang transition, and the influences of these two previous texts are quite obvious.[24] The first part of *Shuo Tang* (approximately the first fourteen chapters) focuses on Qin Shubao and is apparently based on episodes about this same character in *Suishi yiwen* and *Sui Tang yanyi,* although many details are condensed or omitted. One result of such condensation and omission is that there is no longer a consistent emphasis on *ren* as the virtue defining a *haohan.* Most of the direct references to this concept in the two preceding novels are now simply omitted. Instead, as the narrative unfolds, the focus shifts onto other characters, and impulsive fighting and reckless killing, typical of *Shuihu* heroes, once again become the norm for a large group of *haohan.*[25] In other words, although many of the characters have previously appeared in *Suishi yiwen* and *Sui Tang yanyi,* fighting and violence become a much more prominent component of their stories in *Shuo Tang.* In fact, some scenes of killing in *Shuo Tang* are directly reminiscent of those in *Shuihu zhuan.* For example, Wang Shichong (the future king of the state of Zheng) kills the entire family of Shui Yao in revenge for Shui's having killed his parrot (32.252–254); the episode reminds the reader of Wu Song's brutal killing of

Zhang and his entire family in *Shuihu zhuan* (chapter 31). Although the descriptions of violence in *Shuo Tang* are less graphic, the similarities are obvious: repeated killings of the innocent, concubines, maids, and servants. Like Wu Song, Wang kills everyone he happens to come cross in Zhang's house. Moreover, he defiantly announces himself as the perpetrator of the massacre by writing a poem in blood on the walls of his victim's house.

The celebration of violence and physical prowess seems to have reached a new level. All the important *haohan* in *Shuo Tang*—the so-called "Eighteen Doughty Warriors of the Sui"—are ranked in a strict hierarchy that is based exclusively on physical prowess. In the context of *Shuo Tang,* the English word "warrior" is apparently a closer equivalent to the Chinese term *haohan* since the emphasis is now almost exclusively on physical strength and martial skills.[26] The rankings are supposed to be absolutely accurate in that a higher-ranking warrior can always easily outfight any warriors ranked below him. For example, the number 1 warrior, Li Yuanba, is so powerful that he literally tears warrior number 3 into pieces with his bare hands; no warrior under heaven can challenge him in a battle. Consequently, no one can stop Li Yuanba, and military victory is automatically guaranteed when his services are enlisted. With this absolute hierarchy of *haohan* and with so many battles and fight scenes depicted in detail, *Shuo Tang* seems to go even further than *Shuihu zhuan* in emphasizing violence and physical prowess as the important qualities of masculinity.

Compared with *Suishi yiwen* and *Sui Tang yanyi,* which tend to be more realistic, *Shuo Tang,* with its more exaggerated rhetoric, "heavier" characters, and quicker narrative pace, appears to be much more indebted to the oral tradition (*Shuihu zhuan* shares this indebtedness to a considerable degree).[27] In his study of *Shuihu zhuan,* Liangyan Ge has related its characters' tendency toward violence to the influence of oral traditions.[28] It is reasonable to believe that the prevalence of violence and the cult of physical prowess in *Shuo Tang* largely reflect the tastes of the less educated rather than those of the literati. However, because of the comic nature of *Shuo Tang,* the obsession with violence and physical power is not necessarily always safe from the novel's own satire. Given its various hilarious parodies, we have to entertain the possibility that its author is a sophisticated literatus who has appropriated stories from previous sources for his own satirical agenda.[29]

One significant difference from *Shuihu zhuan* is that the violence described in *Shuo Tang* is likely to be much less disturbing to a modern reader, in part because it is presented in much less graphic detail. To avoid detailing the killings of large numbers of people, the narrator often uses the phrase "a sea of blood and a mountain of corpses" (13.102, 25.196, 40.330 and 337). Furthermore, the overall comic tone of the narrative also helps to alleviate the shocking effects of violent incidents. For example, Yuchi Gong, a powerful enemy warrior that Li Shimin admires, once pledged that he would surrender only after his lord, Liu Wuzhou, has died. To convince Yuchi to surrender, Li tries to find someone who resembles Liu Wuzhou and has him killed so that he can convince Yuchi of Liu's death with the head of his look-alike. The beheading of the innocent look-alike could have been a disturbing scene. This, however, is not the case thanks to the comic manner in which the incident is presented:

> The Prince of Qin said [to the look-alike], "I want to borrow a treasure from you, and [as a reward] I will ennoble you as a duke ruling over ten thousand families." Hearing of this, the man was as elated as if the bones of his entire body weighed only a few ounces. "If your humble servant possesses what you want, he is willing to give you whatever he has." The prince said, "What I want to borrow is the head on your shoulders so that I can persuade Yuchi Gong to surrender. I will immediately ennoble your descendants as dukes and reward them with one thousand ounces of gold." The man cries, "Aya! Your Majesty cannot do this! I have to keep this head on my neck so that I can continue to eat food!" Cheng Yaojin interrupted him: "Only this time. We won't borrow your head again." The man becomes hysterical, crying, "If your servant dies, Your Majesty must keep his word. I live at the western end of the Green Cloth Bridge village, outside the east gate of Taiyuan City. There lives an old woman named Aqu, and she is my mother-in-law. My three sons also live there." The prince gave orders to Cheng Yaojin. Cheng Yaojin said, "We will remember this." He went ahead and beheaded the man. (48.378)

Here the beheading of an innocent is turned into a humorous farce.

In the hierarchy rankings of physical prowess, we find that many powerful warriors—such as the number 2 warrior, Yuwen Chengdu, and the number 8 warrior, Yang Lin—are on the side of the "evil forces," but the novel's focus is not on the highly ranked warriors. Rather it is on those at the lower end, such as Qin Shubao (warrior number 16) and Shan Xiongxin (warrior number 18). (Of course, warrior number 7, Luo Cheng, also receives considerable attention in the novel.) In fact, relatively speaking, most of the top six warriors in the hierarchy (Li Yuanba, Yuwen Chengdu, Fei Yuanqing, Xiong Kuahai, Wu Yunzhao, and Wu Tianxi) make rather brief appearances in the novel. Moreover, Li Yuanba, warrior number 1, despite being the son of Li Yuan, the so-called "true ruler," is not presented in a flattering light. He is arrogant and ruthless, and he likes to humiliate those who have already fallen victim to his brutal physical power. Since no one can defeat him, he has to defeat himself. The way in which this absolutely invincible warrior meets his unexpected death is revealing: one day, upset by loud thunder and pouring rain, Li Yuanba throws two heavy hammers into the sky, as if he is trying to overpower Heaven. Accidentally, he is crushed by one of the falling hammers. Li Yuanba's tragic death is apparently designed to call the reader's attention to the self-destructiveness of unchecked physical power, as well as the dangers of blind confidence in one's invincibility. Thus the novel's apparent celebration of physical prowess is by no means unqualified.

This blind confidence in one's physical prowess and invincibility is a trait that can also be seen in other warriors. The number 10 warrior, Shang Shitu, eventually loses battles to Qin Shubao and others largely because of it and because he insists on gentlemanly fair play in fighting. Shang's horse, nick-named the Thundering Leopard, roars like thunder and spews black smoke that literally scares an enemy's horse into total dysfunction. This is why Shang is able to capture Cheng Yaojin without much effort. Qin Shubao challenges Shang's manhood when he implies that the horse is the better fighter. Shang Shitu is so confident about his martial skills and so eager to be a "true man" on the battlefield that he agrees to fight Qin on foot, leaving his horse tied to a spear stuck in the ground. Qin, however, gets back on his horse as soon as his friend, Wang Bodang, steals Shang's horse. In order to get his horse back, Shang has to release Cheng Yaojin to Qin. Shang Shitu is foolish enough to accept Qin's assurance that his horse will not be stolen next time and agrees once more to fight Qin on foot, claiming that as a true man he will not go back on his previous word (37.290). Of course, once again, his horse is stolen and he has to retreat. Shang Shitu's defeat is the direct result of his arrogance and his obsession with his self-image as a mas-culine hero. In battle, the pursuit of the empty title of "true man" is shown to be nothing but a fatal mistake. Shang Shitu is also presented as a warrior who personifies loyalty. He commits suicide when cornered by Qin and his troops. His tragic demise is part of the novel's overall effort to problema-tize many conventional virtues associated with masculinity, such as a loyalty and personal honor, that have been celebrated in novels such as *San'guo yanyi, Shuihu zhuan, Suishi yiwen,* and *Sui Tang yanyi.*

The idea of loyalty is also ridiculed in the lengthy account of how Yuchi Gong finally surrenders to Li Shimin. As we briefly mentioned, Yuchi Gong, following the moral maxim that a chaste woman does not marry twice and a loyal minister does not serve two different lords (48.376), has declared that he will surrender to Li Shimin only after his lord, Liu Wuzhou, has died (48.377). By proposing this specific precondition for surrender, Yuchi Gong has already compromised the ethical principle he says he is following by suggesting that a loyal minister can indeed serve another lord. To make this pledge of loyalty more ironic, Yuchi Gong's precondition for surrender eventually leads to the death of Liu Wuzhou. Yuchi Gong sees through Li Shimin's trick of killing Liu Wuzhou's look-alike, but next time, Li Shimin and his people succeed in killing the real Liu Wuzhou and convince Yuchi Gong that the head he is seeing this time is indeed authentic. Only then does Yuchi Gong realize that it is he who has caused the demise of his lord, the very person to whom he swore loyalty (48.388).

Shan Xiongxin is another character who apparently chooses death to prove his loyalty to the King of the Zheng, Wang Shichong. In *Suishi yiwen* and *Sui Tang yanyi*, Li Yuan's accidental killing of Shan's brother was said to be the main reason for Shan Xiongxin's reluctance to join Qin Shubao and his other sworn brothers in switching allegiance to the Tang. While the killing of his brother remains a factor, loyalty to his lord, the King of Zheng, assumes a more significant role in *Shuo Tang*, where Shan becomes the royal brother-in-law of Wang Shichong by marrying his sister. Even after many of his sworn brothers have deserted Wang Shichong, Shan Xiongxin's loyalty remains unwavering. When the cause of Zheng is already lost, Shan Xiongxin, instead of waiting to be arrested by the Tang troops (as is the case in the two previous novels), charges into the Tang camp. (He does so after a heroic farewell to his wife, reminding the reader of Xiang Yu's farewell to his concubine Yu Ji, as discussed in chapter 1.)[30] He kills many enemy soldiers until he is totally exhausted and taken prisoner. In contrast to the two previous novels, Li Shimin never intends to have Shan executed. Instead, he tries all he can to win him over. He even kneels down to beg Shan to surrender. However, Shan Xiongxin is so adamant in his refusal to surrender that Li Shimin is finally persuaded by his adviser, Xu Maogong, to have him executed. Instead of the ritual of cutting flesh from the thighs that we witnessed in the two previous novels, Shan Xiongxin refuses to accept even a farewell toast from his sworn brothers.[31]

All this seems to underscore Shan's inviolable sense of loyalty. However, what has problematized such insistence on loyalty is Shan's unexpected acceptance of a toast from Cheng Yaojin, who remarks, "You should know my character. If I am willing to surrender, then I will. Now you are not willing to surrender; you will be a happy man even after you are cut down. When I die in the future and meet you in hell, I shall admire you as a *haohan* who would rather die than surrender. You should be considered ten times more worthy than those cowards" (56.447). This is ironic because in *Shuo Tang*, Cheng Yaojin is probably the last character to care about the idea of loyalty, a fact he happily acknowledges in his toast to Shan Xiongxin. After he is taken prisoner by Meng Haigong and his troops (who have come to aid the King of Zheng against the Tang army) Cheng Yaojin quickly indicates his willingness to surrender. First he begs Shan Xiongxin for help but is rebuffed. Then he simply declares, "How can you insist on having me executed if I have already surrendered? I am willing to surrender if you spare my life" (54.424).

Cheng Yaojin surrenders so casually because he considers the whole idea of loyalty meaningless. After the death of Luo Cheng, Cheng Yaojin cries, "The Tang family has no conscience. They have no use for us in times of peace. Now when there is a war, they come with that ox-nosed Taoist [Xu Maogong]. They come here, pretending to deliver their condolences just like a cat crying over the death of a mouse. To conquer more areas and to fight for control of the entire country, they are now trying to trick us into fighting for them again" (62.492–493). Cheng Yaojin's seemingly childish complaint demonstrates some surprising insights into the nature of the ruler-minister relationship, based on the unconditional loyalty of the minister, an ideal celebrated with so much enthusiasm in *Suishi yiwen* and especially in *Sui Tang yanyi*. If the illiterate Cheng Yaojin's lack of interest in loyalty is understandable because of his "lowly" background (he is a smuggler and convicted murderer), then the former blacksmith Yuchi Gong's insistence on loyalty becomes even more ironic. This kind of questioning of the virtues conventionally associated with masculinity permeates *Shuo Tang*.

As mentioned, in *Sui Tang yanyi* the emphasis on loyalty is closely associated with female chastity; its author takes great pains to tell his readers how many of Emperor Yang's palace ladies commit suicide or deface themselves in order to prove their chastity. Now in chapter 40 of *Shuo Tang*, two of the palace ladies do not commit suicide for Emperor Yang. Instead, convinced that the emperor's days are numbered and that Li Yuan is the future true ruler, they force Li Yuan to rebel by getting him drunk and then sleeping with him. Li Yuan has no alternative but to rebel; otherwise he will be punished for violating the chastity of the emperor's women. Under the pretense of helping fulfill the mandate of Heaven, chastity is the least of the concerns of these two palace ladies. This purported motive for Li Yuan's rebellion is absurd to the degree of being comic.[32]

Many other women in *Shuo Tang* share a disregard for chastity. One of Meng Haigong's concubines, the black female warrior, initially refuses to surrender after being captured by Yuchi Gong. However, she changes her mind after being forced to sleep with Yuchi Gong. Apparently, Yuchi Gong's sexual prowess wins her over. Soon she decides to help Yuchi Gong capture another of Meng Haigong's concubines, the white female warrior. Finally, both women are married to Yuchi Gong, and female chastity is a nonissue. If his two concubines are "shameless," Meng Haigong's first wife, Ma Saifei, is no better. Overwhelmed by Luo Cheng's handsome appearance, she flirts with him on the battlefield: "What a handsome lad! If only I could sleep with him one night, it should be better than being a queen" (54.425). This scene in *Shuo Tang* is apparently a parody of the episode in which Luo Cheng and Dou Xianniang find love at first sight on horseback in *Sui Tang yanyi*. However, there is no romance here—only sheer lust. In other words, instead of initiating a touching romance as in *Sui Tang yanyi*, the handsome Luo Cheng only draws the unwanted attentions of a wanton woman.

A man's attitude toward his wife/wives is often believed to be an important index to his masculinity, as we found in *San'guo yanyi* and *Shuihu zhuan*. Many *Shuihu* heroes, such as Shi Xiu and Lu Junyi, consider it their manly duty to execute their adulterous wives. In *San'guo yanyi*, a hunter kills his wife merely to serve her flesh to the starving Liu Bei. The readiness to desert or even sacrifice one's wife for the sake of friends or sworn brothers is often considered a measure of a hero's true manhood. Here we may recall Liu Bei's reasoning: "Brothers are like one's own arms and legs, while wives are like clothes. When clothes are worn out, they can be patched up. When one loses an arm or a leg, it cannot be replaced." In both novels, for a masculine hero, a wife never occupies an important position.

In *Shuo Tang,* while the status of a wife still remains quite low, Liu Bei's reasoning becomes the target of subtle derision. When the thirty-six heroes are debating whether they should rescue their imprisoned sworn brothers You Da and Cheng Yaojin, Xu Maogong cautions that some of them may not want to be involved in a rescue mission because it will put their wives and families at risk. Shan Xiongxin, however, assures Xu, "Elder brother, you are wrong. It has been true ever since ancient times that only those men who base their life-and-death decisions on the interests of friends can be considered true heroes. Wealth is something you cannot bring along with you after you have died. One can always remarry if one's wife dies, while a true friend is virtually irreplaceable" (25.196). After the successful rescue of You Da and Cheng Yaojin, Shan Xiongxin learns that his wife and family have been executed by the local official; he gets very angry and demands to know why Xu Maogong failed to take the necessary measures to protect them. Xu answers that he cautioned him before precisely because he anticipated that a tragic end would befall his family. He implies that Shan cannot blame him now since before the rescue mission he said that friends were far more important than wife and family. The irony does not end here, however. Later, as he had insisted that one could always marry another woman if one's wife died, Shan Xiongxin marries the sister of Wang Shichong, the self-styled King of the Zheng. This marriage proves to be fatal since it further ties him to Wang's doomed cause. Shan Xiongxin eventually pays with his own life for his close association with Wang. It is certainly ironic that Shan Xiongxin should die out of loyalty to his brother-in-law while having such a low opinion of the importance of a wife.

As we discussed, in *Suishi yiwen,* one of the cherished masculine virtues is self-restraint and accommodation *(ren).* How to best adapt to the social environment becomes one of the most important issues for a masculine hero. Eventually a famous general for the newly founded Tang dynasty, Qin Shubao can almost be read as a "tamed" and even Confucianized *haohan* from *Shuihu zhuan:* he is brave, loyal, and yet always prudent. The revisionist tendency exhibited in *Suishi yiwen* continues in *Sui Tang yanyi.* Here the rough image of *haohan* from *Shuihu zhuan* is further softened and even sometimes feminized. The dramatic increase in the presence of women in *Sui Tang yanyi* signals a careful reconceptualization of masculinity. Unlike most *Shuihu* heroes, a *haohan* in *Sui Tang yanyi* is first of all a man capable of tender feelings; romantic sentiments, instead of being viewed as liabilities, are now celebrated as a necessary part of the complete image of a masculine hero. In addition, loyalty receives much more emphasis. Between the conflicting values of loyalty and personal honor, the former is now promoted as the more important.

At first glance, *Shuo Tang,* with its refocus on violence and rough masculinity, reads almost like a nostalgic reversion to the original *haohan* models in *Shuihu zhuan.* However, a closer look should convince us that in this novel the pursuit of masculinity itself is often the target of satire and ridicule. In *Shuo Tang,* the heroes are presented in such an exaggerated fashion that many of them become comic and clown-like. It is within this new low mimetic context that many conventional virtues of masculinity celebrated in *Shuihu zhuan, Suishi yiwen,* and *Sui Tang yanyi* are parodied as well as ridiculed.[33] The unprecedented attention devoted to a *haohan's* physical prowess and martial skills is often mixed with a profound suspicion of his ultimate effectiveness, since the top six warriors all die relatively early in the novel. (The number 1 warrior Li Yuanba's self-inflicted death is particularly revealing in this regard.) In fact the significance of the top warriors in the eventual rise of the Tang is far more limited than that of the warriors ranked at the bottom of the hierarchy, such as Qin Shubao. Violence is at least as dominant a phenomenon here as it is in *Shuihu zhuan,* yet comic figures such as Cheng Yaojin tend to make the violence described in *Shuo Tang* considerably less disturbing than it would have otherwise been. Almost as violent as Li Kui in *Shuihu zhuan,* Cheng Yaojin, who is obviously modeled on Li, is much more clownlike. One of the most hilarious scenes in the novel is Cheng Yaojin engaging his enemy in a fight while suffering from diarrhea (he has to relieve himself during the fight; chapter 49); he also bets repeatedly with his enemies on the battlefield (38.300 and 46.361). Compared with Li Kui, Cheng is sometimes even less concerned with the notion of personal honor, or *yi.* (One notable exception is his acknowledgement of his role in a robbery when he learns that Qin Shubao has been beaten by his boss for failing to capture the culprits of the robbery.) He lies and switches allegiances without hesitation. Some of his remarks and observations, though childish and silly, are often surprisingly insightful. There is a child-like element in this clown figure.

Cheng's child-like quality is shared by other warriors in the novel. In fact, several powerful warriors—such as the number 1 warrior, Li Yuanba; the number 3 warrior, Fei Yuanqing; and the number 7 warrior, Luo Cheng (although he is said to be married)—are presented as "kids." Even when some of the warriors are presented as adults, they tend to behave like children: a fight between Cheng Yaojin and Yuchi Gong over a game of chess (chapter 40); Qin Shubao's underhanded killing of Sun Tianyou (Sun becomes invulnerable to knives and swords whenever he recites a spell, and Qin is able to kill him only after tricking him into forgetting to recite the spell; 38.300); and Cheng Yaojin's request that Luo Cheng fake defeat while they are fighting so that Cheng can boast to his peers about how great a warrior he is (50.395). This kind of mischievousness, prevalent in the novel, often makes us feel that we are reading an entertaining story about unruly children or teenage pranksters. Yet these child-like warriors hate being treated like kids. The most humiliating thing for a hero is to be called a brat. For example, those who despise Li Shimin always address him as "the Tang brat." All these heroes want to act like adults, but their pretense is often so awkward and comic that in the end the adult behavior they are imitating also becomes comic and, ultimately, the target of derision.

Related to this children's mimicking of adults is the narrator's apparent delight in touting the uninspiring appearance of his warriors. In contrast to *Suishi yiwen* and *Sui Tang yanyi*, where *haohan* are often admired for their muscular build and other "masculine" physical qualities (although Luo Cheng's feminine appearance is still presented as "sexy"), in *Shuo Tang* the ugliness or even hideousness of the warriors is underscored. Li Yuanba is said to be a twelve-year-old kid with a protruding mouth and hollow cheeks. He is so skinny that he looks like a sick ghost (34.266). Shan Xiongxin, we are told, is also extremely ugly, although in *Suishi yiwen* and *Sui Tang yanyi* his appearance is not an issue.[34] Shan Xiongxin calls Yuchi Gong an "ugly devil" when they first confront each other on the battlefield. Yuchi Gong retorts that although he may indeed be homely, Shan is hardly more appealing, a comment that incenses Shan tremendously (50.394). Here the two warriors are almost engaged in a contest of ugliness.[35] Luo Cheng's handsome appearance, which is celebrated in the two previous novels, is mentioned in *Shuo Tang* only as a cause for the evil thoughts of a lusty female warrior (54.425).

Shuo Tang is different from many other novels about masculine heroes because the implications of masculinity, as presented, can be appreciated only negatively; the novel constantly exposes and satirizes. The novel is a strange mixture of the vivacious innocence typical of folklore and the witty cynicism of a sophisticated literatus. Child-like "genuineness," which was worshiped by many during the late Ming (one of the reasons behind the tremendous popularity of *Shuihu zhuan*), now has become something to be toyed with in a novel by a cynical mid-Qing literati writer.[36]

If *Shuo Tang* has generated many more warrior narratives in the form of sequels and imitations, most of them are less entertaining and less parodic and probably less literati-ized.[37] *Sui Tang yanyi* points to a new trend in the convergence of *wen* and *wu* in the construction of masculine heroes, a convergence that will pick up momentum in some novels of the late eighteenth and early nineteenth centuries (see chapter 8). In the next chapter, we shall explore in detail the *wen* aspect of masculinity as constructed in novels where romantic love figures prominently.

CHAPTER 7

Effeminacy, Femininity, and Male-Male Passions

Thus far we have explored the images of *yingxiong* and *haohan*—mostly *wu* models of masculinity—in novels where political intrigue, military campaigns, and martial exploits are the main themes. As noted, these macho heroes are often defined *against* the feminine, emphasizing their differences and disassociation from women. (*San'guo yanyi* and *Sui Tang yanyi* are exceptions in a limited sense.) Turning to a group of fictional works that focus on romantic love, we find that the images of men become significantly more feminized; the men tend to be less distinguishable from their female counterparts in terms of both appearance and personality. Here masculinity is often defined in close association or juxtaposition with women. It seems that the notion of masculinity suggested in these works is considerably different from that in *San'guo yanyi, Shuihu zhuan, Suishi yiwen,* and *Shuo Tang quanzhuan.* In fact, this feminizing tendency is already evident in *Sui Tang yanyi,* where, the feminine-looking and handsome warrior Luo Cheng shares many traits with the refined young scholars, or *caizi,* celebrated in many scholar-beauty novels very popular during the second half of the seventeenth century.

Important attributes shared by both male and female protagonists in many seventeenth-century scholar-beauty novels are talent and beauty.[1] To qualify as a *caizi,* a young man has to be handsome as well as talented. While talent is largely defined as poetic talent, male beauty, interestingly, is often presented as a feminine quality, and the most handsome scholar is always said to resemble a beautiful woman.[2] While feminine good looks are shared by the *caizi* protagonists in many scholar-beauty novels, feminine male beauty seems to have received special attention in *Liangjiaohun* (Double Marriages). The novel is about how a talented and extremely beautiful brother and sister overcome all obstacles and marry another pair of equally talented and beautiful siblings.

In the novel, the male protagonist, Gan Ji, is repeatedly said to be as beautiful as a boudoir beauty (1.2 and 1.6). Hearing of the beauty and tal-

135

ent of Miss Xin Gucai, he tries desperately to find a way to approach her. Thanks to his beautiful face and romantic demeanor, Gan Ji is soon able to enlist the help of Li Qing, a courtesan acquaintance of Miss Xin's. Li Qing finds Gan Ji simply too attractive to resist: "Li Qing originally thought about pretending not to help him just in order to make him suffer a bit more. However, she simply could not resist the beautiful smiling face that was inching ever closer to her. His sweet voice and tender feelings were just too much for her" (4.43). Overwhelmed by his charm, Li Qing offers her help. Here the conventional gender roles seem to have been reversed: Gan Ji is using his (feminine) sexual charms to seduce the courtesan Li Qing into serving as a go-between for him and Miss Xin.

As if to reaffirm the reversed gender roles, Li Qing suggests that Gan Ji masquerade as a girl; then he will be able to participate in the poetry contests for talented girls and will have a chance to approach the hostess, who sponsors these contests in order to find a bride for her brother. Trying to convince Gan Ji of the feasibility of her plan, Li Qing assures him, "Fortunately, your appearance is even prettier than that of a woman, although your body is that of a man" (5.46).

Miss Xin is equally impressed with the beauty and poetic talent of Gan Ji in feminine disguise, and she simply wishes that "this endearing one could immediately turn into a man" so that she could marry him (5.55). The two soon develop a close relationship, and they become so attached that they are reluctant to say good-bye—as if they were a loving couple trying to delay the moment of farewell (6.57). A modern reader, who is used to the assumed dichotomy between the masculine and the feminine and between the homosexual and the heterosexual, may infer that Li Qing and Miss Xin feel a lesbian attraction toward Gan Ji (Gan Ji is here mistaken to be a woman), although this is not the novelist's point.

After Li Qing tells Miss Xin that the beautiful and talented "girl" she has just met is actually a young man, Miss Xin wonders to herself, "She is so attractive. Where could one find a handsome man as beautiful as this girl?" (7.74). Obviously, this is not a concept of beauty shared only by women. Miss Xin's brother, Xin Jieyun, himself a handsome scholar with an appearance typical of a female beauty, is equally attracted to Gan Ji. A unique interchangeability seems to be assumed between a refined young scholar and a beautiful and talented woman (*jiaren*) (7.70). This interchangeability enhances the compatibility between a *caizi* and a *jiaren*, making the love between them even more romantic. They resemble each other not only in appearance, but also in their love of poetry and their poetic talent. (Poetry is one of the few venues where a girl is allowed to demonstrate her talent and where she and a young scholar can enjoy a compatible standings.) Courtship between *caizi* and *jiaren* in these novels is almost always in the form of poetry exchanges.[3]

Apparently, in the minds of Li Qing and Miss Xin, Gan Gi's masculinity is enhanced by his feminine beauty because these two women perceive little difference between masculine and feminine beauty. A brilliant young scholar's feminine beauty is by no means a sign of effeminacy. In other words, a romantic *caizi* can be very feminine in appearance but not effeminate. There is a subtle but important difference between "femininity" and "effeminacy" in that the former refers to qualities associated with women that, if found in a man, are to his advantage, while the latter is an attribute that diminishes a man's manliness. A man can appear feminine but still be very competent in his manly duties, such as being a good official or even a brave and virile warrior. In *Liangjiaohun*, Gan Ji, despite or because of his feminine beauty, never doubts that he is a true man (7.73), nor have his feminine looks caused others to consider him less of one (1.3).

Gan Ji's manliness is never in doubt, not the least because Miss Xin is supposed to be the last woman who would fall in love with a man whose masculinity could be questioned. As proof of Miss Xin's unusual insights in judging the manliness of a *caizi* (an ability by no means inconsistent with her taste for feminine-looking scholars), the reader is told that she was once able to pass an extremely accurate judgement on a young scholar just by reading his essays (without seeing him in person). The son of one of her father's close friends, this young scholar has successfully passed the provincial examinations, and his father wants him to marry Miss Xin. Her father is quite impressed with the young scholar's examination essays, but Miss Xin, after reading these same essays, concludes, "Although his writing is impressive on the surface, one can tell from it that [the author's] virility [*jing*] has already been worn out, and so has [his] male energy [*qi*]. . . . His success in the national examinations is unlikely" (3.29). Later, this young man, as Miss Xin has predicted, dies as a result of excessive indulgence in wine and sex. Apparently, Miss Xin has an uncanny knack for evaluating a man's "male essence." Symbolically, this episode seems to suggest that Gan Ji's feminine appearance is anything but an attribute compromising his masculinity since Miss Xin, an expert on "male essence," has done nothing but complement this *caizi* for his stunning beauty and poetic talent.

Cross-dressing is a common motif in the scholar-beauty novel, although it is usually a girl who masquerades as a man in order to pursue her ideal lover or to escape from an unwanted marriage or family disaster.[4] A maiden's adventures outside the confines of her boudoir are "transgressions" that are often needed to make a romantic story more dramatic and exciting. At the same time, cross-dressing makes such transgressions less liable to moral censorship at a time when sex segregation was the norm. The fact that cross-dressing had become such a favorite plot device for so many writers of the scholar-beauty novel also points to the more fluid gender boundaries in contemporary culture, as noted above (although gender fluidity did not necessarily translate into gender equality). In other words, without the assumed interchangeability between feminine and masculine looks, such masquerading would have appeared too implausible to contemporary readers. In *Liangjiaohun,* Gan Ji's ability to pass himself off as a girl is eloquent testimony to this perceived gender fluidity.

Even in the few scholar-beauty novels that emphasize the martial prowess of the male protagonists—most works in this genre tend to focus on literary talent—the men's feminine beauty is presented as a masculinity to be celebrated with great enthusiasm. Take the famous *Haoqiu zhuan* (The Ideal Mates), for example. Its male protagonist, Tie Zhongyu, is a martial arts specialist, and despite his Confucian learning and poetic talent, he is almost a *haohan*-type of character with a chivalrous heart. At the same time, he is presented as a handsome young scholar with a girlish appearance.[5]

In another work from approximately the same period, *Huatu yuan* (The Romance of the Two Magical Maps), the male protagonist, He Tianhua, is said to be a beautiful man (there is repeated emphasis on his fair skin; 1.4).[6] His beauty is again compared to that of a young woman (2.15). Later he meets an even more feminine-looking young man, Liu Qingyun, and helps him and his family to fight off the local bullies who are trying to take advantage of them. Soon these two young men become close friends. It seems that one important aspect of He Tianhua's attachment to Liu Qingyun is his admiration of Liu's feminine beauty; he is quite adamant in letting Liu know of his admiration:

> He Tianhua said, "I have something on my mind that I want to mention to you. But I am afraid you might be offended."
>
> "When two best friends talk to each other, they should be able to say whatever is on their minds. Why should you be afraid of speaking out?" replied Liu Qingyun.
>
> He Tianhua said, "Since Brother Liu doesn't mind, I will speak my mind. As far as I know, Pan An and Wei Jie are supposed to have been the two most beautiful scholars ever since ancient times. However, in my view, they cannot compare with you." (5.60)

Later He Tianhua has to resist sleeping in the same bed with Liu for the curious reason that others will become suspicious, apparently because Liu Qingyun is just too beautiful (5.61). Furthermore, He Tianhua repeatedly swears to Liu Qingyun that he can only marry a girl who is as beautiful as he, seeing little difference between feminine and masculine beauty. Although absolutely nothing happens between the two, a modern reader is once again likely to suspect a possible homoerotic relationship here (more on this point below).

In fact, Liu Qingyun is meant to be a surrogate for his twin sister in the courtship between her and He Tianhua. Though an excellent essay writer, Liu Qingyun is not a great poet.[7] To exchange poems with He, he has to have help from his sister, who often serves as his ghostwriter. In actuality, it is his sister who is engaged in the poetry exchange with He Tianhua. Liu Qingyun is only acting as a double in this ritual of courtship on behalf of his sister. Eventually the true identity of the author of these brilliant poems is revealed, and He is able to marry the real poet.

According to the narrator, He Tianhua is unusual in that, in addition to being a feminine-looking *caizi*, he also possesses tremendous martial prowess and is considered a man of outstanding ability and great aspirations (*haojie;* 1.5). Despite his impressive book learning and literary skills, he aspires to achieve fame on the battlefield rather than in the examination hall. After successfully passing the provincial examinations, he initially refuses to take the national examinations because he does not want to become a civil official (11.133). Eventually, He Tianhua achieves glory both on the battlefield and in the examination hall. Thereafter he marries Liu Qingyun's sister, who is said to be as beautiful as her brother, and he thus fulfills his earlier wish to only marry a girl who is as beautiful as Liu Qingyun. He Tianhua, a feminine-looking *caizi* who also possesses characteristics typical of *wu* masculinity, points to a significantly new notion of masculinity that I shall explore in detail in chapter 8.

In many works of Ming-Qing fiction, feminine male beauty is an attribute associated not only with refined scholars *(shusheng),* but also with men in other professions who are not necessarily distinguished by their book learning. For example, in "The Pearl Shirt Reencountered," the first story in Feng Menglong's *Yushi mingyan* (Clear Words to Instruct the World), the male protagonist, a merchant, is described as having dark brows, fine eyes, white teeth, and ruby lips.[8] In *Shuihu zhuan*, Zhang San, a government clerk who has an affair with Song Jiang's woman, is presented as an attractive young man in exactly the same words.[9] In this same novel, Yan Qing, who has turned the head of the famous courtesan Li Shishi, is also described as a handsome young man with fair skin and a pretty face. That is, a "sexy" man is often feminine in appearance. Such feminine sexiness in a man tends to be more emphasized in a romantic story, while in less romantic contexts, feminine looks are less likely to be considered an important aspect of male beauty. For example, in *San'guo yanyi* Guan Yu represents a quite different type of male beauty. He is tall and known for his long, beautiful beard. Of course, Guan Yu is presented as a famous warrior. In fact, he is known for his ability to resist sexual temptation, and he is certainly the last person the reader would associate with a romantic situation.[10]

Male Same-Sex Love and Masculinity

The image of feminine *caizi* continues to dominate the romantic novels of later ages; among them the nineteenth-century *Pinhua baojian* (A Precious Mirror for Grading Flowers), by Chen Sen (fl. mid-nineteenth century), is probably the only full-length traditional Chinese novel that focuses on male-male love. The novel's central story line evolves around a torturous love affair between the actor/female impersonator Du Qinyan and the young scholar Mei Ziyu. Here the celebration of male feminine beauty reaches an unprecedented scale, and what constitutes it is a topic of serious debate among the characters.

The novel opens with a lengthy discussion between Mei Ziyu and his friends about the relationship between male and female beauties. Presented with a book describing and grading the top female impersonators in the capital, Mei Ziyu insists that he simply cannot believe that men (including even the most charming female impersonators) can ever be more beautiful than women because the former are affected while the latter are natural. Citing many examples from history, his friends, however, point out that ever since ancient times, words such as *meiren* and *jiaren,* both of which mean "beautiful person," have been used to refer to both handsome men and beautiful women. They argue that beauty is not exclusively possessed by the female sex (1.12).[11] To support their arguments, they refer to phenomena beyond the human world; for example, they point out that the part of a plant that faces the sun *(yang)* tends to grow faster and be more luxuriant than the part in the shade *(yin),* which grows more slowly and tends to wither more easily. Of course, *yang* is usually associated with the male gender in Chinese cultural discourse. Furthermore, the friends remind Mei that among animals it is often the males that are more colorful as well as more beautiful, as in the case of peacocks.[12] Contrary to Mei Ziyu's view, they believe that a beautiful woman who relies on powder and rouge is less natural than a beautiful man. Furthermore, they point to Mei Ziyu himself as a ready example of an extremely handsome man and ask him to compare himself with any of his maids to see who is the most beautiful. Quite aware of his own beauty, Mei Ziyu seems persuaded. Obviously, neither side in this debate distinguishes between "masculine" and "feminine" beauty, and the lack of distinction is a premise few question.[13]

This debate provides the general framework within which the novel's models of masculinity are to be constructed and contested. More important, the emphasis on the compatibility between feminine and masculine beauty will serve as the theoretical justification for deemphasizing differences between heterosexual and same-sex love, as declared by a *caizi* character, Tian Chunhang, who is in love with the female impersonator Su Huifang: "I really don't understand why people nowadays consider it normal for men to love women [*nüse;* more literally, female beauty] and think it strange for men to love men [*nanse,* or male beauty]. If one really loves beauty, why should he make any distinction between male and female beauty? If one loves female beauty but not male beauty, then what he has is lust rather than a genuine love of beauty [*haose*]. If he is lustful, then beauty is simply not important to him" (12.170). At the opening of the first chapter (1.1), the narrator underscores *qing* (passion, love, affection) as the novel's central thematic concern and defines it as a deep love of beauty devoid of lust *(haose buyin)*. In chapter 24, Mei Ziyu's cousin, Yan Zhongqing, delivers a lengthy speech on the relationship between *qing* and *haose*, pronouncing that only those who can love beauty without lust are capable of genuine passion (24.337).[14]

In sum, to love beauty without lust becomes an important rationale for the special attachments among males in the novel. Completely different from men who physically lust after other men (no lack of such examples in the novel), the gentlemen of genuine passions, such as Mei Ziyu and his peers, love the female impersonators in *almost* a purely aesthetic way. The rich and chivalrous *caizi* Xu Ziyun "regards these female impersonators as rare treasures, precious birds, or celebrated flowers. For them he has only tender feelings but no lecherous intentions" (5.65). The following is his explanation to his wife about what is so marvelous about female impersonators: "Of course, in your eyes, girls are more beautiful. But we can never go to a party with girls because it will look too vulgar. What is so unique about a female impersonator is that he has the face of a girl but not her body. He not only pleases your eyes [*yumu*], but also disciplines your mind. He gives you pleasure but instills in you no lust. Isn't this perfect?" (11.151).

Female impersonators are better than "real" women because they are the purified version of the feminine, like a work of art that gives a man only aesthetic pleasures and will not lead him astray, as a seductive "real" woman would. Of course, in the novel, Xu Ziyun is presented as a pure aesthete who relishes beautiful things and beautiful men as well as beautiful women. Extremely generous, he is always ready to help female impersonators in distress, even though some of them, such as Du Qinyan, are the lovers of other men. After all, he has paid a huge amount of money to buy out Du's "contract" with the wife of his master.[15] Xu's magnificent garden, a grand world of aesthetic beauty, often serves as a refuge for female impersonators trying to escape from the unaesthetic world of lust. The literati lovers of female impersonators are passionate connoisseurs of great art works, as suggested by the title of the novel. The word *pin* (grading and appreciating) in the title captures the nature of the relationship between these self-proclaimed connoisseurs and the artifacts (flowers or female impersonators) they collect.[16]

Tian Chunhang offers a lengthy speech on the aesthetic principles behind the literati connoisseurship of female impersonators:

This is just like [appreciating] seasonal flowers or beautiful women, the gorgeous moon or graceful clouds, marvelous books or famous paintings. These are extremely beautiful toys [*wanhao*] that every one is crazy about.... These female impersonators are like seasonal flowers, but they are not plants; they are like exquisite jade, but they do not rely on makeup; they are like the gorgeous moon or graceful clouds, but they are reachable and can be played with; they are like marvelous books or famous paintings, but they have a voice and can talk; they are like exquisite toys, but they are capable of an infinite number of charming gestures and mannerisms. (12.169)

An important term in Tian Chunhang's speech is *wanhao,* which, for lack of a better equivalent in English, I have translated as "toys." Separately, *wan* means "play," and "study" or "appreciate," and *hao* means "things that one loves" or "hobby." Consequently, *wanhao* can be understood both as something that one loves to play with as a hobby and something one can spend a long time appreciating and studying. This word also betrays the condescension in this connoisseurship. No matter how great or beautiful the female impersonators are, they are nevertheless "things" (objectified) rather than human beings with whom the *caizi* will stand on a completely equal footing —despite the fact that many *caizi* have repeatedly emphasized their respect for them. They are toys or pets to be cherished, but they still belong to a category or class much below their *caizi* lovers.

In remarks quoted previously, Xu Ziyun emphasized a female impersonator's ability to please the eyes *(yumu).* Here the word *yumu* connects to a conversation between Mei Ziyu and his friends at the beginning of the novel: Shi Nanxiang asks Mei Ziyu, "What can please your eyes and ears the most and move and intoxicate you most?" After Mei Ziyu complains that the question is too general, Shi Nanxiang tries to be more specific, saying that he is referring to a particular kind of people. Mei Ziyu replies that probably a few best friends can please one another most. However, this reply provokes laughter from his friends. Shi Nanxiang even pretends that he is insulted: "What nonsense! How can friends please one another? You must have evil thoughts in your mind." Then he presents Mei Ziyu with a collection of poems that carefully grade all the top female impersonators in the capital, telling him that these are the people who can please one's eyes and ears (1.4–5). Shi Nanxiang is obviously making a clear distinction between female impersonators and friends. Only female impersonators can be appreciated because they, like artifacts, can please one's senses; one's friends, who are one's intellectual peers and from the same social class, cannot be so objectified. The former are things *(wu)* to be desired, while the latter are people who have desires. Of course, in a patriarchal system, a female impersonator, the object of desire, is always relegated to the position of a woman.

The most feminine as well as the most beautiful female impersonator is Du Qinyan, who is often said to be more feminine and beautiful than a beautiful woman.[17] As noted above, Du Qinyan captivates Mei Ziyu. To complicate matters, Mei Ziyu, though definitely a desiring male subject in his relationship with Du Qinyan, is also presented as a feminine-looking male beauty (1.2) who is said to have tremendous appeal to both men and women. When he walks in the streets, women flirt with him (9.124). At the same time, Du Qinyan's love for Mei can also be attributed in large part to his stunning feminine looks (22.320). Mei Ziyu is feminine not only in appearance, but also in personality. When asked about his relationship with Du Qinyan, Mei Ziyu is "as shy as a boudoir maiden peeping at people from behind a screen" (15.215). During the night of the Lantern Festival, a woman accidentally bumps into Mei Ziyu; to avoid falling, she grabs him by the chest. Mei Ziyu is a scared by this contact as if he were a boudoir maiden who had been taken advantage of by a man in the street (9.125). When frustrated in his relationship with Du Qinyan, Mei Ziyu can only "wash his face with tears" or simply get ill.

There are indeed a few moments in the novel when Mei Ziyu's manhood is questioned. One day, after being separated from Du Qinyan for a long time, Mei Ziyu has a dream about meeting him in a boat on a river. After exchanging a few words, Du sits on his lap and leans against him. All this makes Mei Ziyu feels uneasy. All of a sudden, the Du Qinyan in his arms is transformed into a real young woman (probably a prostitute). Alarmed, Mei tries to struggle free, but he is totally powerless. This woman tells him that the love between a man and a woman is as natural as Heaven and Earth and holds him even tighter. When he yells for help, the woman becomes very upset:

> "You fool! Why are you yelling? How on earth can a woman take advantage of a man?"
>
> "What are you trying to do to me?" asked Ziyu.
>
> "I only want to show my love for your beauty and talent," says the woman. "You are a man. How could you be so incompetent in this business?"

Just at this moment of total helplessness, Du Qinyan reappears, and Mei Ziyu again yells for help. Angered, the woman pushes him away, yelling: "I didn't expect to meet such a bookworm in this world! What an outrage!" (53.776). Mei Ziyu's timidity apparently makes the woman wonder about his manhood, and she even begins to suspect that Mei Ziyu cannot function sexually.[18] This incident will become more significant later, when Mei Ziyu is to marry his female cousin, Miss Wang Qionghua. Mei Ziyu convinces himself that his bride is lovable largely because she looks like Du Qinyan. This is why, the narrator tells us, "Mei Ziyu does not behave like that bookworm in the dream. If he had repeated his performance in that dream, Miss Qinghua would have been really upset" (54.790). It seems that Mei Ziyu's masculinity can only be proven by showing that he can function in a heterosexual relationship. Thus the novelist feels obligated to arrange for his protagonist to marry Miss Wang Qionghua; since Mei Ziyu cannot marry Du Qinyan and since he is a man, Heaven takes pity on him and creates a girl who bears a great resemblance to Du (54.769–670). Of course, marrying and carrying on the family line (procreation) was an important part of a man's Confucian duty at that time. By demonstrating that Mei Ziyu is more than capable of fulfilling this important manly duty, the novelist assures the reader of the masculinity of his feminine-looking male protagonist.

The same is true of Tian Chunhang. After the death of his first wife, Tian eventually marries a girl who resembles his male lover, the female imper-sonator Su Huifang. In contrast to Mei Ziyu, Tian Chunhang has demon-strated many masculine qualities, even though he is also as beautiful as a girl. Unlike Mei Ziyu, who guards his chastity vigilantly (*shoushen ruyu;* 1.3), Tian Chunhang squanders all his money in the pleasure quarters, and he considers that being free with money is an important quality of a true man (12.170). Unlike Mei Ziyu, who seems to have never been bothered by any physical desire in his relationship with Du Qinyan, Tian Chunhang some-times has to work hard to suppress his physical longings in the presence of Su Huifang (14.196).[19] It is under the benign influence of Su Huifang that Tian begins to reform and devote himself to diligent study. His relationship with Su Huifang is also quite different from that between Mei Ziyu and Du Qinyan. Tian Chunfang is persuaded to marry Miss Su Wanlan in part because he is told that while his bride resembles Su Huifang, the "real" woman is even more charming and more delicate than the impersonator: "Meixiang [Su Huifang] is a man after all, and he cannot be as delicate as a woman" (49.708). After marrying Miss Su Wanlan, Tian suggests to Su Hui-fang that he should get married too. Indeed Su seems to develop a roman-tic relationship with Sister Three, one of Tian's maids (49.714–716). This is quite different from the case of Du Qinyan, who continues to study with Mei Ziyu (as Mei's father has instructed) after the latter has married Miss Wang Qionghua. There is no hint that Du Qinyan is going to marry any woman. Instead, he remains "faithful" to Mei Ziyu (as a chaste woman is expected to do), while "fidelity" does not seem to be an important issue in Su Huifang's relationship with Tian Chunfang.

At the end of the novel, the reader is told that Mei Ziyu is the happiest man on earth since he now has a charming wife at home and a beautiful friend outside (60.883), implying that heterosexual marriage and male-male love can coexist among the three.[20] Miss Wang Qionghua never seems to have felt uneasy about her husband's relationship with another man. Instead, she admires the deep *qing* between the two men—"Probably he loves him only because he appreciates his beauty and nothing else" (29.414; see also 54.790)—and she is convinced that there is absolutely nothing physical going on between them. Obviously, this happy and harmonious relation among the three reads like a fantasy invented by the novelist, an imaginative solution to the problem created by the different demands of the heterosexual and the homosexual (although the love between Mei Ziyu and Du Qinyan is almost completely Platonic).

In this novel, one's masculinity appears to have very little to do with one's manly appearance.[21] In fact, as in many scholar-beauty novels, a masculine appearance is often assigned to the "negative" characters in *Pinhua baojian*. For example, Xi Shiyi, a bully who tries to rape Du Qinyan, is tall, muscular, and has an air of invincibility (3.35). This kind of macho man can attract only vulgar women, such as Chrysanthemum, a prostitute (18.267). The male beauty celebrated in the novel is "refined gracefulness" and a feminine charm, which, according to these *caizi* connoisseurs, depends on one's cultural refinement and literary sophistication (5.69). Reading books and composing poetry are activities largely conducted inside the home, the domestic space where the presence of women is much more likely (women are closely associated with domesticity, or *nei*).[22] The more one can afford to study or engage in intellectual activities inside the home, instead of working in the fields in the sun or doing other manual labor, the more likely it is that one will have fair skin, a badge of membership in the social elite. Feminine male beauty is a token of cultural sophistication and elite social status. This explains in part why femininity is praised as an important element of the male beauty celebrated in the novel.

Close association with the feminine, however, does not prevent these *caizi* from proving their masculinity by achieving success in the civil examinations and becoming important governmental officials—the ultimate proofs of a man's manhood in late imperial China. Tian Chunhang achieves the top honors in the regular national examinations, which are held every three years, while the more feminine Mei Ziyu achieves even more: he wins the number one prize in the special national examinations held every ten years—an achievement much more glorious than that of the more masculine Tian. This is a subtle but important difference, and one female character deliberately reminds Mei Ziyu's fiancée Wang Qionghua of it (54.780).

Consequently, in *Pinhua baojian*, although many qualities that a modern reader would consider feminine are often admired in a man, people have definite notions of masculinity that are closely associated with the broad concept of *wen* in terms of cultural sophistication (refined literary and artistic tastes, poetic talent, an ability to appreciate beautiful things without lust, and success in the civil examinations).[23] Since certain aspects of cultural sophistication are not inherently masculine (such as refined literary and artistic tastes) and women could at least in theory aspire to them, the boundaries of masculinity in the novel are not always stable. The late imperial Chinese patriarchal system, however, seldom allowed this instability to materialize into meaningful social practice. For example, the social constraints upon women made cultural sophistication almost always an exclusively male achievement. No matter how "pure" Mei Ziyu's relationship is with Du Qin-yan, Mei has to be given the polygamous privilege of a male—he can marry a woman while keeping his male lover as "best friend." No matter how "equal" the relationship between Tian Chunhang and Su Huifang is said to be, Su can only marry one of Tian's maids since as a female impersonator, Su Huifang is condemned to being socially inferior to Tian. The heterosexual gender hierarchies have to be reproduced in the context of same-sex love.[24]

The Reluctance to Be an Adult: Confucian Masculinity Critiqued

As many readers have pointed out, *Pinhua baojian* is deeply indebted to the eighteenth-century classic novel *Honglou meng,* whose male protagonist, Jia Baoyu, is arguably the most famous feminine male protagonist in Chinese literature.[25] A brief look at this famous predecessor of *Pinhua baojian* should allow us to better appreciate the possible different implications of masculinity as they are presented in these two novels. Although both works deal with same-sex love, in *Honglou meng* heterosexual passions are far more prominent.

Like Mei Ziyu, Jia Baoyu is handsome, frail, and feminine-looking; like Mei Ziyu, once he is almost "raped" by a lustful woman (after a visit to the sick Qingwen [Skybright] in chapter 78), although Mei's fearful experience takes place in a dream; when frustrated in love, Jia also gets sick. However, Jia Baoyu appears "feminine" in many different ways, and he likes to participate in girls' activities: he loves to run errands for his female cousins and maids; he is an expert in the arts of makeup and dressing. Quite unlike Mei Ziyu, Jia Baoyu, raised among female relatives and maids, openly praises girls at the expense of boys. Even his close relationships with several young men, such as Qin Zhong and the female impersonator Jiang Yuhan, can be understood as an expression of his admiration for the feminine since all these men, like himself, look feminine.

A much more significant difference is Jia Baoyu's insistence on remaining a child. One of the textual problems associated with the novel are the inconsistencies in Jia Baoyu's age. By carefully studying the complicated history of the novel, some scholars have suggested that age inconsistencies might have been the result of the novelist's repeated attempts to lower the ages of many of his important characters in the long process of rewriting and revision. I have argued elsewhere that the novelist's attempts to make his characters younger parallel a more subtle reluctance on the part of the male protagonist to grow up. Throughout the first eighty chapters of the novel, Jia Baoyu tries to convince himself and others that he is still a child and that he should be allowed to stay with his young female relatives.[26] There is a profound fear of, and strong suspicion about, adulthood in the novel. Jia Baoyu tries desperately to postpone his inevitable growing up by whiling away his time among his female cousins and maids and by refusing to study and prepare for the civil service examinations (as Mei Ziyu successfully did), the most important undertaking of an educated man at that time.

Much has been said about Jia Baoyu's problematic gender identity.[27] However, we have yet to take into serious consideration his apparent reluctance to grow up in our examination of his gender identity and sexual orientation. Jia Baoyu's first sexual experience takes place rather early in the novel (at the beginning of chapter 6), and, curiously enough, this is his only sexual experience for the first eighty chapters—as if sex is not worth another trial (a symbolic rejection of what the adult world is all about?).[28] Not too long after this first sexual experience, Jia Baoyu discovers that his pageboy is mimicking what he has just done by having sex with one of the maids. Not upset at all that his servant is disregarding the rules of the household, he is bothered only by the fact that his pageboy should do this without knowing the maid's name or age. For Jia Baoyu, knowing the "identity" of one's sexual partner is much more important than the sexual act itself. Such a view of sexual relationships is either childish or very sophisticated.

For the first two-thirds of the novel, the reader often wonders whether this is a story about the emotional entanglements of adolescent boys and girls (although there are moments when the implications of adulthood are difficult to miss). Jia Baoyu's "femininity" often appears to have been the result of his being a "child" rather than anything else. For example, like Mei Ziyu, he is easily scared. However, we are told that precisely because he is easily scared, like a typical pampered child, Baoyu always has someone (often his maid) sleep in his bedroom during the night. Sometimes, he will climb into the arms of his mother or grandmother. Furthermore, Baoyu's tumultuous relationship with his cousin Lin Daiyu is largely defined by its adolescent characteristics.

Baoyu's emotional attachment to male characters in the novel seems different from what is usually considered homoerotic since there is hardly anything adult-like in their relationships (not to mention anything physical). More important, such relationships are often nurtured in the context of the adolescent, although the world of physical desire is never far away. For example, the attachment between Baoyu and Qin Zhong is first of all a relationship between two young children, but some readers have referred to Baoyu's remarks that he will "settle accounts" with Qin Zhong during the night upon capturing Qin making love to a young nun; the narrator coyly states that he does not know how the account is finally settled. However, it is difficult to imagine that anything physical could be going on since the reader is specifically told there are many nannies and maids sleeping on the floor in the same room that night, although Baoyu and Qin are supposed to sleep in the same bed (15.207).[29] Even in an account of fighting in the clan school in chapter 9, the mischievous behavior typical of children dominates the scene, and the homoerotic implications of the incident do not necessarily involve Qin Zhong or Baoyu. Furthermore, even if we read this episode as evidence of homoerotic tendencies in these two characters, there are absolutely no references to "chastity" or "jealousy" in their relationship (for example, Qin Zhong is apparently trying to make friends with another boy in the clan school) as we are accustomed to seeing in many Ming-Qing homoerotic stories (including Mei Ziyu's relationship with Du Qinyan in *Pinhua baojian*).

The novel's adult male world—represented by characters such as Jia Rui (Baoyu's distant relative), Jia Lian (Baoyu's cousin), and Jia Zhen (Baoyu's cousin)—is a world of incompetence, greed, corruption, and debauchery. If masculinity refers to the qualities typical of mature adult men, then it is the very qualities with which Baoyu dreads being associated. Reluctant to grow up, Baoyu deliberately refuses to become a man. In a way, we can read the novel as a critique of the notion of masculinity itself: it shows that the world of adult men (together with the cherished masculine dreams of success in the civil service examinations and in an official career) is a world one should avoid as much as possible. Baoyu even tries to stop his nephew, Jia Lan, from practicing "archery and equitation" with the excuse that he might hurt himself physically (26.365). This may remind him of the kind of martial masculinity promoted by the Manchu government (even though the novelist never makes explicit reference to the historical setting of the story). Baoyu also expresses serious doubts about the long-cherished Confucian masculine ideal that a true man dies for the sake of loyalty, or "a scholar dies remonstrating, and a soldier dies fighting" *(wen sijian wu zhansi)*.[30] He considers such acts the crazy behavior of a "whiskered idiot" (36.493). His dream is to remain a carefree child forever, so that gender differentiation is the least of his concerns. In many ways, *Honglou meng*'s suspicions about "masculinity" remind one of the somewhat similar stance adopted in *Shuo Tang* (discussed in chapter 6), despite the obvious fact that the latter is a vastly different work with totally different thematic concerns (not to mention its hilarious parodies).

Effeminacy and Femininity in a Larger Cultural Context

Jia Baoyu's intimate and close relationships with other men and Mei Ziyu's torturous love with Du Qinyan, as well as their shared feminine characteristics, are likely to lead one to wonder whether these characteristics are related to their interest in other men. In a study of late imperial Chinese sexuality, Wu Cuncun argues that the popularity of male "homosexuality" *(tongxing lian)* in Ming-Qing society might have contributed significantly to what she considers to be an increasingly effeminate image of men in the fiction of the period:

Many studies have demonstrated that there is no absolute causal link between homosexuality and cross-dressing and that most male homosexuals do not exhibit the tendency to mimic women. However, homosexuality in traditional China, which was often an unequal sexual relationship between masters and servants or between a male prostitute and his client, is quite different from the kind of egalitarian homosexual relationship typical of modern times. In traditional China, male prostitutes always presented themselves as "women."[31]

Wu's argument seems to be supported by the common impression that the so-called submissive/passive partner in a male-male relationship in various written sources from traditional China is always presented as more feminine in both appearance and manners. Moreover, modern scholars are almost unanimous about the distinctly hierarchical nature of Chinese male "homosexual" tradition (although there were significant exceptions to the norm). There were two basic sets of complementary roles—dominant/submissive and active/passive—and they were determined by three closely interrelated factors: gender, age, and status.[32] In a homoerotic relationship, the submissive (often passive as well) party was almost always a *younger* man who was assumed to be *more* feminine and who tended to be from a *lower* social stratum. This hierarchical pattern seems to have been especially prominent in relations involving male prostitutes and female impersonators, whose sexual appeal often depended on their feminine looks and mannerisms. This is confirmed by several works of vernacular fiction that focus on homoeroticism, such as *Bian er chai* (A Cap beneath the Hairpin; a late Ming collection of homoerotic short stories) and *Pinhua baojian,* under discussion here.[33] In his study of legal cases from late imperial China, Mathew Sommer discusses how penetration was an important engendering act in a man-man sexual relationship in that the penetrated was often considered "feminine" and supposed to assume the social role of a woman; he was often younger and from a lower social class. At the same time, the penetrator was often considered the masculine partner, and in a consensual relationship, he was always the socially superior.[34]

More specifically, Wu Cuncun seems to be arguing that the general fascination with feminine-looking men was a result of the admiration for the passive/submissive lovers in an unequal homosexual relationship. These lovers, in order to please their active/dominant partners, had to make themselves more attractive by presenting themselves as "women," while "real" women were always characterized by their submissiveness and weaker position in traditional Chinese society. To accept this rather totalizing argument we first have to come up with answers for some obvious but difficult questions: Given that a man in a "heterosexual" relationship at that time was supposed to dominate and be pleased rather than to please, why should women admire in a man the qualities associated with the passive and dominated in a male-to-male relationship? Moreover, why should men admire men such as Jia Baoyu and Mei Ziyu for their feminine looks if Jia and Mei are supposed to be "desiring subjects" rather than "desired objects" owing to their higher social positions?

In fact, feminine male beauty had been in vogue long before the Ming-Qing period, which Wu Cuncun considers to be the time when "homosexuality" became widespread and when the concept of male beauty was most likely to have been influenced by the vogue of "homosexual" feminine males. Historians have long noted the fascination with feminine male beauty in the cultural discourse during the Six Dynasties (317–588). It appears that sometime before the Six Dynasties—probably starting with the late Eastern Han dynasty (25–220)—male beauty began to receive increasing attention; at least we begin to see many more references to handsome men in the writings from this period. In these writings, a handsome man has fine eyes and brows *(ming meimu)*, a beautiful beard *(mei xuran)*, and a sonorous voice.[35] We should note that this period overlapped with the Three Kingdoms Period, when the cult of *yingxiong,* or heroes, was in full swing (as discussed in chapter 5). This somewhat masculine image was gradually replaced by a more feminine image in the cultural discourse of the following periods, and it was characterized by a fair complexion and graceful figure. Handsome men were now often called "men of jade."[36] Some of these beautiful men were said to be so delicate physically that they could hardly stand the weight of the light clothes they were wearing. For example, the following is Ji Shao's description of Zhao Jingzhen; it is quoted by Liu Xiaobiao in his notes to "Yanyu," in *Shishuo xinyu* (A New Account of Tales of the World), a famous anthology of anecdotes on the literati of the Six Dynasties attributed to Liu Yiqing (403–444): "Zhi [Zhao Jingzhen] was seven feet and three inches tall. He had fair skin, dark black hair, ruby lips, and fine eyes. He did not have much beard, and his manners were quiet. Physically he was so delicate that he could hardly stand the weight of the clothes he was wearing."[37] Almost all the legendary figures of male beauty celebrated for their feminine looks in Ming-Qing literature, such as Pan An (also known as Pan Yue) and Wei Jie (as mentioned by He Tianhua in *Huatu yuan;* quoted above), were from this period.[38]

The obsession with feminine male beauty certainly did not begin with the Six Dynasties. We can find references from even much earlier ages to such a fascination, albeit often in a derogatory context. For example, in the writings attributed to Xunzi (ca. 312–230 BCE) we find the following:

> It is the custom of the anarchic masses of the present day for the "smart" youth of every village to be beautifully elegant and seductively fascinating. They wear striking clothing with effeminate decorations and are as soft and as weak as young girls. Married women once all hoped to get such a man for a husband. Unmarried girls all hope to get one of them as their knight and would even be willing to abandon their father's house so that they could elope with him and

take the wife's position at his side. Nonetheless, the average lord would be ashamed to have them as ministers, the average father to have them as sons, and the average man to have them as friends.[39]

According to Xunzi, these effeminate "smart" youths, despite the disapproval of many men, seemed to have a particular appeal to women. For the women at that time, a "sexy" man was probably someone with feminine looks or mannerisms. This may explain in part why in traditional literature on romantic love a "sexy" man is always presented as feminine in appearance. Here this fascination with feminine male beauty seems to have nothing to do with same-sex love. If Xunzi's account is credible, this concept of feminine male beauty might have reflected the desires of many women at that time. To accurately describe the relationship between same-sex love and the fascination with feminine male beauty in Ming-Qing cultural discourse is not easy since the distinctions between the heterosexual and homosexual in traditional China were by no means clear.

Inspired by Michel Foucault's influential theories about "the modern invention of sexuality," several cultural historians have demonstrated that in many European countries up until the eighteenth century "men did not define themselves in their sexual behavior, whether homosexual or heterosexual."[40] According to Randolph Trumbach, "In European society before 1700 probably most males felt desire for both males and females. Adult men expressed this by having sexual relations with both adolescent males and with women." However, this began to change around 1700. Increasingly sodomites were considered a "third gender," and men "were now supposed to be either exclusively homosexual or heterosexual. The majority of men now desired only women," while "homosexuals" were increasingly identified as "effeminate" since only women desired men (of course there are other feminizing factors).[41] Trumbach's account of the association of "effeminacy" with the formation of "homosexuals" in European history seems to have lent support to Wu Cuncun's argument with regard to traditional China. However, the concept of a "third gender," later known as "homosexuals," did not gain prevalence in Chinese cultural discourse until the early twentieth century, when Western cultural values and Western medical science began to acquire a hegemonic status in China.[42] In fact, same-sex love in pre-eighteenth-century Europe as described by Trumbach and others bears a certain resemblance to the situation in traditional China, where many men desired both women and other men and one's sexual identity was not determined by the gender of the object of desire.

In sum, there was no gender category of "homosexual" in pre-twentieth-century China as understood in its modern sense.[43] Consequently, there was never a prevalent anxiety over effeminacy as a result of homophobia in traditional China, as has been the case in modern Europe. In pre-twentieth-century Chinese cultural discourse, same-sex passion was seldom blamed for a man's effeminacy since femininity was not associated *only* with males who desired other males, even though it is true that the passive partner in a same-sex relationship was often described as feminine: "In all these texts, both legal and fictional, the male sex object appears attractive to the extent that he possesses a certain feminized standard of beauty. Youth, whiteness and cleanliness, clarity of complexion, red lips and white teeth, a willowy physique—all these features are conflated and eroticized."[44] However, such a "feminized standard of beauty" was by no means confined to the same-sex erotic context, as our discussions of various written sources have demonstrated. In these texts, a man's feminine looks were often admired by "heterosexual" males and "heterosexual" females as well.

The next logical question one has to ask is whether the fascination with feminine male beauty in Ming-Qing cultural discourse reflected the contemporary women's conceptualization of masculinity. This is a difficult question that defies a definitive answer since almost all the available views on the issue were expressed by men.[45] In the very limited number of extant writings by women that touch on this issue, such as works of *tanci* (narratives in verse), which were often authored by women for female audiences, the image of a handsome man remains equally feminine. In these writings, cross-dressing (usually a woman masquerading as a man) is as common as in the scholar-beauty novel, reflecting the assumed interchangeability in appearance between men and women.[46] Of course, it can be argued that in Ming-Qing China women's views on what constituted male beauty could well have internalized the values held by men, which would have dominated the contemporary cultural discourse in every conceivable way.

A much more persuasive explanation for such a long-standing celebration of feminine male beauty in traditional China is that in pre-twentieth-century Chinese cultural discourse, gender distinctions between the feminine and the masculine were never nearly as absolute as they are in the modern West. Even in the West, as studies by scholars such as Thomas Lacqueur have demonstrated, people began to emphasize such distinctions only as recently as the eighteenth century. According to Lacqueur, up until the seventeenth century, sexual differences were only a matter of degree in Western medical discourse, and "to be a man or a woman was to hold a social rank, a place in society, to assume a cultural role, not to be organically one or the other of the two incommensurable sexes. Sex before the seventeenth century, in other words, was still a sociological and not an ontological category."[47] By the end of the eighteenth century, the older understanding of human character as controlled by the specific humoral mix of each individual was replaced by a new theory that gave central place to a more fixed anatomical difference in determining gendered behavior. Now men and women were increasingly considered "naturally" and predeterminedly different, and their characteristics were those of "opposite sexes."[48] Lacqueur further argues that in "pre-Enlightenment texts, and even some later ones, sex, or the body, must be understood as the epi-phenomenon, while *gender,* what we would take to be a cultural category, was primary or 'real.'"[49]

An understanding of the relative newness of the Western theory of "opposite sexes" should position us to better appreciate some of the important assumptions in traditional Chinese gender ideologies, in which the feminine and the masculine are not perceived to be absolutely different but two poles in a continuum (as I discussed in the introduction). By the same token, the "heterosexual" and the "homosexual" were not perceived to be two absolute gender categories but also two polarities in a continuum. However, as noted above, this relativism did not necessarily amount to an equal relationship between men and women or between the active and passive partners in a same-sex relationship.

Pinhua baojian and especially *Honglou meng* are different in that they present an apparent effort toward equality in male-male relationships, although, as I pointed out, hierarchy is sometimes implicit in the former. Since in many relationships described in these two novels love devoid of lust is emphasized, and since there is almost no reference to physical relationships, penetration is not nearly as important as Sommer has emphasized in his discussions of legal cases from late imperial China. (Note too that his sources often involved members of the nonelite.)[50] We can still discern the hierarchical nature of the love between Mei Ziyu and Du Qinyan: Mei Ziyu, as a member of the social elite, enjoys the privileges of a polygamous male, while Du Qinyan, as a female impersonator/male "courtesan," assumes the role of a chaste woman. However, we see little presence of a hierarchy in Jia Baoyu's relationship with Qin Zhong. Although he is from a lower social class, Qin Zhong pursues relationships both with a woman and with other men, and Baoyu does not expect him to remain "faithful" to him. Again, this tolerance must be related to the adolescent nature of Jia and Qin's relationship. As "children," they are much less susceptible to the ideology of hierarchy that dominates the adult world. At the same time, there is no indication that Qin Zhong is necessarily more feminine than Jia Baoyu. In *Honglou meng,* the homoerotic stereotypes—active versus passive, old versus young, and penetrator versus penetrated—tend to break down in Baoyu's relations with other men, although we need more evidence to say conclusively that the relationship between Baoyu and Qin Zhong is completely egalitarian.[51]

Needless to say, the kind of same-sex passion celebrated in *Pinhua baojian* could well have upset an orthodox Confucian such as Master An in *Ernü yingxiong zhuan* (A Tale of Heroic Lovers), a novel where *Pinhua baojian* apparently becomes a target of ridicule. After hearing his friend talk about his disgust with the behavior of female impersonators and their male lovers in the capital, Master An sighs, "This kind of horrible behavior by youngsters should be blamed on their fathers and brothers for failing to teach and discipline properly." [52] In *Honglou meng,* too, Baoyu's father, Jia Zheng, became angry after learning of his son's relationship with the female impersonator Jiang Yuhan. How to properly educate young men and provide appropriate models of masculinity for them to emulate indeed became an important concern in prescriptive advice literature, a topic explored in chapter 9. Before turning to this topic, however, I shall continue to explore in the next chapter the changing ideals of masculinity as presented in other works of fiction from the eighteenth and nineteenth centuries, where a perfect union between *wen* and *wu* and between male heroic spirit and tender romantic feelings are considered the hallmarks of the masculine.

CHAPTER 8

Romantic Heroes in
Yesou puyan and
Sanfen meng quanzhuan

There was a discernable trend in the vernacular fiction of the late eighteenth and early nineteenth centuries toward a significant convergence of narrative elements that in the past could be found only separately in works belonging to quite different genres. The contemporary development of the so-called *caizi jiaren xiaoshuo* (scholar-beauty fiction) may serve to illustrate some aspects of this trend. Historians of Chinese fiction have long noted that many works of this period defy easy classification—for example, *Xue Yue Mei* (Three Women Named Snow, Moon, and Plum) and *Lingnan yishi* (Forgotten Tales of Lingnan).[1] Although these works are often classified as scholar-beauty fiction, the reader will not find in them any sustained focus on romantic elements, such as a celebration of poetic talent, secret rendezvous between lovers in back gardens, or their determined pursuit of happiness against all odds. Now the emphasis is on the male protagonists' achievements on the battlefield rather than in the examination hall or in poetic gatherings; the story's focus becomes much wider, with the love story relegated to the periphery. In fact, this new focus on military achievement *(wu)* is already anticipated in several early Qing scholar-beauty novels, such as *Huatu yuan* and *Tiehua xianshi* (A History of the Immortal and Iron Flower), although the male protagonists of most these novels are still distinguished by their literary achievements *(wen)*.[2]

Sharing this emphasis on *wu* is *Jinshi yuan* (The Romance of Gold and Stone), a work most likely from the mid-eighteenth century. In this novel, poetic talent, which was such an important attribute of both male and female protagonists in the seventeenth-century scholar-beauty fiction, is almost totally irrelevant. On the contrary, poetry now serves only as a vehicle for a lustful anti-heroine, Aizhu, to seduce the virtuous male protagonist, Jin Yu (20.146). Before suffering a deservedly tragic end, Aizhu comes to the painful realization that her talent and beauty are absolutely useless in her pursuit of a *caizi*. Here *jiaren* is redefined as a woman of virtue rather than simply a talented beauty. The redefinition is underscored by the contrast between the talented but immoral Aizhu and her more plain-looking maid/ adopted sister, who is the embodiment of virtue. At the same time, Jin Yu's standing as a desirable *caizi* now has to be proven on the battlefield, in spite of the fact that he has already achieved top honors in the civil service examinations. He leads government troops to quell a large-scale bandit rebellion and defeat some fearsome pirates. These changes testify to the author's subversion of the conventions of scholar-beauty fiction. We could almost read this work as a deliberate critique of the genre, despite the novel's substantial debt to the target of its critique.

Because of the shift in emphasis to military talent as a defining quality of *caizi, Jinshi yuan* may represent an interesting link between *Huatu yuan* and *Tiehua xianshi* of the early Qing and *Xue Yue Mei* and other similar works at the turn of the nineteenth century. The image of a *wenwu shuangquan* (one distinguished in both literary and military arts) receives even more emphasis in *Xue Yue Mei* and *Lingnan yishi*. In *Xue Yue Mei*, although there still are brief accounts of quite a few young couples finally finding happiness, the main focus is on martial prowess and military achievements rather than on romantic entanglements. Whereas Jin Yu in *Jinshi yuan* is still presented as a delicate young scholar with a fair complexion (12.84 and 87) who is able to achieve military victories only with good luck and the help of a mysterious Taoist immortal, his counterpart in *Xue Yue Mei*, Cen Xiu, is known for his literary talent as well as for his martial prowess. He declares, "A true man should be well versed in both the civil and the military. How could one be content with mere literary craftsmanship?" (1.596). Here literary talent is no longer important. In *Lingnan yishi*, the all-around talents of the male protagonist, Huang Qiong, are touted in even more exaggerated terms: he is said to have read all the books that are worth reading, and he is good at composing every kind of verse. Furthermore, he is a man of enormous physical prowess and great swordsmanship.[3]

Despite conscious authorial efforts to underscore the importance of military achievements in *Jinshi yuan, Xue Yue Mei,* and *Lingnan yishi,* all the male protagonists, on a closer reading, appear to be somewhat pathetic as military heroes. In *Jinshi yuan*, when he is first assigned to the task of quelling the bandits, Jin Yu, who has no training in military affairs, panics, believing that he is doomed to fail. His unexpected victory is the result of sheer luck: his father happens to be the tutor of the adopted son of the bandit chief, and this adopted son has always harbored a plan to kill the bandit chief for murdering his biological father. Most of the pages of *Lingnan yishi* are devoted to accounts of the military talents and martial skills of Huang Qiong's three future wives, while Huang Qiong himself is the hopeless object of desire chased after by these three women (especially by the two women warriors Li Xiaohuan and Mei Yingxue). When forced to marry one of the women to protect his "chastity," Huang even attempts to commit suicide (19.102), a feminine gesture usually reserved for female protagonists in many traditional novels. Like many male protagonists in early Qing scholar-beauty novels—such as Shuangxing in *Dingqing ren* (The Worthy Lovers) —Huang Qiong is said to look like a girl (2.18). In contrast to his three would-be wives, Huang Qiong's military competence falls far short of the expectations raised at the beginning of the novel, when the reader is told how proficient he is in both civil and military affairs. Cen Xiu's victories on the battlefield are probably more convincing as evidence of his all-around talents in *Xue Yue Mei.* However, he is still mainly presented as a man of *wen* (14.653 and 16.662), despite the novel's repeated references to his determination to excel in the martial skills and the author's implied complaint that too much importance has been given to *wen* at the expense of *wu* (*zhong-wen qingwu;* 12.642). Cen Xiu's achievements on the battlefield seem to be necessitated at least in part because of his failure to achieve honors in the civil service examinations. (He used some taboo characters in his otherwise excellent examination essays, and he is able to enter officialdom only by the intervention of the emperor. Many believe this is not a legitimate entry; 30.727.)

The masculinizing efforts to transform *caizi* into *yingxiong* in these novels, though obvious, are often hesitant and even timid, as if the authors, reluctant to do away with the refined image of a *caizi,* are still searching for the perfect balance between the civil and the military. A much grander attempt at such a balance is found in the late eighteenth-century novel *Yesou puyan* (The Humble Words of an Old Rustic), which, some modern scholars believe, marked the beginning of an important new trend in Chinese vernacular fiction.[4]

Having noted the convergence of the generic elements of *xiayi xiaoshuo* (fiction of chivalry) and *caizi jiaren xiaoshuo* in many novels of the late eighteenth and nineteenth centuries, Sun Kaidi is probably one of the first to suggest that the term *ernü yingxiong xiaoshuo* (fiction of heroic lovers) be used to differentiate these novels from *caizi jiaren xiaoshuo* (scholar-beauty fiction).[5] Another historian of Chinese fiction, Tan Zhengbi, tries to distinguish *ernü yingxiong* fiction from other scholar-beauty novels by emphasizing that in the former "either the *caizi* must have talent in both the civil and the military realms or the *jiaren* is a martial arts specialist."[6]

Sun Kaidi's choice of the term *ernü yingxiong* must have been inspired by the mid-nineteenth-century novel *Ernü yingxiong zhuan,* where what constitutes a heroic lover becomes a central issue:

> In talking about lover [*ernü*] and hero [*yingxiong*], people tend to treat them as if they were entirely opposite concepts. They mistakenly believe that only those with physical prowess and the will to fight bravely are heroes, while those romantically involved are lovers. They conclude that if someone has an inclination toward romantic love, then he cannot be a hero or if someone is disinterested in

romantic love, then he must be capable of great heroic valor. These people fail
to understand that only those endowed with the disposition of a true hero are
capable of the tender feelings of a lover; only after people have experienced the
genuine sentiments of a lover can they achieve great success as heroes.[7]

Sister Thirteen, the female protagonist of the novel, is the heroic lover—
both a hero distinguished by her martial prowess and a lover capable of tender feelings. She is not only a great female warrior/knight-errant, but also
a devoted and loving wife (as she turns out to be in the second half of the
novel). *Ernü yingxiong zhuan* is thus often considered a work exemplifying
the conscientious convergence of the chivalric tradition with that of the
scholar and beauty.

In his study of Qing fiction, Zhang Jun regards *Yesou puyan* and *Ernü
yingxiong zhuan* as the pioneering work and the last important work in the
development of *ernü yingxiong* fiction respectively.[8] Although the "mani-
festo" of *ernü yingxiong xiaoshuo* appeared only belatedly in *Ernü yingxiong zhuan, Yesou puyan* was indeed the first work that fully articulated the
ernü yingxiong agenda. *Yesou puyan* is an enormous novel (more than 150
chapters) and an extremely complicated work, so of course its thematic concerns go beyond *ernü yingxiong.* In the rest of this chapter, however, I shall
concentrate only on *Yesou puyan*'s painstaking attempts to construct a Confucian superhero and on its re-envisioned masculinity based on the perfect
union between *ernü* and *yingxiong.* Then I shall offer a reading of the little-
studied *Sanfen meng quanzhuan* (Three-Tenths of the Story Is a Dream), a
novel of the early nineteenth century that bears some important similarities
to *Yesou puyan,* to see how the celebration of a heroic lover takes a different turn in some of the novels during the nineteenth century.

Beyond *Caizi:* The Sage Hero in *Yesou puyan*

Unlike many scholar-beauty novels, which often start with the family background of the *caizi* protagonist and with clichés about how handsome and
talented he is, *Yesou puyan* begins with its male protagonist, Wen Suchen,
expounding to the emperor on the true meaning of a Tang dynasty poem.
Consequently, at the very beginning of the novel, Wen Suchen is already well
on his way to success in his political career. This deliberate departure from
the conventions of scholar-beauty fiction should prepare the reader for his
spectacular career successes, which unfold in the rest of the novel in a most
exaggerated fashion.[9] By the end of the novel, Wen Suchen has achieved
the greatest successes imaginable for a literatus in traditional China; he has
become the most powerful man in the country, second only to the emperor,
and many of his descendants have also achieved glory.

Still in the first chapter, however, the narrator flashes back to the days when Wen Suchen was merely a licentiate *(xiucai)*. Like his counterpart in a typical scholar-beauty novel, Wen Suchen is sent off on a study tour around the country.[10] He does not search for a *jiaren* to marry, as a *caizi* would do, because he is already married (a typical *caizi* protagonist is almost always single to start with). Instead the real purpose of Wen Suchen's journey is to investigate political conditions in the country and recruit heroes in preparation for his campaigns to eradicate Taoism and especially Buddhism. However, this does not prevent him from meeting many *jiaren* along the way. Wen Suchen's journey soon turns into a romantic adventure during which he wins the hearts of all too many beautiful women. In this regard the plot conforms to that of many scholar-beauty novels (especially erotic romances such as the late Ming *Langshi* [A History of Debauchery] and its many early Qing imitations, where the male protagonists have a series of erotic encounters with various beautiful women).[11] It is precisely this kind of romantic journey that provides Wen Suchen with many opportunities to simultaneously assume the role of *ernü* and *yingxiong*.

Like a *caizi* protagonist in many scholar-beauty novels, Wen Suchen is extremely learned, but his learning goes well beyond that of a traditional *caizi*, who usually has poetic talent and a knowledge of the Confucian classics. In addition to poetic talent and a mastery of the canon, Wen Suchen is an expert in mathematics and military strategy. Furthermore, he is a martial arts specialist. He is the culmination of the *wenwu shuangquan* trend already evident in his counterparts in works such as *Xue Yue Mei* and *Lingnan yishi*, only Wen Suchen's all-around talents are celebrated in an even more detailed and exaggerated fashion. *Yesou puyan* stands apart, however, in its conscientious attempt to present its male protagonist as both a lover and a hero. In fact, there are many direct references to the concept of *ernü yingxiong* in the novel proper, as well as in the commentaries attached to its several extant late Qing editions.[12] In chapter 6, as Wen Suchen is bidding farewell to Ren Luanchui and her maid Su'e but is reluctant to leave them, his eyes become moist. The narrator characterizes Suchen's show of emotion as "the stout heart of a masculine hero" [turned into] the tender feelings of a lover and his tears as those of a great hero (6.87). In chapter 7, when Suchen finally agrees to accept Xuangu as his concubine after her brother's repeated pleas, the narrator again refers to "the valor of a great hero . . . turned into the tender feelings of a young lover" (7.107). The narrator makes the same observation with regard to Suchen's friend Jin Chengzhi, who is smitten by the talented and beautiful Miss Min (48.776).

The most significant reference to the concept of *ernü yingxiong* as it relates to the masculinities envisioned in the novel is probably in chapter 59. After touring a villa that the landowner Dongfang Qiao is going to lease to Suchen's family, Suchen becomes rather excited. He begins to describe the beauty of the villa in detail to his wives and maids. This upsets his mother, Madam Shui. Apparently feeling that the villa is too luxurious, she insists that if she had had a choice, she would have chosen another place. Suchen tries to assure Madam Shui:

> Mother has said this because she wants me to learn from the example of Tao Kan [259–334]. Even though he was a high official, he carried tiles day and night in order to keep himself mentally and physically fit. Mother is worried that living in such a comfortable environment will lead me to indulge in private romantic sentiments [*ernü qingchang*] and that it will weaken my heroic valor [*yingxiong qiduan*]. Mother is concerned that I will forget my aspirations and become lazy. However, your son is confident that he would never lower himself to the level of being corrupted by wealth and rank. Mother, you really need not worry. (59.930)

Suchen seems to insist that his enterprising spirit will not suffer as a result of his romantic attachments. However, his confident remarks only upsets Madam Shui more, and she even accuses him of behaving recklessly. Apparently she is most concerned by Suchen's audacity in implicitly presenting himself as a truly great man because Suchen has referred to one of the qualities that Mencius considered essential to such a man—the ability to avoid being corrupted by wealth and rank.[13] Madam Shui reminds Shuchen that the most important quality of a sage is moral vigilance and a constant effort to guard against moral failure (*lin ru bingyuan*; 59.931).

Madam Shui's comments are reminiscent of those of the Song Neo-Confucian thinker Zhu Xi, who felt that a true hero was characterized by moral prudence, as if he were "approaching a deep abyss, as if walking on thin ice." In his famous debate with the utilitarian Confucian thinker Chen Liang (discussed in chapter 1), Zhu Xi apparently tried to distinguish his "sages" (whom he called "truly heroic figures") from Chen Liang's "heroes" by emphasizing that the latter were ultimately after profits rather than righteousness. However, the late Ming writer Jiang Yingke believed that Zhu Xi was talking only about sages rather than heroes, implying that Zhu Xi was confusing the two because a real hero could not be constantly bothered by the thought that he might have erred (more on this issue in chapter 9).[14]

Indeed there is an apparent tension between the image of a hero and that of a sage in *Yesou puyan*.[15] The person who comes closest to the ideal of a sage, strangely enough, is not Wen Suchen but his mother, Madam Shui. In contrast, Wen Suchen is first of all an action hero, despite his impressive mastery of the Confucian canon. Often in the novel just after Suchen has said or done something that appears perfectly sound or even morally impeccable to everyone else, Madam Shui will get upset, and, much to the surprise of others, she will manage to point out how self-deluded her son is when judged strictly by the teachings of the sages. Nowhere is Wen Suchen more exposed as too self-confident or arrogant than in the sage presence of his mother.[16] If Wen Suchen's heroics are the central story of the novel, then one of the subplots is that he often runs the risk of being *kuang* (arrogant and reckless) in the eyes of his mother.

An important aspect of the Confucian masculinity envisioned in *Yesou puyan* is its painstaking attempts to present Wen Suchen as a sage hero (i.e., both a sage and a hero). In fact, Wen Suchen's childhood ambition, specifically mentioned early in the novel, was to become a sage (1.5). However, such attempts also foreground the perennial tension between sage and hero, as evidenced in the debate between Zhu Xi and Chen Liang. This tension seems to have led the novelist to associate Wen Suchen more with the image of a hero and Madam Shui with that of a sage. While Wen Suchen's glorious achievements are mainly in the public domain, Madam Shui's are confined to the domestic realm. It is not the female sage Madam Shui but the masculine hero Wen Suchen who leads successful campaigns to save the nation and defeat various heretical forces. The fact that sage status is ultimately assigned to a woman who is largely confined to the private space of a household alerts the reader to the novel's possible implicit questioning of the significance of sages in a time of national crisis.[17]

Despite its enthusiastic celebration of Neo-Confucian orthodoxy, the novel seems also to have subscribed to the theory that the military is more important than the civil in a time of disorder and that the latter becomes more important only after peace is restored; this view is even condoned by the sage Madam Shui herself (60.945). In principle, a sage should have transcended the division between the military and the civil. However, in historical reality, sages such as Mencius, who believed in *wangdao* (the kingly way) rather than *badao* (the hegemonic way), have always been less interested in military affairs. That is why heroes are needed more urgently when there is disorder under Heaven—a view paradoxically advocated by Chen Liang in his debate with Zhu Xi. Of course, it would have been unimaginable for the novelist Xia Jingqu (1705–1787) or his protagonist Wen Suchen, two avowed followers of Zhu Xi's school of Neo-Confucianism, to openly endorse Chen Liang's utilitarian view. However, in his enthusiasm to celebrate his autobiographical protagonist as a superhero in the public arena, Xia might have departed further from Zhu Xi than he was willing to admit, as will be revealed by a closer look at the implications of Madam Shui's gender status in the novel.

While Madam Shui's role in the novel is important and her constant lecturing to her son and others is almost always enlightening, her gender status as a woman determines the passivity of her role as a sage. This draws the reader's attention to the subtle fact that a sage is often too "philosophical" to be an active hero, while a hero is defined by his deeds rather than his verbal eloquence. (Wen Suchen can be very eloquent except in his mother's presence.) Though not as sage as Madam Shui, Wen Suchen is nevertheless presented as a hero with many sage qualities. By presenting Madam Shui as a sage woman and her son as a masculine hero, the novelist implicitly distinguishes sage from hero in terms of their respective associations with the notions of *nei* (inner) and *wai* (outer). Repeated references to the concept of *nei* versus *wai* appear in the crown prince's praise of Wen Suchen as someone who exemplifies the Confucian ideal of *neisheng waiwang* (sage within and king without; 87.1367 and 88.1384) (although the fact that Wen Suchen is less of a sage than his mother seems to have substantially qualified the crown prince's praise). Madam Shui is presented as more of "a sage within" and Wen Suchen as "a king without."[18] The significant fact that the highest qualities of a sage are embodied in a woman tends to underscore the traditional gender implications of the concepts of *nei* (feminine and private domain) and *wai* (masculine and public domain).[19] In *Yesou puyan* the image of a sage is mainly associated with the feminine and that of a hero with the masculine. As if trying to militate against the apparent hierarchical discrimination implied in this gender positioning of sage and hero, the narrator keeps reminding the reader of how filial and submissive Suchen always is to his mother. Such is the delicate and difficult balance our novelist struggles to achieve in face of the inherent conflicts between sage and hero in traditional intellectual discourses.

As we have indicated, Wen Suchen is conceived not only as a sage hero (albeit less sage than his mother), but also a masculine hero capable of the tender feelings of a lover; the juxtaposition is an implicit critique the Taoist idea that a sage is someone who has transcended feelings *(shengren wuqing)*.[20] The different and sometimes even conflicting claims of sage, hero, and lover are carefully foregrounded, although no easy solution is to be found anywhere in the novel.

Furthermore, Suchen's capacity for tender feelings is not confined to his romantic love for beautiful and talented women. It is a factor of his overall compassionate nature. Perhaps most impressive about his compassionate disposition is his strong sense of justice and his willingness to help others *(rechang,* or a warm heart; 21.351). Early in the novel, Wen Suchen's image comes very close to that of a knight-errant, who is always ready to help the mistreated or abused and to fight against injustice. "A born hero, devoted to helping the poor and those in distress" (24.409), he is widely known for his chivalry. He is often compared to Meng Ben and Guo Jie, two legendary masculine heroes from the Warring States and early Han periods (46.751), one of whom was known as a warrior of tremendous physical strength and the other as a knight-errant of great courage. Many stalwarts and women warriors around the country are eager to swear their loyalty to Wen Suchen as soon as they hear his name. He seems to possess the appeal and charisma of the famous Song Jiang in *Shuihu zhuan*—a far cry from the kind of appeal a sage is supposed to have.

Yet in *Yesou puyan* there is also a concern with the possible recklessness of knight-errantry. This concern takes the form of a Confucian critique eloquently expressed by Madam Shui when Suchen is relating his chivalrous adventures to his family.[21] This is another case where the image of a sage tends to conflict with that of a hero. Mindful of the effect of the knight-errant image on his image as a sage hero, Wen Suchen himself is sometimes conscious of the need to distinguish himself from the usual knight-errant. For example, after overpowering some bandits who have tried to rob him, Wen Suchen declares, "I am not one of those stalwarts on the lake and river. Why should I set you free just in order to follow the code of brotherhood?" (12.195).[22] He is in fact suggesting that he will let them go free only if they agree to work for him in the future. Of course, Wen Suchen's resorting to knight-errantry can be explained at least in part as a deliberate strategy to recruit stalwarts for his more important political cause (to appeal to them by behaving or talking in the same way as they do; 46.753).

The novel's simultaneously irrepressible fascination with heroic chivalry militates against its suspicions of knight-errantry, however. This very fascination is also an important part of the novelist's vision of Confucian masculinity, which does not conform that well to the image of a sage defined by a disposition toward tranquility and reverence, as celebrated in Neo-Confucian discourses on self-cultivation (more on this point in chapter 9). The commentator reminds the reader that Wen Suchen should be considered a chivalrous Confucian of great wisdom and tremendous courage, as if without his chivalrous spirit his image as a Confucian masculine hero would remain somehow incomplete (20.331). Elsewhere, the commentator points out that many people know Wen Suchen only as someone with a chivalrous heart and enormous physical prowess (23.391).

As in the case of a typical knight-errant, Wen Suchen's physical prowess plays an important role in his chivalrous missions and is therefore an indispensable aspect of his masculine image. There are repeated references to his physical strength and martial skills. Frequently his strength is described as "godlike" (24.340–25.242). His lifting and throwing of a copper screen frightens two girls, Luancui and Su'e, nearly to death; the episode is reminiscent of a celebrated scene in which Xiang Yu lifts a cauldron—a reference already made elsewhere by the narrator (1.3). Moreover, Wen Suchen is believed to be even more powerful than the number 1 warrior in *Shuo Tang*, Li Yuanba, who is known for his invincible physical prowess and martial skills (90.1414). Suchen is said to be powerful enough to fight with a dragon single-handedly (3.41) and walk so fast that people cannot catch him even when they are on horseback (21.352). The list of Suchen's physical feats goes on.

Upon a closer reading, however, the reader discovers that it is often Wen Suchen's unprecedented medical expertise rather than his fighting skills that enables him to succeed in his chivalrous undertakings. This expertise also brings him into intimate contact with various beautiful women and therefore offers the opportunity for grand shows of the tenderness of this masculine hero. All this alerts the reader that Wen Suchen has two seemingly different and even opposite sides—namely, the side of the lover and that of the hero. When he saves a woman's life, she usually expresses a gratitude that is often also romantic; this, in turn, induces a tender response from him. However, unlike Tie Zhongyu in *Haoqiu zhuan,* who rescues the female protagonist, Shui Bingxin, by physically fighting those trying to harm her, Wen Suchen often comes to the rescue of a woman in intimate or even compromising situations. The most elaborate example is what happens between him and his future concubine Su'e. When Wen Suchen is sick, out of gratitude for saving her mistress Luanchui (and probably out of her own love for him), Su'e, who is also an expert in medicine (as her name suggests)—though not as knowledgeable as Wen Suchen—realizes that the only way to save him and keep his suffering to a minimum is to use her own naked body to keep him warm. Later, when Su'e gets sick, Wen Suchen in turn holds her in his arms and caresses her all over her naked body in order to save her. After mistakenly taking an aphrodisiac, Su'e turns into a lustful animal. With his superb medical knowledge, Suchen is able to cure her with various unconventional treatments (including caressing her private parts and constant kissing). As a genius doctor, his medical strategies are often unconventional, to say the least. In a different episode, Suchen has to rip clothes off of another girl, Xiangling, in order to save her from a fatal illness. He resorts to such radical and seemingly shameless medical "tactics" because fear, shame, and shock are crucial elements of his treatment.[23] Of course, after such physical intimacy, Su'e and Xiangling have to marry him to preserve their reputations, but both consider it a great honor to join his household even as concubines.

In addition to his medical expertise, it appears that Suchen's success as a doctor can be attributed to his uniquely therapeutic male body. While Suchen's knowledge of herbal medicine is almost unparalleled, one of his effective medical treatments often is intimate physical contact between the patient (usually a woman) and the doctor (himself). The novel often refers to the "pure *yang* energy" of his body (67.1057 and 95.1491). Under orders from her elder brother to offer herself as a token of gratitude for saving his life, Xuangu gets into bed with Suchen when he is fast asleep. Here the reader is told in detail how the *yang* elements of Suchen's body excite her sexually. The hot *yang* energy from between his legs almost causes her to lose control (7.102).

In chapter 96, before entering the Miao Grotto to do reconnaissance on the Python King, Suchen is advised to fake a marriage with a Miao girl to avoid suspicion. He is told that the couple will have to share the same bed because they will be subjected to checks during the night if suspicions of a fake marriage are aroused. Suchen agrees to this proposal only after learning that his future "bride" is a "stone girl" (a woman lacking a vaginal opening and thus unable to function sexually). During the wedding night, however, the bride still derives tremendous physical pleasure just from intimate contact with the *yangqi* of Suchen's body and from his caressing. The pleasure is so intense that this stone girl begins to moan as if she were enjoying great sexual pleasure. This is especially interesting since Suchen subscribes to the theory that sexual intercourse, whose only legitimate function is procreation, is totally superfluous as far as genuine love between a man and a woman is concerned (8.125–128).[24] Now a woman derives even more pleasure from Suchen just by sleeping in the same bed with him and having intimate contact with his masculine energy and bodily warmth.

More surprising still, the "healing power" of the *yang* energy emitted from Suchen's body begins to have a magical effect on his bride. Her abnormal sexual anatomy is eventually transformed into that of a normal woman, as if her private parts have been surgically altered. One character in the novel thus concludes that the coldness of the pure *yin* essence in the stone girl could only be driven away by the warmth of a pure *yang* essence like Suchen (98.1530).

As in typical erotic fiction, attention is repeatedly drawn to Suchen's large member, although he is a chaste Confucian moralist *(daoxue xiansheng)*. In fact, the impressive size of his member once gets him into serious trouble: he is chosen as a target for semen collection after a maid, who is sent by a harem master, Li Youquan, to spy on men in the restroom, catches sight of his penis when he is relieving himself. The narrator tells us that since Suchen is full of *qi,* or energy, his endowment is magnificent, and it takes him a long time to finish urinating. His urine is so warm (potent) that it melts a whole bucket of snow, and the steam billows up like smoke and mist (67.1050). Once again, Suchen's male potency is emphasized in terms of the impressive size of his penis and the warm *qi* associated with such *yang* energy.[25]

More bizzare, Suchen's semen has magical properties. After Suchen is drugged, Li Youquan sucks a large quantity of semen from him. The semen turns out to be much more potent than any aphrodisiac Li has ever taken: after drinking it, Li is able to wage "battles" with fourteen of his concubines and achieves total "victory" each time. While other men would soon die from exhaustion after their semen was repeatedly drained, Suchen proves to be remarkably resilient, apparently owing to the potent *yangqi* of his body. This is in part why he is able to remain physically strong enough to escape from Li Youquan (with the help of others). Even Suchen's bodily waste is thought to be tonic. Li Youquan's ninth concubine and maid are said to be eager to drink Suchen's urine for its tonic effects (68.1068–69 and 70.1096). Suchen himself also believes in the medicinal potential of his urine. He once mixed his urine with herbs to make a medicine for Su'e (20.335).

Here Wen Suchen comes very close to the male protagonists in many erotic romances, such as *Langshi* and *Rou putuan* (The Carnal Prayer Mat), despite the fact he, who has absolutely no interest in sex, is supposed to be an exemplar of Confucian manhood. Of course, in those erotic romances, the hero's masculinity is often equated with sexual virility or the ability to perform in bed. Here masculinity is measured in terms of how long one can last during sex and the size of the penis. The reader of *Yesou puyan* is supposed to infer that Suchen must be much more potent than all the libertine protagonists in those erotic romances because his semen is better than any aphrodisiac. In fact, Suchen is worshiped by Li Youquan and many of his concubines as the very reincarnation of the immortal Taoist patriarch Lü Zu or Lü Dongbin, who is presented as the ultimate symbol of pure male potency in some erotic literature (67.1057). Here Wen Suchen becomes a sex symbol rather than a Confucian sage!

At the same time, the novelist constantly reminds the reader of his protagonist's sage qualities in order to keep him from being confused with a hero of erotic literature. We are told that Wen Suchen is different from those libertine protagonists because of his ability to maintain his chastity despite his unusual endowments (his impressive "equipment" and handsome appearance) and their appeal to women. Wen Suchen prides himself on remaining unperturbed even with a beautiful woman in his arms and compares himself to Guan Yu, the celebrated hero in *San'guo yanyi* who is known for his ability to resist sexual temptation (96.1504 and 25.424). But the temptations Suchen faces are much more challenging even than Guan Yu's. Repeatedly, Suchen finds himself in the arms of a naked and desiring woman (as in the case of Su'e, Xuangu, and the stone girl), and the direct physical temptation is tremendous. While he never shies away from his medical duties as a compassionate and chivalrous doctor and never hesitates to make full use of the unique therapeutic properties of his body, he always manages to remain morally impeccable. No wonder that the crown prince, after hearing the story of how Suchen eventually marries three girls as concubines, insists that Suchen's moral caliber is even more impressive than that of the legendary Liuxia Hui of the Spring and Autumn Period, who was famous for his ability to remain unperturbed with a woman in his arms (80.1380). Suchen's successful resistance to the advances of several beautiful women is an important part of the plot pattern in the early chapters of the novel, a fact that the commentator repeatedly calls to our attention (chapter-end comments, 17.280–281). It shows how skillfully our novelist is able to present different challenging situations, and Suchen passes each "chastity test" with flying colors. The ability to resist sexual temptation is certainly an important attribute of a masculine hero in traditional cultural discourses (as emphasized in novels such as *San'guo yanyi* and *Shuihu zhuan*). Suchen's masculinity is even more impressive because of his ability to maintain his chastity in all these extremely tempting situations, as well as the fact that he, who has tremendous appeal to the opposite sex, is by no means a boring, straightlaced Confucian puritan incapable of romantic sentiments. In sum, in addition to his mastery of both civil and military skills, Wen Suchen's masculinity is defined simultaneously by his male "prowess" (sexual and/or martial) and his ability to always use this prowess most effectively for noble causes. His tremendous appeal to women can be matched only by his equally impressive ability to resist sexual temptation, an uncanny combination that is attributable not only to his unique masculine body, but also to his mental discipline—the result of a perfect upbringing by his mother.

Another Frustrated *Caizi:*
Heroic Dreams in *Sanfen meng quanzhuan*

Sanfen meng quanzhuan (hereafter *Sanfen meng*), by Zhang Shideng (fl. late eighteenth and early nineteenth centuries), shares some remarkable similarities with *Yesou puyan,* although there is no evidence that *Sanfen meng* was influenced by it, probably because *Yesou puyan* was circulated in manuscript copies only within a relatively small circle of readers before it saw print during the late nineteenth century.[26] A close reading of *Sanfen meng* should help us to see how masculinities are reimagined, as well as reconstructed differently, by another literati writer whose life was almost as pathetic as that of the author of *Yesou puyan.*

The author's preface to *Sanfen meng* is dated 1819, during the Jiaqing period (1796–1820). However, in the opening verse of the novel, the Daoguang period (1821–1850) is mentioned (1.1b [p. 2]). It is possible that the preface was written before the final draft of the novel was completed. The earliest extant printed edition of the novel (most likely not the first printed edition) is dated 1835. Little is known about the author, Zhang Shideng, except for the information provided in the prefaces attached to the novel and what might be inferred from the novel itself.[27] According to the preface to the novel by Zhang's fellow townsman Miao Gen, Zhang Shideng originally was very ambitious and had many talents but was not successful in the civil service examinations. Later he followed his uncle in serving on the staffs of officials stationed along China's border areas (1a–b [pp. 1–2]). In a prefatory poem to the novel, a certain Li Chenhua from Nanhai (probably a good friend of Zhang's when the latter was working as a clerk for certain officials in southern China) points out that the last name of the protagonist, Zhang[a], is a pun on the novelist's own, Zhang[b] (they are pronounced the same, though written differently). Furthermore, he is convinced that the novel is the author's attempt to make certain points by using his own life experiences as examples and that we can see the author himself in the novel. Finally, he reveals that most of Zhang's novel is a faithful recording of "facts" and that only three-tenths of it is dream-like fiction—an obvious reference to the title (2a–b; [pp. 3–4]). This interpretation of the title is explicitly confirmed in the concluding poem of the novel proper (16.17a [p. 653]), where the author specifically tells the reader that the work is an account of his personal experiences, with only three-tenths of it "fictional" like a dream (16.17a [p. 653]). In his own preface, Zhang Shideng states that having lived in seclusion for thirty years, he is not interested in fame or profit. He wrote the novel as a dream, and people should not be offended if some characters' names happen to be identical to theirs (3a–4a; [pp. 1–3]). As I shall demonstrate below, naming characters after real people known to the author is an important autobiographical strategy of *Sanfen meng*. All these points suggest that *Sanfen meng* should be read as an autobiographical novel, a suggestion validated not long after the novel proper begins to unfold.[28]

The first few chapters of this sixteen-chapter novel are devoted to the lives and careers of the protagonist's father and especially his grandfather. The grandfather, a man of impressive physical prowess and martial skills, turns to a career in the military only after he has suffered repeated failures in the civil service examinations. The protagonist's father is given the position of county magistrate, thanks to the grandfather's service record and the recommendations of others rather than passing the civil service examinations himself. This is significant because, as the reader will learn later (7.18b [p. 294]), the protagonist, Zhang Mengyao, despite having written brilliant examination essays, is disqualified because jealous examinees claim that he has taken the exams under a false name. (Zhang Mengyao probably took the exams as the son of his father-in-law rather than under his own name because his father-in-law presented him as his own son when Zhang Mengyao accompanied him to Guangdong when he was sentenced to exile there.) Thus neither Zhang Mengyao nor his father or grandfather passed the civil service examinations (although the grandfather passed the military service examinations). In an age when the only authentic ladder to an official career was success in the civil service examinations, this must have been a constant source of anxiety for three generations of Zhangs. However, Zhang Mengyao is said to be quite unconcerned about his examination failure, reminiscent of the similar attitude of Wen Suchen in *Yesou puyan* after he has suffered the same fate.[29]

In these early chapters, the novelist seems to have paid close attention to the chronological accuracy of the events he describes. For example, we are told the particular time of day, the day, the month, and the year of the grandfather's death (2.3b [p. 50]), as well as those of the birth of Zhang Mengyao (4.11a [p. 65]); we are also told the particular time, day, and month of the protagonist's mother's death (4.11a [p. 65]) and the day and month of his father's death (4.14a [p. 147]); in the last two cases, no specific years are given, but we are told that his mother dies when he is five years old and his father dies at the age of forty-four.

Given the meticulous recording of these dates and the explicit encouragement from the novelist and his friends to read the novel autobiographically, one is tempted to speculate about the possible implications of these dates. The author himself was probably born in 1771, the thirty-sixth year of the Qianlong period (1736–1795), the same year Zhang Mengyao was said to have been born. The novelist's grandfather might have died in 1752, the seventeenth year of the Qianlong period, the same year that the protagonist's grandfather is said to have died. The novel also mentions that Zhang Mengyao's grandfather was given the task of quelling pirates when the new emperor assumed the throne; historically, Qianlong's reign started in 1736. Of course, a final determination of the exact autobiographical significance of these dates has to be based on more knowledge of the novelist's family background. However, it is significant that Zhang Shideng was so specific in describing the glorious life and military career of his protagonist's grandfather in this relatively short novel. At one point, the narrator even points out that under a special order from the imperial government, the great achievements of the grandfather were recorded in *Wenzhou fu zhi* (Gazetteer of Wenzhou; 2.6b [p. 56]).

Such insistence on historicity by reference to a local gazetteer is so unusual in a novel that a curious reader might feel compelled to verify the narrator's claim. Sure enough, in the section on "Wuhuan" (military officers) in the Qianlong edition of *Wenzhou fu zhi,* there is indeed a brief biography of a certain Zhang Tianjun, and in the novel the grandfather's name is Zhang Tianjun.[30] The pronunciation is the same, but the names are written differently. (As we mentioned above, one of the preface writers already alerted the reader to the pun on the last names of the protagonist and the author.) In the biography, Zhang Tianjun is said to have two sons, Xialing and Ruiling, while in the novel the grandfather's two sons are named Yalin and Ruilin (the latter being the protagonist's father).[31] The parallels become even more obvious when we find that almost all the important details (including the honors) in the life of Zhang Tianjun listed in the biography are duly reproduced for the grandfather in the novel, only in more detailed and exaggerated fashion. They include the fact that his family was originally from the Qiantang area of Hangzhou; the triumphs over the pirates (the pirate leader, Sun Sen and his subordinates Zhao Jiu and Lin Tai even appear in the novel under their real names [1.8b; p. 16]); the grandfather's much admired chivalrous act of paying off a huge debt for his colleague, Commander Jin, when they were stationed in Haitan; the commendations from the emperor; and the promotion to commander of the Fujian navy (1.17 [p. 33]). A slight factual difference is that in the biography Zhang Tianjun is said to have died at the age of sixty-nine, while in the novel the grandfather dies at the age of sixty-eight (2.3a [p. 49]). Obviously Zhang Shideng intended the first two chapters of his novel to be read as a fictionalized biography of his own grandfather. He was proud and confident enough about the historical accuracy of the grandfather's story in his novel to challenge the reader to read the novel *against* the gazetteer biography. This much touted accuracy in the reconstruction of the grandfather's life serves only to under-score the fictional nature of the later chapters about the grandson (the auto-biographical protagonist), where not so many specific dates are provided.

One point repeatedly emphasized in the commentator's "Reading Prin-ciples" is that the first few chapters of the novel may seem a bit uneventful or even humdrum because they strictly follow the facts (5a–b [p. 1]).[32] That is, the author might have been too preoccupied with infusing facts from his own family history into that of his protagonist to present a more dramatic narrative. In other words, our novelist is too honest to write an entertaining story here. However, the glorious achievements so carefully catalogued in the "boring" accounts of the grandfather in the first few chapters set the standard by which the life and career of his grandson will be judged in the rest of the novel.

Zhang Mengyao does not become the focus of the narrative until chap-ter 6. In the next ten chapters, except for parts about his dramatic victories on the battlefield, Zhang Mengyao's life story is rather uneventful and even depressing. It is mostly about the hardships suffered by the then still young Zhang Mengyao and his siblings after the death of their parents, as well as Zhang's life of wandering and hardship owing to the misfortunes of his father-in-law and the suspicious nature of his mother-in-law.[33] As an auto-biographical novel by a frustrated literati author, *Sanfen meng* is indeed quite different from *Yesou puyan*.[34] Here self-healing takes a much more honest and realistic form, although wish fulfillment remains an important part of its autobiographical agenda.

At first glance, like the author of *Yesou puyan*, Zhang Shideng tries to vindicate himself by attributing to his autobiographical protagonist all the successes that he himself had wished for but failed to achieve.[35] However, one important difference is that in *Sanfen meng* the protagonist's successes are presented in such a way that the reader is likely to doubt whether they can be considered real successes. For example, although Zhang Mengyao has achieved major military triumphs more than once, repeatedly he is not recognized for his achievements because of seemingly unexpected turns of events. Almost every time, as soon as the government troops are victorious after having implemented his tactics, his patron either has to leave his post or dies a sudden death, leaving Zhang unrewarded and unrecognized. The narrator does not explicitly mention that the sudden death or departure of Zhang's patrons can cause him great problems simply because Zhang Meng-yao does not have a formal position and because his ties to the patrons are purely personal. This must be a reflection of the author's own experience as a *muyou* (private secretary; more about this point below). In almost every moment of Zhang Mengyao's triumphs, there lurks a deeper sense of frus-tration—despite his claims that he does not care about recognition. Also, the towering figure of his grandfather is always there to make his disappointments even more difficult to swallow (although his grandfather died long before he was born).

Zhang Mengyao's unfulfilled career forms a sharp contrast to that of his grandfather, as well as to the great promise anticipated at his birth. As often happens in Chinese legends and histories, a great person's birth is always associated with ominous dreams. For example, in *Yeson puyan,* Madam Shui dreams of a jade sparrow flying into her arms before she gives birth to Wen Suchen (1.4). In *Sanfen meng,* Mengyao's mother dreams of a goddess telling her that because of the merits the family has accumulated, she is going to give her a gift. She gives her a jade rabbit, which soon magically enters her abdomen. According to the goddess, Mengyao's mother should raise the child carefully because when the child grows up, he will not only make great contributions to contemporary society, but will also enjoy a great posthumous reputation (2.9b [p. 62]).

As the grandson of a famous general, Zhang Mengyao seems destined to distinguish himself on the battlefield, although nowhere in the novel is it mentioned how he acquires his military expertise; early on the narrative focuses on his precocious literary talent and his image as a *caizi.* Unlike his grandfather, who becomes a military officer by passing the military service examinations, Mengyao is first involved in a military campaign—against the pirates—almost by accident. Barely twenty years old, he agrees to help the Surveillance Commissioner Pan Jingtao only because he wants to avenge the deaths of his brother and sister-in-law, who have been killed by the pirates. The government troops soon triumph thanks to Zhang Mengyao's clever strategies. Commissioner Pan has to leave his post due to the death of a parent before he can recommend Zhang Mengyao for a reward and recognition, and Zhang has to return home almost empty-handed.

A second opportunity for demonstrating military expertise presents itself when Pan Jingtao recommends Zhang Mengyao to Commander Cheng, who is leading another military campaign against the same pirates defeated before. Now these pirates are receiving support from the Vietnamese government. Zhang Mengyao agrees to help only after Commander Cheng has invited him three times—an apparent reference to the three visits Liu Bei pays to secure the services of the famous military strategist Zhuge Liang (as celebrated in *San'guo yanyi* and other legends). In fact, in chapter 12, Zhang Mengyao is directly compared to Zhuge Liang, while the formidable pirate leader is compared to the famous strategist Zhou Yu, who is supposed to have been repeatedly outwitted by Zhuge (12.21b [p. 507] and 14.8a [p. 559]). The campaign is going quite well until Commander Cheng suddenly dies. Even worse than in the previous campaign, Zhang Mengyao has to leave before final victory is achieved because Commander Cheng's successor does not want his services. Once more, he returns home empty-handed, without reward or recognition. This episode again shows that Zhang Mengyao, as a *buyi* (someone without an official position), will never achieve major success or recognition, despite the fact that his talent has helped others achieve it.[36] In *Yesou puyan,* Wen Suchen, who also failed to pass the civil service examinations, avoids such misfortunes thanks to the consistent support of the crown prince.

After this second bitter experience, Zhang Mengyao decides to withdraw completely into private life and be a hermit. However, his grandfather's glorious achievements still haunt him, and the opportunity for glory in public service proves to be still too tempting to resist. One day, after drinking some wine, Mengyao falls asleep. In his dream, he is invited by the governments of Siam and other countries to lead their troops against invading Vietnamese troops. The foreign kings receive Mengyao at a place significantly called Jiameng guan (the Great Dream Pass), obviously an ironic reference to the wish-fulfilling nature of the dream. However, what saves our novelist from being accused of engineering a blatantly wish-fulfilling dream is the increasingly explicit allegorical nature of the dream.

In order to defeat the enemy troops, Mengyao's troops have to overrun four heavily defended enemy encampments—namely, Wine Spring County (Jiuquan Jun), the Bridge of Bewitching Beauty (Xiaohun Qiao), Copper Mountain (Tongshan), and Purple Energy Pass (Ziqi Guan). Here the references to the four traditional vices—wine, lust, wealth, and anger *(jiu se cai qi)*—are apparent. The names of the generals serving under Mengyao all carry allegorical implications. For example, one of them is known as Shizhong Wokui, which is a pun on *sezhong e'gui* (the lustful; more literally, a ghost who cannot have enough sex).[37] Sexual imagery abounds in the account of the fight between Shizhong Wokui and two female warriors from the Bridge of Bewitching Beauty:

> Dear readers, how could a cudgel be strong enough to resist two axes? After a while, the arms of Shizhong Wogui became numb, and he could not continue [to fight] any longer. He wanted to withdraw but feared that these two women would laugh at his incompetence. He could only force himself to continue, not expecting that his cudgel would be tightly clasped between the axes of the two sisters. Shizhong Wogui tried to pull his cudgel out, but he could hardly move. With smelly sweat all over his body and totally out of breath, he could not move even an inch. Finally, the sisters cut him through the waist with their axes. (15.1b–2a [pp. 584–585])

Allegorically, this is a comic horror story about how a lustful man dies of sexual exhaustion, a fate shared by many oversexed characters in Chinese erotic fiction.

When confronted by Zhang Mengyao, Princess Jade Face warns him that he and his men will eventually fall victim to her and her women warriors, just as many great masculine heroes have done throughout history. She tells Mengyao there is absolutely no chance for him to win this time, not even in his dreams—again an ironic reference to the illusory nature of this part of the narrative (a fact also noted by the commentator, 15.3a [p. 587]). The next fight scene is between Mengyao's general Yu Se, a pun on *yuse* (lusting after beautiful women), and Yang Meiji, a pun on *yangmei ji* (a prostitute who has syphilis); Yu Se proves to be no rival for Yang Meiji. Then another general, Chang Suchang, a pun on *chang su chang* (a frequent visitor to brothels), tries to take over but is soon killed by Yang Meiji (15.3b–4a). Despite the fact that many of his generals are totally incompetent, Zhang Mengyao is resourceful enough to turn the tide at critical junctures and lead his troops from one victory to another.

After failing to stop Zhang Mengyao with the four vices, the queen of Vietnam recommends that the king call in the monk Zuoyong (a person who initiates bad practices), who has a secret formula for a special drug. This drug, which is known as *afurong* (opium), can emit a poisonous and debilitating gas. The monk claims that this gas is much more deadly than the four vices. Despite the poison gas, however, the allied forces achieve final victory thanks to Mengyao's resourcefulness.

The kings of Siam and other countries (including the Kingdom of Poisoned Bodies—i.e., a country where people have apparently been poisoned by opium) are so grateful to Mengyao that they want to reward him generously, but of course our protagonist declines all treasures. The only gift he will accept is a zither, which he looks forward to playing when he is again a private citizen. Finally, the kings and their entourages see Mengyao off at the Great Dream Pass. Just at that moment, Mengyao is awakened from his dream—he is startled by the sound he accidentally makes by touching the strings of the zither as he raises his hand to bid farewell to the kings in the dream. Now, symbolically, he has regained his hermit status. The wine he was sipping before he fell asleep is, however, still warm, suggesting that the dream, though glorious, was not that long and emphasizing the ephemeral nature of the dream experience. From that time on, Zhang Mengyao is completely content with his fate and begins to live in total seclusion. No one knows what finally happens to him. The novel concludes with a poem that has the following lines: "If people have read three-tenths of my story as a dream, they must not take the other seven-tenths too literally." Here the boundaries between fact and fantasy are deliberately confused.

The last two chapters of the novel are full of comic touches, puns, and hilarious plays on words. Consequently, the reader is compelled to reinterpret the autobiographical bitterness of the previous chapters. These two chapters turn the novel into an elaborate ironic comment on the illusory nature of lived experience and add a new twist to the meaning of the cliché that life is a dream. (After all, our protagonist's first name, Mengyao, may have the implications of "a distant dream"; *meng* means "dream," while *yao* puns on the word "distance," which is also pronounced *yao*.)[38] This is our novelist's final desperate attempt to alleviate the disappointment of his own failed life. Mengyao's dream, though self-glorifying to the point of being absurd, is part of a necessary healing process that both our novelist and his autobiographical protagonist have to undergo before they can reach transcendence.

Even in the moments of seemingly harmless self-celebration on the part of our novelist, the reader can still discern a profound concern for the empire, which appears to be collapsing under widespread moral decay, while an ominous new threat is posed by imported opium, even more deadly than the familiar four vices. This leads one to doubt whether the kind of transcendence the author and his autobiographical protagonist are seeking is truly possible. Even after having lived for thirty years as a hermit, Zhang Shideng could not suppress thoughts of his failed career; he had to vindicate himself by writing a novel. It is this persistent pursuit of transcendence and the simultaneous awareness of its futility that add an interesting dimension to an otherwise rather uneventful autobiographical novel.

Compared with the concluding chapter of *Yesou puyan*, which also focuses on the dreams of its main characters,[39] *Sanfen meng*'s conclusion, with its many explicit metafictional plays and comic touches of self-mockery, is far more self-consciously ironic. It is a testament to Zhang Shideng's much stronger self-awareness as a novelist who is not afraid of poking fun at himself for day-dreaming. In his preface, Miao Gen characterizes the novel as *youxi wenzhang* (a literary game; 1b [p. 2]). Indeed, *Sanfen meng*'s concluding chapters put the novel in a class of its own.[40] No wonder the "Reading Principles" insist that the reader should not be discouraged by the early chapters, since the more one reads, the more fascinating the novel becomes. The last few chapters are the most interesting (5a [p. 1] and 6a [p. 3]).[41]

While indulging in the same game of self-vindication and self-reinvention as Xia Jingqu has done in *Yesou puyan*, Zhang Shideng makes his protagonist more realistic and occasionally even more psychologically complex. Zhang Mengyao is apparently torn between his aspirations for career success and his claims of being a recluse. His high-mindedness forms an interesting contrast with the miseries and hardships he suffers in life. His life can be divided into two parts: his uneventful years as a private citizen and his triumphs as a military hero. The accounts of his three triumphs on the battlefield (two while he is awake and one in his dreams) are structurally so detached from the plot development of the rest of the novel that they all take on a quality of fantasy, which is accentuated by his dreamed triumph at the end of the novel. In other words, there are two characters named Zhang Mengyao in the novel, one "realistic" and the other "fantastic," while in *Yesou puyan* Wen Suchen remains consistently fantastic owing to the novel's unrelentingly exaggerated rhetoric. In *Sanfen meng*, the "realistic" seems to have turned the "fantastic" into an understandable (as well as more acceptable) excuse to escape from the honest but disheartening "realistic" itself. If in *Yesou puyan*, Wen Suchen's Confucian masculinity is somewhat threatened by his sage mother and her constant critiques, in *Sanfen meng*, under the long shadow cast by the towering figure of his grandfather, Zhang Mengyao can redeem his manhood only by dreaming up military triumphs in a foreign land.

Compared with Wen Suchen, Zhang Mengyao, lacking the supervision of a mother like Madam Shui, is much less of an orthodox Confucian and less of an erudite scholar, although the commentator calls him a sage (13.19a [543]). Zhang does not offer lengthy lectures on Confucian classics or history, as Wen Suchen frequently does. At one point, he claims to exemplify a perfect balance between *daoxue* (a serious Confucian) and *fengliu* (a romantic; 9.1a–b [pp. 323–324]).[42] In addition to his heroic achievements on the battlefield and his strong qualifications as a *yingxiong*, Mengyao is also quite capable of romantic sentiments. Although he enjoys a good relationship with his first wife, Sufang, his romantic temperament finds its fullest expression in a three-year love affair with Suzhen that is suddenly cut short when she dies of a tragic illness. While they are together, they compose poetry and play chess and music—everything a *caizi jiaren* couple is supposed to do. The appreciation of a beauty such as Suzhen proves to be especially consoling to Mengyao when his career seems to be going nowhere, as is suggested by the first line of the couplet-title of chapter 11: "Suzhen Has the Insight to Appreciate a Talented Man." After Suzhen's death, Mengyao becomes so sentimental (his lover's sentiments become so strong) that he tries to die with her. He refuses food and medicine when he too falls ill, apparently because of his deep grief over her death (12.7a–7b [pp. 479–480]). Here Mengyao is presented as a pure romantic *caizi*, while in *Yesou puyan* the term *caizi* is reserved for people like Suchen's friend Jin Chengzhi, who is known solely for his poetic talent; Wen Suchen, as a Confucian superhero, is much more than just a brilliant scholar.

Like Suchen, Mengyao also exhibits an inclination toward knight-errantry (2a [p. 325]), and he is likewise known for his ability to resist sexual temptation (9.9b–12b [pp. 340–344]). Like many *caizi* protagonists in scholar-beauty fiction, Mengyao is said to be extremely handsome (2.11a–b (pp. 65–66]). Resembling a beautiful girl (6.3b [p. 218]), he is even sexier than a female impersonator (9.1b [p. 324]; see the discussions of male beauty associated with the female impersonator in chapter 7). Compared with Wen Suchen, Zhang Mengyao is closer to the more feminine *caizi* protagonists in the early Qing scholar-beauty novels. In *Yesou puyan*, although Wen Suchen's fair skin is emphasized, he is never said to be feminine. Zhang Mengyao's girlish appearance also presents an interesting contrast with that of his grandfather, who is said to be tall and muscular (1.3b [p. 6])—probably a reason why in "real" life (not in his dream) Zhang Mengyao can never live up to the standards set by his grandfather as a military hero. He is further feminized by the fact that owing to economic distress after the death of his parents, he is married into his wife's family as a young boy *(ruzhui)*.[43]

At the same time, the author of *Sanfen meng* has tried his best to present his protagonist as a man of great talent. For one thing, he devotes quite a few pages to accounts of Zhang Mengyao's precocity. Zhang is repeatedly praised as a child prodigy (see the titles of chapters 7 and 10) who manages to outwit people many years his senior. Although he is quite proficient in the martial skills, much of the narrative focuses on his literary talents. He is certainly a model of *wenwu shuangquan* (12.11a [p. 487]), despite the fact that his main talent in the military arena is his strategizing ability rather than his martial prowess.

While Suchen claims expertise in medicine, military strategy, poetry, and mathematics, Mengyao is an expert in chess and the zither. To authenticate this claim, the author quotes from a lengthy chess manual that Mengyao wrote, as well as zither music that he scored (11.21b–24b [pp. 452–460]; 12.3b–5a [pp. 472–477]); in the "Reading Principles" the commentator has already identified this "authentication" as a unique feature of the novel (5b [p. 2]).[44] Consequently, Mengyao can also claim expertise in four arts: literary skills, military strategy, chess, and music. Whereas Suchen uses his knowledge in mathematics and especially in medicine in his campaign against Buddhism and other evil forces (a worldly effort, or *rushi*), Mengyao's expertise in chess and the zither is meant only to authenticate his status as a high-minded literati recluse (withdrawing from the world, or *chushi*). Even in his allegorical dream, where he defeats the Vietnamese troops—an eloquent testimony to his invincible masculinity—the only reward he wants is a zither, something associated with his status as a recluse and a somewhat feminine "stage prop." In his reclusivity and with his music Zhang Mengyao tries to come to terms with the failures in his career.

Masculinities beyond the Middle Kingdom

Written only a few decades later than *Yesou puyan*, which expresses a deep confidence in the absolute superiority of the Confucian culture over other civilizations, *Sanfen meng* betrays a deep anxiety over the invasion of foreign influence, as well as an implicit fear of the possible collapse of the empire not because of internal conflicts but because of much more ominous forces from abroad. One is tempted to associate the more masculine image of Wen Suchen with *Yesou puyan*'s Confucian confidence and Zhang Mengyao's anxieties over his manhood with the increasingly precarious position in which China found itself during the early nineteenth century. As *Sanfen meng* warned, opium was to play a crucial role in changing the fate of the empire: the so-called Opium Wars broke out in 1840, approximately two decades after Zhang Shideng completed his novel.[45]

One interesting feature of *Yesou puyan* is its persistent interest in realms beyond what is usually considered "China" and its imperialist imagination. Many chapters of the novel are devoted to accounts of Wen Suchen's adventures on China's periphery—the areas of the aborigine Miao people—and his friends' and offsprings' missionary campaigns in foreign lands. For example, Rijing, a good friend of Wen Suchen, travels to Europe and successfully converts people in many countries to Confucianism. He claims, "The most important thing for a true man is the fulfillment of his ambition. It does not matter whether he achieves this in China or a foreign country" (111.1736). On the one hand, the novel exhibits a surprisingly tolerant attitude toward the customs of other races and cultures. Echoing Rijing's insistence on the need to have a vision beyond the Middle Kingdom, Wen Suchen's brother-in-law Yunbei (his concubine Su'e's brother), who is a Han Chinese and a long-time resident of the Miao areas, declares that the ancient sage kings could be considered as initially belonging to the *yi* (the barbarian; 94.1478). Wen Suchen also demonstrates some respect for Miao social customs, such as shaking hands and kissing between male and female strangers. The Native Sage's discourse on the Miao people's concept of "free love" is presented from a perspective that is not completely unsympathetic.[46]

On the other hand, behind this show of tolerance is a much stronger desire to convert or "civilize" other races or cultures. For example, a part of the traditional Miao ritual of courtship between a young couple is singing love songs to each other. Now with the encouragement of Suchen, one couple decides instead to sing poems from the Confucian classic *Shijing* (94.1481)—indeed an ingenious compromise! Suchen's masculine body is also presented as a potent symbol of the superiority of Confucian civilization. As mentioned above, it is Suchen's *yang* energy that works wonders on the Miao stone girl. A phrase often used in the novel to describe Suchen's fertility-enhancing powers is *po tianhuang* (unprecedented; something that has never happened before). Suchen says to himself, "If I use my body of pure *yang* to warm [the Miao girl's] body of pure *yin*, I can cause what has never happened to happen [*pipo tianhuang*]" (97.1520; see also the title of chapter 97). The commentator attributes much more symbolic meaning to this incident, reminding the reader that it symbolizes that Suchen has successfully brought civilization into the world of the primitive (102.1605). If we agree with the commentator, then we should consider Wen Suchen's adventures in the Miao areas a "civilizing" mission; his act of using his *yang* energy to rid the Miao girl of her sterility (his male body "fertilizing" the female "body" of the Miao people) captures the masculine essence associated with the imperialist project. Confucian civilization is the active *yang* (masculine) while the Miao people are the passive *yin* (feminine).

Of course, *Yesou puyan* is not the only traditional Chinese novel in which aborigine peoples are presented as the "other" to validate the masculine worthiness of the male protagonist or the civilization that he represents.[47] In *Lingnan yishi*, the male protagonist, Huang Qiong, is someone almost every beautiful and talented Yao girl wants to marry. The two Yao princesses are most impressed by his mastery of literary skills—a symbol of Chinese cultural sophistication—while they themselves are fierce female warriors. In contrast to these two, Huang Qiong's first wife, Gui'er, who is a Han Chinese, is known for her military wisdom rather than her martial prowess. In other words, the Han Chinese are presented as civilized and culturally sophisticated, while the Yao are physically stronger and more militant. However, the cultural sophistication of the male protagonist can only be fully authenticated by the two girls of a different ethnicity. Here we are reminded of a similar strategy in *Sanfen meng*, where Zhang Mengyao has to gain recognition by fighting for foreign countries.

In *Yesou puyan*, spreading Confucianism around the world is, as Rijing has stressed, a mission worthy of a truly great man. From one of his letters to Wen Suchen, the reader learns that Rijing has conquered seventy-two countries in Europe and people in these countries now practice Confucianism. In fact, Rijing is so successful in converting Europeans from Christianity to Confucianism that the king of one country wants to marry his daughter to Suchen's grandson, Wen Shi, who has accidentally landed in the country on a dragon ride (chapter 148; the phallic image of a dragon is certainly an appropriate symbol of Chinese masculinity). After Wen Shi helps them defeat the local bandits, they decide to convert a Catholic church into a special temple to worship him (149.2370). Many Europeans are learning Chinese and reading the Confucian classics (148.2382), while some members of royal families have even mastered Wen Suchen's method of "having less desire to produce more male offspring" by sleeping with their wives according to their menstrual cycles. After all, in Suchen's dream at the end of the novel, the Confucian pantheon is said to be located somewhere in Europe—another sign of the dominance of Confucianism around the world. Unfortunately, our novelist's confidence in the superiority of Confucianism is as blind as his knowledge of sea voyages is inaccurate: we are told that it takes three years for Wen Shi's father-in-law to reach China from Europe by sea (although the voyage is specifically said to be perfectly smooth; 149.2395).[48]

No wonder that only a few decades later in *Sanfen meng* such blind confidence begins to turn into a deep concern that the Chinese empire is going to suffer disaster owing to the opium trade. Another possible symbolic reference to the threat from abroad is the image of a prostitute carrying syphilis, or *yangmei ji.* (Syphilis is referred to in Chinese as *yangmei chang, Guangdong chuang,* or *meidu.*) Many historians of Chinese medicine believe that syphilis was brought to Canton, or Guangdong (thus *Guangdong chuang,* or "Canton sores") by the Portuguese from India in the sixteenth century. This was and probably still is the perception shared by many Chinese. (As we have mentioned, in *Sanfen meng*, Guangdong is explicitly condemned as a place of moral decay.)[49] Consequently, although the four vices were a long-standing concept in Chinese culture, in the novel a new element is infused into the concept: now the vice of sex is presented in the form of a prostitute carrying syphilis, a foreign disease that, like opium, is regarded as yet another threat from abroad that the empire has to face.

If in *Yesou puyan* the Chinese empire occupies the masculine position of an imperialist nation, then in *Sanfen meng* this same empire is relegated to the feminine position of the threatened, a victim of European imperialism. At the individual level, if Rijing considers it a manly duty to spread Confucianism in Europe, then Zhang Mengyao's having to distinguish himself by fighting for foreign countries can be read as an implicit protest against the lack of opportunities for a true man in the Middle Kingdom. Despite the differences between these two novels, their visions of masculinity stand apart from those in many other works because of a new and deepening consciousness of "others" beyond the Middle Kingdom.[50]

Marginality and the Search for Alternative Masculinities

Many novelists of the late eighteenth and early nineteenth centuries served as *muyou* (private secretaries), a profession to which an increasing number of literati turned when they failed in the civil service examinations during the Ming and especially Qing dynasties. As far as we know, Xia Jingqu, the author of *Yesou puyan;* Chen Lang (b. ca. 1715), the author of *Xue Yue Mei;* and Zhang Shideng, the author of *Sanfen meng,* all worked as *muyou* sometime during their lives.[51] Serving on the staff of an important official might have provided a *muyou* with opportunities for using his talents or expertise. However, good performance did not necessarily bring recognition. A *muyou* worked for an official as his personal aide, and there was almost no institutional sanction for such a personal relationship. Moreover, even if a *muyou*'s talents and skills resulted in major achievements, his patron was more likely to receive the recognition for them than was the staff who was actually responsible (see the discussion of Xu Wei in chapter 3).[52] The bitterness over the lack of recognition for one's achievements (not just unproven talent) is apparent in the stories of Zhang Mengyao's military triumphs in *Sanfen meng.* The personal frustrations expressed in *Yesou puyan* and *Sanfen meng* are even more bitter than those encountered in many scholar-beauty novels of the early Qing; hence they give rise to a much stronger need for self-vindication.

Being a *muyou* demanded practical learning and skills, among which military strategy was probably the most appreciated if a patron happened to be involved in military campaigns. This may be why in *Sanfen meng* Zhang Mengyao is celebrated for his knowledge of military affairs. Battlefield glory could certainly ease a *muyou*'s anxiety over being feminized and boost his self-image as a man. However, in reality few *muyou* had this kind of opportunity, and few had the appropriate skills if such an opportunity presented itself. A *muyou*'s typical duties involved daily administrative chores and the handling of various official documents.[53] In *Sanfen meng* (12.10b–11a [pp.

486–487]), Zhang Mengyao's administrative efficiency is briefly noted when he is helping one of his friends (who is apparently working as a clerk for an official), but the narrator does not dwell on this unglamorous aspect of his protagonist's *muyou* abilities.

Medicine was another important alternative profession chosen by many literati who had failed the civil service examinations. Gong Weizhai (fl. 1800), who served as a *muyou* throughout his life, complained that he might have been able to avoid the unhappy experience if he had had enough medical knowledge to support his family as a doctor.[54] Historians of Chinese medicine have traced the emergence of *ruyi* (Confucian doctor) to the Song dynasty, when the status of doctors who were also trained in Confucian learning began to rise dramatically. In a well-known story associated with the famous Song literati official Fan Zhongyan (989–1052), Fan defended medicine as a career choice worthy of a true man if one could not be an effective minister because the goal of medicine was to save lives.[55] As a result, the notion that "if one could not be a good minister, then one should strive to be a good doctor" *(buwei liangxiang, zewei liangyi)* became a common justification for literati to choose careers as doctors.[56] It appears that in Ming-Qing China, being a doctor was often a career option not only for literati who had failed to pass the civil service examinations, but also for those who did not want to be in government service.[57]

Xia Jingqu, the author of *Yesou puyan,* is said to have written works on medicine.[58] Although we do not know the exact role of medicine in his life, we have reason to suspect that his deep interest in it was most likely related to his failures in the civil service examinations. This explains at least in part why in *Yesou puyan* Wen Suchen's medical knowledge receives so much attention and praise, although he does not practice medicine to earn a living. As we have seen, it is often Wen Suchen's medical skills rather than his martial prowess that enable him to be an effective knight-errant and a successful leader in his campaigns against evil ministers and Buddhist clergy. Wen Suchen once declares that the principles behind the science of medicine and those of military warfare are basically the same (21.344), implying that practicing medicine is a profession equally worthy of a true man, echoing the observation by Fan Zhongyan mentioned above. Wen Suchen wins the support of many aborigine peoples mainly because of his successful treatment of their illnesses (chapters 92 and 93)—much like many Western missionaries in China during the nineteenth century. He is even able to provide effective medical treatments for members of the royal family, including the emperor and the son of the crown prince. As mentioned above, being a physician affords Suchen many opportunities for romance and a chance to show his tender sentiments, pushing the *caizi jiaren* formula to new limits. Unquestionably, in *Yesou puyan* medicine also helps to showcase the ideal union between *yingxiong* and *ernü,* as exemplified in Wen Suchen's first saving and then falling in love with the same women.

In conclusion, to better appreciate the masculinities envisioned in novels such as *Yesou puyan* and *Sanfen meng* we have to consider the new realities confronting the literati during the late eighteenth and early nineteenth centuries. While still deeply indebted to the narrative conventions of the scholar-beauty fiction of the early Qing, these novels' new fascination with masculine heroics was closely related to their authors' unique marginalizing experiences, such as working as private secretaries. Moreover, since some of the officials for whom they worked were involved in military campaigns, these authors were once close to the real action themselves.[59] Thus they tried to present their protagonists as "action heroes" rather than merely refined *caizi*. No longer content with the old wish-fulfilling strategy of granting their protagonists the examination honors they themselves had been denied in real life, these novelists now sought alternative ways to reconstruct and imagine their denied manhood, such as achieving honors on the battlefield, through knight-errantry, or even as successful doctors. The masculine images of these "action heroes" must have had a special healing effect on these literati authors, who, relegated to the feminized position of a *muyou*, were never at the center of action or attention.

Compared with the scholar-beauty fiction of the early Qing, many novels of the late eighteenth and early nineteenth centuries were more explicitly autobiographical, and some of their authors were quite frank about the therapeutic function of authoring fictional works. The author of *Xue Yue Mei*, Chen Lang, was probably the first to argue explicitly that his writing of fiction was intended as an act of *liyan*,[60] one of the three ways to achieve cultural immortality *(san buxiu)*, a concept celebrated in traditional cultural discourse. Without directly referring to *liyan*, Zhang Shideng, the author of *Sanfen meng*, explains that he wrote the novel because he did not want to be forgotten by posterity after leading a life without any achievements. The commentator points out the similar fascination with dreams in this novel and *Honglou meng* (6b [p. 4]). The author, however, blames his lack of success on prosperity and peace, implying that great heroic achievements are possible only during a time of disorder and crisis (1.2b [p. 3]), as suggested in the traditional saying, "disorder brings about heroes." The author's comment becomes ironic when the reader learns of the chaos and moral decay described in the novel. It is probably most discouraging that conventional military campaigns are simply useless in dealing with such evils as opium and syphilis. In other words, a traditional hero is no longer able to cope with this new type of disorder, and even the novel's protagonist can triumph over these new vices only in a dream. Here the author appears rather pessimistic even in self-celebration since what is needed is a new kind of heroism.

Parallels between the male protagonists and their authors can also be found in *Lingnan yishi* and *Xue Yue Mei*, although, as noted, a better understanding of the exact nature of these parallels has to be based on more biographical knowledge about the authors. Continuing to exhibit the autobiographical sensibility evident in *Honglou meng* and *Rulin waishi* in the mid-eighteenth century, *Yesou puyan* and *Sanfen meng* anticipated a more visible autobiographical trend in several novels of the late Qing: *Baiyu ting* (The White Fish Pavilion), *Huayue hen* (Traces of Flowers and the Moon), *Qinglou meng* (The Dream of the Blue Towers), and *Lao Can youji* (The Travels of Lao Can).[61] In *Baiyu ting,* the author, Huang Han (fl. mid-nineteenth century), appears as an important character under his real name in many chapters of the novel, while Yu Da (d. 1884), the author of *Qinglou meng,* openly acknowledges at the end of the novel that a substantial part of it is about himself.[62]

Such close parallels between the novels and the life experiences of the novelists separate *Yesou puyan* and *Sanfen meng* from many other works of the same period that have also been classified as *ernü yingxiong xiaoshuo*—including *Zhengchun yuan* (The Garden of Competing Springs) and *Lü mudan* (The Green Peony), in which *caizi* tend to occupy a much less conspicuous position, while knights-errant and martial heroes enjoy even more predominance. Much less autobiographical and focusing almost exclusively on martial and military skills, these novels represent a further departure from the scholar-beauty fiction toward the fiction of chivalry; they have been appropriately called "martial romances" for their focus on martial heroes and their romantic entanglements.[63] In these martial romances *caizi* are replaced by martial heroes, and the sentimentality characteristic of *ernü yingxiong* novels is overshadowed by a new fascination with robust action and the knight-errantry often celebrated in the oral tradition.[64] They constitute a rather different trend in the masculinization process that was taking place among many late eighteenth- and nineteenth-century novels, a complicated topic that has to be dealt with on a separate occasion.

PART 3

WHAT A MAN
OUGHT TO BE

CHAPTER 9

Ideals and Fears in
Prescriptive Literature

Masculinity is a prescriptive concept about what a man should be rather than a descriptive notion of what a man actually is. It is a man's ideal of himself or the ideal of man shared in a particular group of men. In this chapter, it should be helpful to have a look at the ethical codes and behavioral models prescribed for men in some advice books in the late imperial period. Nowhere are masculinities presented more directly and more self-consciously as prescriptive ideals than in conduct advice books.

In an investigation of how masculinities were constructed and negotiated in late imperial cultural discourse, moving from fictional narrative to prescriptive literature may not be such a drastic shift since these two genres were in fact not as different as they may at first appear to be. Didacticism, a defining feature of prescriptive literature, was also an important aspect of a large number of works of *xiaoshuo* (fiction) in traditional China. The best example is perhaps the eighteenth-century novel *Qilu deng* (The Warning Light at the Crossroads), by Li Lüyuan (1707–1790). It was circulated in the form of hand-copied manuscript for almost two centuries until a complete modern typeset edition was published in 1980, a fate not unusual among many traditional fictional works.[1] However, unique to *Qilu deng* was the fact that many of the hand-copied versions of the novel also had attached the author's *Jiaxun zhunyan* (Earnest Words of Household Instructions).[2] *Qilu deng,* which is about how the son of a gentry family undergoes a gradual moral decline and brings his family to almost complete ruination before he is able to reform, was apparently written and intended to be read as a lengthy fictional elaboration of the novelist's "household instructions" attached to the end of the novel. (The reader was supposed to read the novel with constant reference to these instructions.)[3]

Some traditional bibliographers in fact classified works of prescriptive literature as *xiaoshuo.* For example, in the classification by the Ming writer Hu Yinglin (1551–1602), one subcategory of *xiaoshuo* is *zhen'gui* (writings of admonishment). Thus, works such as *Yanshi jiaxun* (Yan's Household

185

Instructions) and *Yuanshi shifan* (Yuan's Precepts for Social Life), which have always been considered classic works of household instruction, were classified by Hu as *xiaoshuo*.[4]

In this chapter, I shall focus on works of prescriptive advice literature that can be roughly divided into two large groups: "household instructions" *(jiaxun)* and "collections of aphoristic sayings" *(geyan* or *zhenyan)*. These works were usually written by men with other men as their intended audience. (There was also a small number of works targeting an exclusively female audience, but they are not discussed here.) When broadly defined, *geyan* or *zhenyan* sometimes include *jiaxun*, and therefore the terms *geyan* and *jiaxun* often overlap. The differences between the two genres are by no means always distinct. However, here by *geyan* and *zhenyan* I refer to collections of aphoristic advice on general topics rather than exclusively on household management. Given the central place of family in traditional Chinese culture, household instructions might be a good place for us to start our examination of masculine models, although in this chapter I shall often juxtapose and compare works of the two genres in terms of certain common themes.[5]

The Dangers of the Feminine within the Family

First, a few words about the definition of family. Patricia Ebrey has differentiated between two conceptions of family in imperial China: one is network oriented, associated with the ancient notion of patriarchal lineage *(zong)*, and the other is more materialist, associated with the household as a budgetary unit *(jia)*.[6] *Jia* as defined by Ebrey is quite different from "family" as understood by a modern reader since it can be composed of many nuclear families (made up of a couple and their children). Moreover, in most household instructions, the concerns of a patriarchal lineage and those of a budgetary unit are often simultaneously present, a fact confirmed by the loose usage of the character *jia* in the titles of many collections of both household instructions and clan rules *(zugui* or *zufa)*, as well as the fact that many collections of household instructions are included in clan genealogies *(zongpu* or *zupu)*.[7] While *jia* is the focus of most household instructions, the context of lineage succession is often there to frame the discourse.[8]

Household instructions are different from all the texts we have so far examined in this study in the sense that here a man is first of all looked upon as a male member of a large family (often as a son because household instructions are supposed to be the words of a father or head of a family to his sons or members of the younger generations). Consequently, the masculinity envisioned here is closely associated with the central issue in many household instructions—namely, whether a male member's behavior is beneficial or detrimental to the interests of the patrilineal family as whole. To be an exemplary man is first of all to be an exemplary son, grandson, or brother.

According to many household instruction writers, the most serious threats to the well-being of a patrilineal family come from within the family itself. One of the most likely sources of such threats are women who originally came from different families but are now part of their husbands' families through marriage. Maintaining family harmony often becomes a problem after the sons have married and have started their own *jia* within the larger family unit and after "outside" women have become members of the family as daughters-in-laws. There is disharmony among the sons when they fail to see eye to eye owing to the meddling of their wives. These wives, who have no blood ties to the family, tend to have interests that are not in complete accord with those of the larger patrilineal group.

Probably because of such discord, in many household instructions from the late imperial period the acid test of manhood is whether a son is able to resist his wife's bad influence and whether he can effectively discipline her. In *Lanling jiaxun* (The Household Instructions of Lanling; dated 1610), the reader is cautioned that "there are very few men with a resolute character, and most men tend to follow women's opinions."[9] In *Yijing tang jiaxun* (Household Instructions of the Hall of the Single Classic; dated 1624) we read the following: "One should never follow a woman's opinions. Before making a decision, consider carefully whether it is in accordance with reason. Decide on your own. You should avoid not only seeking a woman's advice, but also following her advice. People simply should not discuss [household] issues with you unless you are a resolute man."[10]

The nefarious influence of women continues to be considered a direct threat to a man's masculinity in many household instructions written in the Qing dynasty. For example, in *Jiafan,* from the Kangxi period (1662–1722), we find the following lament over men's inability to resist their wives' bad influence:

> In a family, very few brothers have a strong sense of righteousness. Because of the women of different surnames who marry into the family, [brothers] begin to compete with each other. Under the daily influence of [their wives], they start to be selfish and prejudiced. This will eventually lead to disputes and even to the disintegration of the family, as if [the brothers] have become enemies. All this is caused by women. Few men, even those with a strong will, can avoid being misled by women. I have seen many such cases.[11]

In his often anthologized *Zhuzi zhijia geyan* (Master Zhu's Aphorisms for Regulating the Family), Zhu Bolu (1617–1688) associated a man's ability to resist a woman's influence directly with his masculinity: "How can one be a true man if he mistreats his blood-related kinsmen as a result of following a woman's opinions?"[12] Zhu seems to be implying that a man must first look after the interests of his closest kinsmen—that is, those who share his last name (his father and brothers are apparently the most important male relatives)—while his wife or wives are merely "outsiders" from another family. Similar concerns over women's potential for disrupting the harmony of a patrilineal family can also be found in many other household instructions from the Qing.[13]

Consequently, owing to the patriarchal nature of a Chinese family, daughters-in-law, "outsiders" with different surnames, are considered one of the most serious challenges to the manhood of the sons because of their potential for compromising the sons' allegiance to the patrilineal family. At the same time, this emphasis on the challenges posed by female "outsiders" also highlights anxieties over the frailty of the bonds among the sons, as well as their fragile masculinity under the pressure of such "emasculating" forces.[14] Accepting the almost inescapable reality that a married son was more likely to first look after the interests of his own small family and that the breakup of a big family consisting of several generations was inevitable, Wang Huizu (1730–1807; *ECCP*, pp. 824–826), in his *Shuangjie tang yong-xun* (Plain Instructions from the Hall of Double Integrity), advised his children to face up to the eventuality and prepare in advance:

> Would it not be great if many generations of a family could live together? How-ever, it is too difficult to maintain harmony in a family made of many members. Forcing people to live together is not wise. A large number of sons also means a large number of daughters-in-law. Women tend to have difficulty finding com-mon goals; this can become even worse in the case of granddaughters-in-law. If the family properties are not divided, unscrupulous women will spend the money of the family like dirt since they are interested in saving only their private money. If the head of a family is careless in keeping books, poverty will soon follow. Once the head passes away, the sons and their wives will quarrel without end, and this will soon develop into a disaster for the family. According to the *Book of Rites,* "upon reaching the age of sixty, one should be considered old." When feeling old, one should prepare the necessary documents oneself, dividing the property properly so that all disputes can be avoided after one's death.[15]

Here once again women are regarded as one of the key factors directly con-tributing to the decline and disintegration of a large family. In this passage we can almost feel a sense of resignation regarding women's destructive roles in the inevitable tragedy of generational succession and the breakup of an extended patrilineal family. Such a stance explains why Wang Huizu frankly admitted that maintaining a good relationship with one's brothers was often more difficult than being filial toward one's parents.[16] Wang believed that the relationships among the sons were the thorniest and yet also the most important issues in household management, not least because of the complicating roles of the daughters-in-law. He therefore argued that the task of regulating a family should start with the discipline and education of its female members.[17]

Less pessimistic, Wang's contemporary Hu Dayuan (1778–1841) emphasized the need to keep women in check in his *Dizi zhenyan* (Advice for Youngsters): "When young, brothers tend to have a deep love for each other because their heaven-endowed nature has not been corrupted. Friction begins among them after marriages and at the instigation of their wives. The harmony of a family can be maintained only when [the brothers'] heaven-endowed nature stays immune from the influence of their women and when they can instead reform their women."[18] Hu Dayuan attributed the long-lasting harmony of his own family to its male members' strict observation of the family regulation *(jiafa)* that "a man should not follow women's opinions" *(buting furen yan).*[19]

In the section on "Regulating the Family" (Qijia) in *Geyan lianbi* (The Complete Anthology of Aphorisms)—attributed to Jin Lansheng (fl. mid-nineteenth cent.) and very popular during the late Qing—we are warned rather graphically about the possible threats posed by women to the stability and harmony of a patrilineal family if these women are not properly disciplined: "Brothers are like a piece of meat and [their] women, a knife."[20]

Such general suspicions toward women in household instructions are reminiscent of similar sentiments in many novels, such as *Shuihu zhuan* (discussed in chapter 5), where maintaining a safe distance from women was considered crucial to one's manhood. In a way, both "country" *(guo)* and "family" *(jia)* were patrilineal institutions where male succession was the only acceptable or legitimate option and where the influence of "outsiders" (women with different surnames) was always perceived to be the biggest threat. In both situations, one's manliness was equated with the ability to keep one's distance from women.

Another perceived threat from "outsiders" to the well-being of a family came from friends. The status of women in a patrilineal family could sometimes be ambivalent since they could be considered at least "semi-insiders" once married into the family, but friends remain unequivocally outsiders. Male friends were dangerous because they tended to undermine the sacred bond among the male members of the family. If a man treated his friends as brothers, then his relationships with his real brothers might suffer. (Consequently, an essential aspect of the patriarchal family would be subverted.) This is why Wu Linzheng (1593–1644) concluded the following in his *Jiajie yaoyan* (Essential Advice for Household Management): "If one treats his friends better than his brothers, it is like favoring the flower petals at the expense of the roots of a plant. One should never behave like this. Never!"[21] A related theme of many household instructions is that a youngster should be extremely cautious in choosing friends.[22] Pan Deyu (1785–1839) even suggested in his *Shi'er changyu* (Earnest Words for My Sons) that a son should not be allowed to make any friends until he was in his late twenties since young people were both very vulnerable and impressionable.[23]

Probably because of such wariness about friendship, the popular late Ming collection of aphorisms *Caigen tan* (Wisdom Acquired after a Hard Life), attributed to Hong Yingming (fl. 1596), offered interesting advice on the education of youngsters (although *Caigen tan* was not a collection of household instructions by any means): "Raising a [male] youngster is just like raising a young maiden. One has to be very cautious as to who is allowed to enter one's house and with whom the youngster is making friends. Once in contact with evil people, one becomes a contaminated seed planted in an otherwise clean field. Consequently, the entire field is ruined, and no good crops can be raised there."[24] The concern over a young man's possible exposure to the evil influence of bad friends was so great that some writers of household instructions urged that a son be completely segregated from outsiders, just like a girl. This concern may explain in part why certain qualities typical of girls, such as a lack of sophistication and bashfulness, were considered good indications of a young man's "moral purity."[25] The dire consequences of bad associations are most vividly illustrated in the quasi-*jiaxun* novel *Qilu deng*, where the male protagonist's moral degeneration is said to have been caused in large part by the corrupting influence of evil friends. (They introduced him to prostitutes, gambling, and money counterfeiting, and they repeatedly lured him back into bad habits when he tried to reform.)[26]

Wary of the threats posed by women, bad friends, and other corrupting elements within and outside the household, almost all the authors of household instructions emphasize the need to come to terms with the seemingly inevitable decay or decline of any patrilineal family. The foremost task of the male members of a family, therefore, is to avoid such decay and maintain family harmony and prosperity as long as possible.[27] In his *Jiazheng xuzhi* (A Guide for Household Governing), the seventeenth-century writer Ding Yaokang (1599–1671), who was also the author of a sequel to the novel *Jin Ping Mei*, devoted two sections (out of a total of ten) to the discussion of specific measures to avoid family decline: "Fangdu" (How to Prevent Corrosion) and "Bai" (Decaying).[28]

In *Jiaxun zhunyan*, Li Lüyuan instructed that "No matter what a man is dealing with in life, as long as he can keep in mind the word 'fear' [*pa*], he will not err too far."[29] In the novel *Qilu deng*, the male protagonist's father appears to be constantly worried that any slight mistakes on his part will lead to the rapid decline of his family. Thus he insists on the need to be in constant fear.[30] In the middle of the novel, the narrator (i.e., the novelist) refers directly to Confucius' disciple Zengzi, who emphasized the importance of moral vigilance in the *Lunyu* (discussed in chapter 1): "A young student should be very careful about where he sets his feet. Being over cautious is at least better than being self-indulgent. Consider the ancient sage, who protected his integrity like a piece of precious jade. Right up to his death, he was still talking about being 'in fear and trembling, as if approaching a deep abyss, as if walking on thin ice. . . .' Lucky youngsters, may you have the word 'fear' implanted in your minds after reading [the novel]."[31] One of the most effective ways to avoid the decline of a family, Li Lüyuan seems to suggest, is to be constantly aware of how easily and quickly a family can decline.

Sages, Heroes, and Other Models

Li Lüyuan's emphasis on the need for caution and especially his reference to Zengzi's quotation from the *Shijing* ("as if approaching a deep abyss, as if walking on thin ice") are perfectly in line with the Neo-Confucian ideal of manhood promoted by Zhu Xi and his followers (discussed in chapters 1 and 8). Ever since Zhu Xi suggested that true heroic spirits were the results of being "in fear and trembling, as if approaching a deep abyss, as if walking on thin ice," many literati have celebrated caution and prudence as the most important virtues of a Confucian masculine hero.[32] These lines became the favorite metaphors of many later writers of conduct books for their own versions of masculinity, while the relationship between hero and sage was one of the central issues in the Confucian discourse on masculinity.

In *Shenyin yu* (The Groaning Words), an influential collection of aphorisms, the late Ming scholar-official Lü Kun (1536–1618; *DMB*, pp. 1006–1010) noted that "One's mind should be as bright and high as the blue sky in daylight, and one's behavior should be as cautious as that of someone approaching a deep abyss or walking on thin ice."[33] Elsewhere in this same work, the author wrote that "A heroic gentleman should always be cautious as if in fear and trembling, but he should be completely fearless whenever confronted with a crisis."[34] In contrast to many authors of household instructions, Lü Kun alluded to the importance of courage and fearlessness, as we will see below. In *Caigen tan* we are told that "If a man hopes for great achievement in life, he first has to be able to walk on thin ice." Elsewhere in the same collection, the reader is again reminded that the ability of a great hero to shape the world is often the result of his being constantly aware of the dangers associated with walking on the edge of an abyss or on thin ice.[35] In other words, to be successful in life and to be a fearless hero, a man first has to learn to be morally vigilant or to constantly cultivate "fear" in his mind so that he can avoid moral failure.

In another popular late Ming collection of aphorisms, *Xiaochuang youji* (Jottings in Seclusion under the Small Window), attributed to Chen Jiru, the author submitted that the successes of a sage were the result of his being constantly cautious and prudent. The comment echoed Zhu Xi's famous earlier definition of a true hero, only Chen Jiru replaced Zhu Xi's hero with his "sage," suggesting that what Zhu Xi had originally meant by "hero" was actually "sage"—just as another late Ming writer, Jiang Yingke, had complained that Zhu Xi should not have confused the two (see chapter 8). Elsewhere, Chen Jiru wrote that a man needed to have qualities associated with both sage and hero: "[A man] should have the moral integrity of a sage [more literally, the bones of a sage] and the courage of a hero [*shengxian wei gu, yingxiong wei dan*]."[36] Chen here seems to imply that the qualities of a sage alone are not enough for ultimate masculinity. Chen's implicit revisionist agenda also pointed to the possible tensions between "sage" and "hero," as we discussed in the case of the male protagonist of *Yesou puyan* in chapter 8. As mentioned in chapter 1, Zhu Xi proposed his definition of a true hero in his famous debate with Chen Liang, whom he accused of overemphasizing profit *(li)* in his celebration of a hero.[37] The most essential quality of a true Confucian hero, according to Zhu Xi, was unrelenting vigilance against possible moral failure and a keen awareness of his own fallibility.

While people such as Jiang Yingke thought that Zhu Xi had confused sage with hero, the early Qing thinker Yan Yuan defended Chen Liang vehemently (although from a rather different perspective), emphasizing the similarities between hero and sage: "This is what the sages called 'appropriateness' and 'timing' or what outstanding men of later ages considered 'expediency' and 'being flexible. . . .' Many Confucian scholars consider this trickery or fraud and try to rule it out as part of the sagely way. Consequently, many heroic figures from the Han and Tang dynasties have not been allowed to share the glories of the sages. This is why Chen Longchuan [Chen Liang] was so upset."[38] Zhu Xi's deep suspicion of Chen Liang's admiration for the enterprising spirit of a hero, in the eyes of people such as Yan Yuan, was the direct result of Zhu's overemphasis of self-cultivation at the expense of practical learning and the need for achievement in public affairs.[39] Yan Yuan's elder contemporary, the thinker and historian Huang Zongxi, pointed out that in his time many people had begun to argue that *ru* (Confucian learning) had no role in bringing about success and achievements in the actual world:

> Confucian learning was originally about managing the concrete things between Heaven and Earth. However, people of later ages consider studying the "quotations" [from the sages] the most important thing. After reading some commentaries by the Song Confucians, they regard themselves as members of *ru* and begin to deceive the world in the name of *ru*. . . . Whenever there is a serious crisis and the country needs their service, they will be at a total loss, with their mouths wide open, as if sitting on clouds. Morality has declined to such a degree that some critics now insist that practical achievement in public service depends on a totally different kind of "learning" that is completely beyond those Confucian scholars.

Huang here was expressing his concerns over what he perceived to be an overemphasis of sagehood at the expense of practical learning. The view that a hero, who is good at getting practical results, cannot be completely replaced by a sage was echoed by Lü Kun when he observed that an official needed to have the heart of a sage and the insights and talents of a hero.[40] Here "the insights and talents of a hero" refers to the practical abilities of a hero, which, it is implied, a sage might not have. However, elsewhere in *Shenyin yu,* Lü Kun offered a more discriminating view that presented a rather different picture: "Someone asked how one should judge [the moral character of] a certain person. I answered, 'Although he could be considered a hero, he still cannot be considered a man of integrity.' Then he said, 'If he could be regarded as a man of integrity, he may not be considered an all-around Confucian gentleman of moral integrity.' I said, 'A hero among men of integrity is a perfect Confucian gentleman of moral integrity.'"[41]

Here "an all-around Confucian gentleman of moral integrity" is obviously the image of a sage in Lü Kun's mind, and on his scale, the status of such a sage is much higher than that of a hero. This valorization of sage is also confirmed by the fact that in *Shenyin yu* Lü devoted an entire section (entitled "Sage") to the question of how to achieve sagehood because he bitterly complained that many heroes had been corrupted by a world full of immoral people.[42] Obviously, for Lü Kun an ordinary hero was still morally vulnerable, and he was especially concerned over the potential harm that an overzealous hero could do: "Though sound and straight, the courage of a hero can be quite rough. One-tenth of this energy is often enough. If the remaining nine-tenths is also used, it may lead instead to disaster."[43] According to Lü Kun, being overactive was a common fault of many heroes: "How many heroes have aged [wasted their youths] in noise and excitement. Only a sage could enjoy the tranquility of the disinterested, and only he could cope with noise and excitement with a cool and disinterested mind. The truth of everything under Heaven can be sought only through the tranquility of being disinterested. Therefore, tranquility is what gives rise to action."[44]

Following the Song Neo-Confucian emphasis on *jing,* or "tranquility," Lü Kun seems to have paid particular attention to the importance of achieving a tranquil mind: "The strength a man can acquire after quieting his mind can overpower a thousand buffaloes, and the resultant courage can enable him to overwhelm ten tigers."[45] Moreover, Lü Kun provided an example of the "noise and excitement" associated with an overactive hero who had failed to quiet his mind: "As soon as he hears a story of injustice, he gets all pumped up with anger and begins to make extreme remarks. This is the behavior of a superficial man, precisely what a true gentleman should never do."[46] Here Lü Kun was apparently denigrating the kind of *haohan* masculinity or knight-errantry celebrated and made famous in *Shuihu zhuan* (see chapter 5). In his view, this kind of hero was totally reckless. Lü Kun's concern over heroism running wild is echoed in two seventeenth-century novels examined in chapter 6, *Suishi yiwen* and *Sui Tang yanyi,* where wild heroes are deliberately tamed, as exemplified in the maturation that their common protagonist, Qin Shubao, is supposed to have undergone.

Lü Kun's ambivalence toward heroes was shared by quite a few Confucian thinkers of later ages. The early Qing savant Wang Fuzhi (1619–1692; *ECCP,* pp. 817–819), for example, warned about potential harm if one did not know how to properly read the biographies of such heroes as Xiang Yu in Sima Qian's *Shiji.* Wang pointed out further that "there have been heroes who were not sages, but there have never been any sages who were not heroes."[47] In his collection of aphorisms, *Youmeng ying* (The Shadow of a Tranquil Dream), the much less orthodox Zhang Chao (fl. late seventeenth century) concurred with Lü Kun when he conceded that it was much easier to be a hero than to be a sage.[48]

Shenyin yu, Caigen tan, and *Xiaochuang youji* were all written during the turbulent late Ming, an age known for its ideological and cultural pluralism. The last two texts have also been classified as works of *qingyan* (pure words), a special genre of aphoristic writings popular during the late Ming and early Qing. (*Youmeng ying* was an early Qing work of *qingyan* greatly influenced by its late Ming predecessors.) Many *qingyan* works are characterized by a hedonistic, and often hermetic, tendency to view life aesthetically, as well as by a prose style that foregrounds its own aesthetic appeal. The philosophy promoted in these writings, though not necessarily heretical, is not always in keeping with orthodox Confucian values.[49] Furthermore, unlike household instructions, *qingyan* collections tend to deal with a greater variety of topics and are therefore more likely to conceptualize masculinity from different and even sometimes conflicting perspectives. Here the focus may not be on the interests of a patrilineal family, so the male roles that are presented are much more diverse and go beyond those of an exemplary son or grandson as prescribed in household instructions. Likewise, Confucian values are not as prevalent in *qingyan* works as they tend to be in many household instructions, although compared with the views of Chen Jiru and other writers of *qingyan,* those of Lü Kun are much more Confucian as well as more orthodox.[50]

Even though moral caution and prudence are still honored in these general collections of aphorisms, now they may be emphasized (especially in *qingyan* writings such as those by Chen Jiru) as qualities that a man needs just in order to survive in a dangerous world rather than as sage qualities for moral self-cultivation. While the Confucian spirit of active engagement with worldly affairs is still endorsed, alternative models of masculinity are also promoted: "While alive, a true man should seek success in his career and reward from the government; when dead, [he should] be remembered and worshiped by posterity. However, he can also cultivate himself by withdrawing into private life and amuse himself with books and poetry."[51]

At least two quite different models of masculinity are here considered equally worthy of emulation. For Chen Jiru, who was probably the most famous recluse during the late Ming, "a hero is the result of being simple and disinterested." [52] Elsewhere, Chen Jiru even suggested that a man should eventually transcend the very concern about whether he was manly enough: "Only after giving up the concerns of a vulgar person can one become a man; only after giving up the concerns of a man can one become an immortal; only after giving up the concerns of an immortal can one be considered to have acquired the Way." [53] The Zen-like rhetoric here points to a transcending spirit that is almost Buddhist as well as Taoist. According to Zhang Chao, a perfect man's life should be comprised of the following four stages: "a child prodigy at ten, a romantic scholar [*caizi*] at twenty or thirty, a famous official at forty or fifty, and an immortal at sixty." [54] These aphorisms underscored that a perfect man should be capable of playing different and even sometimes conflicting roles and succeeding in quite different areas. A man's ability to be multifaceted was being valorized as a virtue that enabled him to adapt to the different and changing environment he might had to face in the different stages of his life. His ability to adapt to changes was the hallmark of a true man. [55]

In contrast, Lü Kun insisted that the ultimate true man could only be a sage: "Not being soft is certainly the quality of a man; being soft and yet not losing one's resoluteness is the sign of a true man. This is how one is able to tell a sage from a wise man." [56] He further observed: "A pedantic scholar can only recite passages from books; a woman is always timid and cautious; a true man behaves in a prompt and straightforward manner; only a sage can be flexible as well as versatile." [57] The most elevated masculine qualities, we are told, can be found only in a sage.

As a literati writer and painter, Chen Jiru was much less moralistic in constructing his models of masculinity. He argued that education (especially book learning) was an important part of being a man: "A sword can overwhelm ten thousand enemies, while a pen can conquer one thousand troops." [58] His observation on the relationship between a hero and love is particularly radical: "There can be no contradiction between heroic valor and romantic love." [59] Such a view could never have been condoned in any household instructions. Romantic love is probably the last thing a writer of household instructions would promote given his typical anxiety about the potential harm a woman could do to the harmony of a patrilineal family. For example, in Wu Linzheng's *Jiajie yaoyan*, we are told, "If one is nearsighted, his great aspirations will dissipate; if one indulges in romantic feelings, his heroic spirit will dwindle." [60] Of course, we are already acquainted with the image of a hero capable of romantic feelings from our discussion in chapter 8.

According to Chen Jiru, before a man can achieve the eloquence of a hero in writing, he has to finish reading three thousand books and visit all the magnificent mountains and rivers under Heaven. [61] Furthermore, Chen Jiru compares befriending all the outstanding men under Heaven to reading all the marvelous books that others have not had a chance to read, insisting that chivalry is a necessary part of any friendship.[62] For Chen Jiru, dying for the sake of a *zhiji* (soulmate) is the most manly thing a man can do.[63] Such admiration for friendship reached new heights in Zhang Chao's *Youmeng ying:* "Seeking a soulmate among one's friends is easy; seeking a soulmate among one's wives and concubines is difficult; seeking a soulmate in a prince one serves as a minister is even much more difficult."[64] Here the hierarchical order assumed in the Confucian "five cardinal relationships" is completely reversed: friendship becomes the most desirable, and the prince and minister relationship is presented as the least pleasant. Zhang Chao appears to have paid particular attention to what he called a "bosom friend": "If the person is someone to whom you can confide what you cannot confide to your wife, then that person must be your bosom friend."[65]

Much more conservative, Lü Kun also attached great importance to friendship:

> Friendship is a very important relationship, and this is why it is grouped together with other important relationships, such as those between prince and minister and between father and son, to constitute the so-called "five cardinal relationships." It would be difficult for a man to have great success in life without friends. A prince rules people with regulations and laws; a father loves his sons and will not always admonish them to be good; brothers cherish harmony, and they will not want to hurt each other's feelings by arguing; women have to do chores at home and cannot follow their husbands and keep an eye on them all the time; to persuade his father to correct his mistakes, a son, though willing to argue, will not risk the accusation of being unfilial; in the presence of a teacher, one tends to control oneself and conceal one's shortcomings; at home, being intimate and loving, people usually avoid talking about serious topics. Only with friends does one spend much time everyday; it is unlike seeing a teacher for only a limited period of time. Only with friends can one speak freely without taboos, as one has in the presence of one's father or brothers. . . . This is why friendship is what the other four cardinal relationships rely on![66]

Here Lü Kun comes close to asserting that friendship should be the most important among the five cardinal relationships. This positive attitude toward friendship forms an interesting contrast with the deep anxiety about friends exhibited in many household instructions discussed above.[67] However, one important difference between Lü Kun and Chen Jiru or Zhang Chao is that the former would never embrace the kind of chivalry admired by the latter two. This may explain why Chen Jiru and Zhang Chao repeatedly praised *Shuihu zhuan,* while the *haohan* heroism celebrated in this novel was precisely what made Lü Kun uneasy.[68] Occasionally for Lü Kun, even Mencius, who (as we discussed in chapter 1) had played a crucial role in the formation of the ideal of manhood cherished by so many later Confucians, might have appeared to be a bit too reckless. According to Lü,

Mencius, not as modest or prudent as Confucius, was sometimes too arrogant and relied too much on his own courage.[69]

According to Lü Kun, a true man was almost always a tragic loner, who, like Confucius, held onto his own convictions despite overwhelming odds: "Relying on many people is not as good as relying on only a select few; relying on a select few is not as good as relying on no one. Relying on no one, one relies on Heaven; relying on Heaven, one alone has the true knowledge. You do not feel isolated even if you are all alone in the whole universe. Being able to remain unmoved whether everyone admires or condemns you is the hallmark of what I call a man."[70] Although sharing many other writers' admiration for the virtue of *ren,* or the capacity to endure hardships and humiliations, Lü Kun appeared to be wary of people's tendency to choose expediency at the expense of principle: "To accept small humiliations for the sake of gaining a big advantage is what a sage would not do."[71] Incidentally, this might be read as a critique of Sima Qian's notion of masculinity which is defined by a man's capacity to cope with humiliation (see chapter 1).

Many modern scholars would probably hesitate to classify *Shenyin yu* as a work of *qingyan,* in part because many of its views are simply too orthodox. However, *Jinyuan xiaoyu* (Insignificant Words from the Garden of Briars), by Shen Hanguang (1618–1677), often considered a work of *qingyan,* shares many of the conservative views of *Shenyin yu.* Lü Kun's influence on Shen was obvious: in *Jingyuan xiaoyu,* Shen specifically referred to *Shenyin yu* as a must-read.[72] Like Lü Kun, Shen criticized people's tendency to swear to brotherhood too easily—again a trait admired by the *haohan* heroes in *Shuihu zhuan.* He cautioned that having too many friends was often a cause for trouble; apparently he was much more conservative than Lü Kun on this point.[73] It is interesting too that Shen shared Wang Huizu's rather realistic view that the eventual split of a big patriarchal family, though deeply regrettable, was inevitable.

The Virtue of *Ren*

Ren (the ability to endure and accommodate) is an important virtue celebrated in both household instructions and other kinds of prescriptive literature, a manly quality we have discussed in relation to the historian Sima Qian (chapter 1) and Qin Shubao, the male protagonist in several novels from the Sui-Tang romance cycle (chapter 6). In fact, a collection of aphoristic sayings entitled *Quanren baizhen* (One Hundred Pieces of Advice on the Need for *Ren*), attributed to the Yuan writer Xu Mingkui (fl. fourteenth century), concentrates exclusively on the need to endure and accommodate. It became so popular during the late imperial period that it also became known as *Renjing* (The Classic of *Ren*).[74]

In *Xiaoyou tang jiaxun* (Household Instructions from the Hall of Filial-

ity and Fraternity), by the early Qing thinker Sun Qifeng, *ren* is a prominent topic: "Han Xin suffered humiliation by crawling between someone's
legs, while Zhang Liang [suffered the same] by picking up shoes for an old
man from under a bridge. These two heroes achieved great success in their
lives because they were able to endure humiliation."[75] Sun Qifeng was here
referring to the particular brand of masculinity promoted by Sima Qian,
defined by a man's ability to cope with humiliation, as exemplified in Sima
Qian's well-known biographies of Han Xin and Zhang Liang, one a famous
general and the other a brilliant military strategist, both of whom fought the
founder of the Han dynasty, Liu Bang (discussed in chapter 1). The author
of *Yijing tang jiaxun* urged his audience to be ready to yield or make con-
cessions: "One has to learn to yield and accept losses. From ancient times,
many heroes and outstanding men have suffered defeat simply because they
refused to yield or take any losses [*chikui*] and because they insisted on
being unyielding and saving face."[76] A clear message is that such heroes can
be remembered only as tragic figures because of their inability to endure
and accommodate. Very similar remarks can be found in Wang Huizu's
Shuangjie tang yongxun.[77] Here the concept of *ren* comes very close to the
modern notion of self-control, an important element in many modern
notions of masculinity in the West. However, a crucial difference is that in
these works of prescriptive literature self-control is understood only in
terms of a man's capacity to endure hardship and especially humiliation.[78]

With *qingyan* losing popularity sometime after the seventeenth century,
general collections of aphorisms became increasingly conservative. At the
same time, the differences between general aphoristic writings and household instructions became less distinct, a fact confirmed by the appearance
of many works that covered topics far beyond those of family governance
but were often included in anthologies of household instructions because
they contained substantial discussions of family issues—for example, *Geyan
lianbi*, *Zidi zhenyan* (Advice for Youngsters) and *Zeng "Guangxian wen"*
(An Expanded Version of "The Writings That Spread Virtue"). Compared
with earlier works of prescriptive literature (especially those written in the
sixteenth and seventeenth centuries), those of the nineteenth century tended
to be less original, although the continuities in the works of prescriptive literature from different ages have always been quite remarkable. (Later
works tended to imitate or simply copy earlier works.) By the same token,
models of masculinity in the later works tended to be more uniform and
more Confucian, and the "heroic spirit" celebrated in the works of the late
Ming and early Qing was largely dissipated.

Needless to say, the models of masculinity presented in prescriptive literature are mostly ideals, and the gaps between these models and the cor-
responding images in other written genres, such as historiography and fiction, are necessarily substantial. In fact, an advice book was more likely to

promote what its author had perceived to be absent in the real world (and therefore needed to be promoted). As far as masculinity is concerned, apprehensions over compromised manhood are almost always present in these prescriptive writings. These apprehensions are more obvious in household instructions, where the bonds among the male members of a patriarchal family are of paramount importance and where such bonds are said to be extremely vulnerable to the threats posed by "outsiders" such as female household members and friends. Here again the (male) reader is supposed to experience anxieties over his manhood; as the authors of many conduct books have warned, it is necessary to heed the Song Neo-Confucian master Zhu Xi's advice: be in constant vigil against any possible moral failures.

EPILOGUE

Masculinity and Modernity

Quite a few scholars of Chinese cultural history have observed that Chinese men became increasingly feminized during the Ming-Qing period in comparison with their counterparts in the Han (206 BCE–220 CE) and Tang (618–907) dynasties. Many of them regard the Song dynasty (960–1279) as a period when this feminization began to accelerate. For example, the scholar Min Jiayin observes the following:

> Before the Song dynasty, China was advanced in many areas, such as the economy, technology, and culture. However, after the Song dynasty, China began to lag behind. Before the Song dynasty, Chinese culture and Chinese men were full of unbending *yang* spirit [*yanggang zhi qi*]. However, after the Song dynasty, the unbending *yang* spirit began to dissipate among the men, while the soft spirit of *yin* [*yinrou*] began to rise. . . . In our eastern neighbor, Japanese culture produced the samurai, who were full of unbending *yang* spirit. Consequently, they were able to help their emperor complete the Taika reforms and catch up with China. Later, after the Meiji reforms, Japan was able to catch up with the West.[1]

Min Jiayin is here asserting a direct correlation between China's advanced status in the world prior to the tenth century and contemporary Chinese men's masculine prowess, as well as between the rise of modern Japan and the masculinity of the Japanese samurai, implying that China's later failure to modernize was somehow closely related to the supposed decline of the manliness of Chinese men.

Claims of the feminization of late imperial Chinese men are at best based on anecdotal evidence, however. The perceived decline of the Middle Kingdom during these long centuries, marked by the defeats of the Han Chinese at the hands of their nomadic neighbors to the north during the Song-Yuan and Ming-Qing transitions, contributed to this impression of a process of feminization. More significant, most of these views on decline are in various ways shaped by an implicit "modernity agenda" of their propagators.

200

In other words, accounts of Chinese men becoming increasingly feminized during the late imperial period are most likely teleological narratives developed to account for China's humiliating encounters with the Western powers, a process that started in approximately the mid-nineteenth century. (Of course, such equating of manhood with nationhood had precedents in Chinese history, as examined in chapter 4.) In a word, they were often constructed by some modern historians to explain China's failures to achieve modernity.

This study is not meant to prove or disprove the veracity of such teleological "histories" of late imperial Chinese masculinity. Whether men in Ming-Qing China appeared more feminized in comparison with their ancestors in Tang China is probably not a fruitful topic of investigation since one can always question the historical validity of the standards by which any such comparison is made. Instead, it would be more fruitful to explore what was unique about the ways in which late imperial Chinese men articulated their gender awareness or how they came to terms with the perceived challenges to their manhood, as I have attempted to do in this study. In conclusion, it would be interesting to see how these teleological narratives were shaped by China's painful experience in its encounter with the Western powers (including Japan) or what their complex ideological as well as historical underpinnings were. Whereas a detailed discussion of these issues is beyond the scope of this epilogue, a brief look should place the above exploration of late imperial masculinities in a broader and more recent historical context, as well as suggest possible directions for future research.

The two novels that we examined in chapter 8, *Yesou puyan* and *Sanfen meng,* despite their sometimes exaggerated masculine self-confidence, already anticipate new foreign threats to Chinese manhood that would fundamentally reshape the Middle Kingdom in almost every aspect during the following century. The shock and despair that many late Qing intellectuals experienced in their initial encounters with the West are reminiscent of the soul-searching of many early Qing thinkers with regard to the survivability of Han Chinese civilization and their own gender identities as the educated males of a conquered nation. Writing on chaste women in the aftermath of the Manchu conquest seems to have provided these male literati with an opportunity to reexamine their own gender identities and search for the reasons behind the failure of so many of them to fulfill their manly duties.[2] Throughout Chinese history, educated males were often compelled to reflect upon their failures as men when a dynasty fell (especially when the fall was the result of an invasion by "outsiders"). During these self-reflective moments, manhood was almost always equated with nationhood. The ruthless "penetration" by the Manchus seemed to have turned Han Chinese men into "women" (that is, the conquered). Another and probably even more profound foreign "penetration"—this time by the Western industrial powers during the late nineteenth century—again forced many educated Chinese men to question their manliness. Many felt that their manhood was being questioned owing to the bruised "nationhood."[3]

Here a small but symbolic incident regarding the late Qing scholar Wang Tao (1828–1890) during a sojourn in England in the late 1860s is revealing. Walking on a street in London, Wang Tao, in Chinese dress and with a long queue, was mistaken for a Chinese lady. Wang was quite humiliated, feeling that his manhood as a Chinese man was seriously challenged. He even wondered if this mistaken gender identity was an ominous prediction *(chenyu)* for the rest of his life.[4] Wang was one of the first Chinese intellectuals who was directly exposed to the Western world and who became keenly aware of the importance of Western learning. His humiliating experience indeed captured the gender implications of what later happened to many of his fellow Chinese men as the citizens of a weak nation.

Min Jiayin's direct equation of "modernity" with "masculinity" was part of the common rhetoric of the nationalist discourse among many late Qing and early Republican reformists at the turn of the twentieth century. The famous reformist Liang Qichao (1873–1929), for example, called on his fellow countrymen to again show their ancestors' warrior spirit, or *bushido (wushi dao),* which, according to him, had characterized many Chinese men before the Han dynasty and which seemed to have disappeared in later periods. It is ironic that the Japanese were believed to have cultivated and maintained their *bushido* so well that Japan eventually became a world-class power while China was relegated to the position of a weak and therefore "feminized" nation, even though the spirit of *bushido* was supposed to have flourished first in the Middle Kingdom.[5]

In the writings of late Qing reformists such as Liang Qichao, the feminization of Chinese men was often described in terms of *dongya bingfu* (the sick man of East Asia). After visiting North America, Liang complained in a travelogue that whenever the Chinese gathered to listen to a lecture, only four kinds of noise could be heard from the audience: coughing, sneezing, yawning, and wiping runny noses.[6] Such anxieties over a "weak body" and its assumed connections with China's status as a weak nation were shared by many reformists. Consequently, physical education and military training became important issues in the reform movement.[7] The focus on deplorable effeminacy (symbolized by men's weak bodies) and the need to remasculinize is reminiscent of Yan Yuan's similar views approximately two centuries ago, when the Chinese empire had just been conquered by the nomadic Manchus. The reformists' intense interest in this early Qing thinker at the turn of the twentieth century was not a coincidence: it was an integral part of the their campaign to modernize and remasculinize the Middle Kingdom.[8]

In "Yan Li xuepai yu xiandai jiaoyu sichao" (The School of Yan Yuan and Li Gong and Its Relationship with Modern Educational Trends), Liang

Qichao applauded Yan Yuan as a great educator; he repeatedly quoted Yan's scathing criticism of Song Neo-Confucianism for its feminizing effects and for its "physical drain" on Chinese men in terms of its overemphasis on quiet sitting and book learning. He hailed Yan Yuan as one of the few who had paid serious attention to *tiyu* (physical education) throughout the two-thousand-year history of imperial China.[9] Elsewhere Liang Qichao asserted that Yan Yuan's emphasis on concrete and practical learning resembled the views of William James and John Dewey, two modern American thinkers very popular among the reformists at that time.[10] Thus Yan Yuan, a seventeenth-century Confucian thinker, was resurrected as a manly hero with even a vision of Chinese modernity.[11]

Given the ingenious late Qing reinvention of Yan Yuan as a cultural hero of modern vision and his celebrated obsession with the martial arts, can we interpret the immense popularity of the image of *xia* (knight-errant) among many reformists (including Liang Qichao) as part of the larger remasculinization and modernization movement of that time?[12] If we can, how does this interpretation complicate our understanding of the gender implications of *wuxia xiaoshuo* (martial arts fiction), which flourished during the same period? How should we explain the continued presence of feminine *caizi* in the so-called *yuanyang hudie pai xiaoshuo* (mandarin ducks and butterflies fiction), which was gaining popularity during the early twentieth century? How were traditional images of *yingxiong* and *haohan* appropriated to help reinvent different models of masculinity in the new environment of a China in pursuit of modernity? What are the gender ramifications of the transition from "traditional literati" to "modern intellectuals" that many educated Chinese men were experiencing at the time? These are some of the interesting questions we may want to investigate in terms of the continuities and discontinuities in the history of modern Chinese masculinities. Regardless of the different answers we may come up with, one thing seems certain: "loyal minister" *(zhongchen),* one of the central symbolic figures explored in this study, is likely to be replaced in any serious study of modern Chinese masculinities by another figure as the focus of investigation: an intellectual burdened by being a male citizen in a weak nation and caught between tradition and modernity. Here nationalism and masculinity are often perceived to be two different aspects of the same issue.[13]

NOTES

INTRODUCTION

1. Yan Yuan, "Xingli ping," in Yan Yuan, *Yan Yuan ji*, p. 62. Unless otherwise noted, translations are mine.

2. Li Gong, *Yan Yuan nianpu*, p. 34.

3. For a more detailed discussion of Yan Yuan, see chapter 4.

4. "Homosocial" is a term borrowed from Sedgwick, *Between Men*. She observes the following: "'Homosocial' is a word occasionally used in history and social sciences, where it describes social bonds between persons of the same sex; it is a neologism, obviously formed by analogy with 'homosexual' . . . and just as obviously meant to be distinguished from 'homosexual.' In fact, it is applied to such activities as 'male bonding,' which may, as in our society, be characterized by intense homophobia, fear and hatred of homosexuality. To draw the 'homosocial' back into the orbit of 'desire,' of the potentially erotic, then, is to hypothesize the potential unbrokenness of a continuum between homosocial and homosexual—a continuum whose visibility, for men, in our society, is radically disrupted" (pp. 1–2).

5. For a more theoretical discussion of this issue from a different perspective, see Rouzer, *Articulated Ladies*, pp. 34–38. Among recent publications in English on gender in Chinese literary history, Rouzer's study is probably most relevant to one of the central concerns of my study—namely, the relationship between the literati's representation of women and their male anxiety. However, in addition to our obviously different approaches, we deal with rather different texts in terms of both genres and historical periods. While a significant part of Rouzer's study concentrates on the male literati's representation of women, I deal with this issue only to the extent that it is relevant to the specific negotiating strategies of masculinization.

6. Black, "Gender and Cosmology in Chinese Correlative Thinking," p. 175.

7. Furth, *A Flourishing Yin*, pp. 48–49.

8. Ibid., p. 46.

9. Ibid., p. 48.

10. In his recent book, *The Fragile Scholar* (pp. 150–182), Geng Song has paid little attention to the women characters in his discussion of masculinity in *San'guo yanyi*.

11. Louie's and Song's studies were not available to me until the draft manuscript of this volume was already completed. Other works are also worth mentioning: Brownell and Wasserstrom, *Chinese Femininities/Chinese Masculinities*, contains several articles related to the concerns of this study. The editors' introduction is particularly helpful in offering an overview of the field of Chinese gender studies. Also relevant are contributions by Susan Mann and Norman Kutcher to a special issue of

the *American Historical Review,* although they do not address the issue of masculinity explicitly. Mention should also be made of Zuyan Zhou's *Androgyny in Late Ming and Early Qing Literature,* which also came to my attention after I had already completed my manuscript. Many cases of what Zhou has characterized as androgyny are related to the arguments of this book, even though the texts on which we concentrate are different. More important, I have reservations about the usefulness and historical validity of the concept of androgyny as Zhou has employed it in his study. In particular, I am quite uncomfortable with his attempts to define androgyny either as a valorizing concept about whether one is seeking "self-liberation" and pursuing a "wholesome identity" (p. 4) or as a "social ideal" (p. 5), and he seems to suggest that the concept was consciously pursued by many men and women in late imperial China. My brief survey here covers only relevant scholarship in English. However, as far as I know, there have been no monographs on this topic in Chinese.

12. Louie translates *wen-wu* as "cultural attainment–martial valour" (*Theorising Chinese Masculinity,* p. 4).

CHAPTER 1: FROM TRUE MAN TO CASTRATO

1. Xu Shen, *Shuowen jiezi zhu,* p. 698. See also "Jiaqu"; in *Baihu tong zhuzi suoyin,* p. 72.

2. Kang Yin, *Wenzi yuanliu qianshuo,* pp. 245 and 412–413, and Li Xiaoding, *Jiagu wenzi jishi,* vol. 1, pp. 159–161. See also Lewis, *Sanctioned Violence in Early China,* p. 32.

3. For a discussion of the early history of *shi,* see Yu Yingshi, *Shi yu Zhongguo wenhua,* pp. 1–112.

4. Zhang Yinlin, *Zhongguo shanggu shigang,* pp. 45–50.

5. See Lewis, "The Warrior Aristocracy," chapter 1 of *Sanctioned Violence in Early China,* pp. 15–52.

6. See Gu Jiegang, "Wushi yu wenshi zhi tuihua." Yu Yingshi believes that *wenshi* did not originate from within *wushi* but rather had a separate origin (*Shi yu Zhongguo wenhua,* pp. 9–33, esp. p. 26). Yu's view is shared by Li Ruilan, "Zhishi fenzi de qiyuan."

7. Cf. Lewis, *Sanctioned Violence in Early China,* pp. 98–103. Lewis has characterized the military strategies that emerged during the Warring States Period as a radical break from the concepts of heroic martiality in the Autumn and Spring Period: "The systematic denial of belligerence or physical prowess on the part of the conqueror constituted a critique of the warrior aristocracy's heroic vision of war. The art of battle no longer consisted in the skills of driving a chariot or handling weapons, but in assessing the terrain and the enemy, organizing multitudes, and devising stratagems. As the master of texts and techniques, it was the commander who now determined the outcome of the battle" (p. 103). See also Li Ruilan, "Zhishi fenzi de qiyuan," p. 14. Here even a military commander took on an identity sometimes closer to *wenshi* than warrior.

8. Cheng Shude, *Lunyu jishi,* 4.132–134; English trans. (modified) from Lau, *The Analects,* 2.24, p. 66. Gu Jiegang argues that Confucius himself did not neglect military affairs and that the "turn toward self-cultivation" at the expense of military prowess probably took place several generations after Confucius ("Wushi yu wenshi zhi tuihua," pp. 86–87). Yu Yingshi, however, argues that Confucius cannot be considered someone good at both the "civil" and the "military" (*Shi yu Zhongguo wenhua,* p. 26).

9. Cheng Shude, *Lunyu jishi,* 35.1241; English trans. (modified) from Lau, *The Analects,* pp. 147–148.

10. Cheng Shude, *Lunyu jishi,* 28.951.

11. Cheng Shude, *Lunyu jishi,* 17.7, and Lau, *The Analects,* p. 145. See also Confucius' observation that "unless a man has the spirit of the rites, in having courage he will become unruly" (Cheng Shude, *Lunyu jishi,* 15.514, and Lau, *The Analects,* p. 92).

12. In *Laozi* we find a flatly negative view of *yong:* "One who is fearless in being bold [*yong*] will meet with his death; he who is fearless in being timid will stay alive. Of the two, one leads to good, the other to harm." See Chen Guying, *Laozi zhushi ji pingjia,* p. 334, and Lau, *Lau Tzu Tao Te Ching,* 73.135. For a view of *yong* attributed to Confucius in *Zhuangzi,* see "Qiushui"; in Chen Guying, *Zhuangzi jinzhu jinyi,* pp. 432–433. In early Taoist writings, *yong* seemed to be something one needed to transcend.

13. Cheng Shude, *Lunyu jishi,* 15.527; Lau, *The Analects,* p. 93.

14. Zhu Xi, *Zhuzi yulei,* 116.2800. "In fear and trembling, as if approaching a deep abyss, as if walking on thin ice," attributed here to Zengzi, is originally from the Confucian classic *Shijing* (The Book of Songs); see *Maoshi zhengyi,* 12.742; Cheng Shude, *Lunyu yishi,* 15.516; Lau, *The Analects,* p. 92.

15. Zhu Xi, *Zhuzi yulei,* 95.2451. A "courageous man of great military skills" is apparently also a quotation from the *Shijing;* see *Maoshi zhengyi,* 1.48.

16. See Jiao Xun, *Mengzi zhengyi,* ch. 29, p. 1014, and Lau, *Mencius,* p. 201.

17. "Da Chen Tongfu shiyi"; in Zhu Xi, *Zhu Xi wenji,* vol. 4, 36.1470.

18. Xu Shen, *Shuowen jiezi zhu,* p. 701. Note that like the character *nan* (adult male), *yong* also contains the strength or *li* radical. Graphically, these two characters look fairly alike, calling our attention to the fact that the notion of valor and courage was closely associated with the masculine in early Chinese texts. *Qi* was an important and broad concept in early Chinese thought. For general discussions of its "history" in traditional China, see Zhang Liwen, *Qi.*

19. Jiao Xun, *Mengzi zhengyi,* ch. 6, pp. 189–202; Lau, *Mencius,* pp. 76–78. The word *haoran* (flood-like) also appears elsewhere in *Mencius* (Jiao Xun, *Mengzi zhengyi,* ch. 9, p. 307). For convenient collections of representative commentaries on this important section of *Mencius,* see Huang Junjie, "Mengzi 'Zhiyan yangqi zhang' jishi xinquan" and "Zhuzi dui Mengzi zhiyan yangqi shuo de quanshi jiqi huixiang."

20. Zhu Xi, *Mengzi zhangju jizhu, juan* 3, in *Sishu zhangju jizhu,* p. 229.

21. Cheng Shude, *Lunyu jishi,* 33.1154, and Lau, *The Analects,* p. 140

22. Jiao Xun, *Mengzi zhengyi,* ch. 4, pp. 113–114; Lau, *Mencius,* pp. 62–63.

23. Elsewhere, Zhu Xi characterized *xueqi* as not arising from *yi;* Zhu Xi, *Zhuzi yulei,* 52.1245.

24. Jiao Xun, *Mengzi zhengyi,* ch. 12, pp. 415–419; Lau, *Mencius,* p. 107 (translation modified); for the use of *xiao zhangfu,* see Jiao Xun, *Mengzi zhengyi,* ch. 9, p. 308, and Lau, *Mencius,* p. 94.

25. The concept of *da zhangfu* also appears in the writings attributed to Laozi, who was believed to be a contemporary of Confucius: "Foreknowledge is the flowery embellishment of the Way and the beginning of folly. Hence a true man [*da zhangfu*] abides in the thick not in the thin, in the fruit not in the flower." See Chen Guying, *Laozi zhushi ji pingjia,* 38.212; English translation (modified) from Lau, *Lao Tzu Tao Te Ching,* p. 99. In Laozi's usage, this term does not have the explicit gender implications that it does in *Mencius.* See also the elaboration by Han Fei (ca.

280–ca. 233 BCE) of Laozi's usage in *Han Fei zi jishi*, p. 340 ("Jie Lao"), where he defines *da zhangfu* as someone who has great wisdom.

26. "Shuoru" was originally published in *Shiyusuo jikan* 4, no. 33 (1934) and later reprinted in Hu Shi, *Hu Shi zhexue sixiang ziliao xuan*, pp. 359–429.

27. For a discussion of the various responses to Hu Shi's essay and for information on more recent scholarship concerning this issue, see Ye Shuxian, *Yan'ge yu kuangjuan*, pp. 199–223. Qian Mu's essay, "Bo Hu Shi zhi shuoru," is probably the most substantial and influential negative response; see Qian Mu, *Zhongguo xueshu sixiang shi luncong*, pp. 373–389. Elsewhere in his study (pp. 192–199), Ye Shuxian tries to corroborate Hu Shi's argument by referring to some "feminine" poems from the Ya and Song sections of *Shijing*, arguing that these might well be the works of the so-called *ru* priests. Without referring to Hu Shi's arguments, C. H. Wang, "Towards Defining a Chinese Heroism," discusses the sentiments of distrust regarding violence and war in *Shijing*.

28. Lewis, *Sanctioned Violence in Early China*, pp. 68 and 95.

29. "Qiren jian Tian Pian" and "Qi si," in *Zhan'guo ce jianzhu*, p. 282.

30. "Jin Biyang zhi sun Yu Rang" and "Zhao yi," in *Zhan'guo ce jianzhu*, p. 425. English translation (modified) from Crump, *Chan-kuo Ts'e*, pp. 165–166.

31. "Cike liezhuan"; in Sima Qian, *Shiji*, 86.2519, and "Bao Ren Shaoqing shu"; in *Quan Shanggu, Sandai Qin Han San'guo Liuchao wen*, vol. 1, p. 501.

32. "Tian Dan liezhuan"; in Sima Qian, *Shiji*, 82.2457. An account of this episode can also be found in *Shuoyuan*, compiled by Liu Xiang; see "Lijie," in Liu Xiang, *Shuoyuan zhuzi suoyin*, p. 30.

33. *Zhouyi zhengyi*, 1.21; translated in Legge, *The Sacred Books of China*, p. 420.

34. Dong Zhongshu, *Chunqiu fanlu*, 12.5b–6a; English translation from Fung Yu-lan, *A History of Chinese Philosophy*, vol. 2, pp. 42–43.

35. Xu Fuguan, *Zhongguo renxinglun shi*, pp. 516–517.

36. Raphals, *Sharing the Light*, p. 168. Raphals argues that theories of *yin* and *yang* shifted from an emphasis on complementarity to a focus on hierarchy in Han correlative thinking (pp. 139–168).

37. Jiao Xun, *Mengzi zhengyi*, ch. 21, p. 721; Lau, *Mencius*, pp. 157–158. For a similar emphasis on the need for a ruler to respect his minister as a teacher, see Jiao Xun, *Mengzi zhengyi*, ch. 8, p. 260, and Lau, *Mencius*, p. 87. Elsewhere Mencius said that when a *shi* was offering his advice to a man of consequence, he should even show some contempt (Jiao Xun, *Mengzi zhengyi*, ch. 29, p. 1014, and Lau, *Mencius*, p. 201).

38. Jiao Xun, *Mengzi zhengyi*, ch. 26, p. 903; Lau, *Mencius*, p. 185.

39. Here Mencius was referring to ministers from families other than those of the royal house *(yixing zhi qing);* ministers of royal blood *(tongxing zhi qing)* could simply depose the prince; see Jiao Xun, *Mengzi zhengyi*, ch. 21, p. 728; Lau, *Mencius*, p. 159. Yu Yingshi observes that the appearance of the School of Jixia during the Warring States Period marked the peak of power enjoyed by *shi* in pre-Qin China (*Shi yu Zhongguo wenhua*, p. 57). For a study of the interesting historical phenomenon of this school, see Bai Xi, *Jixia xue yanjiu*.

40. "Qin Shihuang benji"; in Sima Qian, *Shiji*, 6.254–255; English translation (modified) from Watson, *Records of the Grand Historian: Qin Dynasty*, p. 54.

41. For an account in English of the important political changes in these periods, see Michael Loewe, "The Consolidation of the Empire (141–87 BC)," in Twichett and Loewe, *The Cambridge History of China*, pp. 128–151.

42. Dongfang Shuo, "Da Ke'nan"; in *Quan Shanggu Sandai Qin Han San'guo Liuchao wen*, vol. 1, pp. 492–493; English translation based on Declercq, *Writing against the State*, pp. 27–28. Similar sentiments appear in the works of Yang Xiong (53 BCE–18 CE), a writer of the next generation. See Yang Xiong, "Jiechao"; in *Quan Shanggu, Sandai Qin Han San'guo Liuchao wen*, vol. 1, p. 734. For a discussion of the changes in *shi* status during the Warring States and early imperial periods, see Yu Yingshi, *Shi yu Zhongguo wenhua*, pp. 51–68. For discussions of how *shi* members were trying to come to terms with the new political reality of the unified empire, see Xu Fuguan, "Xi Han zhishi fenzi dui zhuanzhi zhengzhi de yali gan," and Yu Yingchun, *Qin Han shi shi*, pp. 180–246.

43. The Han commentators of the earlier *Shijing* were probably so inspired by the convention initiated by Qu Yuan that they began to read the poems in the anthology allegorically. See Yu, *The Reading of Imagery in the Chinese Poetic Tradition*, pp. 112–117. In chapter 2 I will discuss in more detail the rhetorical tradition in works where *chen* and *qie* are often juxtaposed.

44. The shift from complementarity toward hierarchy in *yin-yang* theories during early imperial China, which Lisa Raphals and other scholars have noted, may be related to the gender rigidity I discuss here. Both of these phenomena, I believe, were in turn related to the new political reality.

45. It is interesting to note that in the first century text *Baihu tong*, a *shi* is defined as one who offers his service (*shi*b *ye;* see "Jue"; in *Baihu tong zhuzi suoyin*, p. 2), while a woman is also defined as "someone who serves another person" (*shiren zhe;* see "Jiaqu" in ibid., p. 72). See also the definition of *shi* in the *Shuowen jiezi* dictionary (Xu Shen, *Shuowen jiezi zhu*, p. 20). Consequently, one important similarity shared by women and *shi* is that they have to serve others.

46. See Zheng Hesheng, *Sima Qian nianpu*, p. 82, and Shi Ding, *Sima Qian xingnian xinkao*, pp. 42–56.

47. Lü Xisheng, "Sima Qian gongxing xiyi."

48. Sima Qian, "Bao Ren Shaoqing shu," p. 501.

49. Ibid., p. 502. English translation (modified) from Watson, *Ssu-ma Ch'ien*, p. 65.

50. Scholars and commentators have repeatedly called attention to the chronological discrepancies in these examples—that is, some of the figures to whom Sima Qian referred in fact produced their works *before* they suffered setbacks. See Liu Zhiji, *Shitong tongshi*, 16.461, and Wai-yee Li, "The Idea of Authority in the *Shih chi*," pp. 362–363. As I discuss below, this problem of chronology later confronted scholars when they tried to interpret *Shiji* as a work Sima Qian wrote after his traumatic experience of castration because he must have already started on it much earlier in his life.

51. Sima Qian, "Bao Ren Shaoqing shu," p. 502.

52. Another interesting reference by Sima Qian to Confucius can be found in his "Taishigong zixu": "My work is only a classification of the materials that have been preserved. Thus it is not innovation, and it is a mistake to compare my work with the *Chunqiu* [Confucius' *Spring and Autumn Annals*]" (in Sima Qian, *Shiji*, 130.3299–3300). When Sima Qian insisted that his work was not innovation and could not be compared to Confucius' *Chunqiu* (thus implying that Confucius was an innovator), he must have had in mind Confucius' remarks that he (Confucius) was not an innovator but a transmitter. Hence, Sima Qian was using the same rhetoric consciously or unconsciously to subvert Confucius' disclaimer of innovation and ulti-

mately his own. He was in fact claiming what he was ostensibly trying to disclaim. For discussions of Sima Qian's complex "relationship" with Confucius, see Durrant, *The Cloudy Mirror*, pp. 1–45.

53. "Bao Ren Shaoqing shu," p. 502; English trans. (modified) from Watson, *Ssu-ma Qian*, p. 66.

54. "Taishigong zixu"; in Sima Qian, *Shiji*, 130.3299. For this positive meaning of *kongwen*, see *Hanyu da cidian*, p. 4899.

55. In "Bao Ren Shaoqing shu" (p. 502), Sima Qian used *wuneng zhi ci* (incompetent words) to describe his own writings, to resonate with the implications of *kongwen* (empty writings).

56. Sima Qian, *Shiji*, 65.2163.

57. Commenting on the later popular story of Sun Bin and the text on military strategy, probably inspired by Sima Qian's account, Lewis observes that "It [the story] is clearly tied to the other stories through the motif of the 'magical' revelation of a military text which granted its possessor victory. Moreover, Sun Bin's mutilation rendered him the very embodiment of physical helplessness, so this story offers the clearest and most extreme development of the recurrent motif of the conqueror as a man of no martial prowess" (*Sanctioned Violence in Early China*, p. 103). Elsewhere Lewis argues that "in place of the old idea of combat as chariot and the bow, the existence of military texts and doctrines implies that battle was a form of wisdom or an art, a mental skill that could be verbally formulated and taught. . . . This emphasis on mental skills based on textual knowledge as the key to power was also part of the general Warring States political transition" (p. 98). Obviously, in Sima Qian's apology, texts or the ability to author texts was presented as the *potent* manifestation of a unique masculine power that should dwarf the physical powers of a man of great martial prowess. Of course, my reading of Sima Qian's story of Sun Bin is contingent upon the fact that this biography as we have it now in *Shiji* was written (or at least revised) by Sima Qian after he had been subjected to the punishment of castration, an issue I discuss in more detail below.

58. Zheng Hesheng, *Sima Qian nianpu*, p. 108.

59. It was rumored that in order to concentrate exclusively on writing a history of the Song dynasty, the Ming official and historian Ke Weiqi (1497–1574) tried to emulate Sima Qian by castrating himself; see Shen Defu (1578–1642), *Wanli yehuo bian*, p. 922. As we shall see in our discussion of the seventeenth-century novel *Sui Tang yanyi* (The Romance of the Sui and Tang Dynasties) in chapter 6, self-castration can even be considered a unique expression of one's masculinity.

60. See the account of the encounter between King Xuan of Qi and the recluse Yan Chu and the latter's assertion that "a *shi* should be honored while a king should not" in *Zhan'guo ce jianzhu*, p. 272 ("Qi Xuanwang jian Yan Chu").

61. Sima Qian, "Bao Ren Shaoqing shu," p. 502.

62. See Wai-yee Li, *Enchantment and Disenchantment*, pp. 17–23.

63. See Wilhelm, "The Scholar's Frustration," and Pankenier, "'The Scholar's Frustration' Reconsidered."

64. "Xianggong ershisi nian"; in *Chunqiu Zuozhuan zhengyi*, 35.1002.

65. See, for example, the reading strategy outlined by Qin Guan (1049–1100) in his "Sima Qian lun"; reprinted in Yang Yanqi, *Lidai mingjia ping "Shiji,"* p. 14. The Qing writer Yuan Wendian (dates unknown) considered Sima Qian's traumatic experience central in interpreting *Shiji* and read many of Sima Qian's biographies of historical figures simply as his own autobiographical postscripts *(zixu);* see his "Du

Shiji"; in ibid., pp. 27–29. On the other hand, other readers criticized Sima Qian precisely for tempering his historical narrative with a personal grudge; see, for example, Wang Ruoxu (1174–1243), "*Shiji* bianhuo"; in *Hunan yilao ji*, 19.14a. Of course, our knowledge about the writing process of *Shiji*—that is, exactly what parts were written or rewritten after the castration—is rather limited, and to complicate the matter further, part of *Shiji* might have been based on what had been written by Sima Qian's father. What we do know are basically the few clues Sima Qian himself left us. In "Bao Ren Shaoqing shu" (p. 503) Sima Qian informed us that when he became implicated in the case of Li Ling he had just started on the draft of *Shiji*. In "Taishigong zixu" (in *Shiji*, 130.3300) he was more specific, mentioning that he had become implicated in the case seven years after he had started working on *Shiji*. Based on this clue, the Tang commentator Zhang Shoujie (fl. 735) suggested in his *Shiji zhengyi* that Sima Qian most likely started writing *Shiji* in the first year of the Taichu period (104 BCE) since the castration was believed to have taken place in the third year of the Tianhan period (98 BCE); the view is shared by many later scholars of *Shiji*. See, for example, Zheng Hesheng, *Sima Qian nianpu*, pp. 69 and 82–89, and Zhao Yi (1727–1814), *Nianer shi zhaji jiaozheng*, 1.1-2. With the explicit reading guidelines issued by Sima Qian and given the fact that a substantial part of *Shiji* was still unfinished when he was implicated in Li Ling's case and the fact that he had ample time to revise or rewrite what he had already drafted before his castration (based on evidence in *Shiji*), Zhang Dake (*Shiji wenxian yanjiu*, pp. 88 and 109–117) argues that Sima Qian's revisions of *Shiji* continued even after the second year of the Zhenghe period (91 BCE); thus it is reasonable to believe that we are able to find traces of his postcastration gender anxiety in this monumental work. More important, Sima Qian's experience of marginalization became only more crystallized after his castration since he must have experienced political marginalization and emasculation as a *shi* long before he was implicated in Li Ling's case.

66. Sima Qian, *Shiji*, 81.2439.

67. Ibid., 81.2443.

68. The Song Neo-Confucian thinker Huang Zhen (1213–1280) argued that both Lin Xiangru and Lian Po could be considered heroes of true manliness (*lie zhangfu*, the same term Sima Qian used to praise Wu Zixu, as we shall see below), although the former was more admirable. See Ling Zhilong and Li Guangjin, *Shiji pinglin*, 81.13a (vol. 4, p. 485).

69. Ibid., 81.2451–2452.

70. Sima Qian, *Shiji*, 66.2183. For many traditional readers, these comments are simply Sima Qian's attempts at an apology. See, for example, Ling Zhilong and Li Guangjin, *Shiji pinglin*, 66.11a (vol. 5, p. 37). For an in-depth discussion of how Sima Qian identified himself with Wu Zixu, see Durrant, *The Cloudy Mirror*, pp. 74–98, esp. 94–97.

71. Sima Qian, *Shiji*, 83.2479.

72. Ibid., 83.2467.

73. See "Huaiyin hou liezhuan"; in Sima Qian, *Shiji*, 92.2610.

74. Ibid., 92. 2610.

75. "Liuhou shijia"; in Sima Qian, *Shiji*, 55.2034–2035.

76. "Ji Bu Luan Bu liezhuan"; in Sima Qian, *Shiji*, 100.2735.

77. Ibid., 100.2729.

78. Ibid., 100.2735.

79. Cf. Cao Lüning, "Shi Qinlü 'baji xumei' ji 'zhanren fajie' jianlun Qin Han de

kunxing." In his letter to Ren Shaoqing (p. 502), Sima Qian listed head shaving right next to amputation and castration as one of the worst corporeal punishments. I shall revisit the symbolic implications of head shaving in chapter 4.

80. Ling Zhilong and Li Guangjin, *Shiji pinglin,* 100.5b–6a (vol. 6, pp. 44–45); see also similar comments by Ding Yan (1794–1885); reprinted in Yang Yanqi, *Lidai mingjia ping Shiji,* p. 654.

81. Sima Qian, *Shiji,* 86.2525.

82. One significant change made by Sima Qian with regard to his sources, as preserved in *Zhan'guo ce,* was his giving Nie Zheng's sister the name of Rong. For a comparative discussion of the story of Nie Zheng in *Shiji* and *Zhan'guo ce,* as well as the significance of the changes Sima Qian made to his source materials, see Durrant, *The Cloudy Mirror,* pp. 105–110. Later readers often questioned the appropriateness of Nie Rong's decision to acknowledge her brother's mutilated corpse against the latter's wishes since this would continue the cycle of revenge and possibly endanger the life of Nie Zheng's patron, Yan Zhongzi—exactly what Nie Zheng had originally tried to avoid by mutilating himself. See, for example, Fang Bao (1668–1749), "Shu 'Cike zhuan' hou"; in Fang Bao, *Fang Bao ji,* 2.54–55.

83. Sima Qian, *Shiji,* 55.2048. Ironically, thanks in part to Sima Qian's famous reference to Zhang Liang's feminine appearance, in some later writings, resembling Zhang Liang became a trademark of a handsome and talented young man (especially as a military strategist). In other words, by the late imperial period, in certain cultural discourses feminine looks were no longer considered to be contradictory to a man's masculine abilities, such as martial arts skills; see, for example, the description of the male protagonist proficient in both literary and military skills in the seventeenth-century scholar-beauty novel *Huatu yuan* (The Romance of the Two Magical Maps), 2.15. More on the relationship between feminine appearance and masculinity is in chapter 7.

84. "Xiang Yu benji"; in Sima Qian, *Shiji,* 7.328 and 334. Here Xiang Yu reminds people of Meng Ben, the famous warrior from the Warring States Period referred to in *Mencius.* It is written in *Lüshi chunqiu* that once Meng Ben angrily glared at *(chenmu)* a boatman after the latter expressed displeasure at Meng's getting into the boat without standing in line. Some passengers in the boat were so scared by his stare that they fell into the water. See "Biji"; in *Lüshi chunqiu jiaoshi,* p. 829. Meng Ben was often remembered as a great warrior by people during the Han dynasty. See the commentaries in Jiao Xun, *Mengzi zhengyi,* pp. 118–119.

85. Sima Qian, *Shiji,* 7.333. English translation (modified) from Watson, *Records of the Grand Historian: Han Dynasty,* p. 45.

86. Sima Qian, *Shiji,* 100.2735.

87. "Huaiyin Hou liezhuan"; in Sima Qian, *Shiji,* 92.2612. People of later ages tended to forget that Han Xin also asserted (p. 2612) that Xiang Yu sometimes acted like a woman in being indecisive, or, more literally, "showing the soft heart of a woman" *(furen zhi ren).* The Yuan writer Yang Weizhen (1296–1370) used these same apparently contradictory phrases to characterize Xiang Yu; see Ling Zhilong and Li Guangjin, *Shiji pinglin,* 7.32a (vol. 2, p. 65).

88. Sima Qian, *Shiji,* 7.295–296.

89. See Jiao Xun, *Mengzi zhengyi,* ch. 4, p. 114.

90. See Durrant, *The Cloudy Mirror,* pp. 131–143, and Hardy, *Worlds of Bronze and Bamboo,* pp. 102–113; see also Qian Zhongshu, *Guanzhui bian,* p. 275.

91. After a series of victories over the Qin army, Xiang Yu summoned the gen-

erals of other states to an audience. All them, after entering the gate, "crawled forward on their knees and none dared look up"; see *Shiji*, 7.307, and Watson, *Records of the Grand Historian: Han Dynasty*, vol. 1, p. 25. Sima Qian was apparently emphasizing Xiang Yu's *qishi* (heroic demeanor).

92. Sima Qian, *Shiji*, 7.339.

93. Cf. Ling Zhilong's (fl. late sixteenth century) marginal note in Ling Zhilong and Li Guangjin, *Shiji pinglin*, 7.35a (vol. 2, p. 69).

94. Cheng Shude, *Lunyu jishi*, 30.1029; English translation (modified) from Lau, *The Analects*, p. 130.

95. As Durrant has noted, *nu* (fury or anger) is a word Sima Qian frequently used to describe Xiang Yu's state of mind (*The Cloudy Mirror*, p. 133).

96. See Zhen Wei (fl. early seventeenth century), *Xi Han yanyi* (dated 1612), in the modern typeset edition *Liang Han yanyi*, 11.20. Cf. *Quan Han zhizhuan* (preface dated 1588), pp. 28–29, and *Liang Han kaiguo zhongxing zhuanzhi* (dated 1605), p. 39. *Liang Han yanyi* was apparently the result of the rewriting based on *Quan Han zhizhuan* and *Liang Han kaiguo zhongxing zhuanzhi*. For a study of these novels, see Ouyang Jian, *Liang Han xilie xiaoshuo*.

97. See Zhen Wei, *Xi Han yanyi*, 83.197–198; *Liang Han kaiguo zhongxing zhuanzhi*, pp. 215–216; and *Quan Han zhizhuan*, pp. 144–146. As the Tang commentator Zhang Shoujie pointed out, Sima Qian might have omitted the words to Lady Yu's song because it was quoted in an earlier text, *Chu Han chunqiu*, attributed to Lu Jia (ca. 228–140 BCE); it was no longer extant after the Song dynasty, but it was certainly available to Sima Qian when he was writing *Shiji*. See Sima Qian, *Shiji*, 7.333, and Zhang's note on p. 334.

98. See Zhen Wei, *Xi Han yanyi*, 83.197–198. In these historical novels on the Han dynasty, it was Xiang Yu's physical prowess that persuaded Lady Yu's father to marry her to him. Consequently, a female beauty was initially presented as an acknowledgement of Xiang Yu's virility, and as a symbol of feminine beauty, she was supposed to enhance his masculine image. See Zhen Wei, *Xi Han yanyi*, 11.21; *Liang Han kaiguo zhongxing zhuanzhi*, p. 40; and *Quan Han zhizhuan*, p. 29. Of course, the episode of Lady Yu's father expressing appreciation of Xiang Yu's physical strength is not found in *Shiji*.

99. The implications of this saying are explored in more detail in chapter 8. Here we may also recall Han Xin's characterization of Xiang Yu as "showing the soft heart of a woman"; "Huaiyin Hou liezhuan"; in Sima Qian, *Shiji*, 92.2612. The romantic side of a masculine hero is explored at length in chapter 8.

100. *Jin Ping Mei cihua*, 1.1–2.

CHAPTER 2: FROM FAITHFUL WIFE TO WHORE

1. *Hanyu da cidian*, p. 5030.

2. Xu Shen, *Shuowen jiezi zhu*, p. 118.

3. Dong Zhongshu's theory of *san'gang*, or the three bonds between husband and wife, father and son, and ruler and subject, was apparently developed from Han Fei's idea on the relationship between loyalty and filiality. See "Zhongxiao"; in *Han Fei Zi jishi*, p. 1107. For a discussion of how later Confucianism became *fajia hua* (legalistic), see Yu Yingshi, "Fanzhi lun yu Zhongguo zhengzhi chuantong," pp. 1–46, esp. 31–46; for discussions of the conventional analogy between a minister and a woman, see Lewis, *Sanctioned Violence in Early China*, pp. 73–76, and Raphals, *Shar-*

ing the Light, pp. 12–14; also cf. Tung, *Fables for the Patriarchs,* pp. 30–40. I have also discussed this analogy in terms of the concept of marginality in my *Literati and Self-Re/Presentation,* pp. 78–81.

4. Mencius was not as influential during the Han dynasty as he would become after the Song dynasty (960–1279), when the Daoxue school of Confucianism (also known in English as Neo-Confucianism) began to dominate intellectual life. This, however, should not affect our discussions since we are dealing with the imperial politics of the Ming dynasty.

5. Lewis, *Sanctioned Violence in Early China,* p. 74.

6. "Waiqi shijia"; in Sima Qian, *Shiji,* 49.1985–1986. It was said that the main reason for Emperor Wu's decision to take such an extreme measure was that the crown prince was only five years old, and he wanted to avoid the situation of a young emperor being controlled by his strong mother.

7. See Sima Qian's comments in *Shiji,* 49.1986. One could argue that Sima Qian's praise was not necessarily sincere since he had to be careful as a subject under Emperor Wu. Although the later commentator Shao Yun took exception to such admiration, he acknowledged that it was the norm in many historical writings; see Ling Zhilong and Li Guangjin, *Shiji pinglin,* 49.15b (p. 580). Shao Yun was not identified in "*Shiji pinglin* xingshi" in ibid., and I have not been able to identify the commentator mentioned. There was a certain Shao Yun from the Song dynasty, who died refusing to surrender to the Jurchen troops. See *Zhongguo renming da cidian,* p. 605. However, I am not sure if the two were the same person.

8. Cheng Yi, *Yichuan wenji,* 2.2b. English translation (modified) from Nivison, "Ho-shen and His Accusers," p. 230. By *siren* it seems to me Cheng Yi was referring to eunuchs rather than monks (as Nivison has translated). Several hundred years later Cheng Yi's advocacy of the authority of scholar-officials as mentors at the expense of the ruler would provoke sharp criticism from Emperor Qianlong (r. 1736–1796) of the Qing dynasty (1644–1911); see Nivison, "Ho-shen and His Accusers," p. 231.

9. *Neiwai* was an important gender differentiating concept in early China, as demonstrated in *Mencius:* "Inside the house, there were no dissatisfied women, and abroad, there were no men who were unmarried"; see Jiao Xun, *Mengzi zhengyi,* ch. 4, p. 139. In this spatial gender scheme, *nei* was always associated with the feminine. For discussions of *neiwai* as a gender differentiating concept, see Raphals, *Sharing the Light,* pp. 195–235.

10. "Yanchen shang," *Mingyi daifang lu;* in Huang Zongxi, *Huang Zongxi quanji,* vol. 1, pp. 44–45; for an English translation, see de Bary, *Waiting for the Dawn,* pp. 166–167. Here we may recall our discussion in chapter 1 regarding the symbolic implications of Sima Qian's castration almost seventeen hundred years ago, when *shi* status began to be redefined in the new power structure. Castration became a potent symbol of marginalization for many *shi* as they were being relegated into the position of the feminine. Of course, the political reality of the Han dynasty was vastly different from that of the Ming dynasty, with which Huang Zongxi was mainly concerned. However, the enduring effectiveness of the political metaphor of emasculation tells us something about the persistent tendency in traditional cultural discourse to conceive political power in gendered terms throughout the imperial period.

11. "Yuanchen," *Mingyi daifang lu;* in Huang Zongxi, *Huang Zongxi quanji,* vol. 1, pp. 4–5; English translation (modified) from de Bary, *Waiting for the Dawn,* pp. 95–96.

12. For Huang Zongxi's interpretation of *Mencius,* see his "Mengzi shishuo" in Huang Zongxi *quanji,* vol. 1, pp. 48–166.

13. "Zhixiang," *Mingyi daifang lu;* in Huang Zongxi, Huang Zongxi *quanji,* vol. 1, p. 8.

14. Hucker, *A Dictionary of Official Titles in Imperial China,* p. 73.

15. For a history of the Grand Secretariat in Ming imperial government, see Wang Qiqu, *Mingdai neige zhidu shi.* For studies of the role of eunuchs in Ming imperial politics, see Tsai, *The Eunuchs in the Ming Dynasty,* and Wei Jianlin, *Mingdai huan'guan zhengzhi.*

16. "Zhixiang," *Mingyi daifanglu;* in Huang Zongxi, Huang Zongxi *quanji,* vol. 1, p. 9.

17. "Yuanjun," *Mingyi daifanglu;* in ibid., vol. 1, p. 2.

18. From the biography of Fang Xiaoru in *Mingshi,* 141.4019.

19. *Qiefu xintai* was the phrase used by Zuo Dongling in his discussion of the scholar-officials of the early Ming (*Wangxue yu Zhongwan Ming shiren xintai,* pp. 13, 15, and 177), although Zuo did not trace the use of *qiefu* to Mencius. My discussion of the minister-concubine complex of the Ming scholar-officials here has benefited from some of his observations. In my *Literati and Self-Re/Presentation* (p. 79), I also discuss the "concubine complex," from which many scholar-officials suffered in imperial politics.

20. See "Mengzi shishuo"; in Huang Zongxi, *Huang Zongxi quanji,* vol. 1, pp. 51 and 105.

21. Zhu Yuanzhang, "Suzhou rencai"; in *Quan Ming wen,* 31.706; see also "Xingfa er"; in *Mingshi,* 94.2318.

22. See Zhu Ronggui, "Cong Liu Sanwu *Mengzi jiewen* lun junquan de xianzhi yu zhishi fengzi zhi zizhu xing."

23. See Wang Chunnan and Zhan Yinglin, *Song Lian, Fang Xiaoru pingzhuan,* pp. 122–130.

24. Chen Jingzong, "Wenjian Huang gong Huai muzhiming"; in Jiao Hong, *Xianzheng lu,* 12.14a–b (p. 392).

25. "Xueshi Xie gong Jin zhuan"; in ibid., 12.13a–13b.

26. *Mingshi,* 147.4123–4124.

27. Huang Huai, *Xingqian ji,* 1.24a.

28. In addition to "Qie boming," see, for example, the seventh poem in "Zashi jiushou" (Nine Miscellaneous Poems), 1.9b; the first, fifth, and sixth poems in "Ke cong yuanfang lai liushou" (Six Poems on Friends from Far Away), 1.11a–13b; "Dai fu da" (A Reply on Behalf of a Lady), 1.15b–16a; "Duijing" (The Self in the Mirror), 1.27a; "Jiaren" (A Beauty), 2.12a; "Jiuri dai fu zuo" (Written on Behalf of a Lady on the Ninth Day), 2.32a; and "Ni qufu cidiao 'Feng ru song'" (In Imitation of an Abandoned Woman's Irregular Poem to the Tune of "Wind Blowing in the Pine Trees"), 2.45a–45b; all in Huang Huai, *Xingqian ji.*

29. See also the biographies of Yang Shiqi, Yang Rong, and Yang Pu in *Mingshi,* 148.4131–4144.

30. "Ti Huang shaobao *Xingqian ji* hou"; in Yang Shiqi, *Dongli wenji,* 10.147–148. It was said that Yang Shiqi and other important officials who served under the Jianwen Emperor once pledged among themselves that they would commit suicide together if the Prince of Yan was victorious. However, only Zhou Sixiu (d. 1402) committed suicide as promised. All the others surrendered to the prince and became important officials when he assumed the throne. Later Yang Shiqi told Zhou's son that had he also committed suicide, no one could have written a biography of his

father. The writer Lang Ying (b. ca. 1487) condemned Yang as utterly shameless; see Lang Ying, *Qilei xiugao*, 16.183; see also Wu Tinghan's (1490–1559) comment, "Wengji"; in Wu Tinghan, *Wu Tinghan ji*, p. 106. Yang Shiqi seems to have tried to justify his failure to commit suicide by insisting that he made this choice so that he could immortalize those who had indeed committed suicide by writing about them. This same not-so-convincing excuse was used by many Ming loyalists in the seventeenth century to justify their decision to live as subjects under the new alien rule of the Manchus: they chose to live because they wanted to write the history of the fallen monarchy as its loyal subjects (more on this in chapter 4). In this they surely followed the model of Sima Qian.

31. "Shou Shaofu Xichang Yang gong"; in Yang Rong, *Wenmin ji*, 2.27a.

32. Ye Sheng, *Shuidong riji*, 5.56.

33. "Xuan'gui fu"; in Li Mengyang, *Kongtong ji*, 1.10a (p. 11).

34. See Chen Shulu, *Mingdai shiwen de yanbian*, pp. 139–152.

35. Here the Governor of Guiji must refer to Zhu Maichen (d. 112 BCE). Zhu was poor for a long time. Unable to endure poverty, his wife left him, despite his prediction that he would become wealthy when he was fifty. Indeed he became an official and was appointed Governor of Guiji. His former wife committed suicide after they were reunited. See *Zhongguo renming da cidian*, p. 261. The story of Zhu and his wife is retold as the prologue of the twenty-seventh story in Feng Menglong's *Yushi mingyan*, pp. 404–406, while an earlier version of the story can be found in the Ming collection *Guose tianxiang* (the seventh story).

36. Li Mengyang, *Kongtong ji*, 18.3a–4a (p. 130).

37. Ibid., 16.2b–3a (p. 113). This poem must have been modeled on Li Bai's (701–762) more famous *yuefu* (music bureau) poem of the same title, which traditional commentators always associated with the poet's political setbacks. For a sampling of these readings, see Zhan Ying et al., *Li Bai quanji jiaozhu huishi jiping*, pp. 796–799.

38. "Lu Zhonglian and Zou Yang liezhuan"; in Sima Qian, *Shiji*, 83.2473.

39. Wang Yangming, *Wang Yangming quanji*, 19.692.

40. Cf. Zuo Dongling's discussion of these poems in *Wangxue yu Zhongwan Ming shiren xintai*, pp. 176–178.

41. Many scholars have explored the relationship between Wang Yangming's experience in Ming politics and the development of his philosophy. See, for example, Zuo Dongling's extensive discussion in *Wangxue yu Zhongwan Ming shiren xintai*, pp. 128–271, esp. 250–271.

42. Sima Xiangru's "Meiren fu" was written on the model of "Dengtu zi haose fu," attributed to Song Yu, a disciple of Qu Yuan. For a discussion of the gender politics of these rhapsodies, see Rouzer, *Articulated Ladies*, pp. 39–72. See also Wai-yee Li, *Enchantment and Disenchantment*, pp. 3–46.

43. *Quan Shanggu, Sandai Qin Han San'guo Liuchao wen*, vol. 1, p. 459.

44. Cheng Shude, *Lunyu jishi*, p. 611.

45. Xu Zhenqing, *Digong ji*, 5.5a.

46. For a discussion of Xu Zhenqing's poetry and his literary theories, see Chen Shulu, *Mingdai shiwen de yanbian*, pp. 241–252.

47. Cf. Ray Huang, *1587*, esp. 75–103.

48. On *tingzhang*, see "Xingfa san"; in *Mingshi*, 95.2329–2331.

49. For accounts of remonstrations by the famous "upright official" Hai Rui

(1514–1587) and the Wanli Emperor's response, as well as his strategy for dealing with other remonstrators, see Yu Shenxing, *Gushan bizhu*, 5.51–54.

50. See Ray Huang, "The Lung-ch'ing and Wan-li Reigns, 1576–1620"; in Mote and Twitchett, *The Cambridge History of China*, vol. 7, pp. 511–584, and Zuo Dongling, *Wangxue yu Zhongwan Ming shiren xintai*, pp. 523–545.

51. For a discussion of how family pressures and other factors repeatedly forced Yuan Hongdao to reluctantly resume his official career, see Wang Junjiang, "Fusheng ning yiwei, duanbu hui jianghu," pp. 35–38 and 34.

52. "Da Mei Kesheng"; in Yuan Hongdao, *Yuan Hongdao ji jianjiao*, 21.748.

53. "Suimu jishi"; in ibid., 3.151.

54. Xiao Difei et al., *Tangshi jianshang cidian*, p. 985.

55. Ibid., pp. 985–987.

56. Yuan Zhongdao, "Libu Yanfengsi langzhong Zhonglang xiansheng xingzhuang"; in Yuan Hongdao, *Yuan Hongdao ji jianjiao*, p. 1651.

57. "Weng Chengmei wen xu"; in Yuan Zhongdao, *Kexuezhai ji*, 10.486. For discussions of the late Ming obsession with *zhen*, see Wai-yee Li, "The Rhetoric of Spontaneity in Late Ming Literature," and Xia Xianchun, *Wan Ming shifeng yu wenxue*, pp. 209–241.

58. Here we are reminded of the close association of *shi*[b] (to serve) with women and *shi* as found in the early Han text *Baihu tong* (see note 45 of chapter 1).

59. "Guan Dongming"; in Yuan Hongdao, *Yuan Hongdao ji jinajiao*, 6.292.

60. "Qiu Changru"; in ibid., 5.208.

61. "Yu Zhuo Yuebo guanglu"; in Jiang Yingke, *Jiang Yingke ji*, 12.564–565.

62. For discussions of Jiang's life and literary works, see Huang Rensheng's long introductory preface in Jiang Yingke, *Jiang Yingke ji*, pp. 11–59, and Barr, "Jiang Yingke's Place in the Gongan School."

63. "Yu Xie Zaihang"; in Jiang Yingke, *Jiang Yingke ji*, 12.577.

64. "Yu Xie Zaihang"; in ibid., 13.608 (a different letter from the one referred to in the previous note). This is a frequent strategy of self-representation in Jiang Yingke's writings; see, for example, two other letters, "Yu Che Shanbu Chunhan," 12.585, and "Yu Xiangtan Zhou nianxiong," 13.613, and a poem, "Gan'huai"; 1.9,— all in ibid.

65. "Da Zhang Yidu"; in ibid., 13.600–601.

66. "Mei Kesheng"; in Yuan Hongdao, *Yuan Hongdao ji jianjiao*, 11.484.

67. Jiang Yingke, *Jiang Yingke ji*, 14.656–657, and "Xuetao shiping"; in ibid., pp. 799–800 and 807.

CHAPTER 3: THE CASE OF XU WEI

1. In this chapter I confine my discussion to Xu Wei's career before he became a serious painter and calligrapher late in his life. He appears to have found release for his emotions and felt more liberated in his painting. Cf. James Cahill's observation: "The tortured inner life of Hsü Wei [Xu Wei], which is the very content of much of his writing, has not been projected with anything like the same self-revelatory pathos into his paintings. . . . While Hsü's paintings convey a high intensity of feeling, impetuosity, sometimes violence, nothing in them would in itself necessarily suggest the tragic character of the man to a viewer who encountered them in ignorance of Hsü's life. . . . They expressed a sense of release rather than of repression. . . . Painting was probably for Hsü Wei more therapeutic than symptomatic. One's

emotional response on retracing empathically the movements recorded by one of his paintings is thus a feeling more of liberation than of discomfort" (*Parting at the Shore*, p. 163). It seems that Xu Wei felt much more at ease making a living from his paintings than by ghostwriting for officials. For a study of Xu Wei's career as a painter and the implications of the commodification of his paintings, see Ryor, "Bright Pearls Hanging in the Marketplace."

2. "Xu Wenchang zhuan"; in Xu Wei, *Xu Wei ji*, p. 1343.

3. One of the very few "feminine" poems (in which the poet presents himself in a feminine position) is "Shedai Linmou da Hu tongzheng" (A Reply to Vice Commissioner Hu on Behalf of Mr. Lin); p. 375. However, as the title of the poem indicates, the poem was apparently written on behalf of a certain Mr. Lin.

4. Xu Wei made repeated references to Jing Ke in his writings; see, for example, the second poem in "Ru Yan sanshou," "Zhengbin yi Riben dao jianzeng, yige dazhi," "Zeng wuju Chen zi," and "Ai Zhu shangshu ci"; in Xu Wei, *Xu Wei ji*, pp. 70, 126, 186, and 663. In his "Ke *Xu Wenchang yishu* xu," Zhang Rulin compared Xu Wei to the legendary knight-errant Yu Rang; see Xu Wei, *Xu Wei ji*, p. 1348. Zhang Rulin was the son of Zhang Yuanbian (1538–1588), who played a major role in winning Xu Wei an early release from prison after he was convicted of killing his wife. Xu Wei mentioned the Zhangs as those to whom he was deeply indebted ("Ji'en") in his "Jipu"; in Xu Wei, *Xu Wei ji*, p. 1333; for an English translation of "Jipu," see Faurot, "Four Cries of a Gibbon," pp. 150–162.

5. For example, see "Xiazhe" and "Wu xiashi muzhiming"; in Xu Wei, *Xu Wei ji*, pp. 1028–1029. For a brief discussion of Xu's fascination with *xia*, or chivalry, see Zhou Mingchu, *Wan Ming shiren xintai ji wenxue ge'an*, pp. 153–157.

6. See, for example, the first poem in "Jinri ge liangshou," "Zhengbin yi Riben dao jianzeng, yige dazhi," "Baojian pian song Lu shanren," "Shen Shuzi jie fandao weizeng ershou," "Zhang Xu guan Gongsun da'nian wu jianqi," "Liuqiu dao ershou," and "Baodao shi"; in Xu Wei, *Xu Wei ji*, pp. 121, 126, 148, 149, 159, 167, and 185.

7. "Jipu"; in ibid., p. 1326.

8. For a brief reference to the strained relationship between Xu Wei and his elder brothers, see "Shang Tixuefushi Zhang gong shu"; in ibid., p. 1107.

9. "Jipu"; in ibid., p. 1326. Because his birth mother was sold, Xu Wei bore some grudge against Miaoshi, to whom he was otherwise very grateful.

10. Ibid., p. 1328.

11. Xu Wei once complained bitterly about the custom in his native town that a groom was supposed to give expensive betrothal gifts to his bride's family. See "Zeng fuweng Pan gong xu"; in Xu Wei, *Xu Wei ji*, p. 546.

12. "Wangqi Pan muzhiming"; in ibid., p. 634. This fact is also noted by Luo Yuming and He Shengsui, *Xu Wenchang pingzhuan*, pp. 22–23.

13. In "Jipu," Xu Wei mentioned this legal dispute in very vague terms (in Xu Wei, *Xu Wei ji*, p. 1327). See also "Ziwei muzhiming"; (in ibid., p. 639), where he noted that he lost the right to inherit the property of his deceased brother in a legal suit. Despite the fact that *ruzhai* could be a rather emasculating experience, several years later, when Xu Wei was thirty-nine, circumstances forced him once again to accept an uxorial marriage arrangement with the Wang family, although that marriage did not last long. See "Jipu," (in ibid., p. 1328). For a discussion of the practice of *ruzhui* and the possible discrimination against a son-in-law in an uxorial marriage, see Guo Songyi, *Lunli yu shenghuo*, pp. 314–336. Although Guo deals with only the Qing period, many of his observations should still be valid for the Ming dynasty.

14. "Ziwei muzhiming"; in Xu Wei, *Xu Wei ji*, p. 639.

15. "Shang Dufu shu"; in ibid., p. 465. It was even rumored that a few of Xu's suggestions on military actions were adopted by Hu Zongxian and that they led to successes on the battlefield. For example, Yuan Hongdao believed that Hu Zongxian sought advice from Xu Wei in his successful campaigns against the notorious pirates Wang Zhi and Xu Hai; see his "Xu Wenchang zhuan"; in ibid., p. 1342. However, the modern scholar Xu Lun argues that this was unlikely since Xu Wei did not join Hu Zongxian's staff until one month after the latter had captured Wang Zhi; see Xu Lun, *Xu Wenchang*, p. 82.

16. The first poem in "Kaige ershou zeng canjiang Qi gong," in Xu Wei, *Xu Weiji*, p. 343.

17. "Kaige sishou zeng Cao jun"; in ibid., pp. 344–345. Elsewhere, Xu Wei deplored that his book learning had brought him no rewards whatsoever; see, for example, the second poem in "Jinri ge liangshou"; in ibid., p. 122. In a note to these two poems, Xu Wei wrote: "That year the barbarians invaded Gubeigou, and I worked as a *muyou* in the capital."

18. "Song Zhang jun zhi Haining jiaoshou"; in ibid., p. 716.

19. Shen Defu, *Wanli yehuo bian*, 10.270.

20. *Qingyan*, 9.3a; in Zheng Zhongkui (fl. 1634), *Yuzhu xintan*.

21. "Chulie pian wei Xu jishi Wang jiangjun zuo"; in Shen Mingchen, *Fengdui lou shixuan*, 5.14b.

22. "Shen jiangjun shi"; in Xu Wei, *Xu Wei ji*, p. 161.

23. See "Guo Xiang Yu gugong"; in ibid., p. 719.

24. "Ai Zhu shangshu ci"; in ibid., p. 663.

25. "Ji Binzhong"; in ibid., p. 232.

26. Xu Wei, *Xu Wei ji*, p. 449.

27. "Zeng Xu mou Baozhou mu xu"; in ibid., pp. 903–904.

28. "Zeng Jin Weizhen xu"; in ibid., pp. 934–935. Similar feelings of ambivalence toward *muyou* can be found in "Song Shen sheng xu"; in ibid., p. 922.

29. For a discussion of this important change, see Guo Runtao, "Zhongguo mufu zhidu de tezheng xingtai he bianqian," esp. pp. 10–12; see also Chen Baoliang, "Mingdai mubin zhidu chutan." I shall return to the significance of the *muyou* experience for some literati in chapter 8.

30. Of course, actual practices were more complicated, and there was another side to this change: as a "friend" or "guest," one could potentially be treated with more respect. Not being a formal subordinate, a *muyou* also enjoyed more freedom in his relationship with his employer.

31. "Baixian"; in Xu Wei, *Xu Wei ji*, p. 179.

32. "*Chaodai ji* xiaoxu"; in ibid., p. 537. See also two other prefaces Xu wrote for the collection of his commissioned writings; in ibid., pp. 537–538.

33. For a discussion of the intimate relationship between *pinshi* and *pinnü* poetry in Chinese literary history, see Chen Wenzhong, *Zhonggo gudian shige jieshou shi yanjiu*, pp. 162–182.

34. "Fu dei wei taren zuo jiayishang"; in Xu Wei, *Xu Wei ji*, p. 251. The Qing literatus Xu Jiacun (fl. mid-nineteenth century), who had served on the staffs of many officials throughout his life, also compared himself to a poor girl who always made new clothes for the weddings of rich girls. In one of his letters to friends he complained: "This spring I again worked as a clerk for an official in Pingshu County. All these years, I have been making clothes [for others]. So far I am still a servant. All this is because I am someone with the appearance of a country girl, and no one

appreciates such a face." For the text of the entire letter, see Xu Jiacun, letter 3, "Yu Zhao Nanhu," *Qiushui xuan chidu;* in Xu Jiacun and Gong Weizhai, *Qiushui xuan, Xuehong xuan chidu,* p. 4.

35. "Jipu"; in Xu Wei, *Xu Wei ji,* p. 1334.

36. Xu Shuofang observes that Xu Wei and Shen Lian might not have been that close when the latter was alive. Shen Lian began to appear much more frequently in Xu Wei's writings after his heroic death. See "Xu Wei nianpu"; in Xu Shuofang, *Xu Shuofang ji,* vol. 3, p. 98. Shen Liang's fame can be confirmed by the fact that the last story of Feng Menglong's (1574–1646) famous collection of short stories, *Gujin xiaoshuo,* is about him and his son; see Feng Menglong, *Yushi mingyan* (also known as *Gujin xiaoshuo*), pp. 612–642. I am grateful to Robert Hegel for calling my attention to this fact; it is also mentioned in Feng's biography in the *Dictionary of Ming Biography,* p. 1184.

37. See, for example, "Shen canjun," "Shen sheng xing," "Shen Shuzi jie fandao weizeng ershou," and "Duanhe pian song Shen zi Shucheng chusai"; in Xu Wei, *Xu Wei ji,* pp. 67, 146, 149, and 717. Some of these poems were addressed to the son of Shen Lian, Shen Rang (Shen Shucheng), after Shen Lian was already dead.

38. "Zeng guanglu Shaoqing Shen gong zhuan"; in ibid., pp. 624–625.

39. See, for example, the observation by Mei Guozhen (*jinshi,* 1583) that is quoted by Yuan Hongdao at the end of his biography of Xu Wei; in ibid., p. 1344.

40. For a biography of Mi Heng, see *Hou Hanshu,* 80(b).2652–2658.

41. For Xu Wei's direct comparison of Shen to Mi Heng, see "Shen canjun," the third poem in "Ai sizi shi," and "Duanhe pian song Shen zi Shucheng chusai"; in Xu Wei, *Xu Wei ji,* pp. 67 and 718.

42. "Jipu"; in ibid., p. 1329.

43. Ibid.

44. See Wang Chang'an, *Xu Wei sanbian,* pp. 61–100.

45. "Ziwei muzhiming"; in Xu Wei, *Xu Wei ji,* p. 639.

46. "Xu Wenchang zhuan"; in ibid., p. 1340.

47. "Ji Shaobao gong wen"; in ibid., p. 658.

48. "Ai Zhu shangshu ci"; in ibid., p. 663. Xu Wei made this statement in a eulogy in memory of another person to whom he felt indebted, Minister Zhu Dashou (*jinshi,* 1556). However, while Minister Zhu had helped to release Xu from his *muyou* contract with Li Chunfang, Xu Wei unquestionably owed much more to Hu Zongxian.

49. "Shen jishi Mingchen"; in Qian Qianyi (1582–1664), *Liechao shiji xiaozhuan,* p. 496.

50. Mao Guojin, "Xian fujun xingshi"; in Mao Kun, *Mao Kun ji,* p. 1377. Mao Kun's attempt to save his former patron is also mentioned in Gu Yingtai, *Mingshi jishi benmo,* 55.866.

51. See, for example, the long poem (one hundred lines) "Shang Dufu gong shengri shi"; in Xu Wei, *Xu Wei ji,* 319–320.

52. Zhu Yizun, *Jingzhi ju shihua;* quoted by Chen Tian, *Mingshi jishi,* 16.2132.

53. "Gongshi zhuan"; in Xu Wei, *Xu Wei ji,* p. 1043.

54. Given his own long forced separation from his birth mother, this must have seemed particularly inhumane to Xu Wei.

55. Xu Wei, *Xu Wei ji,* pp. 51–52; see also "Zhou minfu ji xu"; in ibid., pp. 554–555.

56. The first two couplets of the first poem in "Du mou minfu diaoji ershou," *Xu Wenchang sanji, juan* 7; in ibid., p. 279.

57. "Zhou minfu"; in ibid., p. 212.

58. *Xu Wenchang yigao, juan* 4; in ibid., p. 769.

59. Rao Longsun suggests that these poems might have been written between 1567 and 1573; see *Mingdai Longqing, Wanli jian wenxue sixiang zhuanbian yanjiu*, p. 77.

60. See "Xu Wei nianpu"; in Xu Shuofang, *Xu Shuofang ji*, vol. 3, pp. 126–129.

61. See "Shang Yu Xinzhai"; in Xu Wei, *Xu Wei ji*, p. 886.

62. *Kuang gushi yuyang sannong;* in ibid., p. 1178.

63. The proverb "A donkey's prick points toward the east and a horse's prick points toward the west" is popular in the area of Xu Wei's hometown; it emphasizes that a man should know his place and should not disregard the social hierarchy. See the note on *Kuang gushi yuyang sannong* in Zhu Youdun et al., *Ming Qing zaju juan*, p. 111.

64. In Xu Wei's writings, Mi Heng is usually associated with his friend Shen Lian (all together four times), but on at least two occasions Xu Wei compared himself directly to Mi Heng. See "Xu Wei nianpu"; in Xu Shuofang, *Xu Shuofang ji*, vol. 3, p. 97.

65. The dating of the four plays in the *Sisheng yuan* cycle remains controversial. In general, there are two theories. The first theory dates the plays before 1558 (i.e., they were written before Xu Wei joined Hu Zongxian's staff as a *muyou*) or, at the latest, before 1562. The second theory suggests that the time lapse among the four plays could be quite long: while the first play, *Yu chanshi cuixiang yimeng*, was probably written as early as or before 1552, the other three plays were completed after the downfall of Hu Zongxian in 1563. For versions of the first theory, see Xu Lun, *Xu Wenchang*, pp. 77–78, and "Xu Wei nianpu"; in Xu Shuofang, *Xu Shuofang ji*, pp. 96–99. For versions of the second theory, see the biographical sketch of Xu Wei in Hu Shihou et al., *Zhongguo gudai xiqujia pingzhuan*, pp. 310–311, and Zhang Xinjian, *Xu Wei lun'gao*, pp. 171–176. Among all the discussions I have read so far, Zhang Xinjian is probably the most persuasive (his discussion is also the most substantial). I tend to believe that the high gender anxiety in *Kuang gushi, Ci Mulan,* and *Nü zhuangyuan* (among other things) made it more likely that they were written after Xu Wei had experienced his crisis of masculinity after the downfall of Hu Zongxian.

66. Jeannette Faurot has complained about the play's lack of "dramatic conflicts"; "Four Cries of a Gibbon," p. 94.

67. *Ci Mulan*, scene 2; in Xu Wei, *Xu Wei ji*, p. 1206.

68. Zhang Xinjian, *Xu Wei lun'gao*, pp. 183–184.

69. *Nü zhuangyuan*, act 2; in Xu Wei, *Xu Wei ji*, p. 1211.

70. *Ci Mulan*, act 2; in ibid., p. 1206.

71. *Nü zhuangyuan*, act 5; in ibid., pp. 1225–1226.

72. *Nü zhuangyuan*, act 4; in ibid., p. 1221.

73. Ibid.

74. *Ci Mulan*, act 2; in Xu Wei, *Xu Wei ji*, p. 1204.

75. *Nü zhuangyuan*, act 5; in ibid., pp. 1228–1229. Wilt Idema has noted Xu Wei's fascination with the body in these two plays in his "Female Talent and Female Virtue," pp. 560–561.

76. *Luoshang* is a term used by Xu Wei to characterize Mi Heng in his poem "Shen Canjun," *Xu Wenchang sanji, juan* 4; in Xu Wei, *Xu Wei ji*, p. 67.

CHAPTER 4: MANHOOD AND NATIONHOOD

1. For studies of the role of male literati in the cult of chaste women during the Ming-Qing period, see the following: T'ien, *Male Anxiety and Female Chastity;* Fei Siyan, *You dianfan dao guifan*, pp. 129–166, 236–250, and 305–313; and Carlitz: "Shrine, Governing-Class Identity and the Cult of Widow-Fidelity in Mid-Ming Jiangnan" and "The Daughter, the Singing-Girl, and the Seduction of Suicide." In his introduction to a special issue of *Nan nü* ("Passionate Women: Female Suicide in Late Imperial China"), Paul Ropp provides a useful overview of studies on female suicide; see also the "Bibliography" compiled by Ropp and provided at the end of this issue. In his study, T'ien argues that there was a direct parallel between the number of male literati failing the civil service examinations in a county and the number of chaste women recorded in that locale. In other words, the failed candidates were the main forces behind the cult of chaste women. Some scholars have expressed doubts about some of T'ien's interpretations of his impressive data, and especially his conclusion that a dramatic increase in the number of chaste women recorded necessarily meant an equally dramatic increase of chaste women in reality and the exact role of male literati anxiety as a result of examination failures; see, for example, the reviews by Ropp ("Review of Ju-kang T'ien's *Male Anxiety and Female Chastity*") and Mann ("Review of Ju-kang T'ien's *Male Anxiety and Female Chastity*").

2. For discussions of the Song and Yuan literati's chaste women rhetoric, see Bossler: "Faithful Wives and Heroic Maidens" and "Gender and Empire." Bossler argues that "Women's assumed weakness, and their very real sexual vulnerability, automatically invested their stories with tension and poignance. This made accounts of women very effective as vehicles for didactic messages about loyalty" ("Faithful Wives and Heroic Maidens," p. 773).

3. Gui Youguang, *Zhenchuan xiansheng quanji*, 24.408.

4. "Bingxue tang ji"; in Luo Lun, *Yifeng wenji*, 6.21a–21b.

5. For a brief account of literati debates on this issue in late imperial China, see Dong Jiazun, "Ming Qing xuezhe guanyu zhennü wenti de lunzhan."

6. "Zhennü lun"; in Gui Youguang, *Zhenchuan xiansheng quanji*, 3.41–42.

7. "Xu Lienü jie"; in Jiang Yingke, *Jiang Yingke ji*, 9.479–480. Given Jiang's rather negative views of officialdom (as discussed in chapter 2), it is a bit surprising to find him praising such extreme acts of chastity and comparing them to a male subject's loyalty, although Jiang himself did not necessarily see any contradiction here. Of course, the contexts were different since here he might have been carried away by his enthusiasm for upholding the chastity/loyalty of others, and the double standard was definitely a possibility. Jiang Yingke, like Yuan Hongdao, was a complicated figure, and, as I pointed out in chapter 2, he continued to serve in the government despite his professed disdain for officialdom. Allen Barr has noted Jiang's deep concern with contemporary political issues ("Jiang Yingke's place in the Gong'an School," p. 46).

8. "Shu 'Gu zhennü zhuan' hou"; in Gui Zhuang, *Gui Zhuang ji*, 4.300–301.

9. Ibid., 4.301–302.

10. Zha Jizuo, *Zuiwei lu*, 28.2562; see also his observation that "the choice of dying or not dying in the end is the same, although dying appears to be a more dif-

ficult choice. In fact, not dying, though looking easier, is also very difficult" (ibid., 28.2555).

11. For a discussion of Zha Jizuo's difficult life as a Ming loyalist under Qing rule and the compromises he had to make late in his life, see Ou Zhijian, "Lüelun Ming yimin Zha Jizuo wannian shenghua zhi yanjiu."

12. For the different and often conflicting views of Ming loyalists on the choice of suicide versus that of continuing to live under Manchu rule, see He Guanbiao, *Sheng yu si,* pp. 71–160, and Zhao Yuan, *Ming Qing zhiji shidafu yanjiu,* pp. 23–49 and 373–401.

13. "Ji Shanyin Liu xiansheng wen"; in Chen Que, *Chen Que ji,* 13.307. For a discussion of the Ming loyalists' painful choice between loyalty and filiality, see He Guanbiao, *Sheng yu si,* pp. 71–96.

14. "Bingbu zuoshilang Cangshui Zhang gong muzhiming"; in Huang Zongxi, *Huang Zongxi quanji,* vol. 10, p. 285.

15. *Shishen* was used by the seventeenth-century Ming loyalist savant Gu Yanwu (1613–1682; *ECCP,* pp. 421–426) to refer to Song *yimin* loyalists who began to serve the alien regime late in their lives; "*Guang Song yimin lu* xu"; in Gu Yanwu, *Gu Tinglin shiwen ji,* p. 33.

16. Cheng Shude, *Lunyu jishu,* p. 760, and Lau, *The Analects,* p. 107.

17. "Sijie lun"; in Chen Que, *Chen Que ji,* 5.152–154. Cf. He Guanbiao, *Sheng yu si,* pp. 227–256, and Zhao Yuan, *Ming Qing zhiji shidafu yanjiu,* pp. 49–57.

18. "Shu 'Pan Liefu beiwen' hou"; in Chen Que, *Chen Que ji,* 17.395–396. For a more general discussion of Chen Que's views on women, see Gerristsen, "Women in the Life and Thought of Ch'en Chüeh."

19. "Zhou Qiujia liushi shou xu"; in Qu Dajun, *Qu Dajun quanji,* vol. 3, p. 92. For Chen Que's similar view, see "Ji Wu Pouzhong shu"; in Chen Que, *Chen Que ji,* 2.102.

20. "Weijia xunfu lienü zhuan"; in Qu Dajun, *Qu Dajun quanji,* vol. 3, p. 366.

21. Here we are once again reminded of Sima Qian, who claimed that he had chosen castration in order to complete his unfinished historical work. In fact, many Ming loyalists claimed they had chosen to live for the sake of preserving the history of the former dynasty. For example, the famous writer and historian Zhang Dai (1597–ca. 1684; *ECCP,* pp. 53–54) offered a similar defense in the first poem of his "He wan'ge ci sanshou" and "Mengyi xu"; in Zhang Dai, *Zhang Dai shiwen ji,* pp. 25 and 110.

22. See Chen Yinke, *Liu Rushi biezhuan,* pp. 881–882.

23. It was said that when Liu Rushi was accused of adultery in Qian Qianyi's absence, he defended her: "Given that even many scholar-officials failed to maintain their integrity during the national crisis, how could people blame a woman for failing to protect her chastity?" See Chen Yinke, *Liu Rushi biezhuan,* pp. 885–886.

24. Qian Qianyi, *Muzhai Youxue ji,* 33.1194.

25. For discussions of Yan Yuan's criticism of the feminization of the literati and his attribution of such feminization to Song Neo-Confucianism, see Chen Dengyuan, *Yan Xizhai zhexue sixiang shu,* pp. 37–69, and Jui-sung Yang, "A New Interpretation of Yen Yüan," pp. 73–119. For general discussions of Yan Yuan's philosophical views, see Tu, "Yen Yüan," and Jiang Guanghui, *Yan Li xuepai,* pp. 11–116.

26. "*Qixue ji* xu"; in Yan Yuan, *Yan Yuan ji,* pp. 398–399.

27. See, for example, "Youdao," "Xuebian yi," "Xingli ping," and "Yue Zhangshi *Wangxue zhiyi ping*"; in ibid., pp. 40, 52, 75, and 496. A similar use of *kongwen* to characterize the useless learning of the Song-Ming Confucian scholars can be found

in the writings of Yan Yuan's famous disciple, Li Gong (1659–1733); see, for example, Li Gong, *Lunxue*, 2.5a.

28. "Da He Qianli"; in Yan Yuan, *Yan Yuan ji*, p. 459.

29. "Xingli ping"; in ibid., p. 73.

30. *"Zhu Zi yulei* ping"; in ibid., p. 259.

31. "Youdao"; in ibid., p. 40. Elsewhere, Yan Yuan castigated Zhu Xi for his emphasis on the civil at the expense of the military [*zhongwen qingwu*] and for his bad influence on the literati of later ages. See Dai Wang, *Yanshi xueji*, 1.17a (p. 41).

32. Wang Yuan, "Liguo lun"; in Dai Wang, *Yanshi xueji*, 8.24a (p. 437). For a general discussion of Wang Yuan, see Jiang Guanghui, *Yan Li xuepai*, pp. 142–169. Relevant here also is Lynn Struve's discussion of a group of scholars (including Yan Yuan and Wang Yuan) of the Kangxi period (1662–1722) with a marked preference for "a more martial brand of heroism" and a "distrust of the concept-sealing power of the written, transmitted word-rhetoric, classification, interpretation" ("Ambivalence and Action," esp. pp. 323, 332, and 340).

33. "Xuebian yi"; in Yan Yuan, *Yan Yuan ji*, p. 51.

34. "Xingli ping"; in ibid., p. 62. This couplet was quoted by many early Qing writers, and the wording could vary in their citations. See also "Zuo fu duyushi zeng taizi shaobao zhongjie Siming Shi gong shendao beiming"; in Huang Zongxi, *Huang Zongxi quanji*, vol. 10, p. 232, and Ji Liuqi, *Mingji beilüe*, p. 511.

35. "Zhongyi Liu Ge"; in *Songshi*, vol. 15, p. 13164.

36. In *Wind against the Mountain*, Richard L. Davis discusses what he has considered to be many Song literati's reluctance "to acknowledge any political consciousness in women of the day," although many of them indeed chose to die for political causes: "The reticence of late Song men to acknowledge the civic consciousness of women and their jealously diligent guard against female intrusion into the political domain may well relate to far broader changes in gender relations—perception that women had somehow come to threaten the hegemony of men over political, cultural, or social life" (pp. 184 and 188). This is indeed a far cry from the tendency of the late Ming and early Qing literati to indulge in profuse praise of chaste women. Ironically, Yan Yuan and his like might resemble more the late Song literati, whom Yan criticized so harshly, in their shared uneasiness about the rhetorical power of the trope of a chaste woman. Also relevant is Davis' central argument that what drove Song men to martyrdom was an attempt to overcompensate for the perception that Southern Chinese literati were not masculine enough. It would be interesting to compare this feeling of emasculation of the Song literati with that of their seventeenth-century counterparts since both seem to have felt humiliated and emasculated when their countries were conquered by alien armies. However, this is a complex topic beyond the scope of this study. For a discussion of the concept of loyalty and its relationship to the image of chaste women in Song China from a different perspective, see Bossler, "Faithful Wives and Heroic Maidens."

37. Li Gong, *Yan Yuan nianpu*, p. 34. T'ien (*Male Anxiety and Female Chastity*, p. 15) makes the interesting observation that in late imperial China as suicide methods became more feminine (more males chose hanging or drowning rather than stabbing or throat slashing), suicide was increasingly considered a feminine act. However, T'ien fails to provide enough evidence to substantiate this observation.

38. "Fu Ouyang Bo'an zhangke"; in Hai Rui, *Hai Rui ji*, p. 443.

39. Li Le, *Jianwen zaji, juan* 10, p. 817.

40. "Fufen"; in Shen Defu, *Wanli yehuo bian, juan* 24, pp. 620–621.

41. "*Cangshu* Shiji liezhuang zongmu houlun"; in Li Zhi, *Li Zhi wenji*, vol. 2, p. 37.

42. Many traditional Confucian scholars have defended the Master's refusal to talk about military affairs with Duke Ling of Wei on the grounds that Confucius believed the duke was morally corrupt and therefore needed to be enlightened first (thus the talk about ritual first). See Cheng Shude, *Lunyu jishi*, p. 1050. Liu Xiang (ca. 46 BCE–23 CE) was one of the few who believed that this passage demonstrated that Confucius emphasized ritual while neglecting military affairs; see "Zashi"; in Liu Xiang, *Xinxu zhuzi suoyin*, p. 27. Yan Yuan offered a different interpretation of this passage, arguing that Confucius was knowledgeable about military affairs but refused to discuss them with the duke because he thought the duke's behavior was excessive and some later scholars misunderstood Confucius in blaming him for acting like a woman. Here Yan Yuan might particularly have had in mind Li Zhi's criticism of Confucius ("*Sishu* zhengwu"; in Yan Yuan, *Yan Yuan ji*, pp. 220–221). However, he was far from convincing in his defense of the Master's "bookish activities" of writing and editing. He argued that Confucius originally wanted to establish himself in practical realms but his offers of service were repeatedly rejected. The Master had no other choice but to devote himself to writing and editing books. Yet he does not explain why Confucius' *wen* activities were not "feminine" as was Song Neo-Confucian bookish learning. See "Xingli ping" and "Zhangshi zonglun"; in Yan Yuan, *Yan Yuan ji*, pp. 77–78 and 496.

43. Huang Shuzhen, "Xu"; in Chen Zilong et al., *Ming jingshi wen bian*, p. 15.

44. "Qiao"; in *Xiaochuang youji*, p. 41.

45. See Zou Yi, *Qi Zhen yecheng*, 13.18a (p. 513). Zou Yi includes this biography in the section on men. A more detailed version of Kong Silang's story can be found in *Xinbian Jiao Chuang tongsu xiaoshuo* (1645), a semifictional work composed of miscellaneous writings, including gossip, random notes, memoirs, and poems by different people from the last years of the Ming dynasty. See *Jiao Chuang xiaoshuo* (the shortened title), 5.16a–17a (pp. 165–167). Zhang Dai apparently also considered Kong Silang a man since he included his biography in the section entitled "Yiren liezhuan"; see his *Shikui shu houji*, 57.315.

46. For the enforcement of this policy by the Manchu regime and the fierce resistance it provoked from the Han people, see Wakeman, *The Great Enterprise*, pp. 646–650, and Chen Shengxi, *Ming Qing yidai shi dujian*, pp. 141–192.

47. Qu Dajun, *Qu Dajun quanji*, vol. 3, pp. 471–472.

48. "Cangfa fu"; in ibid., vol. 3, p. 254. In a short essay "Tusong," Qu sarcastically claimed that being bald was the best thing that could ever happen to a man (in ibid., vol. 3, p. 213). Qu's open defiance of the Manchu policy can also be found in "Cangfa zhong ming" and "Zizuo yiguan zhong zhiming" (in ibid., vol. 3, pp. 206 and 146).

49. "Changfa qiren zan"; in ibid., vol. 3, p. 208. The term *xingyu* could refer to men who had been castrated, as Sima Qian used it (as discussed in chapter 1). Wakeman characterizes the forced head shaving as "tonsorial castration" (*The Great Enterprise*, p. 649).

50. This was a contemporary saying to which later scholars and historians often referred; see, for example, Wu Cuncun, *Ming Qing shehui xing'ai fengqi*, p. 234. However, I have yet to determine when and where this saying originated. For how it was appropriated by some anti-Manchu reformists of the late Qing, see Xia Xiaohong, "Lishi jiyi de chonggou."

51. For a discussion of women's footbinding in the context of the Manchu

regime's haircutting policy and its relationship to contemporary Han Chinese men's sense of masculinity in the aftermath of the fall of the Ming, see Ko, "The Body as Attire."

52. "Er liefu zhuan"; in Yan Yuan, *Yan Yuan ji*, p. 485.

53. Wilt Idema has also briefly touched on the limitations of woman as metaphor in male literati discourse in "Female Talent and Female Virtue," pp. 570–571.

54. "Tianchang Ruan zhenxiao zhuan"; in Gui Zhuang, *Gui Zhuang ji*, 7.422.

55. "Li jiefu Yushi zhuan"; in Sun Qifeng, *Xiafeng xiansheng ji*, 5.42b. Elsewhere, Sun bemoaned that among those who had committed suicide after the death of the last Ming emperor, eunuchs greatly outnumbered generals; see "Sili jian Zhangyin Yunfeng Gao gong mubiao"; in ibid., 7.22b. Sun Qifeng appears to have had a particularly deep gender consciousness when he was evaluating the behavior of those who had served the Ming; see also his "Zhangfu shuo" (On Being a True Man); in ibid., 8.34b–35a.

56. See Yenna Wu, "The Inversion of Marital Hierarchy" and *The Chinese Virago*.

57. *Xingshi yinyuan zhuan*, 91.1304.

CHAPTER 5: FROM *YINGXIONG* TO *HAOHAN*

1. Here "hero" is probably the closest English equivalent. However, as we shall see below, the Chinese term is more precise and specific.

2. See Mou Zongsan, *Caixing yu xuanli*, p. 61. The explosion is confirmed by my search for the term *yingxiong* in the electronic versions of the classical texts collected in the online *Zhongyang yanjiu yuan Hanji dianzi wenxian* (www.sinica.edu.tw/ftms-bin/ftmsw3). The term rarely appears in the so-called "thirteen classics," the writings of various pre-Qin philosophers, and even Sima Qian's *Shiji*. It makes only three appearances in Ban Gu's *Hanshu*. However, the number of appearances increases dramatically during the Three Kingdoms Period and in texts of later periods that are concerned with the Three Kingdoms Period. For example, in Chen Shou's *San'guo zhi* (including Pei Songzhi's copious annotations), it appears approximately thirty-three times (not counting its references to *Yingxiong ji*, a work Pei Songzhi quotes frequently in his annotations), at least twenty-one times in *Hou Hanshu*, and twenty times in *Jinshu*. Although these are only approximate figures and are not necessarily reflective of other writings from this period, they contribute to the overall impression that there was a general surge of interest in the concept during this period.

3. The modern scholar Wu Yechun estimates that Pei Songzhi quoted Wang Can's *Yingxiong ji* eighty-two times; see Yang Yaokun and Wu Yechun, *Chen Shou Pei Zongzhi pingzhuan*, p. 256. For an incomplete version of *Yingxiong ji* pieced together by later scholars, see Wang Can, *Wang Can ji*, pp. 53–92.

4. "Yingxiong"; in Liu Shao, *Renwu zhi jiaojian*, p. 145.

5. Ibid., pp. 147–150.

6. Mou Zongsan (*Caixing yu xuanli*, pp. 61–62) complains that while Liu Shao's understanding of *yingxiong* is interesting, his discussion of *shengren* (sage) is far from adequate (for example, Liu did not devote a chapter to the discussion of *shengren*, as he did to *yingxiong*) and that he almost completely ignored the ethical implications of the concept of *yingxiong*. The dangers associated with *yingxiong*, according to Mou, were not adequately addressed until the Song dynasty, when the Neo-Confucians began to reexamine the issue. Mou here must have had in mind Zhu Xi's

well-known debate with Chen Liang on the relationship between sage and hero (already discussed in chapter 1 and to which I will return in chapters 8 and 9).

7. "Xianzhu zhuan"; in Chen Shou, *San'guo zhi*, 32.875.

8. For a much more elaborate account of this episode in *San'guo yanyi*, see *San'guo yanyi huiping ben*, 21.257–259. All my references to the novel, unless otherwise noted, are to this edition since it contains all the important commentaries from different editions published during the Ming and Qing periods. I refer to the so-called Ming Jiajing edition (entitled *San'guo zhi tongsu yanyi*) whenever textual variations become relevant to my discussion. The word *yingxiong* appears a total of seventy-seven times in *San'guo yanyi* and the term *da zhangfu* twenty-eight times (based on search results of the Mao Zonggang edition in the online *Zhongyang yanjiu yuan Hanji dianzi wenxian*). The frequent usage of these two words is certainly an indicator of the novel's unique concern with the issue of masculinity.

9. "Xianzhu zhuan"; in Chen Shou, *San'guo zhi*, 32.892.

10. "Xu Shao zhuan"; in *Hou Hanshu*, 68.2234. The wording of this remark is substantially different in other written sources. For example, in his annotations to the biography of Cao Cao in *San'guo zhi* (1.3), Pei Songzhi quotes Xu Shao's much harsher criticism of Cao Cao from *Cao Man zhuan*. In his criticism Xu characterizes Cao as "a great minister in a world of peace and a crafty evil strong man [*jianxiong*] in a world of disorder." It is believed that Cao Cao's infamous image as a *jianxiong* has a lot to do with Xu's remarks. Xu's remarks are quoted by the early Qing fiction commentator Mao Zonggang in his comments on chapter 1 of *San'guo yanyi*, 1.1 (see below). For a version of this episode closer to the one in *Hou Hanshu* (but in which the remark is attributed to someone else), see "Shijian"; in Liu Yiqing (403–444), *Shishuo xinyu jiaojian*, 7.212–213.

11. "Wudi ji"; in Chen Shuo, *Sang'uo zhi*, 1.55. The concept of *xionghao* (outstanding strong men) used by Chen Shou here later became almost interchangeable with *yingxiong*, as in the common word *haojie* (outstanding man). However, a subtle difference is that *hao* sometimes implies a powerful man who is arrogant, rude, and unreasonable (see *Hanyu da cidian*, p. 5927).

12. See Cao Cao, *Cao Cao ji*, p. 40.

13. For various theories about the complicated textual history of the novel, see Plaks, *The Four Masterworks of the Ming Novel*, pp. 361–378. Many students of Chinese fiction believe that the Mao Zonggang commentary edition must have been a result of the joint efforts of Mao Lun (fl. mid-seventeenth century) and his son, Mao Zonggang (fl. late seventeenth century); see David Rolston's introductory essay to the English translation of the *dufa* (how to read) essay in the Mao Zonggang commentary edition in Rolston, *How to Read the Chinese Novel*, pp. 146–151. For the sake of convenience, I will refer to this edition by the name of the son only.

14. Quite a few scholars have argued that one of Mao Zonggang's central concerns in editing and commenting on *San'guo yanyi* was his Ming loyalist agenda. See, for example, Xiao Xiangkai, "*San'guo yanyi* Maoping de chufadian he jiben qingxiang"; Du Guichen, "Mao Zonggang yong Liu fan Cao yizai fan Qing fu Ming"; and Wang Xianpei and Zhou Weimin, *Ming Qing xiaoshuo lilun piping shi*, pp. 366–373. Although some scholars might have doubts on the coherence of such an agenda in the Mao Zonggang commentary edition, it is probably safe to assume that the fall of the Ming was on the minds of the father and son commentators, as my discussion below will show.

15. See also *San'guo zhi tongsu yanyi* (a facsimile reprint of the so-called Jiajing

edition), pp. 4 and 7. Note that in this edition the novel is divided into 240 *ze* (sections) rather than 100 *hui* (chapters), as is the Mao Zonggang commentary edition. It is most likely that the Maos based their edition on this edition.

16. *San'guo zhi pinghua;* in *Song Yuan pinghua ji,* p. 775.

17. See the biography of Lü Bu in *Hou Hanshu,* 75.2445.

18. *San'guo zhi pinghua;* in *Song Yuan pinghua ji,* pp. 776–777.

19. Cf. *Hou Hanshu,* 75.2450–2451.

20. Liu An's actions are reminiscent of those of the famous military strategist Wu Qi (d. 381 BCE) from the Warring States Period. According to Sima Qian, Wu killed his wife, who was from Qi, in order to dispel suspicions on the part of the people of Lu that he, a military strategist on the side of Lu, might be siding with their enemy, the troops of Qi. See "Sunzi Wu Qi liezhuan"; in Sima Qian, *Shiji,* 65.2165.

21. *Hua Guan Suo zhuan;* in *Ming Chenghua shuochang cihua congkan,* p. 2. For a discussion of this Ming chantefable, see McLaren, *Chinese Popular Culture and Ming Chantefables,* esp. pp. 239–259.

22. Chen Shou, *San'guo zhi,* 36.939. This is only one of many cases in which the author of *San'guo yanyi* deliberately ignored historical facts in order to elevate Guan Yu to the status of hero; it shows that the novelist is probably not always so obsessed with the "limitations of valor," as Andrew Plaks has argued in his otherwise magisterial study, *The Four Masterworks of the Ming Novel.* Some of the ironies Plaks discusses are not necessarily unique to the novel (they may have already been implicitly present in various works of historiography or other popular sources). Furthermore, referring to a hero's character flaws does not always have to be read as an attempt at deflating heroism, as Plaks has suggested in his reading of this novel and *Shuihu zhuan,* since a flawed person could be an even more convincing hero to which an average reader could easily relate. For a brief discussion of "heroes with flaws" in Ming writings, see Chen Baoliang, "Mingchao ren de yingxiong haojie guan," pp. 366–368.

23. Of course, some historians have questioned the "historicity" of many of the sources Pei Songzhi quotes in his annotations to *San'guo zhi,* but historicity is always a relative issue and Pei's annotations are not necessarily less historically accurate than the accounts in *San'guo zhi.*

24. While we cannot find the *bingzhu dadan* episode in any extant Yuan plays, it indeed appears in several Ming plays on Guan Yu, such as *Gucheng ji.* For discussions of this issue, see Kin Bunkyo, "Cong bingzhu dadan tan *San'guo yanyi* he *Tongjian gangmu* de guanxi," and Wang Anqi, *Mingdai xiqu wulun,* pp. 141–202.

25. *San'guo zhi tongsu yanyi,* p. 795.

26. For a Freudian reading of Guan Yu as a sexualized hero of *wu* masculinity, see Louie, *Theorising Chinese Masculinity,* pp. 22–41. I feel that Louie's point on the tendency to desexualize *wu* masculinity in Chinese literature is generally valid, although there are exceptions, as we see in the so-called "martial romances" of the nineteenth century (briefly discussed in chapter 8). However, some readers might have problems with Louie's argument about Guan Yu's repressed sexuality (his incestuous inclination toward Liu Bei's wives) and some of his "readings against the grain." See also Song's discussion of *San'guo yanyi* and *Shuihu zhuan* in terms of "desexualized heroism" (*The Fragile Scholar,* pp. 158–182). Song's discussion of the misogynist tendencies in *San'guo yanyi* fails to take into account the novel's many episodes where women are presented as moral exemplars, as I try to demonstrate below.

27. Chen Shou, *San'guo zhi,* 36.949.

28. English translation from Roberts, *Three Kingdoms.* Hereafter cited in text as "Roberts" plus page numbers.

29. The wording in the Jiajing edition (p. 447) is slightly different.

30. "Tian Dan liezhuan"; in Sima Qian, *Shiji,* 82.2457.

31. This episode is not found in the Jiajing edition; see *San'guo zhi tongsu yanyi,* pp. 3510–3511.

32. In the Jiajing edition of the novel, there is no mention of Madam Sun committing suicide. Mao Zonggang was apparently not the first to associate her with this act of chastity; references to it can be found in earlier sources; see Wang Yanping, "Liu Bei yu Sun furen guanxi kaoshi." Such episodes of chastity and loyalty not found in the Jiajing edition strengthen the impression that these particular Confucian virtues receive more emphasis in Mao Zonggang's commentary edition—perhaps, one is tempted to think, because the father-and-son commentators had just witnessed violent dynastic changes. This probably is also the case with Mao Zonggang's friend Zhu Renhuo, the author of the novel *Sui Tang yanyi.* Compared with the source texts on which it relies, *Sui Tang yanyi* puts more emphasis on the concept of chastity and loyalty (more in chapter 6).

33. See Ogawa Tamaki, "*San'guo yanyi* de yanbian"; for an attempt to trace the changing image of Zhang Fei from Yuan vernacular literature to *San'guo yanyi,* see Besio, "Zhang Fei in Yuan Vernacular Literature."

34. For a discussion of the images of *rujiang* in some traditional Chinese historical novels, see Ji Dejun, *Ming Qing lishi yanyi xiaoshuo yishu lun,* pp. 248–264.

35. This same phrase is used by Zhao Zi to distinguish Sun Quan from other bookish scholars during Zhao's mission to persuade the Wei government not to attack Wu. Zhao Zi praises Sun Quan as well read but not like the bookish men who like to labor over the texts of the classics (82.996).

36. The concept of *jie* seems also to have received more attention in the second half of the novel, where, most acts of *jie* by women (including suicide) take place.

37. See Chen Xianghua, *Zhuge Liang xingxiaong shi yanjiu,* pp. 240–272.

38. See the prefaces attached to the Chongzhen combined edition; reprinted in Zhu Yixuan and Liu Yuchen, *San'guo yanyi ziliao huibian,* pp. 285–287.

39. See Sun Shuyu, *Shuihu zhuan de laili, xintai yu yishu,* pp. 322–345. This obsession with material goods would intensify in the late Ming novel *Jin Ping Mei,* which is deeply indebted to *Shuihu zhuan.* For a discussion of *Jin Ping Mei* in terms of its obsession with materiality, see my *Desire and Fictional Narrative in Late Imperial China,* pp. 86–103.

40. Unless otherwise noted, all references to the novel are to *Rongyu tang ben Shuihu zhuan,* with chapter and page numbers given in parentheses.

41. See *Shuihu zhuan huiping ben,* 35.671 and 676, 36.681 and 694, and 38.714–715. In the Jin Shengtan commentary edition, the first chapter of the original novel is presented as a prelude, so its chapter 35 would be chapter 36 in *Rongyu tang ben Shuihu zhuan,* etc.

42. In the Jin Shengtan commentary edition, Wu Song has eighteen bowls of wine (*Shuihu zhuan huiping ben,* 22.420).

43. For a brief discussion of the taverns where important events take place in the novel, see Wang Bin, *Shuihu de jiudian,* pp. 3–13.

44. *Shuihu zhuan huiping ben,* 4.128. Wine and sex are also shown be closely related in *Jin Ping Mei,* which can in many ways be read as a deliberate critique of *Shuihu zhuan.*

45. Cf. Louie's discussion of Wu Song as a "working-class hero" in *Theorising Chinese Masculinity*, pp. 79–83.

46. "Xianzhu fa Wu"; in Zhu Guozhen, *Yongzhuang xiaopin*, 14.301.

47. *Shuihu zhuan huiping ben*, 11.239.

48. David Ownby argues that many men from the low social strata resorted to banditry in late imperial China because of their frustrating experiences as bachelors; poverty; the uneven ratio of men to women; and the practice of polygamy among the elite. See his "Approximations of Chinese Bandits," pp. 240–245. If Ownby's observation is accurate, then we can say that the inclination of some *Shuihu* heroes toward misogynistic violence may reflect, in a strange way, the frustration of bachelor bandits over the unavailability of women.

49. Ge, *Out of the Margins*, pp. 60–61.

50. See Ma Jigao, *Song Ming lixue yu wenxue*, pp. 215–225.

CHAPTER 6: RECONSTRUCTING *HAOHAN* IN THREE NOVELS FROM THE SUI-TANG ROMANCE CYCLE

1. These novels are part of the Sui-Tang romance cycle because they all focus on events and figures (historical or fictional) from the period of transition from the Sui to the Tang dynasties (roughly sixth to tenth centuries). For a general study of many works in this cycle, see Qi Yukun, *Sui Tang yanyi xilie xiaoshuo*. See also Hegel, "Rewriting the Tang," for a brief summary of the relationships of some of the important works in this cycle.

2. Robert Hegel observes that many episodes in the novel owe their inspiration to *Shuihu zhuan*, but he does not elaborate (*The Novel in Seventeenth-Century China*, p. 124). In the chapter commentaries in the 1633 edition of the novel, *Shuihu zhuan* is repeatedly mentioned as a model for the stories. See, for example, Yuan Yuling, *Suishi yiwen*, 27.214 and 35.279.

3. *Caoze yingxiong* is a term that frequently appears in Yuan Yuling's *Suishi yiwen*—for example, 1.1 and 3.18.

4. Hegel, "Maturation and Conflicting Values," pp. 134 and 138.

5. See the original preface to the novel (*Suishi yiwen*, p. 1), where *xia* is celebrated as the novel's main theme.

6. Cheng Shude, *Lunyu jishi*, 32.1115; Lau, *The Analects*, p. 135.

7. Self-discipline is a virtue also emphasized in many works of prescriptive advice literature (discussed in chapter 9).

8. At the beginning of chapter 44, the narrator (44.359) emphasizes the importance of the virtue of faithfulness and loyalty in terms of "following one lord to death." He is here praising the heroic death of Qin Shubao's former superior, Commander Zhang Xutuo, of the Sui imperial army. Ironically, Zhang is killed by the troops of Li Mi, to whom Qin Shubao has just pledged his loyalty after deserting his superior. Qin Shubao's final switch to the Tang is eventually justified by the fact that Li Mi himself has surrendered first. The narrator nevertheless feels compelled to defend Qin Shubao by claiming that loyalty becomes an issue only when one has found a "true lord" to whom to offer one's services (53.440).

9. For a list of the chapters in *Sui Tang yanyi* that are largely based on those in *Suishi yiwen*, see Hegel, *The Novel in Seventeenth-Century China*, p. 239. See also He Guli (Hegel), Chinese essay: *"Sui Tang yanyi,"* p. 157.

10. Cf. Hegel, "Maturation and Conflicting Values," p. 142. According to Ouyang

Jian, while most of *Sui Tang yanyi* is based on materials derived from earlier sources, Chu Renhuo also wrote a significant number of original paragraphs and episodes ("*Sui Tang yanyi* 'zhuiji chengzhi' kao," pp. 377–382). Curiously, 90 percent of these paragraphs and episodes are related to women.

11. *Sui Yangdi yanshi* is another major source for the first two-thirds of *Sui Tang yanyi*. See Hegel, *"Sui T'ang yen-i,"* pp. 53–69, and Ouyang Jian, "*Sui Tang yanyi* 'zhuiji chengzhi' kao," pp. 358–369. For a discussion of *Sui Yangdi yanshi*, see Hegel, *The Novel in Seventeenth-Century China*, pp. 106–111.

12. Chu Renhuo, *Sui Tang yanyi* (Taipei, 1988), 47.486. All references to the novel in our discussion will be to this edition, with chapter and page numbers in parentheses.

13. Hegel, *The Novel in Seventeenth-Century China*, p. 206. Hegel argues that Chu Renhuo was likely to harbor Ming loyalist sentiments. However, some Chinese scholars believe that Chu was quite sympathetic to the Manchu regime because some of his family members appeared to be receptive to it. See Yu Shengting's biographical sketch of Chu Renhuo in Zhou Juntao and Wang Changyou, *Zhongguo tongsu xiaoshuo jia pingzhuan*, p. 167. Of course, being nostalgic about the old dynasty and being receptive to the new foreign regime were not necessarily mutually exclusive for many seventeenth-century literati writers. In other words, Chu Renhuo could consider the issue of loyalty important even though he did not necessarily regard himself as a Ming subject. For a discussion of the impact of time on Ming loyalists (including the the implications of the "generation gap"), see Zhao Yuan, *Ming Qing zhiji shidafu yanjiu*, pp. 373–401.

14. This episode is apparently incorporated from *Sui Yang di yanshi* (7.868–899), but there are important changes. In *Sui Yang di yanshi*, the castration takes place, and Wang Yi indeed becomes a eunuch as he wished. See Hegel's discussion of Wang (*The Novel in Seventeenth-Century Chinese Novel*, p. 195).

15. Here we are reminded of Sima Qian's postcastration efforts at re/masculinization (discussed in chapter 1).

16. Hegel makes this point in his discussion of the new image of Qin Shubao in the novel ("Maturation and Conflicting Values," pp. 114–115 and 147–149).

17. Hegel, *"Sui T'ang yen-i,"* pp. 6–10.

18. This observation is also made by Qi Yukun, *Sui Tang yanyi xilie xiaoshuo*, pp. 49–51.

19. The emphasis on military skills can also be found elsewhere in *Sui Tang yanyi*—for example, Li Yuan insists that literary talent (such as poetic skills) is utterly useless at a time of disorder (6.53). See also the narrator's condemnation of Chen Shubao, the last ruler of the Southern dynasty, as a weakling poet indulging in wine and poetry (1.3); he also condemns the government's policy of emphasizing the civil over the military (10.93). Such passages seem to echo similar laments by many late Ming and early Qing figures, such as Hai Rui and Yan Yuan, over the incompetence of the *wenren* and the uselessness of their bookish knowledge (examined in chapter 4). Some of the examples mentioned here can also be found in *Suishi yiwen* (1.3, 5.38, and 9.72), which was written when the Ming dynasty was rapidly approaching its demise; its author, Yuan Yuling, certainly shared these sentiments deploring the deficiencies of the male literati. Such sentiments have deepened considerably in *Sui Tang yanyi*.

20. Cf. *Suishi yiwen*, 5.36, with *Sui Tang yanyi*, 6.51.

21. Hsia, "The Military Romance," esp. pp. 371–378. Many Chinese historians of

Chinese fiction tend to categorize the military romances discussed by Hsia as *ying-xiong chuanqi* (heroic tales); see, for example, Pei Shuhai, *Ming Qing yingxiong chuanqi zonglun.*

22. The most famous and elaborate romance between a hero and a female warrior is probably in the eighteenth-century novel *Shuo Tang sanzhuan.* It tells an entertaining story about how Xue Dingshan is forced to marry Fan Lihua after she has captured Xue; later, having deserted Fan (now his wife) three times, Xue eventually succumbs to her after being repeatedly outwitted and humiliated by her. This romance in *Shuo Tang sanzhuan,* itself a sequel to *Shuo Tang quanzhuan,* must have been inspired in part by the romance between Dou Xiannian and Luo Cheng under discussion here.

23. For studies of the scholar-beauty novels, see Lin Chen, *Mingmo Qingchu xiaoshuo shulu,* esp. pp. 55–84; Zhou Jianyu, *Caizi jiaren xiaoshuo yanjiu;* and my *Desire and Fictional Narrative in Late Imperial China,* pp. 206–235.

24. What specific source texts the author of *Shuo Tang quanzhuan* relied on and the degree to which he relied on a particular text are difficult to determine with accuracy since much of *Suishi yiwen* was copied verbatim into *Sui Tang yanyi.* Hegel ("Rewriting the Tang") believes that given the popularity of *Sui Tang yanyi* during the eighteenth century, it had to be *Shuo Tang quanzhuan*'s main written source. Many Chinese scholars have taken it for granted that *Shuo Tang quanzhuan* reflects the values of the less educated masses because of its much greater affinities with the rhetoric of storytelling.

25. Modern scholars have noted many similarities between *Shuihu zhuan* and *Shuo Tang quanzhuan* in terms of plot structure and characterization. See, for example, Zhao Jingshen, *Zhongguo xiaoshuo congkao,* pp. 134–135, and Qi Yukun, *Sui Tang yanyi xilie xiaoshuo,* p. 75.

26. "Doughty warriors" is the term Hegel has used to translate *haohan* in his "Rewriting the Tang."

27. In *Orality and Literacy,* Walter J. Ong observers that "oral memory works effectively with 'heavy' characters, persons whose deeds are monumental, memorable and commonly public. Thus the noetic economy of its nature generates outsize figures, that is, heroic figures . . . to organize experience in some sort of permanently memorable form. Colorless personalities cannot survive oral mnemonics" (p. 70). Ong's characterization of oral literature fits *Shuo Tang* to a remarkable degree.

28. Ge, *Out of the Margins.*

29. This is also Hegel's central argument in his reading of *Shuo Tang* in "Rewriting the Tang."

30. An observation also made by Hegel, "Rewriting the Tang."

31. Interestingly enough, unlike in the two earlier novels, where Qin Shubao is the central figure in the farewell scene, Qin is nowhere to be seen in *Shuo Tang.* He arrives only after Shan Xiongxin is already executed.

32. This episode is not the creation of the author of *Shuo Tang.* It can be found in the much earlier novel *Sui Tang liangchao shizhuan* (9.143–144). However, the comic account as to why Li Yuan rebelled seems to fit better in *Shuo Tang.*

33. Cf. Hegel's observation: "This novel presents all major characters in a low mimetic light, as worthy, at least part of the time, of ridicule. In effect, the *Shuo Tang* text both fantastically romanticizes its protagonists and reduces them to a level of foolishness that evokes the reader's laughter. To me, and I am certain to any reader

familiar with the *Sui Tang yanyi* versions of these stories (that is, the more widely read and most likely better educated reader), *Shuo Tang* can only come across as a parody, glittering with wit and ironic reversals of characters' personalities, their motivations for action, and their dilemmas" ("Rewriting the Tang," p. 169).

34. When Shan Xiongxin is first introduced in *Shuo Tang* (5.35), the reader is told he has a green face and red hair—a rather devilish appearance. However, there is no description of him when he is first introduced in *Suishi yiwen* (7.58) or *Sui Tang yanyi* (8.79).

35. This point is also discussed by Hegel in "Rewriting the Tang."

36. For discussions of mid-Qing cynicism, see my *Literati and Self-Re/Presentation*, pp. 38–39 and 42, and C. Xiao, *Garden as Lyrical Enclave*, pp. 43–59. As we shall see in the next chapter, another mid-Qing fiction writer, Cao Xueqin, will try to critique adult masculinity from a different angle.

37. For brief discussions in English of these works, see Hegel, "Rewriting the Tang," and Hsia, "The Military Romance"; for a discussion in Chinese, see Qi Yukun, *Sui Tang yanyi xilie xiaoshuo*, pp. 77–92.

CHAPTER 7: EFFEMINACY, FEMININITY, AND MALE-MALE PASSIONS

1. See, for example, *Liangjiaohun*, 1.2.

2. Apparently many shared this view at that time. The seventeenth-century writer Zhang Chao believed that "among human beings, the female is more beautiful than the male; among birds, the male is more beautiful than the female; among beasts, however, the differences [in appearance] between the male and the female are not great" (*Youmeng ying*, p. 202).

3. For a discussion of the importance of poetry in scholar-beauty fiction, see Xiao Chi, "Cong caizi jiaren dao *Shitou ji*." In *The Fragile Scholar*, Song associates the *caizi* claim of masculinity with "textual production" (pp. 73–75).

4. Some of the scholar-beauty novels containing cross-dressing are the following: *Yu Jiao Li, Wanruyue, Tiehua xianshi, Jinxiang ting, Fenghuang chi, Xing fengliu, Feihuaxu*, and *Lin'er bao*. Almost all of them are about a girl masquerading as a man. See also the discussion of the cross-dressing motif in Xu Wei's plays in chapter 3.

5. *Haoqiu zhuan*, 1.2. Although this work has been traditionally classified as a scholar-beauty novel, many of its features make it an exception. See my *Desire and Fictional Narrative in Late Imperial China*, pp. 229–235.

6. All references to this novel are to *Huatu yuan* (Shenyang, 1985).

7. This is rather unusual since in scholar-beauty novels a *caizi* is always beautiful and an excellent poet at the same time. Consequently, Liu Qingyun, despite his stunning beauty, is not a typical *caizi*.

8. Feng Menglong, *Yushi mingyan*, 1.1. For a discussion of the feminine image of male characters in vernacular late Ming short stories, see Shen Jinhao, "Lun *Sanyan Erpai* zhong mei nanzi xingxiang."

9. *Rongyu tang ben Shuihu zhuan*, 21.287.

10. Cf. Louie's observation: "Containment of sexual and romantic desire is an integral part of the *wu* virtue. By contrast to the *wu* male's necessary rejection of women, the *wen* man usually more than fulfils his sexual obligations to women" (*Theorising Chinese Masculinity*, p. 19). However, there are important exceptions. In several so-called martial romances of the nineteenth century, such as *Lü mudan* and *Zhengchun yuan*, a handsome male protagonist is often admired for his tall and

strong body, reminding the reader of Guan Yu in *San'guo yanyi.* Here romantic involvement with women is no longer a taboo, although knight-errantry rather than romantic love is the main concern in the hero's life (see chapter 8).

11. All references to the novel are to Chen Sen, *Pinhua baojian* (Shanghai, 1990), with chapter and page numbers in parentheses.

12. They apparently failed to note that Zhang Chao thought the male was more beautiful than the female *only* among birds (see note 2 above).

13. The obsession with feminine male beauty and same-sex love (though the two were not necessarily always related, as I argue below) had become so common by the eighteenth century that it was the target of satire in Wu Jingzi's (1701–1754) famous novel, *Rulin waishi* (30.409–413). In addition, some romantic literati tendencies to grade female impersonators as a show of refined "aesthetic" literati tastes are also satirized in this novel (30.413–417).

14. For a discussion of the important but complicated notion of *qing* in Ming-Qing cultural discourse, see chapter 2 ("The Debates on *Qing* in Late Imperial China") in my *Desire and Fictional Narrative in Late Imperial China*, pp. 23–56. In his essay on *Pinhua baojian*, "Sublime Love and the Ethics of Equality," Keith McMahon emphasizes the sublime and egalitarian aspects of *qing.*

15. Before becoming a female impersonator, a young boy is usually purchased by his master to be trained as an actor. Once an actor, he is supposed to make money for his master, just like a prostitute is supposed to make money for her madam.

16. Sophie Volpp discusses the homoerotic relationship between literati and male actors in terms of the concept of "connoisseurship" in "Literary Consumption of Actors in Seventeenth-Century China." Her study is relevant here, although she focuses on the seventeenth century.

17. The gender identity of a female impersonator can be confusing to readers. Shang Daxiang, a modern scholar of Chinese fiction, uses the female third-personal pronoun "she" to refer to Du Qinyan throughout his entry on the novel in *Zhongguo gudai tongsu xiaoshuo zongmu tiyao*, pp. 695–696. We cannot exclude the possibility that this is simply a case of typographical errors, but the usage is quite consistent. However, in another article, Shang Daxiang changes to the male third-person pronoun to refer to Du; see his biographical sketch of Chen Sen in Zhou Juntao and Wang Changyou, *Zhongguo tongsu xiaoshuo jia pingzhuan*, p. 270.

18. For a different reading of this episode, see Starr, "Shifting Boundaries," pp. 284–285.

19. To test the purity of Mei Ziyu's love for Du Qinyan, Xu Ziyun deliberately has another female impersonator impersonate Du Qinyan (i.e., a double impersonation). Almost persuaded that the impersonated Du is real, Mei Ziyu gets upset when the fake Du tries to get physical with him (chapter 14 of the novel).

20. I am a bit puzzled by Song's assertion that "the *caizi* is a heterosexual hero" (*The Fragile Scholar*, p. 140).

21. Cf. Starr's views on this issue: "Masculinity and outward beauty are portrayed as indeterminate," and "Masculinity and femininity are shown to be social constructs, coterminous with certain roles, and can be adopted or discarded as circumstances dictate" ("Shifting Boundaries," pp. 297 and 299). Whereas the gender boundaries in the novel are indeed very fluid, in the end social and gender hierarchies remain fundamentally intact. Once a female impersonator, Qinyan can never be completely equal with Ziyu, despite the sublimation of their *qing* and Qinyan's final escape from the profession of acting; the same is true of Huifang's relationship with Tian Chunfang.

22. See the discussion of the close relationship between *nei* and women in traditional Chinese cultural discourses in chapter 1.

23. Here Louie's concept of *wen* masculinity is helpful (*Theorising Chinese Masculinity*, p. 14).

24. McMahon offers a different reading of the novel's conclusion in that the "normative" ending of the novel "should not be seen as canceling out the wayward body of the story" ("Sublime Love and the Ethics of Equality," p. 102). We should point out that the novel's normative ending is not a radical departure but is well anticipated from the preceding pages since the sublime *qing* has repeatedly been shown to have its limitations. Cf. Starr's observation: "Qinyan and Ziyu's tender and reciprocal love is doomed to failure: equality in social status is not possible while Qinyan remains in the role of an actor. . . . Qinyan's escape from the unhappy profession and his upward mobility demand the sacrifice of his relationship with Ziyu" ("Shifting Boundaries," p. 284). Moreover, Qinyan will never be a complete equal in relation to Ziyu, even when he is no longer acting, simply because his acting past will always remain a part of his social identity. By the same token, the re/masculinization of these boy actresses at the end of the novel, such as by "leaving the profession of acting and becoming potential husbands" (as discussed by Starr, p. 274), can never render them as "masculine" as are their lovers from the noble families. See also David Wang's argument that "Chen Sen endeavored to write a romance that transgresses the boundaries of both social and sexual normalcy, but he only ended up squarely reiterating those boundaries" (*Fin-de-siècle Splendor*, p. 66).

25. D. Wang, *Fin-de-siècle Splendor*, p. 64.

26. This is the main argument in the last chapter of my *Desire and Fictional Narrative in Late Imperial China*, esp. pp. 271–314.

27. Edwards, "Gender Imperatives in *Honglou meng*," and my *Literati and Self-Re/Presentation*, pp. 89–94.

28. This is important if we accept the attribution of the last forty chapters to someone other than the original author.

29. All references to the novel are to *Honglou meng* (Beijing, 1992).

30. See chapter 2 for a discussion of the Confucian ideal of masculinity—dying as a result of remonstrating against the emperor.

31. Wu Cuncun, *Ming Qing shehui xing'ai fengqi*, p. 282; see also p. 4. Here we have to be careful in using the term *tongxing lian* to describe the phenomenon of same-sex love in traditional China because this term was coined to translate the English word "homosexuality," while "homosexuality" is a concept that began to emerge in the West during the eighteenth and nineteenth centuries (more about this issue below). At the same time, Wu Cuncun does not make any effort to distinguish between "femininity" and "effeminacy," as I have tried to do. (She often uses *nüxing hua* to refer to both.) As I have argued, for many in late imperial China, certain feminine qualities in a man, such as feminine looks, did not necessarily render him effeminate (i.e., less a man), and they were not necessarily thought to be the qualities that compromised a man's masculinity. Terms such as "homosexual" and "heterosexual" are being used here only as heuristic concepts, and therefore they are used within quotation marks. See also Song's discussions on this issue (*The Fragile Scholar*, pp. 43–67 and 125–190).

32. See, for example, Hinsch, *Passions of the Cut Sleeve*, pp. 8–10.

33. Among the four stories collected in *Bian er chai*, "Qingxia ji" is an exception. In this story, such a hierarchy is not obvious. For discussions of *Bian er chai*, see my *Desire and Fictional Narrative in Late Imperial China*, pp. 176–184.

236 Notes to Pages 149–153

34. Sommer, "Dangerous Males, Vulnerable Males, and Polluted Males." I also touch on the gender implications of active and passive lovers in same-sex relationships (both male-male and female-female) in *Desire and Fictional Narrative in Late Imperial China,* pp. 176–205.

35. See, for example, the biographies of Zhang Guang, Sima You, and Lu Ji in *Jinshu,* 57.1563, 38.1123, and 54.1467.

36. See the biography of Pei Kai in *Jinshu,* 35.1048. For a discussion of the obsession with male beauty during this period, see Fan Ziye, *Zhonggu wenren shenghuo yanjiu,* pp. 81–112.

37. No. 15, "Yanyu"; in Liu Yiqing, *Shishuo xinyu jiaojian,* p. 41.

38. See "Rongzhi"; in ibid., pp. 333–342.

39. "Feixiang"; in *Xunzi jijie,* p. 76, and Knoblock, *Xunzi,* p. 205 (translation modified).

40. "Introduction"; in Hitchock and Cohen, *English Masculinities, 1660–1800,* p. 5.

41. "Introduction"; in Trumbach, *Sex and the Gender Revolution,* pp. 5 and 9. See also Trumbach's "Gender and the Homosexual Role in Modern Western Europe" and "Sex, Gender and Sexual Identity in Modern Culture." Agreeing with Trumbach about this important shift, Alan Sinfield *(The Wilde Century)* argues that the situation was much more "confused" and that the association of homsexuality with effeminacy became much more emphasized after Oscar Wilde was prosecuted and imprisoned for his homosexual affairs. See also Bristow, *Effeminate England.*

42. For a study of the impact of Western medical science on early twentieth-century China, see Dikötter, *Sex, Culture, and Modernity in China.*

43. See Rocke, *Forbidden Friendships,* esp. chs. 3 and 4, pp. 87–147. In his study of Qing legal cases involving crimes committed by sodomites, Mathew Sommer concludes that "desire for another male in and of itself seems to have carried little significance in popular attitudes and none at all for law. (In legal texts, homoerotic desire requires no special vocabulary, just the same cliches used to describe heterosexual lust, such as *yin xin*)" *(Sex, Law, and Society in Late Imperial China,* p. 117); see also Hinsch, *Passions of the Cut Sleeve,* pp. 144–145.

44. Sommer, *Sex, Law, and Society in Late Imperial China,* p. 143.

45. Wu Cuncun expresses doubt that the celebration of feminine male beauty in novels by male authors had anything to do with women's views at that time *(Ming Qing shehui xing'ai fenggi,* p. 264). However, to prove otherwise is not easy either.

46. For a discussion of cross-dressing by women in several *tanci* narratives, see Siao-chen Hu, "Literary *Tanci,*" pp. 256–271.

47. Lacqueur, *Making Sex,* p. 8.

48. See Hitchock and Cohen, *English Masculinities, 1660–1800,* p. 7.

49. Lacqueur, *Making Sex,* p. 8. Hitchock and Cohen *(English Masculinities,* p. 9) point out that several scholars have faulted Lacqueur for "underplaying" the variety of medical understandings of gender available to premodern Europeans and his sole reliance on elite sources and neglect of the large literature of popular health texts, which demonstrate that the new assumptions and divisions were only very slowly adopted by the broader population. See, for example, Orgel, *Impersonations,* pp. 19–26, and Porter and Hall, *The Facts of Life.*

50. Sommer, "Dangerous Males, Vulnerable Males, and Polluted Males."

51. As I have already pointed out, hierarchy is also not particularly prominent in the male-male love affair described in "Qingxia ji" in *Bian er chai* (see note 33 above).

52. *Ernü yingxiong zhuan,* 32.616–617. To further complicate matters, Master An's son, Young Master An, the male protagonist of this novel, is presented as a handsome young man with a feminine appearance. This case, along with the satire in *Rulin waishi* (mentioned in note 13), points to the simple but important fact that there were many different and sometimes conflicting views on male beauty and masculinity in late imperial China.

CHAPTER 8: ROMANTIC HEROES IN *YESOU PUYAN* AND
    SANFEN MENG QUAN ZHUAN

1. The author's preface to *Xue Yue Mei* is dated 1775; see Yin Guoguang and Ye Junyuan, *Ming Qing yanqing xiaoshuo daquan,* vol. 3, p. 588. Xiyuan laoren's preface to the earliest extant edition of *Lingnan yishi* is dated 1794. See *Lingnan yishi* (Tianjin, 1995), p. 1. The pseudonymous author of *Lingnan yishi,* Huaxi yishi, has been identified as Huang Nai'an (ca. 1769–ca. 1848). For an account of his life, see the biographical sketch in Zhou Juntao and Wang Changyou, *Zhongguo tongsu xiaoshuo jia pingzhuan,* pp. 258–264.

2. Another exception is the famous early Qing novel *Haoqiu zhuan,* whose male protagonist is known for his martial prowess; for a discussion of this novel as a rather unique example of scholar-beauty fiction, see my *Desire and Fictional Narrative in Late Imperial China,* pp. 231–232.

3. Cf. Zhou Jianyu's discussion of the changing image of *caizi* in *Caizi jiaren xiaoshuo yanjiu,* pp. 188–201. Some of Zhou's observations (for example, his discussion of *Jinshi yuan*'s male protagonist in terms of his military wisdom, pp. 190 and 192), in my opinion, are not completely accurate. Sun Kaidi classifies both *Jinshi yuan* and *Xue Yue Mei* as *caizi jiaren xiaoshuo* and *Lingnan yishi* as a work of *ernü yingxiong xiaoshuo* (fiction of heroic lovers) (*Zhongguo tongsu xiaoshuo shumu,* pp. 163 and 171). (More about this genre of fiction below.) However, Sun (p. 175) also lists the late Qing novel *Yiyong sixia guiying zhuan* as a work of *ernü yingxiong,* apparently unaware that this late Qing novel is almost a verbatim copy of *Xue Yue Mei* (with all the important characters' names changed). Cf. Xiao Xiangkai, *Zhenben jinhui xiaoshuo daguan,* p. 282. (Xiao refers to the novel's title as *Yiyong sixia guiyuan zhuan.*) In his study of Qing fiction, Zhang Jun considers both *Xue Yue Mei* and *Lingnan yishi* works of *ernü yingxiong* (*Qingdai xiaoshuo shi,* pp. 303–304), while Tan Zhengbi considers *Jinshi yuan* simply a novel of manners (see Tan Zhengbi and Tan Xun, *Guben xijian xiaoshuo huikao,* p. 177). Such differences of opinion testify to the hybrid nature of these works and the difficulty of satisfactory genre classification.

4. The dating of *Yesou puyan* is a bit problematic since the earliest extant copy of the novel is a manuscript dated 1878, while the earliest extant printed copy (the so-called Pingling huizhen lou edition) is dated 1881. For accounts in English of the extant editions of the novel, see my *Desire and Fictional Narrative in Late Imperial China,* n. 1, pp. 237–238, and Epstein, *Competing Discourses,* pp. 199–204. However, it is certain that its author, Xia Jingqu, died in 1787 at the age of eighty-three. See Zhao Jingshen, "*Yesou puyan* zuozhe Xia Erming nianpu." Zhao Jingshen suggests (pp. 445–446) that Xia probably completed his novel around 1779. Basing his opinion on a poem attributed to Xia Jingqu, Xiao Xiangkai has more recently argued that the novel might have been completed as early as 1750 ("Zhongguo xiaoshuo shi yanjiu zhong ruogan wenti de kaobian zhiyi," p. 85). Even if Xiao is correct that Xia had already made reference to the novel in a poem dated 1750, it remains pos-

sible that the novel underwent later "reincarnations" (Xia Jingqu might have made substantial changes to later drafts) since it was mainly circulated in hand-copied manuscript until the late nineteenth century.

5. Sun Kaidi, *Zhongguo tongsu xiaoshuo shumu*, pp. 171–175. Sun Kaidi apparently conceives of *ernü yingxiong xiaoshuo* as a subgenre within the genre of *caizi jiaren xiaoshuo*. Elsewhere, he classifies *Yesou puyan* as a work of *caizi jiaren xiaoshuo;* see his "Xia Erming yu *Yesou puyan*," p. 238.

6. Tan Zhengbi and Tan Xun, *Guben xijian xiaoshuo huikao*, p. 177. However, Tan includes in this category many works of scholar-beauty fiction, such as *Haoqiu zhuan* and *Jinxiang ting*, from the early Qing period.

7. *Ernü yingxiong zhuan*, p. 4.

8. Zhang Jun, *Qingdai xiaoshuo shi*, p. 308. In Sun Kaidi's *Zhongguo tongsu xiaoshuo shumu* (p. 171), *Yesou puyan* is the first work listed in the section of *ernü yingxiong* fiction.

9. For discussions of *Yesou puyan*'s indebtedness to and departures from the scholar-beauty fiction, see my *Desire and Fictional Narrative in Late Imperial China*, pp. 244–246, and Epstein, *Competing Discourses*, pp. 229–238. Epstein (p. 230) notes a general shift in the novel from the feminine (characteristic of scholar-beauty fiction) to the masculine (typical of knight-errant fiction).

10. Here travel is associated with masculinity since travel was largely a male privilege in traditional China. According to Wen Sucheng himself, seeing famous mountains and rivers should broaden his outlook (1.14). The implications of travel are rather ambivalent in novels such as *Yesou puyan*. It can also become a feminizing experience, especially when it turns into wandering, as in the case of the male protagonist in *Sanfen meng quanzhuan*, as I discuss below.

11. For discussions of some of these erotic romances, see McMahon, *Misers, Shrews, and Polygamists*, pp. 126–149.

12. In addition to the examples discussed below, references to this concept can also be found in 2.30 and 134.2130. Thus far the commentator's identity has remained unknown. (It is also possible that the commentaries are the work of more than one person.) In the preface to the 1882 printed edition, Ximin shanqiao (the supposed owner of the manuscript version on which this printed edition was based) claims that his great-great-grandfather, Taosou, a close friend of Xia Jingqu's, wrote the commentaries (Xia Jingqu, *Yesou puyan*, p. 2). However, there is no documented evidence to support this claim. Here unless otherwise noted, references to the novel are to this typeset edition (Changchun, 1994), which, as far as I know, is the only modern reprint that is based on the 1881 as well as the 1882 editions, with all the commentaries retained.

13. Jiao Xun, *Mengzi zhengyi*, pp. 415–419; Lau, *Mencius*, p. 107.

14. "Xiang Yu"; in Jiang Yingke, *Jiang Yingke ji*, 6.321.

15. Cf. Song's discussion of the tension between *caizi* and *junzi* (gentleman) in *The Fragile Scholar*, pp. 97–104.

16. For a discussion of other instances in which Madame Shui criticizes her son for his possible departure from the teachings of the sages, see my *Literati and Self-Re/Presentation*, pp. 119–121.

17. For a different reading of the image of Madame Shui, see Roddy, *Literati Identity and Its Fictional Representations in Late Imperial China*, pp. 152–170. Roddy argues that Madame Shui plays a major role in the construction of a Confucian feminist utopia in the novel, pointing to the need for elite Confucianism to accommodate and "acknowledge the presence of feminine and non-literati domains of knowledge"

(p. 162) and that she "speaks for the intuitive and feminine forms of understanding" (p. 168). Roddy refers to Madame Shui's "emotional weakness" as a sign of her association with the "female, aqueous traits" (p. 162). I tend to believe, however, that Wen Suchen suffers much more from "emotional weakness," for which Madame Shui repeatedly criticizes him. Seen in the larger context of the fictional discourse on Confucian masculinity developed here, Roddy's reading seems less than fully convincing.

18. See my *Literati and Self-Re/Presentation*, pp. 121–122.

19. For a discussion of the gender implications of the concepts of *nei* and *wai* in early Chinese texts, see Raphals, *Sharing the Light*, pp. 195–235.

20. See Wen Shuchen's brief remark on this Taoist idea (87.1375).

21. For a discussion of knight-errantry in *Yesou puyan* from a slightly different perspective, see my *Literati and Self-Re/Presentation*, pp. 119–121.

22. See also 23.291–292 for another attempt by Wen Suchen to differentiate himself from an ordinary knight-errant.

23. McMahon refers to possible sources that might have inspired Xia Jingqu to attribute the seemingly strange methods of curing and healing to his protagonist (*Misers, Shrews, and Polygamists*, pp. 160–161).

24. See my *Desire and Fictional Narrative in Late Imperial China*, pp. 239–240. See also McMahon, *Misers, Shrews, and Polygamists*, pp. 150–175, for a discussion of the novel's vision of Confucian sexuality.

25. For a discussion of how Wen Suchen is often associated with the image of *taiyang* (the sun) in the novel, see Huang Yanmei, "Wenming shidai xinde yingxiong shenhua."

26. *Sanfen meng* is usually classified as a work of *caizi jiaren xiaoshuo;* see Sun Kaidi, *Zhongguo tongsu xiaoshuo shumu*, p. 166, and the preface to Zhang Shideng, *Sanfen meng quanzhuan* (Shanghai, 1990), a facsimile reprint of the 1848 printed edition. All references to the novel, unless otherwise noted, are to this edition. The only modern typeset edition of the novel I have so far been able to find is the one collected in *Zhongguo gudai xiaoshuo zhenmi ben wenku* (Xi'an, 1998). However, it does not carry the original prefaces or the commentaries that accompany many Qing printed editions of the novel. Also omitted without explanation are the *qinpu* (musical score for zither) and *qipu* (chess manual) in chapters 11 and 12, even though in the editor's introduction both are mentioned as a feature of the novel. Some key wording is also changed in this typeset edition. (In one place [p. 556], the important name Jiameng guan in the 1848 edition [16.16a] is changed to Jialan guan.) Unfortunately, the editor fails to indicate on which source edition his edition is based. To the best of my knowledge, *Sanfen meng* has never been discussed in English scholarship, and it has received only minimal critical attention in Chinese. I am aware of only two short Chinese articles dealing with this novel, and I will refer to them as they become relevant to my discussion. Given the obscurity of this work, I shall try to provide more general information on the novel and its author.

27. Cf. the biographical sketch in Zhou Juntao and Wang Changyou, *Zhongguo tongsu xiaoshuo jia pingzhuan*, pp. 306–310. The author of this biography has apparently failed to consult the biography of Zhang Shideng's grandfather in the gazetteer *Wenzhou fu zhi*, to which the narrator explicitly refers in the novel, a point I discuss in detail below. This failure is significant given the paucity of the available biographical information about Zhang.

28. It should be pointed out that the attribution of the novel to Zhang Shideng is unequivocal: the attributing remark, "Authored by Zhang Shideng, the immortal historian from Xiaoxiang," is clearly printed on the first page of chapter 1 (1.1a). It was

by no means common in late imperial China for a novelist to use his real name (instead of a pseudonym) to identify himself as the author of a novel.

29. For a discussion of how the author of *Yesou puyan* deliberately seeks vindication for Wen Suchen by having his son, Wen Long, recycle his father's misgraded exam essays as his own to achieve top honors in the exams, see my *Literati and Self-Re/Presentation*, pp. 125–126.

30. *Wenzhou fu zhi*, 18.38b–39a (vol. 4, pp. 1238–1239).

31. Homophones enter into play here. The author was a native of the south, where distinctions in pronunciation between "ing" and "in" and between "xia" and "ya" seem to be ignored. The same is true of the many homophonic puns in the last chapter of the novel, as I will discuss below.

32. I have added the title "Reading Principles" since in the editions that I have consulted there is no title for the section before the novel proper where the commentator's remarks appear.

33. In her brief reading of *Sanfen meng*, Lin Wei, "*Sanfen meng quanzhuan*," focuses on what she has called "the return of a vagrant" and the hardships in Zhang Mengyao's life. While she has appropriately called our attention to the importance of the motif of wandering in the novel, Lin seems to have almost completely ignored the significance of the accounts of the protagonist's military triumphs by simply dismissing them as "superfluous" or "unnecessary."

34. For a discussion of the autobiographical dimension of *Yesou puyan*, see my *Literati and Self-Re/Presentation*, pp. 109–142.

35. Another novel that shares this self-vindication agenda is the nineteenth-century *Ruyijun zhuan* (The Story of the Lord of Complete Satisfaction), by Chen Tianchi (fl. mid-nineteenth century). It is interesting to note that it shares the same historical setting as *Yesou puyan*, the Hongzhi (1488–1505) and Zhengde periods (1506–1521). (The Hongzhi period is extended to at least 1521 in *Yesou puyan;* for a discussion of the possible significance of this extension, see my *Literati and Self-Re/Presentation*, pp. 136–141.) For a discussion of the relationship between Chen Tianchi's *Ruyijun zhuan* and a famous Ming erotic text with the same title, see H. Laura Wu, "Vindication of Patriarchy."

36. Zhang Mengyao uses the term *buyi* later to refer to himself when he is dreaming of being invited by the King of Siam to command his troops to fight the invading Vietnamese (14.b [p. 559]). The commentator notes that *buyi* is the exact word Zhuge Liang used to describe himself in his famous "Chushi biao" (Memorial on the Expedition). See Wang Ruigong, *Zhuge Liang yanjiu jicheng*, p. 303. In the novel (14.8b [559]), Zhang Mengyao even dresses after the traditional image of Zhuge Liang.

37. As I pointed out above, here the author must have been basing his puns on the pronunciation conventions of the southern dialects.

38. When the novel was republished during the late Qing, the publisher changed its title to *Xingmeng lu* (The Story of Being Awakened from a Dream); see Sun Kaidi, *Zhongguo tongsu xiaoshuo shumu*, p. 166.

39. See my *Literati and Self-Re/Presentation*, pp. 113–114.

40. Here, the novel *Kongkong huan* (An Empty Dream) of the Kangxi period (1662–1722) comes to mind. It begins with an ugly but talented young scholar dreaming of becoming a handsome *caizi* and having all kinds of romantic relationships with *jiaren*. It ends with his being brutally awakened, realizing the invalidity of the cliché that a handsome *caizi* must marry a stunning *jiaren*. This satirical novel is apparently meant to be a critique of the scholar-beauty conventions. It is quite remarkable that

a novel intended to be a parody of scholar-beauty fiction could appear during the heyday of the genre. However, there is no evidence suggesting that *Kongkong huan* is autobiographical.

41. Some modern readers, such as Lin Wei, are nonetheless bothered by Mengyao's "fantastic" dream *("Sanfen meng quanzhuan").*

42. In an interlineal comment (9.1b [p. 324]), the commentator points out that this is a self-portrait of the author himself. Here we are reminded of the concept of *fengliu daoxue* (a romantic Confucian) found in the works of the early Qing writer Li Yu (1611–1679). See the concluding poem in the last scene of the play *Shen luanjiao;* in Li Yu, *Li Yu quanji,* vol. 5, p. 528.

43. Cf. the similar feminizing effect on Xu Wei after he accepted such a marriage arrangement (discussed in chapter 3).

44. Quoting from the chess manual and the musical score, as well as the reference to Mengyao's victories in fighting the four vices, point to the possible influence of the more famous *Jinghua yuan,* a novel mentioned by the commentator in the "Reading Principles" (6a [p. 3]).

45. In addition to the allegorical reference to opium in Mengyao's dream in the last chapter of the novel, in chapter 11, the author has already called the reader's attention to opium smoking and to rapidly deteriorating morality in Guangdong, the area most exposed to foreign influence (11.25a–b [pp. 461–462]).

46. Cf. my *Desire and Fictional Narrative in Late Imperial China,* pp. 249–250.

47. For a study of how the people of Miao ethnicity were appropriated as the "feminine other" in contemporary Han Chinese discourses, see Schein, *Minority Rules.*

48. Before the Suez Canal became operational in 1869, it normally took 130–150 days to reach China from Europe by sea; see Peng Deqing, *Zhongguo hanghai shi,* vol. 2, p. 99. Even if we take into account the fact that the same voyage would have taken significantly longer because of less advanced technology in the late eighteenth century, three years would still have been grossly inaccurate. An interesting related fact is that Wen Suchen, despite his heroic status, is quite uncomfortable with water and oceans. See Huang Yanmei, "Wenming shidai xinde yingxong shenhua," pp. 100–101; Epstein, *Competing Discourses,* pp. 221–222; and Roddy, *Literati Identity and Its Fictional Representations in Late Imperial China,* pp. 157–158.

49. See Wong and Wu, *History of Chinese Medicine,* pp. 136–137 and 217–219; Ma Boying, *Zhonggo yixue wenhua shi,* p. 717; and Hershatter, *Dangerous Pleasures,* pp. 233–234.

50. *Jinghua yuan,* which was probably written a few decades after *Yesou puyan,* also shares this consciousness of the foreign "other" to a remarkable degree. Much more critical of China's cultural tradition than the author of *Yesou puyuan,* the author of *Jinghua yuan* nevertheless views the foreign from a largely sinocentric perspective, and he fails to demonstrate an accurate knowledge about realms beyond the Middle Kingdom; see Ouyang Jian, "Hai de tanxian he haiwai shijie de faxian."

51. For a reference to Xia Jingqu's *muyou* experience, see Ximin Shanqiao's preface to the 1882 printed edition of *Yesou puyan* (p. 2); for some brief biographical information on Chen Lang, see Xu Shuofang's preface to the facsimile reprint of *Xue Yue Mei* (Shanghai, 1990); in his preface to *Sanfen meng quanzhuan,* Miao Gen mentions that Zhang has served on the staffs of various officials (1a [p. 1]). Other nineteenth-century fiction writers who also had *muyou* experience include Chen Sen, the author of *Pinhua baojian;* Wei Xiuren (1819–1874), the author of *Huayue*

hen; and Han Bangqing (1856–1894), the author of *Haishang hua liezhuan*. For a brief discussion of the possible impact that the marginalizing experience of *muyou* might have had on some literati's sense of self-identity, see my *Literati and Self-Re/Presentation*, pp. 34–35.

52. The low status of a *muyou* and his own unhappy experience in this profession were probably the reasons why Wang Huizu (b. 1730), who had worked as a *muyou* most of his life, was so grateful to one of his friends for continuing to show him friendship even after he had passed the civil service examinations at the national level and for his kind prediction that Wang would not remain a *muyou* forever. Despite his fame as a succesful *muyou* and his popular advice book on how to be an effective *muyou*, Wang stressed to his children that *muyou* was a profession they should enter only when there were no other alternatives. See Wang Huizu, *Shuangjie tang yongxun*, 5.179 and 6.227. For further discussion of Wang Huizu, see chapter 9.

53. See Guo Runtao, *Guanfu, muyou yu shusheng*, for a study of the *muyou* phenomenon in Qing China.

54. Gong Weizhai, "Yu Wang Yanru," *Xuehong zhai chidu;* in Xu Jiacun and Gong Weizhai, *Qiushu xuan, Xuehong zhai chidu*, p. 34.

55. Chen Yuanming, *Liang Song de shangyi shiren yu ruyi*, esp. pp. 103–111. See also Hymes, "Not Quite Gentlemen?"

56. For the earliest attribution of this saying to Fan Zhongyan, see Wu Zeng (ca. 1127–1160), *Nenggai zhai manlu*, 13.4a–b.

57. See Leung, "Organized Medicine in Ming-Qing China," esp. pp. 151–153. In the famous eighteenth-century novel *Rulin waishi* (The Scholars), by Wu Jingzi, the high-minded Yu Yude, totally disillusioned with governmental service, advises his son to turn to medicine for his career. See Wu Jingzi, *Rulin waishi huijiao huiping ben*, 46.623.

58. Xia Jingqu is said to have authored *Yixue fameng* (An Introductory Study of Medicine), which is probably no longer extant; see Zhao Jingshen, "*Yesou puyan* zuozhe Xia Erming nianpu," p. 437. Xia's contemporary, Huang Nai'an, the author of *Lingnan yishi*, was known as a *ruyi;* he published two medical books, both of which are still extant. See the biographical sketch of Huang Nai'an in Zhou Juntao and Wang Changyou, *Zhongguo tongsu xiaoshuo jia pingzhuan*, pp. 258–259.

59. We have yet to find any direct hard evidence that Xia Jingqu and Zhang Shideng participated in any military campaigns while they worked as *muyou*, although this was not unlikely (as noted, Zhang is said to have worked for officials stationed in the border areas). Yu Wanchun (1794–1849), the author of the novel *Dangkou zhi* (The Quelling of the Bandits), was indeed directly involved in military campaigns against the aborigine peoples and peasant uprisings when his father was an official stationed in various areas in southern China. Interestingly enough, later in life Yu became a practicing doctor. See the biographical essay of Yu in Zhou Juntao and Wang Changyou, *Zhongguo tongsu xiaoshuo jia pingzhuan*, pp. 275–276. Of course, a novelist who had once been a *muyou* did not necessarily construct his autobiographical protagonist in the same mold. For example, the author of *Huayue hen*, Wei Xiuren, who also once served as a *muyou*, adopts a quite different autobiographical approach in his novel. His two male protagonists, who are supposed to be the respective "real" and "idealized" halves of his autobiographical self, are both presented as *caizi*. However, at least one of them is said have achieved recognition by leading successful military campaigns.

60. "Zixu"; in Chen Lang, *Xue Yue Mei*, p. 588.

61. For a study of the autobiographical sensibilities in *Honglou meng, Rulin waishi*, and *Yesou puyan*, see my *Literati and Self-Re/Presentation*.

62. Yu Da, *Qinglou meng*, 64.417. For a brief discussion of *Baiyu ting* and its author, see the biographical sketch of Huang Han in Zhou Juntao and Wang Changyou, *Zhongguo tongsu xiaoshuo jia pingzhuan*, pp. 301–305. For an examination of the autobiographical implications of *Lao Can youji* and its sequel, see my essay, "From Self-Vindication to Self-Celebration: The Autobiographical Journey in *Lao Can youji* and Its Sequel," in M. W. Huang, *Snakes' Legs*.

63. See Wan, "*Green Peony* as New Popular Fiction," for a study of these novels, especially *Lü mudan*.

64. In this regard, *Ernü yingxiong zhuan* is unique. A sophisticated literati novel, it also conscientiously imitates the conventions of oral tradition. In this novel, the *yingxiong* is a woman knight-errant, with a feminine *caizi* occupying a much less glorious position. The strategy of gender reversal is reminiscent of that in *Lingnan yishi*. However, these two works are very different, despite the fact that both have been classified as works of *ernü yingxiong xiaoshuo*.

CHAPTER 9: IDEALS AND FEARS IN PRESCRIPTIVE LITERATURE

1. For an account of the circulation history of the novel, see Luan Xing's essays accompanying the modern typeset edition: Li Lüyuan, *Qilu deng*, pp. 3, 14, 1015–1019. For a biography of the author and his writing of the novel, see Luan Xing, "*Qilu deng*" *yanjiu ziliao*, pp. 1–65.

2. For the text of *Jiaxun zhunyan* (eighty one items in all), see Luan Xing, "*Qilu deng*" *yanjiu ziliao*, pp. 141–152.

3. For a detailed discussion of the relationship between the novel and *Jiaxun zhunyan*, see my "*Xiaoshuo* as 'Family Instructions.'"

4. Hu Yinglin, *Shaoshi shanfang bicong;* in Huang Lin and Han Tongwen, *Zhongguo lidai xiaoshuo lunzhu xuan*, p. 146. In the massive eighteenth-century catalogue *Siku quanshu zongmu tiyao*, which was compiled by Ji Yun (1724–1805) under imperial sponsorship, *Yuanshi shifan* was reclassified as belonging to the category of *rujia* (Confucianism) rather than *zajia* (miscellaneous doctrines), where most previous bibliographers had put it, a change reflecting the elevated status of works of *jiaxun* during that period, as noted by Patricia Ebrey, *Family and Property in Sung China*, note 13, p. 170. In fact, many other *jiaxun-* (household instruction-) like works, such as Liu Qingzhi's (1130–1195) *Jiezi tonglu*, were elevated to the genre of *rujia* in *Siku quanshu*. See my "*Xiaoshuo* as 'Family Instructions,'" pp. 67–70.

5. The number of volumes of household instruction extant from late imperial China is enormous; in comparison, there are only a few book-length studies devoted to this important genre. Ebrey's *Family and Property in Sung China*, which contains an English translation of Yuan Cai's Song dynasty classic *Yuanshi shifan* and a lengthy introduction, is one of these. Another is Taga Akigorō, *Sōfu no kenkyū* (An Analytic Study of Chinese Genealogical Books). It contains three sections: the first has several long introductory essays; the second has a helpful and detailed bibliography of various collections of household instructions held in libraries in Japan, China, and the United States; the third contains the texts of many not easily available collections of household instructions from the late imperial period. The recently published *Zhongguo jiaxun shi*, by Xu Shaojin and Chen Yanbin, is also useful, but it did not become available to me until the final draft of this study was already completed. Mention also should be made of Lu Lin, *Zhonghua jiaxun daguan*, which contains a

section of descriptive entries on some important collections of household instructions (pp. 119–222), as well as a substantial bibliography in its appendixes (pp. 793–835). See also *Zhongguo congshu zonglu*, vol. 2 *(Zimu)*, pp. 751–756, for relevant bibliographical information. Charlotte Furth's "The Patriarch's Legacy" is a useful introductory essay on household instructions. In contrast, there are quite a few monographs devoted to the study of household and clan regulations, such as H. W. Liu, *The Traditional Chinese Clan Rules*, and Fei Chengkang, *Zhongguo de jiafa zugui*. However, these studies focus on regulations and punishment rather than instructions and admonishments, although *jiaxun* and *zugui* (clan regulations) are closely related.

6. Ebrey, "Conceptions of the Family in the Sung Dynasty."

7. See H. W. Liu, *The Traditional Chinese Clan Rules*, pp. 25–30. As noted, Taga's study, which covers a great number of *jiaxun*, is entitled *An Analytic Study of Chinese Genealogical Books*.

8. Under the rubric of *jiaxun*, several subgenres such as *zuxun* (lineage instructions), are often included.

9. Reprinted in Taga, *Sōfu no kenkyū*, p. 606.

10. Reprinted in ibid., p. 611.

11. Reprinted in ibid., p. 618.

12. Reprinted in Qu Bo, *Zhongguo Jiaxun jingdian*, p. 658.

13. See, for example, Wang Huizu, *Shuangjie tang yongxun*, 3.55 and 59.

14. This anxiety over masculinity in household instructions can be related to the images of henpecked husbands and their shrewish wives often found in many fictional and semifictional works from the Ming-Qing period. See Yenna Wu, *The Chinese Virago*. In a survey of fictional works from this period, we also discern a trend of male degeneration—the husband becomes increasingly incompetent and increasingly dominated by women. This trend seems to have started with the character of Chen Jingji in the late Ming novel *Jin Ping Mei*, and it became a more prominent aspect of the plots of many later works, such as *Cu hulu, Xingshi yinyuan zhuan, Guwangyan*, and *Qilu deng;* see my *Desire and Fictional Narrative in Late Imperial China*, p. 110.

15. "Zhijia"; in Wang Huizu, *Shuangjie tang yongxun*, 3.101. Wang's deep pessimism on the inevitable disintegration of a large patriarchal family can also be seen in his advice that a family patriarch should retain sufficient property for himself when he is dividing the family property among his children and grandchildren because they might not be reliable in the future when he begins to need financial support (ibid., 3.102).

16. Wang Huizu, *Shuangjie tang yongxiong, juan* 3.55.

17. Ibid., 3.57.

18. *Dizi zhenyan*, 5.7a; in Wu Dacheng, *Wu Dacheng shoupi ben "Dizi zhenyan,"* p. 157. Hu Dayuan was the father of Hu Linyi (1812–1861; *ECCP*, pp. 333–335), the famous general who, together with Zeng Guofan (1811–1872; *ECCP*, pp. 751–756), played a crucial role in the suppression of the Taiping Rebellion.

19. Ibid., 5.11b, p. 166.

20. Qu Bo, *Zhongguo jiaxun jingdian*, p. 796. In his *Jiazheng xuzhi*, Ding Yaokang considered "one's distancing oneself from one's blood-related kinsman as a result of following women's opinions" as one of the causes that would lead to the rapid decline of a family. See Ding Yaokang, *Ding Yaokang quanji*, vol. 3, p. 256. Such concerns over the dangers posed by the female members of a family are also quite prominent in works of *jiaxun* from much earlier periods. In his famous *Yanshi*

jiaxun, Yan Zhitui (531–ca. 595) devoted an entire section, entitled "Brothers," to the question of how to maintain harmony among male siblings; "Xiongdi"; in Yan Zhitui, *Yanshi jiaxun jijie*, pp. 23–30. Elsewhere in *Yanshi jiaxun*, Yan Zhitui warned about the dangers of allowing women to run a household ("Zhijia," p. 47). Similar sentiments can be found in the *jiaxun* classic by Yuan Cai (*jinshi*, 1163); see Yuan Cai, *Yuanshi shifan, juan shang*, p. 31.

21. Wu Linzheng, *Jiajie yaoyan*, p. 10.

22. Taga, *Sōfu no kenkyū*, 615–616.

23. Reprinted in Lu Lin, *Zhonghua jiaxun daguan*, p. 741. For a discussion of the general suspicion toward friendship in Confucian culture, see Kutcher, "The Fifth Relationship."

24. Hong Yingming, *Caigen tan*, p. 410. Coming up with a satisfactory English rendering of this title has been frustrating. I have chosen the clumsy translation above because during the Ming-Qing period *yao caigen* (chewing vegetable stalks) was a common metaphor to describe someone leading a hard and impoverished life. A literal but much more awkward translation could be "the vegetable stalk talks." More about the generic nature of *Caigen tan* in terms of its differences from *jiaxun* below.

25. Here we are reminded of the girlish male protagonist in the nineteenth-century novel *Ernü yingxiong zhuan*. In *Geyan lianbi*, several aphorisms evoke the image of an exemplary woman as a model for men to follow. For example, "A man should maintain his integrity as a maiden guards her virginity," or "A licentiate [*xiu-cai*] should be shy of seeing strangers just like a maiden; once having entered officialdom, one has to take of care of others just like a daughter-in-law; once retired, one has to assume the task of educating others just like a mother-in-law." See Qu Bo, *Zhongguo jiaxun jingdian*, pp. 801 and 779. That a licentiate should act like a cautious maiden was a common expectation among the literati in late imperial China. For example, Hai Rui once complained that in his time many licentiates acted like sluts rather than maidens; "Xingge tiaoli"; in Hai Rui, *Hai Rui ji*, p. 54. As I have mentioned in previous chapters (especially in discussions of chaste women in chapters 4 and 5), on the one hand, women appear often to have been assigned the heavy burden of being "natural" moral exemplars for men; on the other hand, they could also be viewed with deep suspicion and regarded as the sources of evil that led men astray. Either way women carried the huge responsibility of men's moral ups and downs.

26. See my "*Xiaoshuo* as Family Instructions."

27. Cf. Furth, "The Patriarch's Legacy," p. 187.

28. Ding Yaokang, *Ding Yaokang quanji*, vol. 3, pp. 252 and 256.

29. *Jiaxun chunyan;* in Luan Xing, *"Qilu deng" yanjiu ziliao*, p. 149.

30. Li Lüyuan, *Qilu deng*, 3.33.

31. Ibid., 58.544.

32. Not too long after Zhu Xi's death, his formulation of Confucian masculinity received much attention. See, for example, Luo Dajing's comments, "Zhenzheng yingxiong"; in Luo Dajing, *Helin yulu*, p. 239. Luo was probably one or two generations younger than Zhu Xi. This Neo-Confucian notion of masculinity became even more popular during the Ming. See, for example, "Zeng Huang Guangtai siqin baiyong xu"; in Hai Rui, *Hai Rui ji*, p. 331, and "Zhenzheng yingxiong cong zhanzhan jingjing lai"; in Yuan Zongdao (1560–1600), *Baisuzhai leiji*, 7.79–80. Of course, as I discuss below, there were also people who strongly disagreed with Zhu Xi on this issue.

33. "Xiushen"; in Lü Kun, *Shenyin yu*, p. 84.

34. "Pincao"; in ibid., p. 249.

35. Hong Yingming, *Caigen tan*, pp. 373 and 421.

36. "Qi"; in Chen Jiru, *Xiaochuang youji*, p. 113.

37. Elsewhere, Zhu Xi sarcastically termed Chen Liang's learning as *yingxiong zhi xue* (the learning of heroes), in apparent contrast with his own *shenxian zhi xue* (the learning of sages). See Zhu Xi, *Zhuzi yulei*, 116.2801. For Chen Liang's correspondence with Zhu Xi on this issue, see Chen Liang, *Chen Liang ji, juan* 28, pp. 333–355; Zhu Xi's related correspondence is also reprinted in *Chen Liang ji* as part of the appendix, pp. 356–376. Zhu and Chen's debate focused on a perennial issue in Chinese political thought—namely, the relationship between *wang* (the kingly way) and *ba* (the hegemonic way). For a brief history of this issue, see Zhang Liwen, *Zhongguo zhexue fanchou fazhan shi*, pp. 677–708. For the debate between Zhu Xi and Chen Liang, see C. Chang, *The Development of Neo-Confucian Thought*, vol. 1, pp. 309–332; for a study of the overall relationship between these two Song thinkers, see Tillman, *Utilitarian Confucianism.*

38. Li Gong, *Yan Yuan nianpu*, p. 53.

39. Here we are reminded of the definition in the Han text *Baihu tong*, mentioned in chapter 1: a *nan* (man) is someone who is capable of achieving success in a public career *(gongye)*.

40. "Zhidao"; in Lü Kun, *Shenyin yu*, p. 294.

41. "Pincao"; in ibid., p. 262.

42. "Zhidao"; in ibid., p. 302.

43. "Yingwu"; in ibid., p. 186.

44. Ibid., p. 176.

45. "Cunxin"; in Lü Kun, *Shenyin yu*, p. 17. For a discussion of the important concept of *jing* in Lü Kun's theory of self-cultivation, see Ma Tao, *Lü Kun pingzhuan*, pp. 238–248.

46. "Xiushen"; in ibid., pp. 108–109.

47. *Sijie;* in Wang Fuzhi, *Chuanshan quanshu*, vol. 12, pp. 477–479.

48. Zhang Chao, *Youmeng ying*, p. 201. However, Lü Kun's contemporary Li Zhi tended to emphasize the affinities between sage and hero: "Throughout history, all sages have been made of heroes. There has never been a case in which someone who is not a hero has becomes a sage" ("Yu Jiao Ruohou," *Fenshu, juan* 1; in Li Zhi, *Li Zhi wenji*, vol. 1, p. 3). For a general survey of different concepts of hero in Ming cultural discourse, see Chen Baoliang, "Mingchao ren de yingxiong haojie guan."

49. For a discussion of *qingyan* as a subgenre of *xiaopin wen* (informal essays), popular during the late Ming and early Qing, see Wu Chengxue, *Zhongguo gudai wenti xingtai yanjiu*, pp. 287–306.

50. Although *Shenyin yu* has been considered by some to be a work of *xiaopin wen*, it was certainly quite different from a typical work of *qingyan*. The picture of Lü Kun (mainly based on *Shenyin yu*) presented here is necessarily incomplete. For a discussion of different aspects of Lü Kun and especially his achievements in various "pragmatic" areas, see Handlin, *Action in Ming Thought.* Handlin's exploration of Lü Kun's "crisis mentality" is relevant to my discussion here. In *Guifan* (Precepts for Women), Lü Kun criticized the view commonly presented in household instructions that a man should not listen to a woman, although Lü Kun's context was that of imperial politics rather than household management. See Lü Kun, *Guifan*, 3.110a–110b (pp. 541–542). For a discussion of Lü Kun's views on women, see Handlin, "Lü K'un's New Audience."

51. "Hao"; in Chen Jiru *Xiaochuang youji,* p. 134. This passage seems to have been quoted from "Liang Tong liezhuan," *Hou Hanshu,* 34.1172.

52. "Xing"; in Chen Jiru, *Xiaochuang youji,* p. 12.

53. "Qiao"; in ibid., p. 41

54. Zhang Chao, *Youmeng ying,* p. 182.

55. For a discussion of the philosophy of *shishi* (adapting to the world), popular during the late Ming, see Zhou Mingchu, *Wan Ming shiren xintai ji wenxue ge'an,* pp. 251–264.

56. "Shengxian"; in Lü Kun, *Shenyin yu,* p. 224.

57. "Pincao"; in ibid., p. 249.

58. "Hao"; in Chen Jiru, *Xiaochuang youji,* p. 137.

59. Ibid., p. 138. Similar views can be found elsewhere in Chen Jiru's writings. See, for example, "Fan Muzi waizhuan"; in Chen Jiru, *Chen Meigong xiaopin,* p. 79. See also similar remarks by another late Ming figure, Zhou Quan (ca. 1600): "I think what makes heroes is that they have love [*qing*] in greater measure than others and are capable of greater devotion to something, with their heart and soul in it. . . . When the country called, they responded. There is no mystery about it. They had a big heart and merely transferred that great love from one thing to something else. Therefore, as I say, love is not confined to any one thing. Only those who make some great sacrifice can love truly" ("Yingxiong qiduan shuo"; cited in Wei Yong [fl. seventeenth century], *Bingxue xie,* vol. 2, p. 144; English translation [with modifications] from Lin Yutang, *The Importance of Understanding,* pp. 117–118). Such views of hero were closely related to the late Ming cult of *qing.* For a discussion of the status of "desire" in late Ming culture, see my *Desire and Fictional Narrative in Late Imperial China,* pp. 23–56.

60. Wu Linzheng, *Jiajie yaoyan,* p. 5.

61. "Hao"; in Chen Jiru, *Xiaochuang youji,* p. 135.

62. Ibid., p. 133; see also Chen's observation on the delights of the company of different friends in "Qian"; in ibid., p. 159.

63. "Hao"; in ibid., p. 138.

64. Zhang Chao, *Youmeng ying,* p. 184.

65. Ibid., p. 186; see also the lengthier observation on a "true friend" on the same page.

66. "Lunli"; in Lü Kun, *Shenyin yu,* pp. 35–36.

67. There are many possible factors contributing to the enthusiasm for friendship found in Lü Kun and Chen Jiru. Scholars have noted the elevation of the status of friendship and an increasing admiration for *xia* (chivalry or knight-errantry) among the literati during the late Ming. See, for example, McDermott, "Friendship and Its Friends in the Late Ming," and Zhou Mingchu, *Wan Ming shiren xintai ji wenxue ge'an,* pp. 153–157. However, we should be aware of the implications of the generic differences between *jiaxun* and *qingyan.* That is, since the well-being and stability of a family are the central concerns in household instructions, anything from the "outside" is viewed with suspicion, especially since friends are thought to have the power to pull a man away from his family.

68. See, for example, "Fa"; in Chen Jiru, *Xiaochuan youji,* p. 151, and Zhang Chao, *Youmeng ying,* pp. 181 and 186.

69. "Wenxue"; in Lü Kun, *Shenyin yu,* p. 148; see also critique of Mencius' famous theory of "flood-like *qi*" (*haoran zhi qi*), which we discussed in chapter 1.

70. "Xiushen"; in ibid., p. 87.

71. Ibid., p. 88.

72. Shen Hanguang, *Jingyuan xiaoyu,* p. 247.

73. Ibid., pp. 229 and 256.

74. There are quite a few modern annotated editions of this work. See, for example, Ma Da, *Zhongguo renshu.*

75. Sun Qifeng, *Xiaoyou tang jiaxun,* 3b.

76. Reprinted in Taga, *Sōfu no kenkyū,* p. 611; see also "Yingshi"; in Wang Huizu, *Shuangjie tang yongxun,* 4.116, for a discussion of the importance of *ren'nai* (endurance and patience).

77. Wang Huizu, *Shuangjie tang yongxun,* 4.114.

78. For example, in reference to a man's self-control in the face of sexual temptation the concept of *ren* is seldom evoked. This is certainly the case with Qin Shubao in *Suishi yiwen* (discussed in chapter 6).

Epilogue: Masculinity and Modernity

1. Min Jiayin, *Yanggang yu yinrou de bianzou,* p. 427 (see also pp. 202–205 and 425–429). Ye Shuxian has a general discussion of this issue in *Yan'ge yu kuangjuan,* pp. 151–223. The Dutch sinologist Van Gulik offers a slightly different and more specific observation that this "feminization," as reflected in paintings, began during the late Ming and accelerated during the Qing (*Sexual Life in Ancient China,* p. 294). For discussions of the triumph of *wen* over *wu* in the imperial power structure of the Song dynasty, see Davis, *Wind against the Mountain,* pp. 143–147; Liu Zijian (James T. C. Liu), "Lüelun Songdai wuguan zai tongzhi jieji zhong de diwei"; and Huang Kuanzhong, "Zhongguo lishi shang wuren diwei de zhuanbian." James T. C. Liu ("Polo and Cultural Change") discusses the cultural change from the Tang to the Song in terms of the declining popularity of polo (a sign of decreasing interest in athleticism in Song China). However, Chen Gaohua ("Song Yuan he Mingchu de maqiu") argues that polo was still quite popular during the early Ming.

2. Much of the "chaste women" rhetoric shared by the Ming loyalists and other early Qing literati (examined in chapter 4) was appropriated by many male late Qing reformists and revolutionaries to promote their modernization agenda. See Xia Xiaohong, "Lishi jiyi de chonggon."

3. Here we may recall the terms used by the seventeenth-century literati to deplore the effeminacy of their fellow countrymen (discussed in Chapter 4)—for example, *xumei er furen zhe* (literally, a woman with a beard) and *guan er ji zhe* (literally, a woman in man's clothing). Very similar terms, such as *xumei er jin'guo* (literally, a lady with a beard), are employed by late Qing reformists to criticize the effeminacy of their male contemporaries. See, for example, the radical social activist Jin Tianhe's (1874–1947) *Nüjie zhong,* p. 39. Elsewhere Jin (pp. 35–36) describes Chinese women as the "slaves of slaves" (i.e., women were enslaved by men who were slaves themselves); he deplores that Chinese men have lost their self-respect and that traditional culture has turned them into slaves who cannot think independently.

4. Wang Tao, *Manyou suilu, Fusang youji,* p. 144. For a study of Wang Tao's life and career, see Cohen, *Between Tradition and Modernity.*

5. See Liang Qichao's preface to his "Zhongguo zhi wushi dao," pp. 17–23, and his "Lun shangwu" in his "Xinmin shuo," pp. 108–118.

6. Liang Qichao, "Xin dalu youji jielu," p. 125.

7. See Brownell, *Training the Body for China,* pp. 37–48. See especially Brownell's reference (p. 40) to an American sociology professor's enthusiasm in 1911 for

the "manliness" of Western sports and his contempt for "effeminate" Chinese intellectuals (accentuated by their braids and long gowns).

8. For an account of the revival of Yan Yuan at the turn of the twentieth century, see Jui-sung Yang, "A New Interpretation of Yen Yüan," pp. 210–259.

9. Liang Qichao, "Yan Li xuepai yu xiandai jiaoyu sichao," pp. 12–20. For Yan Yuan's views on the martial arts and physical exercise, see Ma Mingda, "Yan Li xuepai yu wushu."

10. Liang Qichao, "Ming Qing zhijiao Zhongguo sixiang jie jiqi daibiao renwu," p. 33.

11. Many late Qing reformists maintained that the *bushido* spirit began to dissipate among Chinese men only after the Han dynasty (Confucius could therefore still be considered a symbol of such masculine spirit), but more radical May Fourth intellectuals, such as Hu Shi, began to reevaluate the entire Confucian heritage as a "feminizing" ideology. Hu Shi's interpretation of *ru* (a word that later came to denote what is considered Confucian) as "soft" and "feminine" (discussed in chapter 1) has to be understood in the context of the reformists' even more radical modernization and remasculinization endeavors.

12. See Chen Pingyuan, "Wan Qing zhishi de youxia xintai," and Wang Yue, "Zhang Taiyan de ruxia guan jiqi lishi yiyi," for discussions of the late Qing intellectuals' fascination with *xia*.

13. In Zhong's recent study, *Masculinity Besieged?*, which focuses on Chinese masculinity in the late twentieth century, "modernity" continues to be a central issue.

GLOSSARY

afurong 阿芙蓉

ai qi shen 愛其身

"Ai sizi shi" 哀四子詩

"Ai Zhu shangshu ci" 哀諸尚書辭

badao 霸道

"Bai" 敗

Baihu tong 白虎通

"Baixian" 白鷴

Baiyu ting 白魚亭

Ban Gu 班固

"Bao Ren Shaoqing shu" 報任少卿書

"Baodao shi" 寶刀詩

"Baojian pian song Lu shanren" 寶劍篇送
    陸山人

Bian er chai 弁而釵

"Biji" 必己

bing 病

"Bingbu zuoshilang Cangshui Zhang gong
    muzhiming" 兵部左侍郎倉水張公墓誌銘

"Bingxue tang ji" 冰雪堂記

bishang Liangshan 逼上梁山

"Bo Hu Shi zhi shuoru" 駁胡適之說儒

bukeyong 不可用

buting furen yan 不聽婦人言

buwei liangxiang, zewei liangyi 不為良相，
    則為良醫

buyi 布衣

buyu 不遇

Caigen tan 菜根譚

caizi 才子

caizi jiaren 才子佳人

caizi jiaren xiaoshuo 才子佳人小說

"Cangfa fu" 藏髮賦

"Cangfa zhong ming" 藏髮塚銘

"*Cangshu* Shiji liezhuang zongmu houlun"
    藏書世紀列傳總目後論

Cao Cao 曹操

Cao Man zhuan 曹瞞傳

caoze yingxiong 草澤英雄

Chang Shoujing 常守經

chang su chang 常宿娼

Chang Suchang 常夙昌

"Changfa qiren zan" 長髮乞人贊

changyou 倡優

chaochen 朝臣

"*Chaodai ji* xiaoxu" 抄代集小序

chaonan 朝南

chen 臣

Chen Jingzong 陳敬宗

Chen Jiru 陳繼儒

Chen Lang 陳朗

Chen Liang 陳亮

Chen Que 陳確

Chen Sen 陳森

Chen Shou 陳壽

Chen Tianchi 陳天池

Chen Zilong 陳子龍

Cheng Yi 程頤

chenmu 瞋目

chi 恥

chikui 吃虧

chonggang 重剛

chongxin huanguan 崇信宦官

"Chounü fu" 醜女賦

Chu bawang 楚霸王

Chu Han chunqiu 楚漢春秋

Chu Renhuo 褚人獲

chuangdi jian shi 床第間事

"Chulie pian wei Xu jishi Wang jiangjun
    zuo" 出獵篇為徐記室王將軍作

Chunqiu 春秋

chushi 出世

"Chushi biao" 出師表

ci 雌

Ci Mulan tifu congjun 雌木蘭替父從軍
ciji hua xiong 雌雞化雄
"Cike liezhuan" 刺客列傳
cixiong 雌雄
Cu hulu 醋葫蘆
"Cunxin" 存心
"Da Chen Tongfu shiyi" 答陳同甫十一
"Da He Qianli" 答何千里
"Da Ke'nan" 答客難
Da Xueshi 大學士
"Da Zhang Yidu" 答張異度
da zhangfu 大丈夫
dachi 大恥
"Dagao" 大誥
"Dai fu da" 代婦答
Dangkou zhi 蕩寇誌
Daoxue 道學
daoxue xiansheng 道學先生
datoujin 大頭巾
Daxue zhangju 大學章句
dayi 大義
dayitong 大一統
dayong 大勇
"Dengtu zi haose fu" 登徒子好色賦
deshi zhe qiang, shishi zhe wang 得士者強,
　失士者亡
di wanren 敵萬人
di yiren 敵一人
dimei 低眉
dimei shiren 低眉事人
Ding Yan 丁晏
Ding Yaokang 丁耀亢
Dingqing ren 定情人
Dizi zhenyan 弟子箴言
Dong Zhongshu 董仲舒
Dongfang Shuo 東方朔
"Du mou minfu diaoji ershou" 讀某愍婦弔
　集二首
"Du *Shiji*" 讀史記
Duan Yucai 段玉裁
"Duanhe pian song Shen zi Shucheng
　chusai" 短褐篇送沈子叔成出塞
dufa 讀法
"Duijing" 對鏡
duoqing de ren 多情的人
duxing qi dao 獨行其道
"Er liefu zhuan" 二烈婦傳
erchen 貳臣
ernü qingchang 兒女情長
ernü yingxiong xiaoshuo 兒女英雄小說

Ernü yingxiong zhuan 兒女英雄傳
"Fa" 法
fajia hua 法家化
"Fan Muzhi waizhuan" 范牧之外傳
Fan Zhongyan 范仲淹
Fang Xiaoru 方孝孺
"Fangdu" 防蠹
Feihuaxu 飛花絮
"Feixiang" 非相
Feng Menglong 馮夢龍
Fenghuang chi 鳳凰池
fengliu 風流
Fenshu 焚書
fu 賦
"Fu dei wei taren zuo jiayishang" 賦得為他
　人作嫁衣裳
"Fu Ouyang Bo'an zhangke" 復歐陽柏菴掌
　科
fu si ganzheng 婦寺干政
"Fufen" 傅粉
"Fulie" 婦烈
furen ganzheng 婦人干政
furen zhi ren 婦人之仁
gang 剛
"Ganhuai" 感懷
"Gaozu benji" 高祖本紀
geyan 格言
Geyan lianbi 格言聯璧
gong 公
Gong Weizhai 龔未齋
Gong'an pai 公安派
gongnu 宮奴
"Gongshi zhuan" 贡氏傳
gongye 功業
Gu Yanwu 顧炎武
guafu zhi yeku 寡婦之夜哭
"Guan Dongming" 管東溟
guan er ji zhe 冠而笄者
"Guang Song yimin lu xu" 廣宋遺民錄序
Guangdong chuang 廣東瘡
Guben xiaoshuo jicheng 古本小說集成
Gucheng ji 古城記
Gui Youguang 歸有光
Gui Zhuang 歸莊
guizhen 貴真
guizhong yifu 閨中義婦
Gujin xiaoshuo 古今小說
guo 國
Guo Jie 郭解
"Guo Xiang Yu gugong" 過項羽故宮

Guose tianxiang 國色天香
guoshi zhi dai 國士之待
Guwangyan 姑妄言
Hai Rui 海瑞
Haishang hua liezhuan 海上花列傳
Han Bangqing 韓邦慶
Han Fei 韓非
Han Xin 韓信
"Handan cairen jiawei siyang zu fu" 邯鄲
才人嫁為廝養卒婦
Hanshu 漢書
hao 豪
"Hao" 豪
haode ru haose 好德如好色
haohan 好漢
haojie 豪傑
Haoqiu zhuan 好逑傳
haoran zhi qi 浩然之氣
haose buyin 好色不淫
haose jiande 好色賤德
haoyong 好勇
"He wan'ge ci sanshou" 和輓歌辭三首
Hong Yingming 洪應明
hongyi 弘義
Hu Dayuan 胡達源
Hu Linyi 胡林翼
Hu Shi 胡適
Hu Yinglin 胡應麟
Hu Zongxian 胡宗憲
Hua Guan Suo zhuan 花關索傳
Huainanzi 淮南子
"Huaiyin hou liezhuan" 淮陰侯列傳
Huang Han 黃瀚
Huang Huai 黃淮
Huang Nai'an 黃耐庵
Huang Shu 黃澍
Huang Zhen 黃震
Huang Zongxi 黃宗羲
Huatu yuan 畫圖緣
Huayue hen 花月痕
hui 回
"Ji Binzhong" 寄彬仲
"Ji Bu Luan Bu liezhuan" 季布欒布列傳
ji er guan zhe 笄而冠者
"Ji Shanyin Liu xiansheng wen" 祭山陰劉
先生文
"Ji Shaobao gong wen" 祭少保公文
"Ji Wu Pouzhong shu" 寄吳裒仲書
Ji Yun 紀昀
jia 家

jiafa 家法
Jiafan 家范
Jiajie yaoyan 家戒要言
Jialan guan 佳蘭關
Jiameng guan 佳夢關
Jiang Yingke 江盈科
jianghu 江湖
jianren 賤人
jianxiong 奸雄
"Jiaqu" 嫁娶
jiaren 佳人
"Jiaren" 佳人
Jiashen xunnan lu 甲申殉難錄
jiaxun 家訓
Jiaxun zhunyan 家訓諄言
Jiazheng xuzhi 家政須知
jie 節
"Jie Lao" 解老
"Jiechao" 解嘲
"Jiefu pian" 節婦篇
"Ji'en" 紀恩
Jiezi tonglu 戒子通錄
"Jin Biyang zhi sun Yu Rang" 晉畢陽之孫
豫讓
Jin Lansheng 金蘭生
Jin Ping Mei 金瓶梅
Jin Shengtan 金聖歎
Jin Tianhe 金天翮
jing 精
jing 靜
Jing Ke 荊軻
Jinghua yuan 鏡花緣
Jingzhi ju shihua 靜志居詩話
jingnan 靖難
jingquan 經權
Jingyuan xiaoyu 荊園小語
"Jinri ge liangshou" 今日歌兩首
jinshi 進士
Jinshi yuan 金石緣
"Jinshi Zhang Shuibu" 近試張水部
Jinxiang ting 錦香亭
"Jipu" 畸譜
"Jiren shuo" 畸人說
jiu se cai qi 酒色財氣
Jiuquan jun 酒泉郡
"Jiuri dai fu zuo" 九日代婦作
jiuse 酒色
jizhi 紀知
"Jue" 爵
jueyi cixiong 決一雌雄

junshi 軍師
junzi 君子
"Kaige ershou zeng canjiang Qi gong" 凱歌二首贈參將戚公
"Kaige sishou zeng Cao jun" 凱歌四首贈曹君
ke 客
"Ke cong yuanfang lai liushou" 客從遠方來六首
Ke Weiqi 柯維騏
"Ke *Xu Wenchang yishu* xu" 刻徐文長佚書序
Kong Silong 孔四郎
Kongkong huan 空空幻
kongwen 空文
Kuang gushi Yuyang sannong 狂鼓士漁陽三弄
kun[a] 坤
kun[b] 髡
kunqian 髡鉗
Langshi 浪史
langzi 浪子
Lanling jiaxun 蘭陵家訓
Lao Can youji 老殘游記
Laozi 老子
li 力
li 利
Li Bai 李白
Li Chunfang 李春芳
Li Gong 李塨
"Li jiefu Yushi zhuan" 李節婦于氏傳
Li Le 李樂
Li Ling 李陵
Li Lüyuan 李綠園
Li Mengyang 李夢陽
Li Shimin 李世民
Li Si 李斯
Li Yuan 李淵
Li Zhi 李贄
Li Zicheng 李自成
"Lian Po Lin Xiangru liezhuan" 廉頗藺相如列傳
Liang Qichao 梁啟超
"Liang Tong liezhuan" 梁統列傳
Liangjiaohun 兩交婚
lianqi 戀妻
liao 僚
"Libu Yanfengsi langzhong Zhonglang xiansheng xingzhuang" 吏部驗封司郎中中朗先生行狀
lide, ligong, liyan 立德, 立功, 立言

lie zhangfu 烈丈夫
Lienü zhuan 列女傳
"Liguo lun" 立國論
Liji 禮記
"Lijie" 立節
lin ru bingyuan 臨如冰淵
Lin'er bao 麟兒報
Lingnan yishi 嶺南逸史
Lisao 離騷
Liu Bang 劉邦
Liu Bei 劉備
Liu Ge 劉韐
liu gusui 溜骨髓
Liu Jin 劉瑾
Liu Qingzhi 劉清之
Liu Rushi 柳如是
Liu Shao 劉邵
Liu Xiang 劉向
Liu Xiaobiao 劉孝標
Liu Zongzhou 劉宗周
"Liuhou shijia" 留侯世家
"Liuqiu dao ershou" 琉球刀二首
Liuxia Hui 柳下惠
liyan 立言
liyin 吏隱
liyin chengyang 厲陰乘陽
Longchang wudao 龍場悟道
louyi 螻蟻
Lü Dongbin 呂洞賓
Lu Jia 陸賈
lü liaozi 驢臁子
Lü mudan 綠牡丹
Lü Kun 呂坤
Lü zu 呂祖
"Lu Zhonglian Zou Yang liezhuan" 魯仲連鄒陽列傳
luanshi chu yingxiong 亂世出英雄
"Lun shangwu" 論尚武
"Lunli" 倫理
Lunyu 論語
Luo Dajing 羅大經
Luo Lun 羅倫
luoshang 裸裳
Lüshi chunqiu 呂氏春秋
maliaozi 馬臁子
Mao Guojin 茅國縉
Mao Kun 茅坤
Mao Lun 毛綸
Mao Zonggang 毛宗崗
mashang di yinyuan 馬上締姻緣

Mei Guozhen 梅國禎
"Mei Kesheng" 梅客生
meidu 梅毒
meiren 美人
"Meiren fu" 美人賦
meixuran 美鬚髯
Meng Ben 孟賁
Mengyao 夢瑤
"Mengyi xu" 夢憶序
"Mengzi shishuo" 孟子師說
Mi Heng 襧衡
"Ming jingbiao jiefu cong zumu Xushi
　muzhiming" 明旌表節婦從祖母徐氏墓誌銘
ming meimu 明眉目
Mingyi daifang lu 明夷待訪錄
mu 幕
muke zhi 幕客制
muliao zhi 幕僚制
muyou 幕友
muyou zhi 幕友制
nan 男
nanse 男色
nanxiang nü buxiang 男降女不降
nanzi tai 男子態
nei 內
neichen 內臣
neige 內閣
Neijing 內經
neisheng waiwang 內聖外王
neisheng zhi dao 內聖之道
neiwai youbie 內外有別
"Ni qufu cidiao 'Feng ru song'" 擬去婦詞
　調風入松
Nie Zheng 聶政
nu 怒
nü duo nan zhi 女奪男質
Nü zhuangyuan cifeng dehuang 女狀元辭鳳
　得凰
nügong 女紅
nuo 懦
nüse 女色
nüxing hua 女性化
pa 怕
Pan An 潘安
Pan Deyu 潘德輿
Pan Yue 潘岳
Pei Kai 裴楷
Pei Songzhi 裴松之
piao'ni 票擬
pifu zhi yong 匹夫之勇

pin 品
"Pincao" 品操
pingmin 平民
Pinhua baojian 品花寶鑒
pinjin 聘金
pinnü 貧女
pinshi 貧士
pipo tianhuang 劈破天荒
po tianhuang 破天荒
puqie 仆妾
qi 氣
qi 奇
"Qi" 奇
Qi Jiguang 戚繼光
"Qi si" 齊四
"Qi Xuanwang jian Yan Chu" 齊宣王見顏
　斶
"Qian" 倩
Qian Qianyi 錢謙益
qianwan shi zhi ru jie wei furen 千萬世之儒
　皆為婦人
"Qiao" 哨
qie 妾
"Qie boming" 妾薄命
qiefu 妾婦
qiefu xintai 妾婦心態
qiefu zhi dao 妾婦之道
"Qijia" 齊家
Qilu deng 歧路燈
Qin Guan 秦觀
"Qin Shihuang benji" 秦始皇本紀
Qin Taoyu 秦韜玉
qing 情
qingci 青詞
Qinglou meng 青樓夢
qingyan 清言
qinpu 琴譜
qipu 棋譜
qiqi 棄妻
qiren 奇人
"Qiren jian Tian Pian" 齊人見田駢
qishi 氣勢
"Qiu Changru" 邱長孺
"Qiushui" 秋水
"Qiuxian ling" 求賢令
qiuzhen 求真
"Qixue ji xu" 泣血集序
Qu Dajun 屈大均
qu qi zhi qi 屈其志氣
Qu Yuan 屈原

Quanren baizhen 勸忍百箴
"Qufu ci" 去婦辭
"Qufu tan" 去婦嘆
qushen yangmu 屈身養母
rechang 熱腸
ren 忍
Renjing 忍經
ren'nai 忍耐
Renwu zhi 人物志
Rong 榮
"Rongzhi" 容止
rongyue 容悅
rongyue zhe 容悅者
rou 柔
Rou putuan 肉蒲團
roudao 柔道
ru 儒
ru 辱
"Ru Yan sanshou" 入燕三首
ruan 軟
Ruilin 瑞麟
Ruiling 瑞齡
rujia 儒家
rujiang 儒將
rushi 入世
ruyi 儒醫
Ruyijun zhuan 如意君傳
ruzhui 入贅
san buxiu 三不朽
San Yang 三楊
Sanfen meng quanzhuan 三分夢全傳
san'gang 三綱
San'guo yanyi 三國演義
San'guo zhi 三國志
San'guo zhi pinghua 三國志平話
sangwo 喪我
se 色
sezhong e'gui 色中餓鬼
"Shang Dufu shu" 上督府書
"Shang Dufu gong shengri shi" 上督府公生
    日詩
"Shang Tixuefushi Zhang gong shu" 上提
    學副使張公書
"Shang Yu Xinzhai" 上郁心齋
Shao Yun 邵雲
Shaoshi shanfang bicong 少氏山房筆叢
shaqi 殺妻
"Shedai Linmou da Hu tongzheng" 設代林
    某答胡通政
"Shen canjun" 沈參軍

Shen Defu 沈德符
Shen Hanguang 申涵光
"Shen jiangjun shi" 沈將軍詩
"Shen jishi Mingchen" 沈記室明臣
Shen Lian 沈鍊
Shen luanjiao 慎鸞交
Shen Mingchen 沈明臣
Shen Rang 沈襄
"Shen sheng xing" 沈生行
"Shen Shuzi jie fandao weizeng ershou"
    沈叔子解番刀為贈二首
shengbu 聲怖
shengren 聖人
shengxian 聖賢
"Shengxian" 聖賢
shengxian wei gu, yingxiong wei dan 聖賢
    為骨，英雄為膽
shengxian zhi xue 聖賢之學
Shenyin yu 呻吟語
shi 士
shi[a] 師
shi[b] 事
Shi Bangyao 施邦曜
shi buyu 士不遇
shi[b] *ye* 事也
shi you nü ye 士猶女也
shidafu 士大夫
Shi'er changyu 示兒長語
Shiji 史記
"Shiji pinglin xingshi" 史記評林姓氏
Shiji zhengyi 史記正義
"Shijian" 識鑒
Shijing 詩經
shiren zhe 事人者
shishen 失身
Shiyusuo jikan 史語所集刊
Shizhong Wokui 式鍾臥傀
"Shou Shaofu Xichang Yang gong" 壽少傅
    西昌楊公
shoushen ruyu 守身如玉
"Shu Chai Jixun 'Gu ruren zhuan' hou" 書
    柴集勳顧孺人傳後
"Shu 'Cike zhuan' hou" 書刺客傳後
"Shu 'Gu zhennü zhuan' hou" 書顧貞女傳
    後
"Shu 'Pan liefu beiwen' hou" 書潘烈婦碑文
    後
Shuangjie tang yongxun 雙節堂庸訓
Shuihu zhuan 水滸傳
Shuji 蜀記

Shuo Tang quanzhuan 說唐全傳
Shuo Tang sanzhuan 說唐三傳
"Shuoru" 說儒
Shuowen jiezi 說文解字
Shuoyuan 說苑
shusheng 書生
si 私
Sichao chengren lu 四朝成仁錄
Sijie 俟解
"Sijie lun" 死節論
Siku quanshu zongmu tiyao 四庫全書總目
    提要
Sili jian 司禮監
"Sili jian zhangyin Yunfeng Gao gong
    mubiao" 司禮監掌印雲峰高公墓表
Siliu wen 四六文
Sima Qian 司馬遷
"Sima Qian lun" 司馬遷論
Sima Xiangru 司馬相如
siren gongnü 寺人宮女
Sisheng yuan 四聲猿
"Sishu zhengwu" 四書正誤
Song 頌
"Song Shen sheng xu" 送沈生序
Song Yu 宋玉
"Song Zhang jun zhi Haining jiaoshou" 送
    章君之海寧教授
Sui Tang yanyi 隋唐演義
Sui Yangdi yanshi 隋煬帝艷史
"Suimu jishi" 歲暮即事
Suishi yiwen 隋史遺文
Sun Bin 孫臏
Sun Qifeng 孫奇逢
"Sunzi Wu Qi liezhuan" 孫子吳起列傳
"Suzhou rencai" 蘇州人才
"Taishigong zixu" 太史公自序
taiyang 太陽
tanci 彈詞
Tao Wangling 陶望齡
"Ti Huang shaobao *Xingqian ji* hou" 題黃
    少保省愆集後
tian 田
"Tian Dan liezhuan" 田單列傳
"Tianchang Ruan zhenxiao zhuan" 天長阮
    貞孝傳
Tiehua xianshi 鐵花仙史
tingchen 庭臣
tingzhang 廷杖
tiyu 體育
Tongshan 銅山

tongxing lian 同性戀
tongxing zhi qing 同姓之卿
"Tusong" 禿頌
waichen 外臣
waiqi 外戚
"Waiqi shijia" 外戚世家
waiwang zhi dao 外王之道
Wang Can 王粲
Wang Fuzhi 王夫之
Wang Huizu 汪輝祖
Wang Ruoxu 王若虛
Wang Shouren 王守仁
Wang Tao 王韜
Wang Yangming 王陽明
Wang Yuan 王源
wangdao 王道
"Wangqi Pan muzhiming" 亡妻潘墓誌銘
wangsheng 罔生
wangsi 罔死
wanhao 玩好
Wanruyue 婉如約
Wei Jie 衛玠
wei taren zuo jiayishang 為他人作嫁衣裳
Wei Xiuren 魏秀仁
"Weijia xunfu lienü zhuan" 未嫁殉夫烈女
    傳
wen 文
wen sijian wu zhansi 文死諫武戰死
"Weng Chengmei wen xu" 翁承嫩文序
"Wengji" 甕記
wen'guan 文官
"Wenjian Huang gong Huai muzhiming"
    文簡黃公准墓志銘
wenren 文人
wenren hua 文人化
wenshi 文士
wenwu shuangquan 文武雙全
"Wenxue" 問學
"Wenyan" 文言
Wenzhou fu zhi 溫州府志
wu 物
wu 武
Wu Linzheng 吳麟徵
Wu Qi 吳起
Wu Tinghan 吳廷瀚
"Wu xiashi muzhiming" 吳俠士墓誌銘
"Wu Zixu liezhuan" 伍子胥列傳
"Wudi ji" 武帝記
wuhuan 武宦
wuneng zhi ci 無能之辭

wushi 武士
wuwei zhi zhi 無為之治
wuxia xiaoshuo 武俠小說
xia 俠
Xia Jingqu 夏敬渠
Xialing 遐齡
"Xian fujun xingshi" 先府君行實
Xiang Yu 項羽
"Xiang Yu" 項羽
"Xiang Yu benji" 項羽本紀
"Xianggong ershisi nian" 襄公二十四年
"Xianzhu fa Wu" 先主伐吳
"Xianzhu zhuan" 先主傳
xiao zhangfu 小丈夫
xiaochi 小恥
Xiaochuang youji 小窗幽記
Xiaohun Qiao 銷魂橋
xiaojie 小節
xiaopin wen 小品文
xiaoshuo 小說
xiaoyi 小義
xiaoyong 小勇
Xiaoyou tang jiaxun 孝友堂家訓
xiayi xiaoshuo 狹義小說
"Xiazhe" 俠者
xicheng funü tai 習成婦女態
"Xie Dufu Hu gong qi" 謝督府胡公啟
Xie Jin 解縉
Xinbian Jiao Chuang tongsu xiaoshuo 新編
  剿闖通俗小說
"Xing" 醒
Xing fengliu 醒風流
"Xingfa er" 刑法二
"Xingfa san" 刑法三
"Xingge tiaoli" 興革條例
"Xingli ping" 性理評
xinglu 刑戮
Xingmeng lu 醒夢錄
Xingqian ji 省愆集
Xingshi yinyuan zhuan 醒世姻緣傳
xingyu 刑餘
xingyu zhi ren 刑餘之人
xingzhi 婞直
Xinxue 心學
xiong 雄
"Xiongdi" 兄弟
xionghao 雄豪
xiucai 秀才
"Xiushen" 修身
xu 需

"Xu" 序
Xu Jiacun 徐葭村
Xu Jie 徐階
"Xu Lienü jie" 徐烈女解
Xu Mingkui 許名奎
"Xu Shao zhuan" 許邵傳
Xu Shen 許慎
Xu Wei 徐渭
"Xu Wei nianpu" 徐渭年譜
"Xu Wenchang zhuan" 徐文長傳
Xu Zhenqing 徐禎卿
"Xuan'gui fu" 宣歸賦
xue 學
Xue Yue Mei 雪月梅
"Xuebian yi" 學辯一
xuejian 學劍
xueqi 血氣
xueqi cuhao 血氣麤豪
xueqi fanggang 血氣方剛
xueqi weiding 血氣未定
xueqi zhi yong 血氣之勇
"Xueshi Xie gong Jin zhuan" 學士解公縉傳
xueshu 學書
xueshu xuejian di wanren 學書學劍敵萬人
"Xuetao shiping" 雪濤詩評
xumei 鬚眉
xumei er furen zhe 鬚眉而婦人者
xumei er jin'guo 鬚眉而巾幗
Xunzi 荀子
Ya 雅
Yalin 迓麟
Yan Chu 顏斶
Yan Song 嚴嵩
Yan Yuan 顏元
Yan Zhitui 顏之推
yanbi zhi xiu 掩鼻之羞
"Yanchen shang" 奄臣上
yang 陽
Yang Meiji 羊玫芰
Yang Meiji 楊梅妓
Yang Pu 楊溥
Yang Rong 楊榮
Yang Shiqi 楊士奇
Yang Weizhen 楊維禎
Yang Xiong 楊雄
yanggang zhi qi 陽剛之氣
yangmei chuang 楊梅瘡
yangxiao yinzhang 陽消陰長
Yanshi jiaxun 顏氏家訓
"Yanyu" 言語

yao 遙

yao caigen 咬菜根

Yesou puyan 野叟曝言

yi 義

yi 夷

yi shili dai zhi 以師禮待之

Yijing 易經

yijing 遺精

Yijing tang jiaxun 一經堂家訓

yin 陰

ying 英

"Yingshi" 應世

"Yingwu" 應務

yingxiong 英雄

yingxiong chuanqi 英雄傳奇

Yingxiong ji 英雄記

yingxiong meiren 英雄美人

yingxiong qiduan, ernü qingchang 英雄氣短, 兒女情長

"Yingxiong qiduan shuo" 英雄氣短說

yingxiong shilu, tuozu wumen 英雄失路, 投足無門

yingxiong zhi xue 英雄之學

yinrou 陰柔

"Yiren liezhuan" 義人列傳

yishe weidao 以舌為刀

yishi xingqi 一時性起

yixing zhi qing 異姓之卿

Yixue fameng 醫學發蒙

Yiyong sixia guiying zhuan 義勇四俠围英傳

Yiyong sixia guiyuan zhuan 義勇四俠围媛傳

yize 遺泽

yong 勇

yongshi 勇士

you 友

"Youdao" 由道

Youmeng ying 幽夢影

youxi wenzhang 遊戲文章

Yu chanshi Cuixiang yimeng 玉禪師翠乡一夢

"Yu Che Shanbu Chunhan" 與車膳部春涵

Yu Da 俞達

Yu Ji 虞姬

Yu Jiao Li 玉嬌梨

"Yu Jiao Ruohou" 與焦弱侯

Yu Rang 豫讓

Yu Se 俞瑟

Yu Wanchun 俞萬春

"Yu Wang Yanru" 與王言如

"Yu Xiangtan Zhou nianxiong" 與湘潭周年兄

"Yu Xie Zaihang" 與謝在杭

"Yu Zhao Nanhu" 與趙南湖

"Yu Zhuo Yuebo guanglu" 與卓月波光祿

Yuan Hongdao 袁宏道

Yuan Wendian 袁文典

Yuan Zhongdao 袁中道

Yuan Zongdao 袁宗道

"Yuanchen" 原臣

"Yuanjun" 原君

Yuanshi shifan 袁氏世範

yuanyang hudie pai xiaoshuo 駕鸯蝴蝶派小說

"Yue Zhangshi *Wangxue zhiyi ping*" 閱張氏王學質疑評

yuefu 樂府

yulei 語類

yumu 娛目

yuse 漁色

zajia 雜家

"Zashi" 雜事

"Zashi jiushou" 雜詩九首

ze 則

"Zeng fuweng Pan gong xu" 贈婦翁潘公序

"Zeng guanglu Shaoqing Shen gong zhuan" 贈光祿少卿沈公傳

Zeng "Guang xianwen" 增廣賢文

Zeng Guofan 曾國藩

"Zeng Huang Guangtai siqin baiyong xu" 贈黃廣臺思親百詠序

"Zeng Jin Weizhen xu" 贈金衛鎮序

"Zeng wuju Chen zi" 贈武舉陳子

"Zeng Xu mou Baozhou mu xu" 贈徐某保州幕序

Zengzi 曾子

Zha Jizuo 查繼佐

Zhang[a] 章

Zhang[b] 張

Zhang Chao 張潮

Zhang Dai 張岱

Zhang Guang 張光

Zhang Ji 張籍

Zhang Liang 張良

Zhang Rulin 張汝霖

Zhang Shideng 張士登

Zhang Shoujie 張守節

Zhang Tianjun 章天峻

Zhang Tianjun 張天駿

Zhang Yuanbian 張元忭

"Zhang Xu guan Gongsun da'niang wu jianqi" 張旭觀公孫大娘舞劍器
zhangfu 丈夫
"Zhangfu shuo" 丈夫說
"Zhangshi zonglun" 張氏總論
Zhan'guo ce 戰國策
zhangyi shucai 仗義疏財
zhanzhan jingjing, rulin shenyuan, rulü bobing 戰戰兢兢，如臨深淵，如履薄冰
"Zhao yi" 趙一
zhen 真
"Zhengbin yi Riben dao jianzeng, yige dazhi" 正賓以日本刀見贈，以歌答之
Zheng Chenggong 鄭成功
Zhengchun yuan 爭春園
zhen'gui 箴規
"Zhennü lun" 貞女論
zhenren 真人
zhenyan 箴言
zhenzheng da yingxiong ren 真正大英雄人
"Zhenzheng yingxiong" 真正英雄
"Zhenzheng yingxiong cong zhanzhan jingjing lai" 真正英雄從戰戰兢兢來
zhenzhu 真主
"Zhidao" 治道
zhiji 知己
zhishi 志士
"Zhixiang" 置相
zhongchen 忠臣
Zhongshu ling 中書令
zhongwen qingwu 重文輕武
"Zhongxiao" 忠孝
Zhongyang yanjiu yuan Hanji dianzi wenxian 中央研究院漢籍電子文獻
"Zhongyi Liu Ge" 忠義劉馉
"Zhou minfu" 周愍婦
"Zhou minfu ji xu" 周愍婦集序
"Zhou Qiujia liushi shou xu" 周秋駕六十壽序

Zhou Quan 周銓
Zhou Sixiu 周斯修
"Zhoushi nü ershou" 周氏女二首
Zhu Bolu 朱柏盧
Zhu Dashou 諸大綬
Zhu Di 朱棣
Zhu Guozhen 朱國禎
Zhu Maichen 朱買臣
Zhu Qingyu 朱慶餘
Zhu Xi 朱熹
Zhu Yizun 朱彝尊
Zhu Youjian 朱由檢
Zhu Yuanzhang 朱元璋
Zhu Yunwen 朱允炆
"Zhuzi yulei ping" 朱子語類評
Zhuzi zhijia geyan 朱子治家格言
"Zimu" 子目
Ziqi guan 紫氣關
"Ziwei muzhiming" 自為墓誌銘
"Zixu" 自序
zixu 自序
"Zizuo yiguan zhong zhiming" 自作衣冠冢誌銘
zong 宗
zongpu 宗譜
Zou Yi 鄒漪
zufa 族法
zugui 族規
zuo shuzhai ren 坐書齋人
"Zuo fu duyushi zeng taizi shaobao zhongjie Siming Shi gong shendao beiming" 左副都御史贈太子少保忠介四明施公神道碑銘
Zuoyong 作俑
zuozhe 作者
Zuozhuan 左傳
Zupu 族譜
zuxun 族訓

BIBLIOGRAPHY

The following two abbreviations are used in the text:

DMB   *Dictionary of Ming Biography, 1368–1644.* Ed. Carrington L. Goodrich and Chaoying Fang. New York: Columbia University Press, 1976.

ECCP   *Eminent Chinese of the Ch'ing Period.* Ed. Arthur W. Hummel. Washington, D.C.: U.S. Government Printing Office, 1943.

Ames, Roger. *Sun-Tzu: The Art of Warfare.* New York: Ballantine Books, 1993.

Bai Xi 白奚. *Jixia xue yanjiu: Zhongguo gudai de sixiang ziyou yu baijia zhengming* 稷下學研究: 中國古代的思想自由與百家爭鳴. Beijing: Sanlian shudian, 1998.

Baihu tong zhuzi suoyin 白虎通逐字索引. Comp. Liu Dianjue 劉殿爵 et al. Hong Kong: Shangwu yinshuguan, 1992.

Barr, Allen. "Jiang Yingke's Place in the Gongan School." *Ming Studies,* no. 45–46 (2001): 41–68.

Besio, Kimberly. "Zhang Fei in Yuan Vernacular Literature: Legend, Heroism, and History in the Reproduction of the Three Kingdoms Story Cycle." *Journal of Sung-Yuan Studies* 27 (1997): 63–96.

Black, Alison. "Gender and Cosmology in Chinese Correlative Thinking." In *Gender and Religion: On the Complexity of Symbols.* Ed. Caroline Walker Bynum, Stevan Harrell, and Paula Richman, 166–195. Boston: Beacon Press, 1986.

Bossler, Beverly. "Faithful Wives and Heroic Maidens: Politics, Virtue, and Gender in Song China." In *Tang Song nüxing yu shehui* 唐宋女性與社會. Ed. Deng Xiaonan 鄧小南 et al., 751–784. Shanghai: Shanghai cishu, 2003.

———. "Gender and Empire: A View from Yuan China." *Journal of Medieval and Early Modern Studies* 34, no. 1 (2004): 197–223.

Bristow, Joseph. *Effeminate England: Homoerotic Writing after 1885.* Buckingham, England: Open University Press, 1995.

Brownell, Susan. *Training the Body for China: Sports in the Moral Order of the People's Republic.* Chicago: University of Chicago Press, 1995.

Brownell, Susan, and Jeffrey N. Wasserstrom, eds. *Chinese Femininities/Chinese Masculinities: A Reader.* Berkeley: University of California Press, 2002.

Cahill, James. *Parting at the Shore: Chinese Painting of the Early and Middle Ming Dynasty, 1368–1580.* New York: Weatherhill, 1978.

Cao Cao 曹操. *Cao Cao ji* 曹操集. Beijing: Zhonghua shuju, 1959.

Cao Lüning 曹旅寧. "Shi Qinlü 'baqi xumei' ji 'zhanren fajie' jianlun Qin Han de kunxing" 釋秦律"拔其鬚眉"及"斬人髮結"兼論秦漢的髡刑. *Zhongguo shi yanjiu* 中國史研究 89, no. 1 (2000): 166–170.

Carlitz, Katherine. "The Daughter, the Singing-Girl, and the Seduction of Suicide." *Nan nü* 3, no. 1 (2001): 24–44. Special issue on "Passionate Women: Female Suicide in Late Imperial China."

———. "Shrine, Governing-Class Identity and the Cult of Widow-Fidelity in Mid-Ming Jiangnan." *Journal of Asian Studies* 56, no. 3 (1997): 612–640.

Carter, Philip. *Men and the Emergence of Polite Society, Britain 1660–1800.* Essex, England: Pearson Education, 2001.

Chang, Carsun. *The Development of Neo-Confucian Thought.* New York: Bookman Associates, 1957.

Chang, Kang-i Sun. *The Late Ming Poet Ch'en Tzu-lung: Crisis in Love and Loyalism.* New Haven, Conn.: Yale University Press, 1991.

Chen Baoliang 陳寶良. "Mingchao ren de yingxiong haojie guan" 明朝人的英雄豪傑觀. *Zhongguo wenhua yanjiu suo xuebao* 中國文化研究所學報 10 (2001): 349–375.

———. "Mingdai mubin zhidu chutan" 明代幕賓制度初探. *Zhongguo shi yanjiu* 中國史研究, no. 2 (2001): 135–147.

Chen Chen 陳忱. *Shuihu houzhuan* 水滸後傳. Shanghai: Shanghai guji, 1993.

Chen Dengyuan 陳登原. *Yan Xizhai zhexue sixiang shu* 顏習齋哲學思想述. Shanghai: Dongfang chuban zhongxin, 1996. First ed. 1934.

Chen Gaohua 陳高華. "Song Yuan he Mingchu de maqiu" 宋元和明初的馬球. In Chen Gaohua, *Song Yuan shi yanjiu lun'gao* 宋元史研究論稿, 408–415. Beijing: Zhonghua shuju, 1991.

Chen Guying 陳鼓應, ed. *Laozi zhushi ji pingjia* 老子注譯及評價. Beijing: Zhonghua shuju, 1984.

———, annot. and trans. *Zhuangzi jinzhu jinyi* 庄子今注今譯. Hong Kong: Zhonghua shuju, 1990.

Chen Jiru 陳繼儒. *Chen Meigong xiaopin* 陳眉公小品. Beijing: Wenhua yishu, 1996.

———. *Xiaochuang youji* 小窗幽記. In *Xiaochuang youji (wai erzhong).*

Chen Lang 陳朗. *Xue Yue Mei* 雪月梅. Shanghai: Shanghai guji, 1990. Also in Yin Guoguang and Ye Junyuan, *Ming Qing yanqing xiaoshuo daquan.*

Chen Liang 陳亮. *Chen Liang ji* 陳亮集. Ed. Deng Guangming 鄧廣銘. Beijing: Zhonghua shuju, 1987.

Chen Pingyuan 陳平原. "Wan Qing zhishi de youxia xintai" 晚清志士的遊俠心態. In *Xia yu Zhongguo wenhua* 俠與中國文化. Ed. Danjiang daxue Zhongwen xi 淡江大學中文系, 227–268. Taipei: Xuesheng shuju, 1993.

Chen Que 陳確. *Chen Que ji* 陳確集. Shanghai: Shanghai guji, 1984.

Chen Sen 陳森. *Pinhua baojian* 品花寶鑒. Shanghai: Shanghai guji, 1990.

Chen Shengxi 陳生璽. *Ming Qing yidai shi dujian* 明清易代史獨見. Zhengzhou: Zhongzhou guji, 1991.

Chen Shou 陳壽. *Sanguo zhi* 三國志. Beijing: Zhonghua shuju, 1982.

Chen Shulu 陳書錄. *Mingdai shiwen de yanbian* 明代詩文的演變. Nanjing: Nanjing daxue, 1996.

Chen Tian 陳田. *Mingshi jishi* 明詩紀事. Shanghai: Shanghai guji, 1990.

Chen Wenzhong 陳文忠. *Zhongguo gudian shige jieshou shi yanjiu* 中國古典詩歌接受史研究. Hefei: Anhui daxue, 1998.

Chen Xianghua 陳翔華. *Zhuge Liang xingxiang shi yanjiu* 諸葛亮形象史研究. Hangzhou: Zhejiang guji, 1990.

Chen Yinke 陳寅恪. *Liu Rushi biezhuan* 柳如是別傳. Reprinted in Chen Yinke, *Chen Yinke ji* 陳寅恪集. Beijing: Sanlian, 2001.

Chen Yuanming 陳元明. *Liang Song de shangyi shiren yu ruyi: Qianlun qi zai Jin Yuan de liu bian* 兩宋的尚醫士人與儒醫: 兼論其在金元的流變. Taipei: Guoli Taiwan daxue chuban weiyuanhui, 1997.

Chen Zilong 陳子龍 et al., eds. *Ming jingshi wen bian* 明經世文編. Ming Chongzhen reprint ed. Beijing: Zhonghua shuju, 1962.

Cheng Bushi 程不識, ed. *Ming Qing qingyan xiaopin* 明清清言小品. Wuhan: Hubei cishu, 1993.

Cheng Shude 程樹德, comp. *Lunyu jishi* 論語集釋. Beijing: Zhonghua shuju, 1990.

Cheng Yi 程頤. *Yichuan wenji* 伊川文集. In *Er Cheng quanshu* 二程全書. Sibu beiyao edition.

Chu Renhuo 褚人獲. *Sui Tang yanyi* 隋唐演義. Taipei: Wenhua tushu, 1988.

Chunqiu Zuozhuan zhengyi 春秋左傳正義. In *Shisan jing zhushu* 十三經注疏. Ed. Li Xueqin 李學勤 et al. Beijing: Beijing daxue, 1999.

Cohen, Paul A. *Between Tradition and Modernity: Wang T'ao and Reform in Late Ch'ing China.* Cambridge, Mass.: Harvard University Press, 1974.

Crump, J. R., Jr., trans. *Chan-kuo Ts'e.* Oxford: Oxford University Press, 1970.

Dai Wang 戴望, ed. *Yanshi xueji* 顏氏學記. Taipei: Mingwen shuju, 1985.

Davis, Richard L. *Wind against the Mountain: The Crisis of Politics and Culture in Thirteenth-Century China.* Cambridge, Mass.: Council on East Asian Studies, Harvard University, 1996.

de Bary, Wm. Theodore, trans. *Waiting for the Dawn: A Plan for the Prince.* New York: Columbia University Press, 1993.

Declercq, Dominik. *Writing against the State: Political Rhetorics in Third and Fourth Century China.* Leiden: Brill, 1998.

Dikötter, Frank. *Sex, Culture, Modernity in China.* London: Hurst, 1995.

Ding Yaokang 丁耀亢. *Ding Yaokang quanji* 丁耀亢全集. Zhengzhou: Zhongzhou guji, 1999.

Dong Jiazun 董家遵. "Ming Qing xuezhe guanyu zhennü wenti de lunzhan" 明清學者關於貞女問題的論戰. *Xiandai shixue* 現代史學 3, no. 1 (1936). Reprint in Dong Jiazun, *Zhongguo gudai hunyin shi yanjiu* 中國古代婚姻史研究, 345–351. Guangzhou: Guangdong renmin, 1995.

Dong Zhongshu 董仲舒. *Chunqiu fanlu* 春秋繁露. Sibu beiyao edition.

Du Guichen 杜貴晨. "Mao Zonggang yong Liu fan Cao yizai fan Qing fu Ming" 毛宗崗擁劉反曹意在反清復明. *San'guo yanyi xuekan* 三國演義學刊 1 (1985): 279–284.

Durrant, Stephen. *The Cloudy Mirror: Tension and Conflict in the Writings of Sima Qian.* Albany: State University of New York Press, 1995.

Ebrey, Patricia. "Conceptions of the Family in the Sung Dynasty." *Journal of Asian Studies* 43, no. 2 (1984): 219–245.

———. *Family and Property in Sung China: Yüan Ts'ai's "Precepts for Social Life."* Princeton, N.J.: Princeton University Press, 1984.

———. *The Inner Quarters: Marriage and the Lives of Chinese Women in the Sung Period.* Berkeley: University of California Press, 1993.

Edwards, Louise. "Gender Imperatives in *Honglou meng:* Baoyu's Bisexuality." *Chinese Literature: Essays, Articles, and Reviews* 12 (1990): 69–81.

Epstein, Maram. *Competing Discourses: Orthodoxy, Authenticity, and Engendered Meanings in Late Imperial Chinese Fiction.* Cambridge, Mass.: Harvard University Asia Center, 2001.

Ernü yingxiong zhuan 兒女英雄傳. Beijing: Renmin wenxue, 1983.

Fan Ziye 范子燁. *Zhonggu wenren shenghuo yanjiu* 中古文人生活研究. Ji'nan: Shangdong jiaoyu, 2001.

Fang Bao 方苞. *Fang Bao ji* 方苞集. Shanghai: Shanghai guji, 1983.

Faurot, Jeannette Louise. "Four Cries of a Gibbon: A Tsa-chü Cycle by the Ming Dramatist Hsü Wei (1521–1593)." Ph.D. dissertation, University of California, Berkeley, 1972.

Fei Chengkang 費成康, ed. *Zhongguo de jiafa zugui* 中國的家法族規. Shanghai: Shanghai shehui kexueyuan, 1998.

Fei Siyan 費絲言. *You dianfan dao guifan: Cong Mingdai zhenjie lienü de bianshi yu liuchuan kan zhenjie guannian de yan'ge hua* 由典範到規範: 從明代貞節烈女的辨識與流傳看貞節觀念的嚴格化. Taipei: Taida chuban huiyuanhui, 1998.

Feng Menglong 馮夢龍. *Yushi mingyan* 喻世明言. Hong Kong: Zhonghua shuju, 1985.

Fung Yu-lan. *A History of Chinese Philosophy.* Trans. Derk Bodde. Princeton, N.J.: Princeton University Press, 1953.

Furth, Charlotte. "Androgynous Males and Deficient Females: Biology and Gender Boundaries in Sixteenth- and Seventeenth-Century China." *Late Imperial China* 9, no. 2 (December 1988): 1–31.

———. *A Flourishing Yin: Gender in China's Medical History, 960–1665.* Berkeley: University of California Press, 1999.

———. "The Patriarch's Legacy: Household Instructions and the Transmission of Orthodox Values." In *Orthodoxy in Late Imperial China.* Ed. Kwang-ching Liu, 187–211. Berkeley: University of California Press, 1990.

Ge, Liangyan. *Out of the Margins: The Rise of Chinese Vernacular Fiction.* Honolulu: University of Hawai'i Press, 2000.

Gerritsen, Anne T. "Women in the Life and Thought of Ch'en Chüeh: The Perspective of the Seventeenth Century." In *Chinese Women in the Imperial Past: New Perspectives.* Ed. Harriet T. Zurndorfer, 223–257. Leiden: Brill, 1999.

Gu Jiegang 顧頡剛. "Wushi yu wenshi zhi tuihua" 武士與文士之蛻化. In Gu Jiegang, *Shilin zashi* 史林雜識, 85–91. Beijing: Zhonghua shuju, 1963.

Gu Yenwu 顧炎武. *Gu Tinglin shiwen ji* 顧亭林詩文集. Beijing: Zhonghua shuju, 1959.

Gu Yingtai 谷應泰. *Mingshi jishi benmo* 明史紀事本末. Beijing: Zhonghua shuju, 1977.

Gui Youguang 歸有光. *Zhenchuan xiansheng quanji* 震川先生全集. Shanghai: Shangwu yinshuguan, 1935.

Gui Zhuang 歸莊. *Gui Zhuang ji* 歸莊集. Shanghai: Shanghai juji, 1984.

Guo Runtao 郭潤濤. *Guanfu, muyou yu shusheng: "Shaoxing shiye" yanjiu* 官府幕友與書生: 紹興師爺研究. Beijing: Zhongguo shehui kexue, 1996.

———. "Zhongguo mufu zhidu de tezheng xingtai he bianqian" 中國幕府制度的特徵, 形態和變遷. *Zhongguo shi yanjiu* 中國史研究, no. 1 (1997): 3–14.

Guo Songyi 郭松義. *Lunli yu shenghuo: Qingdai de hunyin guanxi* 倫理與生活: 清代的婚姻關係. Beijing: Shangwu, 2000.

Hai Rui 海瑞. *Hai Rui ji* 海瑞集. Beijing: Zhonghua shuju, 1983.

Han Fei zi jishi 韓非子集釋. Comp. Chen Qiyou 陳奇猷. Taipei: Huazheng shuju, 1974.

Handlin, Joanna F. *Action in Ming Thought: The Reorientation of Lü K'un and Other Scholar-Officials.* Berkeley: University of California Press, 1983.

———. "Lü K'un's New Audience: The Influence of Women's Literacy on Sixteenth-Century Thought." In *Women in Chinese Society.* Ed. Margery Wolf and Roxane Witke, 13–38. Stanford, Calif.: Stanford University Press, 1975.

Hanyu da cidian 漢語大詞典. Shanghai: Hanyu da cidian, 1997. Small-print version.

Haoqiu zhuan 好逑傳. Zhengzhou: Zhongzhou guji, 1991.

Hardy, Grant. *Worlds of Bronze and Bamboo: Sima Qian's Conquest of History.* New York: Columbia University Press, 1999.

He Guanbiao 何冠彪. *Sheng yu si: Mingji shidafu de jueze* 生與死: 明季士大夫的抉擇. Taipei: Liangjing, 1997.

He Guli 何谷理 (Robert Hegel). *"Sui Tang yanyi: Qi shidai, laiyuan yu gouzao"* 隋唐演義: 其時代、來源與構造. In *Zhongguo gudian xiaoshuo lunji (dier ji)* 中國古典小說論集 (第二集). Ed. Xia Zhiqing (Hsia Chih-tsing) 夏志清, 153–166. Taipei: Youshi, 1975.

Hegel, Robert E. "Maturation and Conflicting Values: Two Novelists' Portraits of the Chinese Hero Ch'in Shu-pao." In *Critical Essays on Chinese Fiction.* Ed. Winston L. S. Yang and Curtis P. Adkins, 115–150. Hong Kong: Chinese University of Hong Kong Press, 1980.

———. *The Novel in Seventeenth-Century China.* New York: Columbia University Press, 1981.

———. "Rewriting the Tang: Humor, Heroics, and Imaginative Reading." In Huang, *Snakes' Legs,* 159–189.

———. *"Sui T'ang yen-i:* The Sources and Narrative Techniques of a Traditional Chinese Novel." Ph.D. dissertation, Columbia University, 1973.

Hershatter, Gail. *Dangerous Pleasures: Prostitution and Modernity in Twentieth-Century Shanghai.* Berkeley: University of California Press, 1997.

Hinsch, Bret. *Passions of the Cut Sleeve: The Male Homosexual Tradition in China.* Berkeley: University of California Press, 1990.

Hitchcock, Tim, and Michele Cohen, eds. *English Masculinities, 1660–1800.* London and New York: Longman, 1999.

Hong Yingming 洪應明. *Caigen tan* 菜根譚. In *Shenyin yu, Caigen tan.*

Honglou meng 紅樓夢. Beijing: Renmin wenxue, 1992.

Hou Hanshu 後漢書. Beijing: Zhonghua shuju, 1982.

Hsia, C. T. "The Military Romance: A Genre of Chinese Fiction." In *Studies in Chinese Literary Genres.* Ed. Cyril Birch, 339–390. Berkeley: University of California Press, 1974.

Hu Shi 胡適. *Hu Shi zhexue sixiang ziliao xuan* 胡適哲學思想資料選. Ed. Ge Maochun 葛懋春 and Li Xingzhi 李興芝. Shanghai: Huadong shida, 1981.

Hu Shihou 胡世厚 et al., eds. *Zhongguo gudai xiqujia pingzhuan* 中國古代戲曲家評傳. Zhengzhou: Zhongzhou guji, 1992.

Hu, Siao-chen. "Literary *Tanci:* A Woman's Tradition of Narrative in Verse." Ph.D. dissertation, Harvard University, 1994.

Huang Huai 黃淮. *Xingqian ji* 省愆集. Siku zhenben edition.

Huang Junjie 黃俊傑. "Mengzi 'Zhiyan yangqi zhang' jishi xinquan" 孟子知言養氣章集釋新詮. In Huang Junjie, *Mengzi sixiang shilun* 孟子思想史論, 335–413. Taipei: Dongda tushu youxian gongsi, 1991.

———. "Zhuzi dui Mengzi zhiyan yangqi shuo de quanshi jiqi huixiang" 朱子對孟子知言養氣說的詮釋及其回響. *Qinghua xuebao* 清華學報 (*Tsing Hua Journal of Chinese Studies*), new series 18, no. 2 (1988): 305–343.

Huang Kuanzhong 黃寬重. "Zhongguo lishi shang wuren diwei de zhuanbian: Yi Songdai weili" 中國歷史上武人地位的轉變: 以宋代為例. In Huang Kuanzhong, *Nan Song junzheng yu wenxian tansuo* 南宋軍政與文獻探索, 387–399. Taipei: Xinwenfeng, 1990.

Huang Lin 黃霖 and Han Tongwen 韓同文, eds. *Zhongguo lidai xiaoshuo lunzhu xuan* 中國 歷代小說論著選, vol. 1. Nanchang: Jiangxi renmin, 1982.

Huang, Martin W. *Desire and Fictional Narrative in Late Imperial China.* Cambridge, Mass.: Harvard University Asia Center, 2001.

———. "From Self-Vindication to Self-Celebration: The Autobiographical Journey in *Lao Can youji* and Its Sequel." In Huang, *Snakes' Legs,* 237–262.

———. *Literati and Self-Re/Presentation: Autobiographical Sensibility in the Eighteenth-Century Chinese Fiction.* Stanford, Calif.: Stanford University Press, 1995.

———, ed. *Snakes' Legs: Sequels, Continuations, Rewritings, and Chinese Fiction.* Honolulu: University of Hawai'i Press, 2004.

———. "*Xiaoshuo* as 'Family Instructions': The Rhetoric of Didacticism in the Eighteenth-Century Chinese Novel *Qilu deng.*" *Qinghua xuebao* 清華學報 (*Tsing Hua Journal of Chinese Studies*), new series 30, no. 1 (2000): 67–91.

Huang, Ray. *1587: A Year of No Significance: The Ming Dynasty in Decline.* New Haven, Conn.: Yale University Press, 1981.

Huang Yanmei 黃燕梅. "Wenming shidai xinde yingxiong shenhua: *Yesou puyan* shenhua yixiang ji siwei yanjiu" 文明時代新的英雄神話：野叟曝言神話意象及思維研究. *Wenxue yichan* 文學遺產, no. 2 (1997): 97–105.

Huang Zongxi 黃宗羲. *Huang Zongxi quanji* 黃宗羲全集. Hangzhou: Zhejiang guji, 1985–1993.

Huatu yuan 畫圖緣. Shenyang: Chunfeng wenyi, 1985.

Hucker, Charles O., comp. *A Dictionary of Official Titles in Imperial China.* Stanford, Calif.: Stanford University Press, 1985.

Hymes, Robert. "Not Quite Gentlemen? Doctors in Sung and Yuan." *Chinese Science* 8 (1987): 9–76.

Idema, Wilt. "Cannon, Clocks and Clever Monkeys: Europeana, Europeans and Europe in Some Early Ch'ing Novels." In *Development and Decline of Fukien Province in the 17th and 18th Centuries.* Ed. E. B. Vermeer, 459–488. Leiden: Brill, 1990.

———. "Female Talent and Female Virtue: Xu Wei's *Nü Zhuangyuan* and Meng Chengshun's *Zhenwen ji.*" In *Ming Qing xiqu guoji yantaoui lunwen ji* 明清戲曲國際研討會論文集. Ed. Hua Wei 華瑋 and Wang Ailing 王瓔玲. Taipei: Zhongyang yanjiu yuan Zhongguo wenzhe yanjiu suo choubeichu, 1998.

Ji Dejun 紀德君. *Ming Qing lishi yanyi xiaoshuo yishu lun* 明清歷史演義小說藝術論. Beijing: Beijing shifan daxue, 2000.

Ji Liuqi 計六奇. *Mingji beilüe* 明季北略. Beijing: Zhonghua shuju, 1984.

Jiang Guanghui 姜光輝. *Yan Li xuepai* 顏李學派. Beijing: Zhongguo shehui kexue, 1987.

Jiang Yingke 江盈科. *Jiang Yingke ji* 江盈科集. Chengdu: Yuelu shushe, 1997.

Jiao Hong 焦竑, comp. *Xianzheng lu* 獻徵錄. Shanghai: Shanghai guji, 1988. Facsimile reprint of Ming edition.

Jiao Xun 焦循, comp. *Mengzi zhengyi* 孟子正義. Beijing: Zhonghua shuju, 1987.

Jin Ping Mei cihua 金瓶梅詞話. Ed. Mei Jie 梅節. Hong Kong: Xinhai wenhua youxian gongsi, 1987.

Jin Tianhe 金天翮. *Nüjie zhong* 女界鍾. Shanghai: Shanghai guji, 2003.

Jinshi yuan 金石緣. Beijing: Beijing shifan daxue, 1992.

Jinshu 晉書. Beijing: Zhonghua shuju, 1982.

Kang Yin 康殷. *Wenzi yuanliu qianshuo* 文字源流淺說. Beijing: Rongbao zhai, 1979.

Kin Bunkyo 金文京. "Cong bingzhu dadan tan *San'guo yanyi* he *Tongjian gangmu* de guanxi" 從秉燭達旦談三國演義和通鑑綱目的關係. In *San'guo yanyi congkao* 三國演義叢考. Ed. Zhou Zhaoxin 周兆新, 26–54. Beijing: Beijing daxue, 1995.

Knoblock, John, trans. *Xunzi: A Translation and Study of the Complete Works,* vol. 1. Stanford, Calif.: Stanford University Press, 1988.

Ko, Dorothy. "The Body as Attire: The Shifting Meanings of Footbinding in Seventeenth-Century China." *Journal of Women's History* 8, no. 4 (1997): 19–22.

Kutcher, Norman. "The Fifth Relationship: Dangerous Friendships in the Confucian Context." *American Historical Review* 106, no. 5 (December 2000): 1615–1629.

Lacqueur, Thomas. *Making Sex: Body and Gender from the Greeks to Freud.* Cambridge, Mass.: Harvard University Press, 1990.

Lang Ying 朗瑛. *Qilei xiugao* 七類修稿. Beijing: Wenhua yishu, 1998.

Lau, D. C., trans. *The Analects.* Harmondsworth, England: Penguin Books, 1979.

———, trans. *Lao Tzu Tao Te Ching.* Harmondsworth, England: Penguin Books, 1963.

———, trans. *Mencius.* Harmondsworth, England: Penguin Books, 1976.

Legge, James, trans. *The Sacred Books of China: The Texts of Confucianism, Part II: The Yi King.* Oxford: Clarendon Press, 1899.

Leung, Angela Ki Che. "Organized Medicine in Ming-Qing China: State and Private Medical Institutions in the Lower Yangzi Region." *Late Imperial China* 8, no. 1 (1987): 134–166.

Lewis, Mark Edward. *Sanctioned Violence in Early China.* Albany: New York State University Press, 1990.

Li Gong 李塨. *Lunxue* 論學. Baibu congshu jicheng edition.

———. *Yan Yuan nianpu* 顏元年譜. Beijing: Zhonghua shuju, 1992.

Li Hanqiu 李漢秋, ed. *Rulin waishi huijiao huiping ben* 儒林外史會校會評本. Shanghai: Shanghai guji, 1984.

Li Le 李樂. *Jianwen zaji* 見聞雜記. Shanghai: Shanghai guji, 1986.

Li Lüyuan 李綠園. *Qilu deng* 歧路燈. Ed. Luan Xing 欒星. Zhengzhou: Zhongzhou shuhuashe, 1980.

Li Mengyang 李東陽. *Kongtong ji* 空同集. Siku quanshu edition.

Li Ruilan 李瑞蘭. "Zhishi fenzi de qiyuan" 知識分子的起源. In *Shi yu shehui (Xian Qin juan)* 士與社會(先秦卷). Ed. Liu Zehua 劉澤華, 1–19. Tianjin: Tianjin renmin, 1988.

Li, Wai-yee. *Enchantment and Disenchantment: Love and Illusion in Chinese Literature.* Princeton, N.J.: Princeton University Press, 1993.

———. "The Idea of Authority in the *Shih chi (Records of the Historian)*." *Harvard Journal of Asiatic Studies* 54, no. 1 (1994): 345–405.

———. "The Rhetoric of Spontaneity in Late Ming Literature." *Ming Studies* 35 (1995): 32–52.

Li Xiaoding 李孝定. *Jiagu wenzi jishi* 甲骨文字集釋. Nanyang: Zhongyang yanjiuyuan Lishi Yuyan yanjiusuo, 1965.

Li Yu 李漁. *Li Yu quanji* 李漁全集. Hangzhou: Zhejiang guji, 1992.

Li Zhi 李贄. *Li Zhi wenji* 李贄文集. Beijing: Shehui kexue wenxian, 2000.

Liang Han kaiguo zhongxing zhuanzhi 兩漢開國中興傳志. Shanghai: Shanghai guji, 1990.

Liang Qichao 梁啟超. "Ming Qing zhijiao Zhongguo sixiang jie jiqi daibiao renwu" 明清之交中國思想界及其代表人物. Reprinted in Liang Qichao, *Yinbing shi heji,* vol. 5.

———. "Xin dalu youji jielu" 新大陸游記節錄. Reprinted in Liang Qichao, *Yinbing shi heji,* vol. 7.

———. "Xinmin shuo" 新民說. In Liang Qichao, *Yinbing shi heji,* vol. 6.

———. "Yan Li xuepai yu xiandai jiaoyu sichao" 顏李學派與現代教育思潮. Reprinted in Liang Qichao, *Yinbing shi heji,* vol. 5.

———. *Yinbing shi heji* 飲冰室合集. 12 vols. Beijing: Zhonghua shuju, 1988.

———. "Zhongguo zhi wushi dao" 中國之武士道. Reprinted in Liang Qichao, *Yinbing shi heji,* vol. 7.

Liangjiaohun 兩交婚. Shenyang: Chunwen wenyi, 1983.

Lin Chen 林辰. Mingmo Qingchu xiaoshuo shulu 明末清初小說述錄. Shenyang: Chunfeng wenyi, 1988.

Lin Wei 林薇. *"Sanfen meng quanzhuan:* Youzi huanxiang de wenxue muti" 三分夢全傳：游子還鄉的文學母題. In Lin Wei 林薇, *Qingdai xiaoshuo lungao* 清代小說論稿, 129–132. Beijing: Beijing guangbo xueyuan, 2000.

Lin Yutang. *The Importance of Understanding.* Cleveland: World Publishing, 1960.

Ling Zhilong 凌稚龍 and Li Guangjin 李光縉, comps. *Shiji pinglin* 史記評林. Tianjin: Tianjin guji, 1998. Facsimile reprint of Wanli edition.

Lingnan yishi 岭南逸史. Tianjin: Baihua wenyi, 1995. Also Shanghai: Shanghai guji, 1990.

Liu, Hui-chen Wang. *The Traditional Chinese Clan Rules.* Locust Valley, N.Y.: J. J. Augustin, 1959. Published for the Association for Asian Studies.

Liu, James T. C. "Polo and Cultural Change: From T'ang to Sung China." *Harvard Journal of Asiatic Studies* 45, no. 1 (1985): 203–224.

Liu Shao 劉邵. *Renwu zhi jiaojian* 人物志校箋. Annot. Li Chongzhi 李崇智. Chengdu: Bashu shushe, 2001.

Liu Xiang 劉向. *Shuoyuan zhuzi suoyin* 說苑逐字索引. Comp. Liu Dianjue 劉殿爵 et al. Hong Kong: Shangwu yinshuguan, 1992.

———. *Xinxu zhuzi suoyin* 新序逐字索引. Comp. Liu Dianjue 劉殿爵 et al. Hong Kong: Shangwu yinshuguan, 1992.

Liu Yiqing 劉義慶. *Shishuo xinyu jiaojian* 世說新語校箋. Ed. and annot. Xu Zhen'e 徐震堮. Hong Kong: Zhonghua shuju, 1987.

Liu Zhiji 劉知幾. *Shitong tongshi* 史通通釋. Annot. Pu Qilong 浦起龍. Shanghai: Shanghai guji, 1978.

Liu Zijian 劉子健 (James T. C. Liu). "Lüelun Songdai wuguan zai tongzhi jieji zhong de diwei" 略論宋代武官在統治階級中的地位. In Liu Zijian, *Liang Song shi yanjiu huibian* 兩宋史研究彙編, 173–184. Taipei: Liangjing, 1987.

Louie, Kam. *Theorising Chinese Masculinity: Gender and Society in China.* Cambridge: Cambridge University Press, 2002.

Lü Kun 呂坤. *Guifan* 閨範. Shanghai: Shanghai guji, 1994. Facsimile reprint of Fuchun tang 富春堂 edition of the Ming Wanli period.

———. *Shenyin yu* 呻吟語. In *Shenyin yu, Caigen tan.*

Lu Lin 陸林, ed. *Zhonghua jiaxun daguan* 中華家訓大觀. Hefei: Anhui renmin, 1994.

Lü mudan quanzhuan 綠牡丹全傳. Shanghai: Shanghai guji, 1986.

Lü Xisheng 呂錫生. "Sima Qian gongxing xiyi" 司馬遷宮刑析疑. *Zhongguo shi yanjiu* 中國史研究, no. 4 (1983): 68.

Luan Xing 欒星, ed. *"Qilu deng" yanjiu ziliao* 歧路燈研究資料. Zhengzhou: Zhongzhou shuhuashe, 1982.

Luo Dajing 羅大經. *Helin yulu* 鶴林玉露. Beijing: Zhonghua shuju, 1983.

Luo Lun 羅倫. *Yifeng wenji* 一峰文集. Siku zhenben edition.

Luo Yuming 駱玉明 and He Shengsui 賀聖遂. *Xu Wenchang pingzhuan* 徐文長評傳. Hangzhou: Zhejiang guji, 1987.

Lüshi chunqiu jiaoshi 呂氏春秋校釋. Comp. Chen Qiyou 陳奇猷. Shanghai: Xuelin, 1984.

Ma Boying 馬伯英. *Zhongguo yixue wenhua shi* 中國醫學文化史. Shanghai: Shanghai renmin, 1994.

Ma Da 馬達, ed. *Zhongguo renshu: "Quanren baizhen" baihua shiping* 中國忍術：勸忍百箴白話釋評. Beijing: Zhongguo renmin, 1992.

Ma Jigao 馬積高. *Song Ming lixue yu wenxue* 宋明理學與文學. Changsha: Hu'nan shifan daxue, 1989.

Ma Mingda 馬明達. "Yan Li xuepai yu wushu" 顏李學派與武術. In Ma Mingda, *Shuojian conggao* 說劍叢稿, 112–119. Lanzhou: Lanzhou daxue, 2000.

Ma Tao 馬濤. *Lü Kun pingzhuan* 呂坤評傳. Nanjing: Nanjing daxue, 2000.

McDermott, Joseph P. "Friendship and Its Friends in the Late Ming." In *Jinshi jiazu yu zhengzhi bijiao lishi lunwen ji* 近世家族與政治比較歷史論文. Ed. Zhongyang yanjiu yuan jindai shi yanjiu suo 中央研究院近代史研究所, 67–96. Taipei: Zhongyan yanjiu yuan jindai shi yanjiu suo, 1992.

McLaren, Anne E. *Chinese Popular Culture and Ming Chantefables*. Leiden: Brill, 1998.

McMahon, Keith. *Misers, Shrews, and Polygamists: Sexuality and Male-Female Relations in Eighteenth-Century Chinese Fiction*. Durham, N.C.: Duke University Press, 1995.

———. "Sublime Love and the Ethics of Equality in a Homoerotic Novel of the Nineteenth Century: *Precious Mirror of Boy Actresses*." *Nan nü* 4, no. 1 (2002): 70–109.

Mann, Susan. Introduction to *AHR* Forum on "The Male Bond in Chinese History and Culture." *American Historical Review* 106, no. 5 (December 2000): 1600–1614.

———. "Review of Ju-kang T'ien's *Male Anxiety and Female Chastity: A Comparative Study of Chinese Ethical Values in Ming-Ch'ing Times*." *Harvard Journal of Asiatic Studies* 52, no. 1 (1992): 362–369.

Mao Kun 茅坤. *Mao Kun ji* 茅坤集. Comp. Zhang Dazhi 張大芝 and Zhang Mengxin 張夢新. Hangzhou: Zhejiang guji, 1993.

Maoshi zhengyi 毛詩正義. In *Shisan jing zhushu* 十三經注疏. Ed. Li Xueqin 李學勤 et al. Beijing: Beijing daxue, 1999.

Min Jiayin 閔家胤, ed. *Yanggang yu yinrou de bianzou: Liangxing guanxi yu shehui moshi* 陽剛與陰柔的變奏：兩性關係和社會模式. Beijing: Zhongguo shehui kexue, 1995.

Ming Chenghua shuochang cihua congkan 明成化說唱詞話叢刊. Ed. Zhu Yixuan 朱一玄. Zhengzhou: Zhongzhou guji, 1997.

Mingshi 明史. Beijing: Zhonghua shuju, 1982.

Mote, Frederick W., and Denis Twitchett, eds. *The Cambridge History of China*, vol. 7: *The Ming Dynasty, 1364–1644, Part 1*. Cambridge: Cambridge University Press, 1988.

Mou Zongsan 牟宗三. *Caixing yu xuanli* 才性與玄理. Taipei: Xuesheng shuju, 1989.

Nivison, David. "Ho-shen and His Accusers: Ideology and Political Behavior in the Eighteenth Century." In *Confucianism in Action*. Ed. David S. Nivison and Arthur F. Wright, 209–245. Stanford, Calif.: Stanford University Press, 1959.

Ogawa Tamaki 小川環樹. "*San'guo yanyi* de yanbian" 三國演義的演變. *San'guo yanyi xuekan* 三國演義學刊 1 (1985): 323–334.

Ong, Walter J. *Orality and Literacy: The Technologizing of the Word*. London and New York: Methuen, 1982.

Orgel, Stephen. *Impersonations: The Performance of Gender in Shakespeare's England*. Cambridge: Cambridge University Press, 1996.

Ou Zhijian 區志堅. "Lüelun Ming yimin Zha Jizuo wannian shenghuo zhi yanjiu" 略論明遺民查繼佐晚年生活之研究. *Zhongguo wenhua yanjiu* 中華文化研究 14 (1996): 50–56.

Ouyang Jian 歐陽健. "Hai de tanxian he haiwai shijie de faxian: *Jinghua yuan* lishi jiazhi chuyi" 海的探險和海外世界的發現：鏡花緣歷史價值芻議. In Ouyang Jian, *Ming Qing xiaoshuo caizheng* 明清小說采正, 368–388. Taipei: Guanya, 1992.

———. *Liang Han xilie xiaoshuo* 兩漢系列小說. Shenyang: Liaoning jiaoyu, 1992.

———. "*Sui Tang yanyi* 'zhuiji chengzhi' kao" 隋唐演義綴集成帙考. In Ouyang Jian, *Ming Qing xiaoshuo xinkao* 明清小說新考, 353–396. Beijing: Zhongguo wenlian, 1992.

Ownby, David "Approximations of Chinese Bandits: Perverse Rebels, Romantic Heroes, or Frustrated Bachelors?" In Brownell and Wasserstrom, *Chinese Femininities/ Chinese Masculinities,* 226–250.

Pankenier, David W. "'The Scholar's Frustration' Reconsidered: Melancholia or Credo?" *Journal of the American Oriental Society* 110, no. 3 (1990): 434–459.

Pei Shuhai 裴樹海. *Ming Qing yingxiong chuanqi zonglun* 明清英雄傳奇綜論. Wuhan: Wuhan daxue, 1994.

Peng Deqing 彭德清 et al., eds. *Zhongguo hanghai shi* 中國航海史. Beijing: Renmin jiaotong, 1988.

Plaks, Andrew. *The Four Masterworks of the Ming Novel.* Princeton, N.J.: Princeton University Press, 1987.

Porter, Roy, and Lesley Hall. *The Facts of Life: The Creation of Sexual Knowledge in Britain, 1650–1950.* New Haven, Conn.: Yale University Press, 1995.

Qi Yukun 齊裕焜. *Sui Tang yanyi xilie xiaoshuo* 隋唐演義系列小說. Shenyang: Liaoning jiaoyu, 1993.

Qian Mu 錢穆. *Zhongguo xueshu sixiang shi luncong* 中國學術思想史論叢. Taipei: Dongda dushu gongsi, 1977.

Qian Qianyi 錢謙益. *Liechao shiji xiaozhuan* 列朝詩集小傳. Shanghai: Shanghai guji, 1983.

———. *Muzhai Youxue ji* 牧齋有學集. Shanghai: Shanghai guji, 1998.

Qian Zhongshu 錢鍾書. *Guanzhui bian* 管錐編. Hong Kong: Zhonghua shuju, 1990.

Qu Bo 瞿博 et al., eds. *Zhongguo jiaxun jingdian* 中國家訓經典. Haikou: Hainan, 1993.

Qu Dajun 屈大均. *Qu Dajun quanji* 屈大均全集. Beijng: Renmin wenxue, 1996.

Quan Han zhizhuan 全漢志傳. Shanghai: Shanghai guji, 1990.

Quan Ming wen 全明文. Ed. Qian Bocheng 錢伯城 et al. Shanghai: Shanghai guji, 1992.

Quan Shanggu, Sandai Qin Han San'guo Liuchao wen 全上古三代秦漢三國六朝文. Shijiazhuang: Hebei jiaoyu chubanshe, 1999.

Quan Tang wen 全唐文. Beijing: Zhonghua shuju, 1983.

Rao Longsun 饒龍隼. *Mingdai Longqing, Wanli jian wenxue sixiang zhuanbian yanjiu: Shiwen bufen* 明代隆慶萬曆間文學思想轉變研究：詩文部分. Zhongqing: Xi'nan shifan daxue, 1995.

Raphals, Lisa. *Sharing the Light: Representations of Women in Early China.* Albany: State University of New York Press, 1998.

Roberts, Moss, trans. *Three Kingdoms: A Historical Novel.* Berkeley: University of California Press, 1991.

Rocke, Michael. *Forbidden Friendships: Homosexuality and Male Culture in Renaissance Florence.* Oxford: Oxford University Press, 1996.

Roddy, Stephen. *Literati Identity and Its Fictional Representations in Late Imperial China.* Stanford, Calif.: Stanford University Press, 1998.

Rolston, David, ed. *How to Read the Chinese Novel*. Princeton, N.J.: Princeton University Press, 1990.

Rongyu tang ben Shuihu zhuan 容與堂本水滸傳. Shanghai: Shanghai guji, 1988.

Ropp, Paul. "Bibliography." *Nan nü* 3, no. 1 (2001): 143–152. Special issue on "Passionate Women: Female Suicide in Late Imperial China."

———. "Passionate Women: Female Suicide in Late Imperial China—Introduction." *Nan nü* 3, no. 1 (2001): 3–21.

———. "Review of Ju-kang T'ien's *Male Anxiety and Female Chastity: A Comparative Study of Chinese Ethical Values in Ming-Ch'ing Times*." *Journal of Asian Studies* 49, no. 3 (1989): 605–606.

Rouzer, Paul. *Articulated Ladies: Gender and the Male Community in Early Chinese Texts*. Cambridge, Mass.: Harvard University Asia Center, 2001.

Ryor, Kathleen M. "Bright Pearls Hanging in the Marketplace: Self-Expression and Commodification in the Painting of Xu Wei." Ph. D. dissertation, New York University, 1998.

San'guo yanyi huiping ben 三國演義會評本. Ed. Chen Xizhong 陳曦鍾 et al. Beijing: Beijing daxue, 1986.

San'guo zhi tongsu yanyi 三國志通俗演義. Shanghai: Shanghai guji, 1990. Fascimile reprint of Jiajing edition.

Schein, Louisa. *Minority Rules: The Miao and the Feminine in China's Cultural Politics*. Durham, N.C.: Duke University Press, 2000.

Sedgwick, Eve Kosofsky. *Between Men: English Literature and Male Homosocial Desire*. New York: Columbia University Press, 1985.

Shen Defu 沈德符. *Wanli yehuo bian* 萬曆野獲編. Beijing: Zhonghua shuju, 1997.

Shen Hanguang 申涵光. *Jingyuan xiaoyu* 荊園小語. In Cheng Bushi, *Ming Qing qingyan xiaopin*.

Shen Jinhao 沈金浩. "Lun *Sanyan Erpai* zhong mei nanzi xingxiang" 論三言二拍中美男子形象. *Ming Qing xiaoshuo yanjiu* 明清小說研究 54, no. 4 (1999): 183–187.

Shen Mingchen 沈明臣. *Fengdui lou shixuan* 風對樓詩選. *In* Siku quanshu chunmu congshu 四庫全書存目叢書. Ji'nan: Qi Lu shushe, 1997.

Shenyin yu, Caigen tan 呻吟語, 菜根譚. Shanghai: Shanghai guji, 2000.

Shi Ding 施丁. *Sima Qian xingnian xinkao* 司馬遷行年新考. Xi'an: Shanxi renmin jiaoyu, 1995.

Shuihu zhuan huiping ben 水滸傳會評本. Ed. Chen Xizhong 陳曦鍾 et al. Beijing: Beijing daxue, 1987.

Shuo Tang quanzhuan 說唐全傳. Shanghai: Shanghai guji, 2000.

Sima Qian 司馬遷. "Bao Ren Shaoqing shu" 報任少卿書. In *Quan Shanggu Sandai Qin Han San'guo Liuchao wen*, vol. 1.

———. *Shiji* 史記. Beijing: Zhonghua shuju, 1959.

Sinfield, Alan. *The Wilde Century: Effeminacy, Oscar Wilde and the Queer Movement*. London: Cassell, 1994.

Sommer, Mathew. "Dangerous Males, Vulnerable Males, and Polluted Males: The Regulation of Masculinity in Qing Dynasty Law." In Brownell and Wasserstrom, *Chinese Femininities/Chinese Masculinities*, 67–88.

———. *Sex, Law, and Society in Late Imperial China*. Stanford, Calif.: Stanford University Press, 2000.

Song, Geng. *The Fragile Scholar: Power and Masculinity in Chinese Culture*. Hong Kong: Hong Kong University Press, 2004.

Song Yuan pinghua ji 宋元平話集. Ed. Ding Xigen 丁錫根. Shanghai: Shanghai guji, 1990.

Songshi 宋史. Beijing: Zhonghua shuju, 1970.

Starr, Chloe. "Shifting Boundaries: Gender in *Pinhua Baojian.*" *Nan nü* 1, no. 2 (1999): 268–301.

Struve, Lynn. "Ambivalence and Action: Some Frustrated Scholars of the K'ang-hsi Period." In *From Ming to Ch'ing: Conquest, Region, and Continuity in Seventeenth-Century China.* Ed. Jonathan D. Spence and John E. Wills Jr., 323–365. New Haven, Conn.: Yale University Press, 1979.

Sui Tang liangchao shizhuan 隋唐兩朝史傳. In *Mingdai xiashuo jikan (Disan ji)* 明代小說輯刊 (第三輯). Chengdu: Bashu shushe, 1999.

Sun Kaidi 孫楷第. "Xia Erming yu *Yesou puyan*" 夏二銘與野叟曝言. In Sun Kaidi, *Cangzhou houji* 滄州後集, 238–247. Beijing: Zhonghua shuju, 1985.

———. *Zhongguo tongsu xiaoshuo shumu* 中國通俗小說書目. Beijing: Renmin wenxue, 1982.

Sun Qifeng 孫奇逢. *Xiafeng xiansheng ji* 夏峰先生集. Baibu congshu jicheng edition.

———. *Xiaoyou tang jiaxun* 孝友堂家訓. Baibu congshu jicheng edition.

Sun Shuyu 孫述宇. *Shuihu zhuan de laili, xintai yu yishu* 水滸傳的來歷心態與藝術. Taipei: Shibao wenhua, 1981.

Taga Akigorō 多賀秋五郎. *Sōfu no kenkyū* 宗譜の研究. Tokyo: Tōyō Bunko, 1960.

Tan Zhengbi 譚正璧 and Tan Xun 譚尋. *Guben xijian xiaoshuo huikao* 古本希見小說匯考. Hangzhou: Zhejiang wenyi, 1984.

T'ien, Ju-kang. *Male Anxiety and Female Chastity: A Comparative Study of Chinese Ethical Values in Ming-Ch'ing Times.* Leiden: Brill, 1988.

Tillman, Hoyt Cleveland. *Utilitarian Confucianism: Ch'en Liang's Challenge to Chu Hsi.* Cambridge, Mass.: Council on East Asian Studies, Harvard University, 1982.

Trumbach, Randolph. "Gender and the Homosexual Role in Modern Western Culture: The 18th and 19th Centuries Compared." In *Which Homosexuality?* Ed. Dennis Altman et al., 149–169. London: GMP Press, 1989.

———. *Sex and the Gender Revolution,* vol. 1. Chicago: University of Chicago Press, 1998.

———. "Sex, Gender and Sexual Identity in Modern Culture: Male Sodomy and Female Prostitution in Enlightenment England." In *Forbidden History: The State, Society, and the Regulation of Sexuality in Modern Europe.* Ed. John C. Fout, 89–106. Chicago: University of Chicago Press, 1992.

Tsai, Shih-shan Henry. *The Eunuchs in the Ming Dynasty.* Albany: State University of New York Press, 1996.

Tu, Wei-ming. "Yen Yüan: From Inner Experience to Lived Concreteness." In *The Unfolding of Neo-Confucianism.* Ed. Wm. T. de Bary et al., 511–541. New York: Columbia University Press, 1975.

Tung, Jowen R. *Fables for the Patriarchs: Gender Politics in Tang Discourse.* Lanham, Md.: Rowman and Littlefield, 2000.

Twichett, Denis, and Michael Loewe, eds. *The Cambridge History of China: The Ch'in and Han Empires, 221 BC–AD 220.* Cambridge: Cambridge University Press, 1986.

Van Gulik, R. H. *Sexual Life in Ancient China.* Leiden: Brill, 1961.

Volpp, Sophie. "The Literary Consumption of Actors in Seventeenth-Century China." In *Writing and Materiality in China: Essays in Honor of Patrick Hanan.* Ed. Judith Zeitlin et al., 153–183. Cambridge, Mass.: Harvard University Asia Center, 2003.

Wakeman, Frederic. *The Great Enterprise: The Manchu Reconstruction of Imperial Order in Seventeenth-Century China.* Berkeley: University of California Press, 1985.

Wan, Margaret Baptist. "*Green Peony* as New Popular Fiction: The Birth of Martial Romance in Early Nineteenth-Century China." Ph.D. dissertation, Harvard University, 2000.

Wang Anqi 王安祈. *Mingdai xiqu wulun* 明代戲曲五論. Taipei: Da'an, 1990.

Wang Bin 王彬. *Shuihu de jiudian* 水滸的酒店. Beijing: Zhongguo Sanxia chubanshe, 1997.

Wang, C. H. "Towards Defining a Chinese Heroism." *Journal of the American Oriental Society* 95, no. 1 (1995): 25–35.

Wang Can 王粲. *Wang Can ji* 王粲集. Ed. Yu Shaochu 俞紹初. Beijing: Zhonghua shuju, 1980.

Wang Chang'an 王長安. *Xu Wei sanbian* 徐渭三辨. Beijing: Zhongguo xiju, 1995.

Wang Chunnan 王春南 and Zhao Yinglin 趙映林. *Song Lian, Fang Xiaoru pingzhuan* 宋濂方孝孺評傳. Nanjing: Nanjing daxue, 1998.

Wang, David. *Fin-de-siècle Splendor: Repressed Modernities of Late Qing Fiction, 1849–1911.* Stanford, Calif.: Stanford University Press, 1997.

Wang Fuzhi 王夫之. *Chuanshan quanshu* 船山全書. Changsha: Yuelu shushe, 1988.

Wang Huizu 汪輝祖. *Shuangjie tang yongxun* 雙節堂庸訓. Tianjin: Tianjin guji, 1995.

Wang Junjiang 王均江. "Fusheng ning yiwei, duanbu hui jianghu: Shilun paihuai zai shiyin zhijian de Yuan Hongdao" 浮生寧曳尾斷不悔江湖：試論徘徊在仕隱之間的袁宏道. *Ezhou daxue xuebao* 鄂州大學學報, no. 10 (1997): 35–38. (Conclusion of the article on p. 34.)

Wang Qiqu 王其矩. *Mingdai neige zhidu shi* 明代內閣制度史. Beijing: Zhonghua shuju, 1989.

Wang Ruigong 王瑞功, ed. *Zhuge Liang yanjiu jicheng* 諸葛亮研究集成. Ji'nan: Qi Lu shushe, 1997.

Wang Ruoxu 王若虛. *Hunan yilao ji* 滹南遺老集. Siku quanshu edition.

Wang Tao 王韜. *Manyou suilu, Fusang youji* 漫游隨錄，扶桑游記. Changsha: Hunan renmin, 1982.

Wang Xianpei 王先霈 and Zhou Weimin 周偉民. *Ming Qing xiaoshuo lilun piping shi* 明清小說理論批評史. Guangzhou: Huacheng, 1988.

Wang Yangming 王陽明. *Wang Yangming quanji* 王陽明全集. Ed. Wu Guang 吳光 et al. Shanghai: Shanghai guji, 1992.

Wang Yanping 王炎平. "Liu Bei yu Sun furen guanxi kaoshi" 劉備與孫夫人關係考釋. *Sichuan daxue xuebao* 四川大學學報, no. 3 (1995): 80–86.

Wang Yue 王樾. "Zhang Taiyan de ruxia guan jiqi lishi yiyi" 章太炎的儒俠觀及其歷史意義. In *Xia yu Zhongguo wenhua* 俠與中國文化. Ed. Danjiang daxue Zhongwen xi 淡江大學中文系, 269–285. Taipei: Xuesheng shuju, 1993.

Watson, Burton, trans. *Records of the Grand Historian: Han Dynasty.* 2 vols. New York: Columbia University Press, 1993.

———. *Records of the Grand Historian: Qin Dynasty.* New York: Columbia University Press, 1993.

———. *Ssu-ma Ch'ien: Grand Historian of China.* New York: Columbia University Press, 1958.

Wei Jianlin 衛建林. *Mingdai huan'guan zhengzhi* 明代宦官政治. Shijiazhuang: Huashan wenyi, 1998.

Wei Yong 衛泳, comp. *Bingxue xie* 冰雪攜 (Guoxue zhenben wenku 國學珍本文庫.) Shanghai: Zhongyan shudian, 1935.

Wenzhou fu zhi 溫州府志. Taipei: Chengwen, 1983. Facsimile reprint of 1914 edition, which is in turn a reprint (*buke ben* 補刻本) of the 1760 printed edition.

Wilhelm, Hellmut. "The Scholar's Frustration: A Note on a Type of 'fu.'" In *Chinese Thought and Institutions.* Ed. John K. Fairbank, 310–319. Chicago: University of Chicago Press, 1957.

Wong, K. Chimin, and Lien-the Wu. *History of Chinese Medicine,* 2nd ed. Shanghai: National Quarantine Service. Reprint New York: AMS Press, 1973.

Wu Chengxue 吳承學. *Zhongguo gudai wenti xingtai yanjiu* 中國古代文體形態研究. Guangzhou: Zhongshan daxue, 2000.

Wu Cuncun 吳存存. *Ming Qing shehui xing'ai fengqi* 明清社會性愛風氣. Beijing: Renmin wenxue, 2000.

Wu Dacheng 吳大澂. *Wu Dacheng shoupi ben "Dizi zhenyan"* 吳大澂手批本弟子箴言. Beijing: Zhonghua quan'guo tushuguan wenxian suowei fuzhi zhongxin, 1997.

Wu, H. Laura. "Vindication of Patriarchy: Chen Tianchi's *Ruyijun zhuan* as a Critique of the Ming *Ruyijun zhuan.*" In Huang, *Snakes' Legs,* 190–209.

Wu Jingzi 吳敬梓. *Rulin waishi huijiao huiping ben* 儒林外史會校會評本. Ed. Li Hanqiu 李漢秋. Shanghai: Shanghai guji, 1984.

Wu Linzheng 吳麟徵. *Jiajie yaoyan* 家誡要言. In *Zhijia geyan, Zeng "Guang xianwen," Nüer jing,* 5–17.

Wu Tinghan 吳廷瀚. *Wu Tinghan ji* 吳廷瀚集. Beijing: Zhonghua shuju, 1984.

Wu, Yenna. *The Chinese Virago: A Literary Theme.* Cambridge, Mass.: Council on East Asian Studies, Harvard University, 1995.

———. "The Inversion of Marital Hierarchy: Shrewish Wives and Henpecked Husbands in Seventeenth-Century Chinese Literature." *Harvard Journal of Asiatic Studies* 48, no. 2 (1988): 363–382.

Wu Zeng 吳曾. *Nenggai zhai manlu* 能改齋漫錄. Baibu congshu jicheng edition.

Xia Jingqu 夏敬渠. *Yesou puyan* 野叟曝言. Changchun: Jilin wenshi, 1994.

Xia Xianchun 夏咸淳. *Wan Ming shifeng yu wenxue* 晚明士風與文學. Beijing: Zhongguo shehui kexue, 1994.

Xia Xiaohong 夏曉虹. "Lishi jiyi de chonggou: Wan Qing 'Nanxiang nü buxiang' shiyi" 歷史記憶的重構: 晚清男降女不降釋義. In *Wan Ming yu Wan Qing: Lishi chuancheng yu wenhua chuangxin* 晚明與晚清: 歷史傳承與文化創新. Ed. Chen Pingyuan 陳平原 et al., 257–271. Wuhan: Hubei jiaoyu, 2002.

Xiao Chi 蕭馳. "Cong caizi jiaren dao *Shitou ji:* Wenren xiaoshuo yu shuqing chuantong de yiduan qingjie" 從才子佳人到石頭記: 文人小說與抒情傳統的一段情結. *Hanxue yanjiu* 漢學研究 (Chinese Studies) 14, no. 1 (June 1996): 249–278. Reprinted in Xiao Chi, *Zhongguo shuqing chuantong* 中國抒情傳統, 275–320. Taipei: Yunchen wenhua shiye gufen youxian gongsi, 1999.

———. *Garden as Lyrical Enclave: A Generic Study of "The Story of the Stone."* Ann Arbor: Center for Chinese Studies, University of Michigan, 2001.

Xiao Difei 蕭滌非 et al. *Tangshi jianshang cidian* 唐詩鑒賞辭典. Shanghai: Shanghai cishu, 1983.

Xiao Xiangkai 蕭相愷. "*San'guo yanyi* Maoping de chufadian he jiben qingxiang" 三國演義毛評的出發點和基本傾向. *San'guo yanyi xuekan* 三國演義學刊 1 (1985): 267–278.

———. *Zhenben jinhui xiaoshuo daguan: Baihai fangshu lu* 珍本禁毀小說大觀: 稗海訪書錄. Zhengzhou: Zhongzhou guji, 1992.

———. "Zhongguo xiaoshuo shi yanjiu zhong ruogan wenti de kaobian zhiyi" 中國小說史研究中若干問題的考辨之一. In Xiao Xiangkai and Zhang Hong, *Zhongguo gudian tongsu xiaoshuo shilun* 中國古典通俗小說史論, 79–85. Nanjing: Nanjing chubanshe, 1994.

Xiaochuang youji (wai erzhong) 小窗幽記 (外二種). Shanghai: Shanghai guji, 2000.

Xinbian Jiao Chuang tongsu xiaoshuo 新編剿闖通俗小說. In *Jiao Chuang xiaoshuo* 剿闖小說. Shanghai: Shanghai guji, 1990.

Xingshi yinyuan zhuan 醒世姻緣傳. Shanghai: Shanghai guji, 1981.

Xu Fuguan 徐復觀. "Xi Han zhishi fenzi dui zhuanzhi zhengzhi de yali gan" 西漢知識分子對專制政治的壓力感. In Xu Fuguan, *Liang Han shixiang shi* 兩漢思想史, vol. 1, 281–294. Taipei: Xuesheng shuju, 1978.

———. *Zhongguo renxinglun shi: Xian Qin pian* 中國人性論史：先秦篇. Taipei: Shangwu yinshu guan, 1969.

Xu Jiacun 許葭村 and Gong Weizhai 龔未齋. *Qiushui xuan, Xuehong xuan chidu* 秋水軒雪鴻軒尺牘. Shanghai: Shanghai guji, 1986.

Xu Lun 徐崙. *Xu Wenchang* 徐文長. Shanghai: Shanghai renmin, 1962.

Xu Shaojin 徐少錦 and Chen Yanbin 陳延斌. *Zhongguo jiaxun shi* 中國家訓史. Xi'an: Shanxi renmin, 2003.

Xu Shen 許慎. *Shuowen jiezi zhu* 說文解字注. Annot. Duan Yucai 段玉裁. Shanghai: Shanghai guji, 1988.

Xu Shuofang 徐朔方. *Xu Shuofang ji* 徐朔方集. Hangzhou: Zhejiang guji, 1995.

Xu Wei 徐渭. *Xu Wei ji* 徐渭集. Beijing: Zhonghua shuju, 1983.

Xu Zhenqing 徐禎卿. *Digong ji* 迪功集. Siku quanshu edition.

Xunzi jijie 荀子集解. Annot. Wang Xianqian 王先謙. Beijing: Zhonghua shuju, 1988.

Yan Yuan 顏元. *Yan Yuan ji* 顏元集. Beijing: Zhonghua shuju, 1987.

Yan Zhitui 顏之推. *Yanshi jiaxun jijie* 顏氏家訓集解. Ed. Wang Liqi 王利器. Beijing: Zhonghua shuju, 1993.

Yang, Jui-sung. "A New Interpretation of Yen Yüan (1635–1704) and Early Ch'ing Confucianism in North China." Ph.D. dissertation, University of California, Los Angeles, 1997.

Yang Rong 楊榮. *Wenmin ji* 文敏集. Siku zhenben edition.

Yang Shiqi 楊士奇. *Dongli wenji* 東里文集. Beijing: Zhonghua shuju, 1999.

Yang Yanqi 楊燕起 et al., comps. *Lidai mingjia ping "Shiji"* 歷代名家評史記. Beijing: Beijing shifan daxue, 1986.

Yang Yaokun 楊耀坤 and Wu Yechun 伍野春. *Chen Shou Pei Songzhi pingzhuan* 陳壽裴松之評傳. Nanjing: Nanjing daxue, 1998.

Ye Sheng 葉盛. *Shuidong riji* 水東日記. Beijing: Zhonghua shuju, 1997.

Ye Shuxian 葉舒憲. *Yan'ge yu kuangjuan* 閹割與狂狷. Shanghai: Shanghai wenyi, 1999.

Yin Guoguang 殷國光 and Ye Junyuan 葉君遠, eds. *Ming Qing yanqing xiaoshuo daquan* 明清言情小說大觀. Beijing: Huaxia, 1993.

Yu Da 俞達. *Qinglou meng* 青樓夢. Beijing: Dazhong wenyi, 1999.

Yu Jiao Li 玉嬌梨. Shenyang: Chunfeng wenyi, 1982.

Yu, Pauline. *The Reading of Imagery in the Chinese Poetic Tradition.* Princeton, N.J.: Princeton University Press, 1987.

Yu Shenxing 于慎行. *Gushan bizhu* 穀山筆麈. Beijing: Zhonghua shuju, 1984.

Yu Yingchun 于迎春. *Qin Han shi shi* 秦漢士史. Beijing: Beijing daxue, 2000.

Yu Yingshi 余英時. "Fanzhi lun yu Zhongguo zhengzhi chuantong" 反智論與中國政治傳統. In Yu Yingshi, *Lishi yu sixiang* 歷史與思想. Taipei: Lianjing, 1976.

———. *Shi yu Zhongguo wenhua* 士與中國文化. Shanghai: Shanghai renmin chubanshe, 1987.

Yuan Cai 袁采. *Yuanshi shifan* 袁氏世範. Tianjin: Tianjin guji, 1995.

Yuan Hongdao 袁宏道. *Yuan Hongdao ji jianjiao* 袁宏道集箋校. Ed. and annot. Qian Bocheng 錢伯城. Shanghai: Shanghai guji, 1981.

Yuan Yuling 袁于令. *Suishi yiwen* 隋史遺文. Beijing: Renmin wenxue, 1989.

Yuan Zhongdao 袁中道. *Kexuezhai ji* 珂雪齋集. Ed. Qian Bocheng 錢伯城. Shanghai: Shanghai guji, 1989.

Yuan Zongdao 袁宗道. *Baisuzhai leiji* 白蘇齋類集. Shanghai: Shanghai guji, 1989.

Zha Jizuo 查繼佐. *Zuiwei lu* 罪惟錄. Hangzhou: Zhejiang guji, 1986.

Zhan Ying 詹瑛 et al., comps. *Li Bai quanji jiaozhu huishi jiping* 李白全集校注彙釋集評. Tianjin: Baihua wenyi, 1996.

Zhang Chao 張潮. *Youmeng ying* 幽夢影. In *Xiaochuang youji (wai erzhong)*.

Zhang Dai 張岱. *Zhang Dai shiwen ji* 張岱詩文集. Ed. Xia Xianchun 夏咸淳. Shanghai: Shanghai guji, 1991.

———. *Shikui shu houji* 石匱書後集. Beijing: Zhonghua shuju, 1959.

Zhang Dake 張大可. *Shiji wenxian yanjiu* 史記文獻研究. Beijing: Minzu, 1999.

Zhang Jun 張俊. *Qingdai xiaoshuo shi* 清代小說史. Hangzhou: Zhejiang guji, 1997.

Zhang Liwen 張立文, ed. *Qi* 氣. In *Zhongguo zhexue fanchou jingcui congshu* 中國哲學範疇精粹叢書. Beijing: Zhongguo renmin daxue, 1990.

———. *Zhongguo zhexue fanchou fazhan shi (rendao pian)* 中國哲學範疇發展史(人道篇). Beijing: Zhongguo renmin daxue, 1995.

Zhang Shideng 張士登. *Sanfen meng quanzhuan* 三分夢全傳. Shanghai: Shanghai guji, 1990.

———. *Sanfen meng quanzhuan*. In *Zhongguo gudai xiaoshuo zhenmi ben wenku* 中國古代小說珍秘本文庫, vol. 5. Ed. Fu Xuanzong 傅璇琮 et al., 403–557. Xi'an: San Qin, 1998.

Zhang Xinjian 張新建. *Xu Wei lun'gao* 徐渭論稿. Beijing: Wenhua yishu, 1990.

Zhang Yinlin 張蔭麟. *Zhongguo shanggu shigang* 中國上古史綱. Taipei: Huagang chuban youxian gongsi, 1974.

Zhan'guo ce jianzhu 戰國策箋注. Annot. and trans. Zhang Qingchang 張清常 and Wang Yandong 王延棟. Tianjin: Nankai daxue chubanshe, 1993.

Zhao Jingshen 趙景深. "*Yesou puyan* zuozhe Xia Erming nianpu" 野叟曝言作者夏二銘年譜. In Zhao Jingshen, *Zhongguo xiaoshuo congkao*, 433–447.

———. *Zhongguo xiaoshuo congkao* 中國小說叢考. Ji'nan: Qi Lu shushe, 1983.

Zhao Yi 趙翼. *Nianer shi zhaji jiaozheng* 廿二史箚記校正. Ed. Wang Shumin 王樹民. Beijing: Zhongshu shuju, 1984.

Zhao Yuan 趙園. *Ming Qing zhiji shidafu yanjiu* 明清之際士大夫研究. Beijing: Beijing daxue, 1999.

Zhen Wei 甄偉. *Xi Han yanyi* 西漢演義. In *Liang Han yanyi* 兩漢演義. Shanghai: Shijie shuju, 1936.

Zheng Hesheng 鄭鶴生. *Sima Qian nianpu* 司馬遷年譜. Shanghai: Shangwu, 1957. First ed. 1933.

Zheng Zhongkui 鄭仲夔. *Yuzhu xintan* 玉麈新譚. Shanghai: Shanghai guji shudian, 1980.

Zhijia geyan, Zeng "Guang xianwen," Nüer jing: Zhijia xiuyang geyan shizhong 治家格言, 增廣賢文, 女兒經: 治家修養格言十種. Shanghai: Shanghai guji, 1991.

Zhong, Xueping. *Masculinity Besieged? Issues of Modernity and Male Subjectivity in Chinese Literature of the Late Twentieth Century*. Durham, N.C.: Duke University Press, 2000.

Zhongguo congshu zonglu 中國叢書綜錄. Shanghai: Shanghai guji, 1986.

Zhongguo renming da cidian 中國人名大辭典. Shanghai: Shangwu yinshuguan, 1934.

Zhongguo gudai tongsu xiaoshuo zongmu tiyao 中國通俗小說總目提要. Ed. Jiangsu sheng shehui kexueyuan Ming Qing xiaoshuo yanjiu zhongxin 江蘇省社會科學院明清小說研究中心. Beijing: Zhongguo wenlian chuban gongsi, 1990.

Zhou Jianyu 周建渝. *Caizi jiaren xiaoshuo yanjiu* 才子佳人小說研究. Taipei: Wenshizhe, 1998.

Zhou Juntao 周鈞韜 and Wang Changyou 王長友, eds. *Zhongguo tongsu xiaoshuo jia pingzhuan* 中國通俗小說家評傳. Zhengzhou: Zhongzhou guji, 1993.

Zhou Mingchu 周明初. *Wan Ming shiren xintai ji wenxue ge'an* 晚明士人心態及文學個案. Beijing: Dongfang, 1997.

Zhou, Zuyan. *Androgyny in Late Ming and Early Qing Literature.* Honolulu: University of Hawai'i Press, 2003.

Zhouyi zhengyi 周易正義. In *Shisan jing zhushu* 十三經注疏. Ed. Li Xueqin 李學勤. Beijing: Beijing daxue, 1999.

Zhu Guozhen 朱國禎. *Yongzhuang xiaopin* 湧幢小品. Beijing: Wenhua yishu, 1998.

Zhu Ronggui 朱榮貴. "Cong Liu Sanwu *Mengzi jiewen* lun junquan de xianzhi yu zhishi fengzi zhi zizhu xing" 從劉三吾孟子節文論君權的限制與知識分子之自主性. *Zhongguo wenzhe yanjiu jikan* 中國文哲研究集刊 6, no. 3 (1995): 173–198.

Zhu Xi 朱熹. *Sishu zhangju jizhu* 四書章句集注. Beijing: Zhonghua shuju, 1984.

———. *Zhu Xi wenji* 朱熹文集. Ed. Chen Junmin 陳俊民. Taipei: Zhongyang yanjiu yuan lishi yu yuyan yanjiu suo, 2000.

———. *Zhuzi yulei* 朱子語類. Ed. Li Jingde 黎靖德. Beijing: Zhonghua shuju, 1990.

Zhu Yixuan 朱一玄 and Liu Yuchen 劉毓忱, comps. *San'guo yanyi ziliao huibian* 三國演義資料匯編. Tianjin: Baihua wenyi, 1983.

Zhu Youdun 朱有燉 et al. *Ming Qing zaju juan* 明清雜劇卷. Annot. Dai Shen 戴申. Beijing: Huaxia, 2000.

Zou Yi 鄒漪. *Qi Zhen yecheng* 啟禎野乘. *Mingdai zhuanji congkan* 明代傳記叢刊. Taipei: Mingwen shuju, 1991.

Zuo Dongling 左東岭. *Wangxue yu Zhongwan Ming shiren xintai* 王學與中晚明士人心態. Beijing: Renmin wenxue, 1999.

INDEX

ABOUT THE AUTHOR

Martin W. Huang, professor of Chinese at the University of California, Irvine, has authored numerous books and articles, most recently *Desire and Fictional Narrative in Late Imperial China* (2001) and *Snakes' Legs: Sequels, Continuations, Rewritings, and Chinese Fiction* (ed., 2004). His research focuses on traditional Chinese fiction and late imperial Chinese cultural history, and he is currently working on a new book about male friendship in Ming-Qing China.

Production Notes for Huang / Negotiating Masculinities
in Late Imperial China

Designed by Liz Demeter with text in Times Ten and
display in Charlemagne

Composition by Josie Herr

Printing and binding by Integrated Book Technology, Inc.

Printed on 60# Sebago Eggshell, 420 ppi